Toward Digital Equity

Bridging the Divide in Education

EDITED BY

Gwen Solomon

TechLearning.com

Nancy J. Allen

Texas A&M University

Paul Resta

University of Texas at Austin

Boston   New York   San Francisco
Mexico City   Montreal   Toronto   London   Madrid   Munich   Paris
Hong Kong   Singapore   Tokyo   Cape Town   Sydney

Series Editor: *Arnis E. Burvikovs*
Editorial Assistant: *Christine Lyons*
Marketing Manager: *Tara Whorf*
Editorial-Production Service: *Chestnut Hill Enterprises, Inc.*
Composition and Prepress Buyer: *Linda Cox*
Manufacturing Buyer: *Andrew Turso*
Cover Administrator: *Kristina Mose-Libon*
Electronic Composition: *Omegatype Typography, Inc.*

For related titles and support materials, visit our online catalog at www.ablongman.com.

Between the time Website information is gathered and then published, some sites may have closed. Also, the transcription of URLs can result in typographical errors. The publisher would appreciate notification where these occur so that they may be corrected in subsequent editions.

Library of Congress Cataloging-in-Publication Data

Toward digital equity : bridging the divide in education / edited by Gwen Solomon, Nancy J. Allen, Paul Resta.—1st ed.
    p. cm.
  Includes bibliographical references and index.
  ISBN 0-205-36055-6
    1. Information technology—Social aspects—United States. 2. Digital divide—Government policy—United States. 3. Education—Effect of technological innovations on—United States. I. Solomon, Gwen, 1944– II. Allen, Nancy (Nancy J.) III. Resta, Paul E.

T14.5 .T69   2003
303.48'33'0973—dc21   2002027672

Printed in the United States of America

10 9 8 7 6 5 4 3 2 1   08 07 06 05 04 03 02

CONTENTS

ABOUT THE AUTHORS

Nancy J. Allen, Ph.D.

Nancy J. Allen, Assistant Professor, Department of Teaching, Learning, and Culture, at Texas A & M University has a B.A. in zoology and an M.Ed. and Ph.D. in science education from the University of Texas. Her research interests are focused on the use of technology with multicultural populations. She was curriculum specialist for the Four Directions Challenge in Technology Project, a collaborative effort between Native American schools, universities, parents, elders, and students to create culturally relevant education through technology. She has been curriculum director at summer institutes for teachers of Native Americans and has served as science consultant, instructional designer, and curriculum expert on numerous educational software projects. The projects included the EcoExpert series in environmental education, and the SALUT Project, a collaboration among Texas Learning Technology Group and Texas school districts to produce CD-ROM–based science instruction for limited English proficient students. She received the 1996 National Association for Research in Science Teaching Outstanding Paper Award for her presentation, "Voices from the Bridge: Kickapoo Middle School Students and Science Education—A Worldview Comparison." Dr. Allen currently serves as a curriculum consultant for the Bureau of Indian Affairs and numerous tribal schools and colleges.

Bonnie Bracey, M.Ed.

Bonnie Bracey is a technology pioneer. She is an outspoken advocate for teacher involvement in the exploration and visioning for the use of technology as a tool. She is a George Lucas Education Foundation Fellow. She is currently learning about Next Generation Internet and resources in visualization and modeling from ACCESS and NCSA. She was a member of the National Information Infrastructure Advisory Council appointed by former President Clinton, working with former Vice President Gore and the Department of Commerce in helping to frame the documents that provided the national visions for the use of technology. She continues to help teachers all over the world in global and national outreach on special initiatives.

Julia F. Butler, M.Ed.

Julia Friend Butler is Coordinator of Southside Virginia Learning Network, a technology consortium made up of Longwood College, St. Paul's College, and local school divisions. While a classroom teacher, reading specialist, and elementary and central office administrator, she developed the first West Virginia "Newspaper in Education Week" program, served as state president for the International Reading Association, and was a member of the Virginia Regional Staff Development Council. She worked with the Virginia Department of Education and Japanese Ministry of Education to bring Japanese teachers to Southside. She collaborated on the development of a regional alternative school, worked with AEL on curriculum alignment, and has made several national and state presentations, including the National School Boards Technology Excellence Fair, the Society for Information Technology in Education, and the National Educational Computing Conference. She has been very active promoting the integration of technology in Virginia schools through working with the K–12, business, and higher education communities.

Ms. Butler earned her Bachelor of Science from Radford College in Political Science and her Master of Education from George Mason University. She is currently a doctoral candidate in Educational Leadership and Policy Studies at Virginia Polytechnic Institute, with a research focus on technology and the leadership role of K–12 administrators.

Vivian Delgado, Ph.D.

Vivian Delgado is the former Director of Oksale Native Teacher Preparation Program at Northwest Indian College and has also taught in the teacher preparation program at Washington State University. Northwest Indian College is located on the Lummi reservation in the northwest part of the state of Washington. Dr. Delgado received a B.S. in Elementary Education from the University of South Dakota, a Master's degree in Education Administration from the University of Mary at Bismarck, North Dakota, and a doctorate from the University of North Dakota in Grand Forks. Dr. Delgado's professional goal is to prepare Native American teachers who understand that Native American education involves more than language and culture; it also involves developing in students a Native worldview that focuses on the mindset.

Kathleen Fulton, M.A.

Kathleen Fulton is an educational technology consultant with ThinkQuest and the University of Northern Iowa in support of their work with the Department of Education's Preparing Tomorrow's Teachers to Use Technology (PT3) Program. She served as the Project Director for the congressional Web-based Education Commission where she was responsible for researching and writing *The Power of the Internet for Learning: Moving from Promise to Practice.* This report, released to Congress and the President on December 19, 2000, has been called the most comprehensive report to date on the impact of the World Wide Web on education.

Ms. Fulton was Associate Director of the Center for Learning and Educational Technology at the University of Maryland, where her work focused on establishing a research, development, and demonstration center for advancing technology-facilitated learning and professional development. While at Maryland, Fulton wrote two national reports: *Closing the Gap: Delivering Quality Educational Content in the Digital Age,* the report from the July 1999 NCTET Tahoe Institute; and *The Skills Students Need for Technological Fluency,* for the Milken Exchange on Educational Technology. She also worked for the Office of Technology Assessment (OTA) for the U.S. Congress, where she helped write OTA's education and technology studies.

Sandra Geisler, M.A.

Sandra K. Geisler recently completed her Master's Degree in Instructional Technology at the University of Georgia in Athens. Her main focus is on instructional design and development as well as electronic curriculum development.

Carmen Gonzales, Ph.D.

Carmen Gonzales is a faculty member of the Department of Curriculum and Instruction in the Learning Technologies Program at New Mexico State University. She was Chair of the New Mexico Council on Technology in Education and a member of the Board of Directors of the International Society of Technology in Education. She is Project Director for a statewide professional development project, Regional Educational Technology Assistance (RETA), funded by a Technology Innovation Challenge Grant from the U.S. Department of Education. RETA is a partnership of public schools, universities, the New Mexico State Department of Education, and local business, whose mission is to develop the capacity to integrate technology into classroom instruction of New Mexico's schools to improve student learning and teacher performance.

Dr. Gonzales has served on national committees and evaluation projects such as Star

Schools–Distance Education Projects, Secretary Riley's Distance Education Think Tank, and the National Science Foundation's Alliance for Minority Participation. She has conducted research in educational technology, distance education, and telecommunications for teaching and learning and has taught a number of distance courses via the World Wide Web.

Cheryl Grable, Ed.D.

Cheryl Grable is Director of Preparing Tomorrow's Teachers to Use Technology and an Associate Professor of Teacher Education at the University of Arkansas at Little Rock, where she is an instructor of middle level and secondary science methods and curriculum design. Dr. Grable taught mathematics and science in middle school through community college, directed a program for underrepresented students in mathematics and science at a community college, and co-directed a Youth Opportunities Unlimited program that worked with at-risk high school students to improve their skills in mathematics, facilitate graduation from high school, and encourage college attendance. Her PT3 grant focuses on developing technology-rich classroom and field experiences for aspiring teachers and technology-centered learning communities—composed of the College of Education, other colleges across the UALR campus, and area metropolitan and rural schools—to support and encourage digital equity for underserved populations.

Henry T. Ingle, Ph.D.

Henry T. Ingle holds the rank of tenured Professor of Communication and Associate Academic Affairs Vice President for Technology Planning and Distance Learning at the University of Texas at El Paso (UTEP). His responsibilities focus on campus planning for developing alternative instructional delivery to promote educational equity and access to instructional programs and training opportunities for historically underserved diverse populations in the region.

Dr. Ingle holds a B.A. degree in Mass Media and Communications from Texas Western College (now the University of Texas at El Paso); a Master of Science in Communication Media with a concentration in educational telecommunications from the Newhouse School of Communication at Syracuse University in New York; and a Ph.D. from Stanford University in Palo Alto, California. His doctoral studies reflect interdisciplinary study emphasis in international education and cross-cultural communication, educational media and technology, curriculum and instructional design, educational program planning and evaluation, and the diffusion and adoption of educational innovations.

Joan Karp, Ph.D.

Joan Karp is currently on the founding faculty of California State University Channel Islands in Camarillo, California. Formerly, she was the Co-Director of the Arrowhead Preparing Tomorrow's Teachers to Use Technology Project. This project involved changing the ways in which teachers are prepared to use technology by integrating technology tools into coursework throughout campus and strengthening the relationships among the university and Duluth Public Schools and Fond du Lac Ojibwe Schools. As professor of special education at University of Minnesota, Duluth, she has been instrumental in developing a number of innovative uses of technology with undergraduate and graduate students. Strongly committed to diversity issues, she co-authored a textbook on preparing teachers who have disabilities, titled *Enhancing Diversity: Educators with Disabilities*, published by Gallaudet University Press (1998).

Karen M. Keenan

Karen Keenan, a teacher on special assignment and former staff developer with the Duluth Public Schools, is currently Co-Director of the Arrowhead Preparing Tomorrow's Teachers to Use Technology (APT3) Project at the University of

Minnesota, Duluth. Additionally, Ms. Keenan is an organization development doctoral student at the University of St. Thomas's Minneapolis, Minnesota, campus. She believes the body of knowledge generated by professionals in the organization development field is particularly useful to educational communities as they work to shift from industrial model learning environments to those that use the educational advantages that electronic technologies can provide. With the APT3 Project, Ms. Keenan collaboratively applies sound organization development practices to initiate and facilitate change in educational environments.

Robert T. McLaughlin, Ph.D.

Robert T. McLaughlin is founder and executive director of MC Squared (www.teacherednet.org/mc2.html), which is committed to assisting educational institutions to undertake initiatives that foster local economic and social well-being, especially in economically distressed communities. He directs a five-year grant from the U.S. Department of Education to assist 30 school partnerships in nine states with the infusion of technology into K–12 classrooms and with teacher preparation and teacher professional development. He is also the director of a three-year $2.1-million catalyst grant from the U.S. Department of Education's Preparing Tomorrow's Teachers to Use Technology (PT3) program to assist national leaders in teacher preparation reform to infuse technology into their work.

Dr. McLaughlin serves on the PT3 Program's Coordinating Council. He helped form the PT3 Digital Equity Initiative, which is overseeing development by MC Squared of a web-based database on digital equity strategies to provide K–12 educators and teacher educators with information on practical means by which they can address critical dimensions of the nation's digital divide. Under his leadership, MC Squared provides a virtual campus, national listserv, and virtual library assisting educators to learn about and implement digital equity strategies and materials.

Joyce Pittman, Ph.D.

Joyce Pittman is an educational history and philosophy scholar; University of Cincinnati professor of curriculum, instruction, and technology; Director of Education and Technology Research, Principal Investigator and Project Director for the U.S. Department of Education's Preparing Tomorrow's Teachers division. Dr. Pittman's degrees are in Business Education, Occupational and Career Technology Education from Southern Illinois and Chicago State Universities, cum laude. She has a Ph.D. with an emphasis in instructional technology from Iowa State University.

Dr. Pittman is a member of several national and state organizations including: National Educational Technology Standards Writing Team for the International Society for Technology in Education (ISTE), National Commission for the Accreditation of Teacher Education (NCATE), Society for Information and Technology in Teacher Education (SITE), American Association of Colleges of Education (AACE), American Association of Women in Media and Communication, World Council for Curriculum and Instruction (WCCI), and the Cincinnati Minority Women's Leadership Council.

Dr. Pittman's research on national assessment of teacher training in new technologies, learning and teaching with technology, and urban student achievement has landed her recognition in national and international educational, corporate, and government arenas. She is an active participant in ISTE's National Minority Symposium on Technology, which examines technology and education issues in urban schools, higher education, and communities.

J. David Ramirez, Ph.D.

J. David Ramirez is a former teacher, counselor, and school psychologist. His program, evaluation, and research experience spans several areas, including: child development/state preschool, desegregation, migrant education, immigrant education, bilingual education, home/school/community collaboration, special education, integration of technology in education for diverse populations, alcohol and other drug use prevention, community college, adult literacy, school-to-work, juvenile justice systems, seasonal agricultural workers, and U.S. foreign aid technical training programs. He works with student, parent, and community groups as well as staff from local, county, state, and federal education and non-education agencies within the United States, Mexico, Central and South America, China, Korea, Vietnam, and Africa. He is a specialist in the design and evaluation of education programs for language-minority students. Currently, Dr. Ramirez is the Executive Director for the Center for Language Minority Education and Research and Professor in the College of Education at California State University, Long Beach.

Paul Resta, Ph.D.

Paul E. Resta holds the Ruth Knight Millikan Centennial Professorship in Instructional Technology and serves as Director of the Learning Technology Center at the University of Texas at Austin. He is the founder of ENAN, the Educational Native American Network, which enables hundreds of Indian schools to access the Internet and other educational and information resources and provides opportunities to communicate and collaborate across the country and globe. He served as Chair of The Smithsonian Institution National Museum of the American Indian Off-Site Technology Committee, is Chair of the Association for Teacher Educators National Commission on Technology and the Future of Teacher Education, and serves on the International Children's Art Foundation Advisory Board and the Board of Governors for the Online Academy.

He directs the University of Texas Four Directions project funded by the Department of Education. The project involves nineteen rural Indian schools and explores the use of new telecommunications and multimedia technologies to enhance the quality of education in schools in remote areas. The project recently received the 1997 Award for Outstanding and Innovative Use of Technology

from *Government Executive Magazine* and the Government Executive Leadership Institute. He also directs the Technology Leadership Academy and Project INSITE.

Kevin Rocap, M.A.

Kevin Rocap, Director of Programs and Development at the Center for Language Minority Education and Research at California State University, Long Beach, has a Master's in International Education from Harvard University and is pursuing a doctorate in Educational Technology and Leadership from Pepperdine University. He has developed multilingual, multicultural, and antiracist materials and programs for K–12 teaching and learning, for teacher education, and for adult ESL and literacy. Prior work experience includes: education and outreach specialist in hunger relief and international development, evaluator of a federal program in bilingual education, technology trainer, and systems analyst at Children's National Medical Center in Washington, D.C.

Mr. Rocap is the director of the Pacific Southwest Regional Technology in Education Consortium (PSRTEC), which includes seven states and island entities of the Pacific. PSRTEC addresses issues of multilingual, multicultural, diversity-responsive education and the integration of current and emerging technologies for learning. Mr. Rocap has worked at federal, regional, state, and local levels, as well as K–12 and community settings, on a range of learning and equity issues associated with digital technologies. He is director of a Preparing Tomorrow's Teachers to Use Technology catalyst grant designed to integrate diversity-responsiveness practices and meaningful uses of technology into teacher education.

Steven A. Sánchez, M.A.

Steven A. Sánchez is currently the Director of Curriculum, Instruction, and Learning Technologies for the New Mexico State Department of Education. Prior to this position, he served 19 years of his 23-year professional career as an elementary and middle school classroom teacher. In addition to his K–12 responsibilities, Mr. Sánchez served as an adjunct faculty member at the University of New Mexico–Valencia Campus, working with adult learners in the Adult Basic Education program and the Department of Mathematics, facilitating learning for pre- and in-service teachers. In addition, Mr. Sánchez completed a two-year term at the National Science Foundation as an Associate Program Manager in the Education and Human Resources Division, Networking Infrastructure for Education Program, and worked closely with the research community interested in systemic reform, educational technology, and the development and application of advanced technologies.

Lynne Schrum, Ph.D.

Lynne Schrum is an Associate Professor in the Department of Instructional Technology at the University of Georgia. She received a Ph.D. in Curriculum and Instruction from the University of Oregon in 1991, and has an M.A. in Elementary Education and Learning Disabilities from the University of Evansville. Prior to her university work, she taught in elementary schools. She has taught courses on distance learning, telecommunications, research methods, and introduction to instructional technology.

Dr. Schrum's research and teaching focus on online and distance learning, implementation of technological innovations in education, and appropriate uses of information technology in K–12 education. She is a former president of the International Society for Technology in Education (ISTE). She has written two books and numerous articles and monographs on these subjects and consults and speaks with post-secondary and K–12 educators and administrators and policymakers throughout the U.S. and in many countries around the world. Her most recent book is *Connect Online: Web Learning Adventures* (with Gwen Solomon).

Robert Sibley, Ed.M.

Robert Sibley is the Manager of Educational Projects for the non-profit ThinkQuest Organization, where he has been involved in numerous projects since 1997. His current projects include: ScienceQuest, a collaborative program with the Education Development Center and HUD Neighborhood Networks centers, partially funded by the National Science Foundation; ThinkQuest Live; and ThinkQuest for Tomorrow's Teachers, a U.S. Department of Education PT3 catalyst grant program. Sibley also serves as co-director of the PT3 digital equity taskforce.

Prior to joining ThinkQuest, Mr. Sibley taught secondary English and social studies and held management positions in both the private and public sectors. He has had articles published in the *ASCD Curriculum/Technology Quarterly;* has presented papers at numerous regional, national, and international education conferences; and has represented ThinkQuest on the CEO Forum for Education and Technology. He has a B.A. in History from the State University of New York at Buffalo and a Master's in Education from Harvard University.

Gwen Solomon, M.A.

Gwen Solomon is Director of TechLearning.com, the website created from the merger of her NSF-funded Well Connected Educator K–12 publishing center, and *Technology & Learning* magazine. In addition, she is Director of Publication and Dissemination for ThinkQuest's PT3 grant. Prior to this work, Ms. Solomon was Senior Analyst in the U.S. Department of Education's Office of Educational Technology. She also served New York City Public Schools as Coordinator of Instructional Technology Planning and as founding Director of New York City's School of the Future. In the past, she also was a teacher and computer coordinator.

Ms. Solomon writes extensively about all areas of educational technology and particularly about telecommunications. Her most recent book is *Connect Online: Web Learning Adventures* (with Lynne Schrum). Her other books concern teaching writing with computers, and the software she designed for Scholastic also helps students improve writing skills. She is a Contributing Editor for *Technology & Learning* magazine and has been a Contributing Editor for *Electronic Learning* magazine. She has published articles, columns, and reviews on educational technology. Ms. Solomon is a former Chairperson of the Consortium for School Networking (CoSN).

Amy Staples, Ph.D.

Amy Staples is a Visiting Assistant Professor in the Department of Exceptional Education at the University of Wisconsin–Milwaukee, teaching courses in early childhood intervention, literacy, and instructional and assistive technology. She serves as Co-Principal Investigator for several federal- and state-funded technology grants. Among those grants is the Technology and Urban Teaching Project, a Department of Education PT3 grant supporting the integration of technology into UW–Milwaukee's Collaborative Teacher Education Program for Urban Communities. Dr. Staples earned her doctorate in educational psychology at the University of North Carolina at Chapel Hill, where she focused on literacy learning. Prior to relocating to Milwaukee, she worked at the Center for Literacy and Disability Studies, studying how children with disabilities learn to read and write and how teachers and instructional and assistive technologies can best support that process. Her research interests focus on exploring the effective-

ness of technology supports on literacy learning for children with diverse needs.

Karin M. Wiburg, Ed.D.

Karin M. Wiburg is an associate professor and co-ordinator of the Learning Technologies program in the College of Education at New Mexico State University. Her research interest is the design, implementation, and evaluation of technology-integrated learning environments in K–12 and higher education. She has published widely in the field and supervises multiple university/public school collaborative projects. She has worked for over 25 years as a teacher and administrator both in K–12 schools and in higher education.

Linda C. Wing, Ph.D.

Linda C. Wing is the Co-Director of the Urban Superintendents Program and Lecturer on Education at the Harvard Graduate School of Education. She has experience teaching high school history and English, conducting national projects focused on the development of bilingual curriculum materials for elementary school students and the study of test policies in education and employment, and establishing educational technology partnerships with urban school districts for a Silicon Valley company. Dr. Wing has published work on issues such as the education of immigrant children, leadership and technology, and school-to-work policy. She serves on the boards of the ERIC Clearinghouse on Urban Education, the Institute for Responsive Education, and the Massachusetts Asian American Educators Association.

PREFACE

Digital Equity and the Future

This book, *Toward Digital Equity: Bridging the Divide in Education,* brings together nationally recognized educators to address the challenges, opportunities, and strategies for bridging the digital divide in schools and communities. The title begins with the words *toward digital equity,* a positive phrase that supports the authors' belief that the solutions and success stories described in this book—among others—will indeed make the difference.

Surveys show that low-income areas and high-risk students are least likely to receive the benefits of exemplary uses of educational technology and telecommunications. The reasons are multiple and solutions to the problems elusive. This book addresses many of the issues as it attempts to promote understanding and change. Unless there is awareness of both the challenges and potential solutions among those who care about our nation's students, schools and communities will not be able to change.

As readers will learn, minority households, especially low-income minority households, are least likely to have computers or to be online. The hope is that schools, as they deal with the multiplicity of tasks in educating children, can compensate for this lack and help students learn with technology. The news is both good and not good enough. The E-Rate Program, which was designed to make Internet access and internal connections available at discounted rates to schools and libraries, is one reason for the growth in schools' Internet access. Yet we learn that the schools with the highest levels of poverty and minority students have the least amount of access. As readers will see, access is only part of the story. Other issues, such as curriculum, professional development, and leadership, also play major roles in the crisis that is at issue in this book—digital equity.

We begin with the meaning of the term *digital equity.* The authors collaborated online to shape this definition:

> Digital equity in education means ensuring that every student, regardless of socioeconomic status, language, race, geography, physical restrictions, cultural background, gender, or other attribute historically associated with inequities, has equitable access to advanced technologies, communication and information resources, and the learning experiences they provide.
>
> Digital equity also means that all learners have opportunities to develop the means and capacity to be full participants in the digital age, including being designers and producers (not only users) of current and future technologies and communication and information resources.
>
> Teachers, administrators, other adults, and community members who help to integrate digital technologies into empowering teaching and learning practices are important to ensure equitable educational opportunities, experiences, and expectations that support all learners as full political participants, academically prepared lifelong learners, and economically engaged citizens in our democratic society.

How does a book like this get started? To begin with, some of the authors have been involved for years with getting computers and Internet access into classrooms and making sure that technology is used appropriately. In addition, many have worked in low-income areas with high-risk populations, in which technology can make a tremendous difference for student learning and lifelong success. Our intent with this book, as with other aspects of our professional lives, is to make a difference and improve the status quo.

The catalyst for our embarking on this book was the U.S. Department of Education's Preparing Tomorrow's Teachers to Use Technology grant program (PT3) and its Digital Equity Task Force. The PT3 Program began in 1999 to bring new ideas, new collaborations, and new models to teacher education. The PT3 program has made $150 million in federal funding available to 441 programs for teacher preparation institutions to develop capacity, to implement new programs, and to provide innovative catalysts for broader change. These programs are just beginning to take root, but they offer promise for the future.

Within the PT3 program, many grantees are focusing on preparing preservice teachers to work in low-income, high-poverty areas where the digital divide is but one of many challenges. For this reason, Robert McLaughlin, Robert Sibley, and others within the PT3 community initiated an effort known as the PT3 Digital Equity Task Force to address digital equity issues within the context of PT3 grants and communities. The effort focuses on identifying and disseminating digital equity strategies to the nation's preservice educators, policymakers, and other interested stakeholders.

At a December 2000 meeting, participants identified five tasks. Among these was to disseminate information about digital equity issues to PT3 grantees and beyond. The method selected to disseminate information on the challenges and solutions to PT3 grantees, preservice educators, policymakers, educational leaders, and others was to write this book.

In this book, we examine some of the factors that collectively create and sustain the present digital divide and discuss some of the challenges and opportunities that exist in addressing it. More important, we present a vision of digital equity and a framework for understanding and action. The book is divided into five sections, each of which represents a key element of digital equity.

In Section One, Setting the Stage, we examine the notion of access. While many people have yet to achieve equitable access to equipment and to this country's telecommunications infrastructure, there are other issues related to access to consider as well. This section presents the perspective that while historically this country has provided access to whatever infrastructure has been deemed essential, it has overlooked many barriers to effective use. We further learn of the multiple barriers to achieving the best uses of technology for learning, and we read about the factors affecting digital equity at the K–12 and higher education levels from educators who provide authentic context for the hypotheses, assertions, and suggestions of this set of chapters.

Section Two, Power and Literacy, explores the philosophical, sociocultural, and sociopolitical aspects of digital equity. What does it really mean to be *literate* in the 21st century? How does the concept of literacy play out in a technological world? How do issues of power interact with our understanding of digital equity, historically and conceptually? Insights from these chapters provide a theoretical and historical framework for the chapters that follow.

In Section Three, Learners and Technology, we consider the needs of particular populations of learners. This section raises key questions about how educators are employing technology to provide equal opportunity to learn to all students. We explore the problems and possibilities of technology in the education of culturally and linguistically diverse students, for students with physical challenges, and students of both genders. This section concludes with a chapter on curriculum to provide the reader with models of what technology-enhanced instruction really looks like in the equitable classroom.

Section Four, Road Map to the Future, looks ahead. It focuses on institutions rather than on individual learners or classrooms. It discusses the kinds of organizational structures, policies, actions, and plans that must be in place for systemic change to occur. Although each chapter explores a different facet of institutional reform, together they provide an in-depth look at where institutions need to be heading and how to get there. The section provides authentic examples of change within institutions that are moving toward digital equity.

As society becomes increasingly interconnected, those who are prepared to take advantage of advanced technologies will benefit and thrive. Those who are not prepared will not be able to participate fully in the new workplace or take advantage of lifelong learning opportunities to keep pace with rapid changes and improve their skills. Inequity of access, resources, and training will further widen disparities between the haves and have-nots in our society; but technology can provide both a potential solution and the opportunity to create a more equitable society. We hope that this book will create an awareness that can promote a more focused effort to create the conditions for digital equity—both in schools and in communities.

Acknowledgments

We would like to express our appreciation to the persons who have contributed in significant ways to this publication. Cheryl Grable has been an invaluable member of the editorial team. She has taken on much more than she bargained for and made our lives much easier. Deborah Stirling joined the team as our final eyes and ears—editing, overseeing, assembling—that enrich the book in ways we had not imagined. She thanks Rachel Horwitz for editing assistance. We also thank Karin Wiburg and Christine Sherk for providing additional expert assistance in reviewing chapters. Finally, we thank Tom Carroll and Lavona Grow of the U.S. Department of Education for their encouragement throughout the process. In addition, chapter authors have chosen to thank many other individuals, who are listed below.

JOYCE PITTMAN thanks her husband, Brian McLaughlin, Freelance Photojournalist, and her late mother, Maggie Jackson, an International Missionary for Human Rights, who was so excited about this effort and so encouraging, but did not live to see it through. She also thanks her two sons, Derrick Newby and Kenneth Newby, her graduate research assistants, and the CERTI PT3 Management Team at the University of Cincinnati, who all served as readers/advisors, especially Dr. Estela Matriano, Professor Emeritus and Coordinator of Multicultural Studies at UC.

NANCY ALLEN thanks Yueming Jia, Graduate Assistant in the Department of Teaching, Learning, and Culture, in Teaching English as a Second Language, for her work on the citations.

CHERYL GRABLE thanks Pat Laster, PT3 Research Assistant, University of Arkansas at Little Rock, for providing resources and research on gender, and LaKeitha Austin, PT3 Graduate Student, University of Arkansas at Little Rock, also for providing research on gender.

HENRY T. INGLE provides special thanks to the students in his online class, Technology and a Changing Student Demography, for sharing their ideas and perspectives on cultural differences and the evolving relationship with new information media and technology. In particular, he wishes to acknowledge Marcela Morales, Rosemary Echevarria, Ana Lia Gomez, Josefina Parga, Martha Idalia Chew, Claudia Dominguez, Isabel Vallejo, Edgar Reynoso, Iliana Zuniga, Thelia A. Lisle, Sherrie A. Owens, Paige M. Ragsdale, Lem Railsback, Lona F. Sandon, Barbara A. Shaw, and Marla Wyatt.

KATHLEEN FULTON acknowledges Barbara Reeves, Director of Technology for the Maryland State Department of Education, for reviewing and offering suggestions, and Henry Becker, University of California at Irvine, for suggestions and guidance.

KAREN KEENAN and JOAN KARP would like to acknowledge the following people: University of Minnesota, Duluth, Education Department Faculty, Staff, and Dean Paul Deputy; University of Minnesota Chancellor Kathryn Martin; Duluth Public Schools Superintendent Julio Almanza; Fond du Lac Ojibwe Schools Superintendent Michael F. Rabideaux and Grants Director Dan Anderson.

KARIN WIBURG wishes to thank the following scholars from New Mexico State University, who were her co-authors of the collaboratively written chapter, Factors of the Divide: Doctors Rudolfo Chavez, Jeanette Haynes Writer, Maria Mercardo, Jim O'Donnell, Elisa Poel, and Paula Wolfe. Without their writing, this chapter would not exist. She also thanks Marv Wiburg, Library Technologist at New Mexico State University, for his assistance in finding information on the history of libraries and telcommunication services.

INTRODUCTION

Educational Technology and Equity

GWEN SOLOMON

NANCY J. ALLEN

Computers and networked technologies serve as fact and symbol of history's latest great revolution, the movement from an industrial to an information society. The nature of living, learning, and working will be very different from that which we have previously known. The business world has adopted technology to such an extent that much of future work will require it, which means that future workers—today's students—must know how to use technology and information as never before. Schools must teach students in new ways in order to meet this challenge.

Using digital technologies to teach students in new ways, however, is no simple task. Access to equipment is not enough; teachers must also have the expertise to use the equipment to promote learning (Lemke & Coughlin, 1998; Wenglinsky, 1998). These are not tasks that we will accomplish overnight. We are slowly getting computers and connectivity into schools and finding optimal ways to use them for student learning, but we still have much more to accomplish.

The barriers are many and complex. Our framework for this book is that serious inequities in society exist and that digital inequities are extensions of them. The digital divide is thus the result of inequities in a technological world rather than a divide resulting solely from an increasing dependency on technology. One facet of the problem is the "significant difference in the access to and equity of technology experience based on categories such as income, race, gender, location, or education" (Swain & Pearson, 2001, p. 10).

This book explores the digital divide and the factors that cause it and provides a hopeful look at where the future can take us. The title, *Toward Digital Equity: Bridging the Divide in Education,* is the clue. It promises that we can move forward on the road to equity in this technological revolution in education and offers a look at the obstacles to be overcome and some promising solutions.

Technology, Society, and Schools

Technology proficiency has become an economic imperative. Today 60 percent of jobs require skills with technology, and people who use computers on the job earn 43 percent more than other workers (Irving, 1998). Schools take seriously their responsibility to prepare students for the workplace, and today a high school education and basic technology skills are minimum requirements for entry into the labor market.

Various federal, state, and local technology grant programs and corporate and private initiatives have greatly extended educational technology opportunities for many U.S. students. Central to most of these programs are two clear values:

1. Technology is important to student learning.
2. A special effort must be made to provide technology to underrepresented groups.

These two values reflect two significant social and demographic changes occurring in our nation today: increasing dependence on technology and increasing diversification of the population.

Are schools prepared? From 1994 to 1999, the percentage of public schools in the U.S. connected to the Internet rose from 35 percent to 95 percent, and the percentage of connected instructional rooms rose from 3 percent to 63 percent (Lewis, Parsad, Carey, Bartfai, & Farris, 1999). Years one and two of the E-Rate Program provided nearly $4 billion in discounts on the cost of telecommunications services and equipment to schools and libraries. The most disadvantaged districts received nearly ten times as much in discounts on goods and services per student as the least disadvantaged (Puma, Chaplin, & Pape, 2000).

Are all schools equally prepared? Swain and Pearson stated, "Exploring Digital Divide issues in the schools requires educators to examine the access students have *to* technology as well as the equity in the educational experiences students have *with* technology" (2001, p. 11). Neuman stated:

> Economically disadvantaged students, who often use the computer for remediation and basic skills, learn to do what the computer tells them, while more affluent students, who use it to learn programming and tool applications, learn to tell the computer what to do (Neuman in Conte, 1997, ¶ 43).

Are all students equally proficient? Unless disadvantaged students are introduced to more challenging uses of computers, they may be consigned to a new technological underclass, warned Piller.

> Those who cannot claim computers as their own tool for exploring the world never grasp the power of technology. Such students become passive consumers of electronic information. . . . Once out of school, they are relegated to low-wage jobs where they may operate electronic cash registers or bar-code readers. They may catch on as data-entry clerks, typing page after page in deadly monotony. They are controlled by technology as adults—just as drill-and-practice routines controlled them as students (Piller in Conte, 1997, ¶ 44).

Serious inequities exist, and the economic and social forces that underlie those inequities are complex. Race, gender, cultural heritage, linguistic ability, physical ability, and income still define who has access and the quality of that access. For example, urban families whose annual income is $75,000 or more have Internet access at levels 25 times greater than rural low-income families—50 percent compared with 2 percent (Irving, 1999), and White and Asian American and Pacific Islander households own far more computers and have access at rates more than double that of Black and Hispanic households (Mineta, 2000).

In addition, access involves far more than hardware, software, and bandwidth. It involves complex issues, such as the quality of instruction, the availability of appropriate content, and the opportunity to participate in the production of knowledge (Lazarus & Mora, 2000; Lemke & Coughlin, 1998; Wenglinsky, 1999). Technology has the potential to level the playing field for all students—perhaps for the first time in history—by providing almost limitless resources, powerful tools for the creation and publication of knowledge, individualized and assisted educational experiences, and global interaction with experts, mentors, and peers. Yet it can also increase inequity. If some students lack equitable opportunities as technology use becomes routine in business and society, then these students will become increasingly disempowered, and the digital divide will widen.

Access

The Pew Research Center's Internet and American Life Project's report, "Who's Not Online," reinforces the fact that there is still a digital divide. Statistics indicate that minority households, especially low-income minority households, are least likely to be online. For example, whereas 68 percent of poor Whites (households earning less than $30,000) are not online, 75 percent of Blacks and 74 percent of Hispanics are not online (Pew, 2001, p. 5). In fact, the U.S. Department of Commerce (Mineta, 2000) points out that "the August 2000 data show that noticeable divides still exist between those with different levels of income and education, different racial and ethnic groups, old and young, single and dual-parent families, and those with and without disabilities" (p. 1). With home access thus limited, the hope is that schools can compensate and help students learn with technology.

Schools have made some progress in this regard. Access to the Internet has indeed grown. A report by the U.S. Department of Education's NCES (Cattagni & Farris, 2001) stated that the government's E-Rate Program, which was designed to make Internet access and internal connections available at discounted rates to schools and libraries, is one reason for the growth in schools' Internet access. The NCES report found that Internet access in classrooms rose to 77 percent; however, the report suggested that schools with the highest levels of poverty and minority students had the least amount of access (p. 2). Also, Stellin (2001) stated that ". . . schools are reaching the limits of what their network infrastructure can handle—which in turn may limit the types of applications educators can take advantage of for teaching and administrative tasks" (p. 9).

Poverty

A major contributor to the digital divide, and to a general educational divide as well, is the unrelenting poverty that exists among many of our students. Americans resolutely believe that education can help people overcome poverty and that with hard work anyone can be successful. The reality is that many roadblocks caused by poverty exist, and they are not easily overcome. According to the 2000 Census, the poverty rate for adults is 11 percent, but the rate among children under 18 is 17 percent (*NY Times* editorial August 9, 2001), and research has shown that poverty generates a negative impact on student learning and future success (Payne, 1998). Researcher Ron Renchler stated, "The price these children pay for being born poor is enormous" (1993, p. 1). He cited sources indicating that low socioeconomic status (SES) children living in inner cities are much more likely to have educationally damaging circumstances as part of their life experiences than are higher SES children. "Poverty adversely affects children's growth, cognitive development, academic achievement, and physical and emotional health" (Alaimo, Olson, & Frongillo, 2001, p. 781).

Any student at such risk academically could benefit from the immense potential of technology for learning. Effective uses of technology could help these at-risk students to become part of a technologically savvy generation that will command good jobs and high salaries. If students in need are not provided with access to technology and guidance in how to use it, these students may be left out of yet another life opportunity.

Spending on Education and Technology

Attempts to bridge the digital divide are firmly based in historical precedent of this country's commitment to provide access to essentials such as education, public libraries, electricity, and universal phone service. The current effort is the E-Rate Program to connect schools and libraries to the Internet, starting with the lowest SES schools. However, access to technology and wires alone do not tell the whole story. Access to trained teachers and appropriate content is key.

In terms of equipment, the quality of the technology to which students have access and how much access they have make a difference. We know that many students at higher economic levels have home computers that can provide access to learning at any time and can utilize all the latest software and Web sites. For example, in one small upscale southern California community, school leaders recently included laptop computers as suggested school supplies for third, fourth, and fifth graders (Garrison & Yi, 2001). In contrast, although many schools may have computers, the equipment may lack multimedia capability and connections to Internet resources and thus cannot provide the quality of instruction students need.

Statistics tell us that in 1999, 86.3 percent of households earning $75,000 and above per year not only had computers in the home but also had Internet access (Rowand, 2000). Meanwhile, many poor families cannot even afford homes with room for children to play indoors on cold days, a place for a desk for homework, or even a table to gather around for family dinner (Ojito, 2001). Children living in conditions such as these are not likely to perform as well in school as their more affluent counterparts, and these students are unlikely to have access to a computer to help them with homework.

If home access is not possible, at the very least, schools should provide technology on a par with better-off districts. In general, however, educational spending is inequitable. "While suburban school districts may spend $12,000 to $15,000 on every student, city and rural school districts are fortunate if they can raise $7,000" (Clinchy, 2001). In one study, researchers found that the highest 40 percent of the schools spent well over twice as much per capita as the lowest 10 percent (Anderson & Becker, 2001).

While data from the NCES tell us that access to technology and to the Internet has improved, in large part thanks to the E-Rate Program, there is still cause for concern

> if the goal is student Internet access, rather than school Internet access. In 1999, almost three-quarters of instructional rooms in wealthy schools (where less than 11 percent of students receive federal lunch assistance) had Internet access. For high-poverty schools, only 39 percent of the classrooms had access. That gap in Internet access has actually widened over the last five years between rich and poor schools. Also widening in the last two years is the student-per-computer ratio. In high-poverty schools, the current ratio is about 16 students per computer; in wealthy schools, the ratio is only seven to one (Rose, 2001, p. 11).

School Environment

Poor children live in neighborhoods with limited physical, economic, and cultural opportunities. They go to schools with conditions that mirror the conditions in their neighborhoods. These conditions demoralize children for whom there is no escape and who may see the world around them as a reflection of their self-worth.

> Many poor and minority students cope daily with school facilities with peeling paint, crumbling plaster, overflowing or malfunctioning toilets, poor lighting, poor ventilation, and malfunctioning or non-existent cooling and heating systems. [They] find themselves daily in environments that adversely affect their morale and their performance (Wilson & Martin, 2000, p. 24).

The likelihood that these students will have access to advanced technology is slim. Even with access, the likelihood that they will use technology for advanced learning opportunities is even lower.

There is an invisible layer of prejudice toward those who have not succeeded in our society. The Horatio Alger myth is part of our heritage: Anyone can lift himself or herself by the bootstraps and succeed. If you do not, you have only yourself to blame. Thus we deem poor people and their children unworthy and then extend that attitude to language-minority children, to disabled children, and to anyone who does not appear to be mainstream.

Prejudice is so insidious and unconscious that most of society does not recognize its existence. For instance, the language of the Internet is English and few sites exist for linguistically diverse populations. Many sites present information only in the terms of the mainstream culture. Yet Franklin (2001) points out, "In Los Angeles alone, there are at least 80 spoken languages, each representing a group of children who are being brought up with particular cultural behavioral traits" (p. 3). These differences are not limited to race or linguistics. "You have to consider religious differences, gender-equity issues, children who have disabilities, children coming from single parent or same-sex households, and others" (p. 3).

Disabled individuals suffer at the hands of a society that ignores the extent of their need for equitable access to technology. We think in terms of our successes—assistive technologies that give physically handicapped children the tools to communicate. We are often less cognizant of children without sight or hearing or children with other special needs.

Another group of children often underserved by technology is girls. In today's world, electronic and visual media play a large role in shaping our identities, and common stereotypes exist in various media that suggest that girls cannot become scientists, mathematicians, or engineers and that computers are for boys. Thus, these stereotypes serve to limit the participation of girls in technology, while real differences, such as the learning preferences of girls and boys, which could be addressed in classrooms to increase the effectiveness of instruction, go ignored.

Uses of Technology

Merely having computers scattered throughout classrooms does not ensure that they will be used to their best advantage. Opportunities exist for playing games and doing lower-level work online as well as for doing research and engaging in higher-level and creative thinking activities.

The Children's Partnership has found that it is as important to create useful content on the Internet—material and applications that serve the needs and interests of millions of low-income and underserved Internet users—as it is to provide computers and Internet connections. For Americans at risk of being left behind, useful content includes employment, education, business, and other information presented so that limited literacy users can understand it. "Children and youth want participation and self-expression; high-impact packaging with interactivity; multimedia; and youth-friendly tutorials. Both adults and youth want easier searching and usability; encouragement; and involvement" (Lazarus & Mora, 2000, pp. 4–5).

Inequity further exists in the way technology is used with different kinds of students. The attitude that even with technology, poor and minority students should be working on basic skills and test preparation rather than engaging in activities that promote higher-order thinking skills is destructive and inherently biased. As Wenglinsky pointed out, "Disadvantaged eighth graders seem to be less likely to be exposed to higher-order learning through computer . . . and using computers for drill and practice, the lower-order skills, is negatively related to academic achievement" (1998, paragraph 4).

Learning that is Web-infused, collaborative, and project-based may not be easily measurable or measured on standardized tests. However, in Wenglinsky's study, the results show that ". . . higher-order thinking [is] positively related to academic achievement" (paragraph 5). The long-term result is that students who are exposed to such challenging learning experiences are better prepared for our information-based world.

How does technology provide higher-order thinking? There are examples of students communicating with archeologists on expeditions, space scientists in outer space, museum curators, and other professionals who can help students view their work as authentic rather than dull and prescribed. There are examples of students becoming active learners, gathering and analyzing environmental data such as local air and water quality, and comparing the data with other students globally. There are examples of students working collaboratively to research a topic and create learning materials for their peers. When they explore ideas together, they must explain and defend their reasoning and thus must understand the topic at a much deeper level than when they read a textbook passage about it. Such experiences empower students as learners and can influence their commitment to learning in the future. Such empowering instruction is the right of all of America's students.

Teachers

The best way to provide this sort of learning is to have teachers who understand teaching, learning, technology, and more—in other words, capable, experienced teachers. Becker and Riel (2000), in a study of educators, found:

> The most professional engaged teachers—teachers who are leaders in their communities—are exploiting computers in a constructivist manner. Their use of computers with students is not limited to gaining computer competence, but extends to involvement in cognitively challenging tasks where computers are tools used to achieve greater outcomes of students communicating, thinking, producing, and presenting their ideas (paragraph 1).

However, too often, the best teachers migrate to better districts where the best opportunities exist for them as well as for students. The result is that there is constant teacher turnover in poor schools. Schools in poor neighborhoods are likely to have teachers with less experience and less education than those in middle class neighborhoods, which makes a difference in test scores (Levy, Melstner, & Wildavsky, 1974).

Of all the adverse conditions that deprive students of their right to equal educational opportunities, the one that stands out most prominently is teacher preparation and quality. Darling-Hammond (2000), for example, using data from a 50-state survey of policy, found that teacher preparation and certification are by far the strongest correlates of student achievement in reading and mathematics, both before and after controlling for student poverty and language status.

Poorly qualified teachers are not likely to know how to use technology themselves, let alone know the best uses to enhance student learning. Students must have trained teachers who in turn have technical support, professional development so they can enhance their skills with new technologies, and leaders who understand and guide appropriate uses in their schools and districts.

> The widespread consensus among those in government and research who have been studying computer use in education is that effective use of educational technology depends most strongly on the human element—on having teachers and support personnel who have not only technical skills in using computers but practical pedagogical knowledge about designing computer activities that create intellectually powerful learning environments for students (Anderson & Becker, 2001, p. 1).

Yet statistics show that "schools with large concentrations of lower income students spend a smaller portion of their technology funds on teacher training and support than do schools serving wealthier students" (Anderson & Becker, 2001, p. 19).

Professional Development

The U.S. Department of Education (2000), in its National Educational Technology Plan, offers as its second goal: "All teachers will use technology effectively to help students achieve high academic standards" (p. 1). The report expands on the idea that, "Most teachers have been prepared for a model of teaching dramatically out of step with what is needed to prepare the nation's students for the challenges they will face in the future" (p. 5). This lack of preparation results in a lack of technology self-efficacy on the part of the teachers. As an NCES survey reported, "Relatively few teachers reported feeling very well prepared to integrate educational technology into classroom instruction (20 percent)" (Lewis, et al., 1999, p. 2).

This effect is not limited to new teachers. The U.S. Department of Education's Web-based Education Commission reported that both older teachers who were educated before computers and who may be introduced to them for the first time in their own classroom, as well as younger teachers who may know how to use technology themselves, "do not know how to apply these skills in classroom instruction" (Rowand, 2000, p. 26).

Although school districts and state education agencies offer workshops, courses, seminars, and the like to help teachers learn to integrate technology, with teacher attrition and the entrance of so many new teachers each year, districts are fighting an uphill battle.

Preparing Future Teachers

Today there is a new emphasis on preservice educators. According to the Web-based Education Commission (U.S. Department of Education, 2000), ". . . unless new teachers enter the classroom ready to teach with technology, we will never catch up. If teacher education programs do not address this issue head on, we will lose the opportunity to get it right with a whole generation of new teachers and the students they teach" (p. 30). As the Commission has pointed out, most of today's teacher education programs do not yet offer courses that provide instruction on integrating technology (p. 31).

The U.S. Department of Education's Preparing Tomorrow's Teachers to Use Technology (PT3) Program began in 1999. It is bringing new ideas, new collaborations, and new models to teacher education. The PT3 program has made $150 million in federal funding available to 441 programs for teacher preparation institutions to develop capacity, implement new programs, and provide innovative catalysts for broader change. These programs are beginning to take root and offer promise for the future.

Leadership

Even if some teachers understand how to use technology optimally, it will take a concerted effort and organizational change to institutionalize their efforts. The priorities of school administrators determine what happens in the classroom. If administrators are committed to having teachers use technology well and commit resources to professional development and support, change will happen. If administrators at the school or district level pay only lip service to technology use, classroom priorities will not include technology.

Anderson and Dexter (2001) state:

> Because technology implementation requires policy, budget and finance, and various other organizational mechanisms, technology programs are doomed unless key administrators, as well as teachers, play active roles in these programs. Charismatic people may contribute to

technology integration as well, but it is even more essential for a school to distribute leadership and become a "technology learning organization," where administrators, teachers, students, and parents together work on how best to adapt new technologies to improve learning (p. 17).

Empowerment

The key to change is in empowering individuals, schools, and communities to believe in themselves and to adapt technology to their own purposes. Although in the past we have focused on technology literacy—knowing how to use the tools of this information age—the focus now must shift to information literacy—knowing how to get needed information, knowing how to assess and analyze information, and knowing how to create knowledge from information—in other words, empowering people (students in this case) to reach their potential by providing the rich array of technology and learning tools to everyone and making sure everyone is prepared to use such tools appropriately. The goal is for people to realize their potential and find self-fulfillment, which Maslow, in pre-computer times, called "self-actualization" (1943).

Most educators would agree with Parks (1999), that although

school programs must ensure a quality education for all children, past and present conditions of racism contribute to reduced expectations, opportunities, and resources for many poor students and students of color. The influences of racism result in policies and conditions that are debilitating for children and young adults, perpetuating rather than reducing the cycle of poverty (p. 18).

While few people believe that racism, especially in educational institutions, is deliberate, it certainly exists on a covert level. While it is often invisible to those who inadvertently perpetuate it, racism damages both the individuals who are its targets and the society as a whole. It leads to an "internalization of racism," which Weissglass (2001) defines as

. . . the process in which people of color believe and act on the negative messages they receive about themselves and their group. Internalized racism causes people to give up, become hopeless, or believe that they are not as intelligent or as worthwhile as whites. Internalized racism undermines people's confidence and, as a result, their ability to function well (p. 49).

Without a belief in oneself, success is elusive.

Conclusion

This introduction was designed to frame issues of digital equity and its opposite, the digital divide, within the context of societal and educational problems. Many of these problems may seem impossibly complex and intractable. However, this book provides examples that demonstrate the potential of reform.

Access to online information resources and to the use of technology tools for learning can enable more poor and otherwise disenfranchised children to succeed. Technology, with its concomitant contribution of personal power—in accessing information, creating knowledge, and presenting one's work electronically—may do much to promote students' sense of empowerment and the belief in their own abilities.

Technology can make a real difference. The book will demonstrate that with access to technology, technology-proficient teachers, appropriate content, and student-centered instruction, disenfranchised students may experience significant educational gains. If technology provides access to information, experts, and appropriate and varied means of expression, digital equity may be a way to break the cycle of poverty through the only valid path our society offers—education.

1 Creating Educational Access

KARIN M. WIBURG

JULIA F. BUTLER

access: the right to enter, approach, or use; admittance.
—*Webster's New World Dictionary,* 2000

FOCUS QUESTIONS

1. What efforts have been made to ensure access for all to public education and information resources?
2. How have technology tools changed, and how do these changes affect access to digital learning resources?
3. How have educators approached technological innovation in schools, and how does this influence access?
4. What are the different components of digital access, and how do these components relate to educational opportunities?

Access to political power in America was once limited to White, Protestant males who owned property. At the same time a democratic spirit has always existed in the United States, perhaps because of the many immigrants who came here to escape political persecution. The history of American society and the related history of access are largely about the movements and laws that were intended to expand citizen participation from this original narrow political base. It is also about how and why those laws were not always effective. Digital equity is now the latest battle in the effort to keep access to power open to all—to avoid having a technological Berlin Wall between those who have access to electronic information and communication and those who do not.

This chapter provides a historical context for understanding issues of digital access; however, it starts long before access to computers or even electricity became politically important. In many ways access is about the right to learn and to know, the right to an education. It is about who has a right to know and who decides what it is important to know. The history of access begins in the local schools that were established during the very beginning of the United States and continues with the fight for equal educational opportunities for all children. With the invention of electricity, new forms of transportation, telephones, and eventually computers and networks, access to information and knowledge has changed in form but not necessarily in substance. While technologies have changed from the storyteller to one-room schoolhouses to large, online universities, the larger issue has remained the same and that issue is access.

Before looking at current equity and access issues the authors explore the following historical issues: access and free education; access and racial equity; access for special populations; access to electricity, phones, and information; and finally access to computers and networks. The chapter ends with an expanded definition of four components of digital access:

- Access to up-to-date hardware, software, and connectivity
- Access to meaningful, high-quality, and culturally responsive content along with the opportunity to contribute to the knowledge base represented in online content
- Access to educators who know how to use digital tools and resources effectively
- Access to systems sustained by leaders with vision and support for change through technology

All of that, however, comes later. Let us begin our historical journey by going back to the days of the Pilgrims.

Access and Free Education

To put digital access in context, consider the history of equitable access to education. In the United States, public policy providing access to a free education began as early as shortly after the landing of the Pilgrims. People in Massachusetts in 1647 passed the Old Deluder Satan Act that required each township to appoint someone to teach any interested children to read and write. It also required that any township with one hundred families establish a grammar school to prepare students to attend a university. The name of the act reflects the purpose of keeping its youth informed—so they would maintain their religious culture. In 1787, under the Northwest Ordinance, townships were created reserving a portion of each township for a local school. State and national governments established provisions for access to public colleges as well as elementary and secondary schools. In 1862, the Morrill Act designated one land grant college for each state. The law was intended to ensure a higher education for the working classes and for those who could not afford private colleges. These colleges emphasized education and military and mechanical arts, but also insisted that classical studies be included.

Access and the Color Line

In early American history, such free education was intended primarily for the children of White families only. After the civil war, African American children began to attend White schools although they were often not welcomed in the new public schools. The desire to maintain a color line led, in 1896, to the *Plessy v. Ferguson* Supreme Court decision that officially established separate Black schools. According to this ruling such schools were to be designed to be "separate and equal." This ruling caused the continuation of segregation for more than 50 years. Smith (1996) tells the story of Farmville, Virginia, and the impact of "separate but equal" on the schools in that community. He includes pictures of schools built during this time. The White schools were often made of brick while the separate Black schools were little more than tarpaper shacks. The White schools had gymnasiums, infirmaries, and cafeterias while the Black schools were asked to function without those specialized facilities and in very overcrowded conditions. The same size school held 187 Whites and more than 400 Blacks. Yes, the students all had educational facilities but the environment in the White schools was certainly more conducive to learning.

In 1954, the historic court decision of *Brown v. Board of Education of Topeka, Kansas* finally overturned the Plessy case declaring that "separate schools are inherently not equal." The parents of an African American girl who wanted to attend a White school that was much closer to her home than the Black school brought the case. This historic case effectively began the movement for integration of all races in public schools. This court decision and others that supported it were based on the fourteenth amendment to the constitution, which guarantees equal protection and due process to all. The law now supports children of any race attending their neighborhood schools; however, segregation continues to exist due to the economic inequities of neighborhoods and districts.

Children of color, who are most likely to live in poor communities, are still not receiving equal access to a quality education because of inadequate funding of their neighborhood schools. Property taxes are lower or nonexistent in communities that lack expensive homes and businesses. Darling-Hammond (1997) report that schools at the 90th percentile of school funding spend nearly ten times more than schools at the 10th percentile. Poor schools also have the most rapid turnover of teachers and the most difficulty keeping teaching staff (Ingersoll, 2001) and their teachers receive the least professional development (Darling-Hammond, 1997). They are often without textbooks, paper, furniture, and even adequate bathrooms (Kozol, 1991). Until the economic issues of school funding are adequately addressed there will continue to be color and poverty lines.

Access and Language

The United States has always been a multilingual country, a country of immigrants who represent many languages and cultures. Schools have traditionally been the places where students have learned English. In simpler times, when schools were charged with teaching a smaller, fairly homogenous body of knowledge, and when students speaking other languages lived in communities in which English was the common goal, schools seem to have largely succeeded in helping students gain English. The complexity of teaching English has recently increased; however, there are now places such as the Southwest border area of the United States, where large groups of children attending schools are living in communities where the dominant language is not English. In addition Spanish-speaking immigrants are the fastest growing immigration group (*Newsweek,* 2000, September 18). In some states, like New Mexico, Hispanic students are now the majority. The United States is rapidly becoming a bilingual rather than a primarily English-speaking country.

Debates continue about the way in which to integrate bilingual children into American schools and society and whether to support both the native and the English language. Research indicates that children do best in school if they are given the opportunity to first become literate in their first language and then helped to gain a second language, English. For example, Ramirez (1992) reports positive effects of long-term primary instruction over structured English immersion. However, when children enter school in the United States without having had opportunities to gain literacy in their home language the issues become more complex. Gersten and Woodward (1994) describe no differences between student achievement in a bilingual transitional program and a structured English immersion program as long as the primary language is used to support conceptual development.

The bottom line is that all children must have access to a good education. When students are not taught in a language they can understand, they do not have this access. The failure of the San Francisco School District to provide English language instruction to 1800 Chinese children or to provide them with other access to learning resulted in the *Lau v. Nichols* court case. This case established the rule that equal treatment may not be equitable. For example, if a student who doe not speak English is in a class in which the teacher provides information only in English, the student is not receiving equal treatment in terms of getting an education.

Access and Special Education

Individuals with special needs have had to fight similar battles for equitable treatment. In 1975, Public law 94-142 was first passed; it stipulated that all children must receive a free and appropriate public education regardless of their degree of disability. In 1990 this law was reauthorized as the Individuals with Disabilities Education Act (IDEA). The 1997 amendments to IDEA focused specifically on students in the general education classroom. These students comprise 10–12 percent of the nation's student population. Roughly 5.6 million students receive IDEA services (IdeaData.org, 2000). The courts have interpreted these laws to mean that students need to be placed in the least possible restrictive environment, in other words, be placed in as normal a classroom as possible and resources provided to help them learn as well as other students.

Technology has played an essential role in providing access to children with special needs. Many of these students require a special technology called *assistive technology,* without which they could not access a good education. For example, a child might have to type using a special mouthpiece in order to communicate in class or access resources on the Web. Special text-to-speech devices also offer access to electronic educational resources that would not be usable without assistive technology. A student may with the help of technology control the speed of his or her reading or use special devices to access information even when visually or hearing impaired. These are just some of the examples in which technology used appropriately is placing special needs students in an active learning role with access to rich educational resources. Factors involving special education, language, culture, and poverty as related to access to digital resources are discussed more fully in other chapters.

Access to Information and Communication

The Telephone System

In 1934, as telephones became commonly available, the U.S. Congress passed the Communications Act of 1934 to ensure that the pricing of telephone service was economical enough that all Americans could have access to this service. In addition, the Federal Communication Commission (FCC), created as part of Franklin Roosevelt's New Deal, was designed to provide a rapid and efficient national and worldwide access to wire and radio communication services. The FCC now oversees new communication technologies such as satellite, microwave, and private radio communication. The pricing structures created as a result of this act and the 1996 Revised Act, while helpful, have still not made telecommunications available to all U.S. citizens and the goal of universal access has not yet been achieved as service is still prohibitively expensive in some parts of rural American and on some American Indian reservations.

Karen Buller (1999) who heads the National Indian Telecommunications Institute (NITI) described how telephone use is not universal on Indian reservations because of both economic and technical problems. Getting the phone lines to the reservation in very rural areas is difficult and companies are reluctant to invest in infrastructure in these areas. The residents also pay higher amounts in many cases due to the fact that calls even within the reservations are often long distance. Costs can also be different due to state laws—for example on a reservation in the state of Washington service is $16.00 a month, whereas in Santa Fe, New Mexico, it is $30.00 per month. In spite of current inequities in telephone service—inequities that are slowly being addressed at the federal level through agencies such as The Commerce Department's National Telecommunications and Information Administration (NTIA)—the situation in the United States is still better than in many parts of the world where people must wait months to obtain a telephone and then pay high fees for access.

Access to telephone lines is the foundation on which the development of the Internet and thus digital equity rests. Without phone access many students in rural and poor schools can literally not be hooked up to the vast information resources available on the Internet. Phone companies are not always willing to invest in telephone connections in communities that have no commercial infrastructure. In these very poor and inaccessible areas the government will have to take a larger role either through government efforts or through incentives for private industry to serve rural and poorer areas.

Electricity

The Rural Electrification Act of 1936 helped bring safe electric power as well as telephone services to rural communities. Poor farmers and communities could apply for low-cost loans for telephone and electrical services. This government act facilitated the development of infrastructure throughout rural America. Eventually the U.S. Department of Agriculture became the branch of government that continued to facilitate access to electricity and telephones for rural areas. Information about how to get electricity loans is now available via the Web. On May 21, 1999 the USDA Rural Development marked the 63rd anniversary of the Rural Electrification Act by unveiling a new user-friendly Web site to help borrowers and the public learn about the USDA electric program. According to a recent press release from the U.S. Department of Agriculture (2001) rural communities have some of the highest "telephone penetration" rates in the America. The same article (U.S. Dept. of Agriculture, 2001) states that USDA's electric program has helped build about 50% of the nation's power lines.

Building Infrastructure

In 1993, Clinton established the National Information Infrastructure Initiative (NIII). Clinton's agenda under the NII Initiative included the goal of making information resources available to all at affordable prices by extending the *universal service* concept. In order to assist poor schools in obtaining access to telecommunications services, Congress passed the Telecommunications Act of 1996 that provided discounted rates on goods and services to poor districts. This popular program became known as the E-Rate and did help many poorer districts get access to the Internet from their schools and classrooms. The E-Rate provides supplemental funding for districts to acquire access to electronic networks, file servers, and other devices needed to bring the Internet into their schools and classrooms. For example a school district in which 90 percent of its students are on free or reduced lunches (the way in which socioeconomic status is assessed in schools) would receive 90 percent of the funding for equipment from the federal government. A school in which half the children were considered living in poverty would receive half of their funding from the government for networking. The E-Rate, however, is limited to schools and libraries and cannot be used to obtain resources for other community organizations.

There are a growing number of organizations that are focused on building community technology structures. The Community Technology Centers is a national nonprofit membership organization of more than 600 independent community technology centers where people get free or low-cost access to computers and computer-related technology. CTC envisions a society in which all people are equitably empowered by technology skills and usage. Their mission statement is very clear.

> CTCNet shares with Playing To Win, its founding organization, a recognition that, in an increasingly technologically dominated society, people who are socially and/or economically disadvantaged will become further disadvantaged if they lack access to computers and computer-related technologies. CTCNet brings together agencies and programs that provide opportunities whereby people of all ages who typically lack access to computers and related technologies can learn to use these technologies in an environment that encourages exploration and discovery and, through this experience, develop personal skills and self-confidence (Chang, Honey, Light, Light, Moeller, & Roth, 1998).

Kevin Rocap, from the Center for Language Minority Education and Research (CLMER), tells in Chapter 5 of this book the following story about the origin of Break Away Technologies, a community technology center initiative:

During the 1992 "disturbances," or uprisings, in South-Central Los Angeles one African American community leader, Joseph Loeb, watched his community literally go up in flames fueled by anger and historical patterns of neglect. Joseph decided he had to do what he could to make a difference. He quit his job, sold his car, and cleared out his garage to set up a makeshift computer lab to start teaching computer skills to inner-city children and youth, as a way of providing new skills and hope for an economically brighter future. Joseph and many more committed members of the community then opened two small community technology centers before the newly formed Break Away Technologies. This group found a home in a 15,000 square foot facility near Jefferson and Crenshaw in Los Angeles. Break Away Technologies became an after-school and weekend center for K–12 inner-city children, youth and adults; became a point of training and access for community-based arts, nonprofit and economic development organizations; and initiated a successful CyberSeniors program, with many seniors developing high-tech entrepreneurial skills and becoming mentors to neighborhood youth. In collaboration with the Center for Language Minority Education and Research (CLMER), Break Away has became a successful applicant for the "Computers in Our Future" (CIOF) Initiative of The California Wellness Foundation. Over four years Break-Away collaborated with 10 similar sites statewide to develop new operational visions for community-based and managed open access, education, training and support centers where underserved youth can gain access to and develop competencies in using, building and maintaining computer and network technologies, use computers and the Internet for other learning activities and engage in web page development, multimedia, animation and graphic design courses, as well as develop work readiness and preparation skills.

Grants are becoming increasingly available to help build community infrastructure. For example, the Commerce Department's National Telecommunications and Information Administration (NTIA) announced the award in 2001 of $42.8 million in Technology Opportunities Program (TOP) grants to 74 nonprofit organizations, including state and local governments across the country and in Puerto Rico. TOP grants, matched by $46.7 million in contributions from the private sector and state and local organizations, extend the benefits of advanced telecommunications technologies to underserved communities and neighborhoods. In 2002, Congress has appropriated $12.4 million for new grants through the Commerce Department's Technology Opportunities Program (TOP) for Fiscal Year 2002 (TOP, 2002).

At the same time as the notion of technology literacy has extended to include community infrastructure, ideas about information have changed the nature of libraries in the United States. The next section discusses the changing nature of libraries in this country.

Access to Information

In addition to free access to education, telephony, and other infrastructure items, United States leaders as early as the 1800s began to establish free public libraries. The Library of Congress, which was established in 1800, lost many of its books in a fire after the British bombardment in 1814. Much of the loss of the materials was made up soon after by the purchase of Thomas Jefferson's Library. The Library of Congress was required by law to be open to all citizens in order to continue to receive federal funding. During the second half of the 18th century cities began to establish libraries, although at first they were only available to people who could pay the required rental fees. The Boston Public Library was established in 1848 as the first library free to the public and tax-supported. In the late 1800s Andrew Carnegie used his steel fortune to further the status of libraries in most major cities in the United States.

Public libraries meant a great deal to the poor people who lived in cities that had libraries. For the first time it was possible to have a library card and borrow books for free. Adults could access information that would help them learn new skills and prepare for jobs as well as check out books for themselves and their children.

In 1988, the American Association of School Librarians & Association for Educational Communications and Technology published *Information Power: Guidelines for School Library Media Programs*. This book had a profound influence on libraries and led them to expand their mission from being keepers of texts to purveyors of information. As new media became available the library expanded to provide electronic recordings, videos, books on tapes, and access to computers. For many people the library is now their best source of access to the Internet and to electronic mail. Jeffrey Kaye (1999) describes in a PBS NewsHour online issue on the digital divide how people wait for an hour or more to have access to the Internet in the New York Public Library. He also contrasts this situation of limited access with the situation of a family in Tempe, Arizona, who has paid for Internet connections through cable television. While libraries are an essential place for access, people who use them still have less access than those who can receive full access at home.

Technological Change and Issues of Access

While economics continues to be a key factor in dividing those who have computers from those who don't, computers grow more and more powerful and are available at less and less cost. This phenomenon is known as Moore's Law, after Gordan Moore, a co-founder of Intel Corporation. Moore predicted that the number of transistors the industry would be able to place on a computer chip would double every year. While originally intended as a rule of thumb in 1965, it has become the guiding principle for the industry to deliver ever-more-powerful semiconductor chips at proportionate decreases in cost. As the power of the computer chip increases, you can buy a computer with twice the power 18 months after the previous purchase, yet pay the same price (Provenzo, Brett, & McCluskey, 1999). The cost of computing power is decreasing, making it possible for people in lower socioeconomic levels to own home computers.

Changing Functions of Computers

Relevant to understanding issues of access is an overview of how the functions of computers have changed in fundamental ways since the first electromechanical computer, the ENIAC, was first brought into action in 1946. This section describes how computer functions have changed from number crunching to data processing to communication and most recently to knowledge environments.

Number Crunching

The ENIAC's development in the 1940s was partly a response to the needs of the military to decipher enemy codes. The ENIAC made possible much faster numerical calculations and was about 1,000 times faster then the previous generation of relay computers. The ENIAC used 18,000 vacuum tubes; about 1,800 square feet of floor space, and consumed about 180,000 watts of electrical power. The executable instructions for making up a program were embodied in the separate "units" of ENIAC, which were plugged together to form a "route" for the flow of information. These connections had to be redone after each computation, together with presetting function tables and switches. This "wire your own" technique was inconvenient (for obvious reasons). Ironically, a pocket calculator that you can buy at the grocery store for under $5.00 does more than these early computers.

Data Processing

In the 1960s and 1970s the computer became primarily a data machine. By the end of the 1970s about 80 percent of the information processed was text. As computing power grew, a type of smaller mainframe, called a *mini-system,* was developed. Such mini-systems made it possible for businesses and organizations to begin to use computers and moved computing out of the hands of the government and a few universities. Businesses used mini-systems to process batch orders, while the initial use of computers in schools involved connections to either mini-systems or mainframes with tutorials and practice programs for students. During this period software for running the computers was also developed. Additional operating systems such as CPM (Control Program for Microcomputers) and DOS (the Disk Operating System) were developed.

Computers as Communicating Tools

Bell Laboratories invented the transistor in 1958 and with it came the birth of the microcomputer. Microcomputers put significant computing power in the hands of individuals, causing a redistribution of power from the hands of the technical gurus to ordinary people. With the help of two college dropouts, Steve Jobs and Steve Wozniak, microcomputers also became available to schools and to teachers and students in the form of the Apple computer. The computer became both a personal and an educational tool. With the development of the Internet in the 1990s, these microcomputers began to function as tools for communication. Power came not just from the computer itself, but also from its ability to link to networks of worldwide and local information. Computer operating systems also evolved to include graphical interfaces and broader the definition of communication to include not only text, but also pictures, video, and sound. Communication via multimedia became affordable, and the educational implications of using multimedia for learning grew. One example of the potential of computers as communication tools is the expanded use of multimedia programs today to help students who are English language learners.

Knowledge Environments

As computer capacity has grown and network resources increased exponentially, computers have changed from what were at first glorified typing and teaching machines to systems in which it is now possible to create as well as distribute materials. High levels of access allow teachers and students to participate with others in the community and to generate new community knowledge environments. In such environments, when people from different locations develop new ideas together on the computer network, new knowledge results. The computer is no longer just a means for the distribution of curriculum—its function has been further expanded to include the creation of knowledge.

This idea of changing functions and how this affects what is possible is an important one. As Don Norman (1993) has suggested, the technology itself is not neutral. The capacity of the tools matter. Norman (1993) used the term *affordance* to describe what an environment or tool allows us to do. For example a chair affords sitting, a television affords watching, and a computer affords interaction. Certain software affords only right or wrong answers while more open-ended software might support collaborative and generative work and afford multiple solutions to problems. Norman's position is well developed in his book, *Things That Make Us Smart* (1993). He suggested that while previous technologies in schools—such as radio, film, instructional television, and language labs—have not had the impact that the developers expected, interactive capability means this new innovation will have a great deal more impact.

The point of Norman's work is that when hardware and software are evaluated they must be considered in terms of the kinds of learning and activity they afford. Schools may have computers but if they are not powerful enough, for example, to allow teachers to run multimedia programs with sound, required for early literacy learning, then the computers do not afford the desired learning. If students in a poor community want to learn more about the world and don't have Internet access at a reasonable speed to world geography sites, the computers they have do not afford the intended learning. While computer access has increased significantly over the last few years, with reported ratios of 1 computer to 6 students (NTIA, 1998), what is important is not their numbers but their capacity to support communication and learning.

Teachers and Computers

In order for students to have access to computers it is necessary for their teachers to want to use them. Unfortunately the inventions of new technology for education have not had that result. There are many reasons for this, not the least of which is the current organization of schooling and the role of teachers in those schools. Larry Cuban has written an interesting history of how teachers have interacted with technological innovations in schools from 1920 to the late 1980s. He begins the first chapter with a 1922 quote from Thomas Edison: "I believe that the motion picture is destined to revolutionize our educational system and that in a few years it will supplant largely, if not entirely, the use of textbooks" (Cuban, 1986, p. 9).

Developers from outside the school culture have introduced each new educational technology with similar strong words as to how this new device will fundamentally change education. In reality, many of these innovations have had very little impact on teacher practice. It is useful to examine the history of some of these innovations in view of the current promise of computer-based technologies to create fundamental changes in teaching and learning. Is the computer such a fundamentally different machine that its integration into school practice is likely to be different, as suggested by Norman, or is the institution and culture of K–12 education fundamentally in conflict with the potential of computers to create changes in educational practice? What are the limitations of the current educational structure in the United States, and how does this limit what is possible in terms of student access?

Cuban's term for how schools and structures shape behavior and practice is *situationally constrained choice* (p. 66). He provides a historical outline of the introduction of film, radio, and instructional television into the schools and demonstrates the remarkably similar and low impact of each invention on actual classroom practice. For example, researchers gave the following reasons in the 1930s for low integration of films into the curriculum (Cuban, 1986, p. 18):

- Teachers' lack of skill in using the equipment
- Cost of films, equipment, and upkeep
- Inaccessibility of equipment when needed
- Finding and fitting the right films to the class

The book provides similar reasons for the low integration of radio programs: lack of radio receiving equipment, school scheduling problems, and programs not related to the curriculum. In each case there were small groups of teachers who did integrate these new technologies, but most teachers found little reason for using them. Cuban concluded that no one was paying attention to the teachers' point of view. Teachers will embrace innovations such as new forms of grouping, chalkboards, and textbooks when these "advances" solve what teachers consider to be problems. Teachers' needs are anchored in the classroom, an arena largely foreign to researchers and policymakers. Cuban concluded that technologies will be adopted to the extent that they solve classroom problems and when their benefit to the teacher outweighs the cost of learning to use them.

Pedagogy, Technology, and Access

Teachers first used computers the way people almost always use new technologies—to do more efficiently things they have always done. During the 1960s and the 1970s the computer was used for drill-and-practice (tutorial) programs with students. This was known as computer assisted instruction (CAI) or computer assisted learning (CAL). Students would type in answers and the machine would indicate whether the answer was right or wrong. If it was wrong then the computer would indicate that the answer was wrong and then present a new question at the same level of difficulty. If the answer was correct, the computer would present a progressively more difficult question. Educators believed that students could learn more in a shorter period of time using this type of technology.

One of the purposes of CAI was to make education more cost effective. In many cases CAI has been useful in improving student achievement. Cuban, however, noted a study by Levin, Glass, and Meister (1984) that found that peer tutoring was actually more cost effective in terms of learning gains than the use of computers. Hativa (1988) did an extensive meta-analysis of the use of computer-based drill and practice in arithmetic and suggested it was widening the gap between high-achieving and low-achieving students. In other words the high achievers were benefiting while the lower achievers were not improving their skills. CAI is often least effective with English language learners since their problem may stem from language rather than content (Butler-Pascoe & Wiburg, in press; Wetzel & Chisholm, 1998). Repeating the same level of words over and over does not help if the user does not understand the words.

Most current leaders in the field of learning and technology suggest that it is only by tying the use of computers to new forms of instruction—such as constructivism and social-constructivism—that the power of the computer for learning can be tapped (Bereiter, 1994: Dede, 1998a; Norton & Wiburg, 1998). A recent large-scale study by Wenglinsky (1998) found that those children whose teachers used computers in constructivist ways to teach mathematics (simulations, spreadsheets) scored significantly higher in mathematics achievement than those who used the computers as tutorial and drill-and-practice machines. A powerful synthesis is emerging that connects new theories of how students learn by constructing and sharing knowledge and the capacity of new computer-based technologies to support these types of learning strategies. Access to these best uses, however, will not occur until teachers in classrooms choose to embrace these new methodologies with technology. Questions related to pedagogy and access are discussed more fully in the next chapter as related to a *didactic divide.*

Access and Educational Opportunity

Access, as it relates to the digital divide, is often discussed as if it were a simple problem of just *hooking everyone up.* While this in itself is still a significant problem in many parts of the United States, access requires more than mere access to hardware and software. This paper considers four components of access:

1. *Access to up-to-date hardware, software, and connectivity*   While access to hardware, networks, and programs is a minimum condition for full participation and the use of digital resources, the *quality* of access is also important. North Central Regional Educational Lab (NCREL) (2001) defines *high-performance technology* as one in which users can take advantage of digital resources interactively and move effortlessly from application to application, routinely using the technology for constructing and managing their own learning.

2. *Access to meaningful, high-quality, and culturally responsive content and the opportunity to contribute to that content*   The Children's Partnership, as part of its work to bridge the digital divide, has done extensive audits of content on the Internet. They believe low-income groups need web content that includes (a) employment and education information, (b) reading levels appropriate to limited-literacy users; (c) multiple languages; and (d) ways for underserved users to create and interact with content so that it is culturally relevant (access level 4). They found significant barriers to usefulness of the Internet for the 22 million Americans who live on under $14,500/year. In addition, 44 million Americans do not have a high enough literacy level to use the Internet. They also found significant language barriers and suggested the greatest need for underserved Americans was useful local information related to jobs and community resources. Such local information is rarely available (Lazarus & Lipper, 2000).

3. *Access to educators who know how to use digital tools and resources*   While schools were quick to hop on the hardware-acquisition bandwagon, they dedicated very small percentages of budgets to training in how to use these resources. The 1995 Office of Technology Assessment (OTA) report, *Teachers & Technology: Making the Connection,* raised two important points: (1) that "technology is not central to the teacher preparation experience" and (2) that "most technology instruction . . . is teaching about technology . . . not teaching with technology across the curriculum" (p. 165). This lack of training is true not only at the preservice level but also in terms of the lack of in-service available for professional development offered in technology integration with teaching. The situation is, however, getting better in terms of increased integration of technology in teacher education (Beck & Wynn, 1998). Many credit the Department of Education's current PT3 (Preparing Tomorrow's Teachers to use Technology) program for increased integration of technology in teacher education institutions.

4. *Access to systems sustained by leaders with vision and support for change via technology*   Participation as learners and citizens is a key criterion for evaluating levels of access for people in all levels of society. This component of access requires that everyone's voice be heard. Participation is made possible only when there are opportunities to learn how to use technological resources in ways in which all people can participate in creating new digital knowledge. Leadership and systems, which support participation, are necessary for this fourth component of access to occur. The development of systems and leadership for overcoming the barriers to access are discussed in the next chapter.

As new technologies become available, such as the Internet II with its broadband capability for truly interactive information and learning, leaders and policymakers will play a crucial role in determining who gets access to these new information tools. Legislative bodies and citizen groups will need help from leaders in education to understand what types of technology and what kinds of training are essential if teachers are to help students gain the skills they need for the 21st century.

Conclusion

This chapter has served as a historical framework for many of the questions related to how best to achieve digital equity. It began by connecting the current digital divide to other divides in education including access to quality schools and equal educational treatment for all students regardless of color, language, or economic status. The authors gave numerous examples related to how national leaders, the government, and the courts have been committed to providing access to education and information for those who cannot afford it. Such efforts ranged from early public schools to the current E-rate program. We also discussed the importance of tools and the capacity of those tools in terms of providing equity of access. The chapter concluded with an expanded definition of digital access, which will underlie much of the discussion on digital equity in this book. Many of the issues raised in this chapter will be discussed more fully in the following chapters.

2

Barriers to Equity

KATHLEEN FULTON

ROBERT SIBLEY

FOCUS QUESTIONS

1. What factors hinder the achievement of digital equity in education?
2. Why might different groups have dissimilar opinions about what creates and sustains digital inequity?
3. How do these differing understandings about barriers to digital equity affect our ability to bring about change?
4. Which barriers do you see as being the most difficult to address and why?
5. Which barriers are the most amenable to change and why?

In today's knowledge-based economy, access to technology determines access to the resources needed for building knowledge and learning throughout your lifetime. Access to these resources—and having the skills to use them productively—is critical for success in education, in work, and in society in general. The previous chapter on access documented our society's long-term, if flawed, commitment to equitable access to education, and how this now translates to a commitment to equitable educational access to information and communication technologies. This commitment is not a coincidence, or simply a noble gesture. It stands at the foundation of the American principal of equality of opportunity, the principal upon which our social, political, and economic systems are built. It is within this context that it is most appropriate to examine the barriers to digital equity, because digital and networking technologies represent the convergence of vital communication, information, and education resources. Lack of effective access to what we call "technology" is in fact lack of access to the opportunity to fully participate in American life.

In this chapter, we will examine in greater detail the four critical components of access to digital participation presented in the previous chapter, in a sense looking at the flip side of the digital equity equation. That is, if these components are essential for full participation in an equitable educational environment in the digital age, the absence or diminishment of any one of these components presents a barrier that hinders or prohibits various groups and individuals from equitable access to educational opportunity. We will also examine why these barriers exist and why they are so difficult to dismantle or overcome. We focus primarily on the barriers of educational vision, which create a didactic divide that may be the most significant barrier of all.

Four Critical Components for Educational Equity in a Digital Age

The previous chapter laid out the framework of essential components necessary for full educational opportunity in our digital age. They are:

- Access to up-to-date hardware, software, and connectivity
- Access to meaningful, high-quality, and culturally responsive content along with the opportunity to contribute to the knowledge base represented in online content
- Access to educators who know how to use digital tools and resources effectively
- Access to systems sustained by leaders with vision and support for change through technology

Barrier 1:   Access to Up-to-Date Hardware, Software, and Connectivity

For the education community, much of the focus on bridging the digital divide over the last several decades has revolved around the challenges of providing hardware, software, and connectivity to schools that were lagging behind in acquiring these assets. Especially since the mid 1990s, the federal government has set in place funding programs that have gone a long way to lessening the gap in school access to hardware, software, and networking technologies. These programs, (including the Technology Literacy Challenge Fund to States, the E-rate program providing discounts for school and library connections to the Internet, funding in Title I for schools with high numbers of students in poverty, and other programs) have begun to lessen the digital divide in terms of school infrastructure. A number of state and district programs have added resources that have helped bridge the technology divide in public schools in their regions. More than $5 billion in state, local, and federal funds has been invested annually for K–12 learning technologies (Milken Exchange, 1999).

Success in bridging the technology gap is measured in lowered student-to-computer ratios and higher percentages of school classrooms with Internet access, and improvements are being registered all across the nation, even in low-income communities. Despite the good news of these dramatic improvements, closer examination of the data reveals several critical flaws in the sound bites that have made the headlines. Increases in computer access and the lower student-to-computer ratios they represent have been more dramatic in schools serving low-income or minority students, but these gains came from such low starting points that the actual difference between the numbers of students without Internet access or reasonable student-to-computer ratios actually stayed the same or rose. Thus, even as late as 1999, in schools where more than 70 percent of students received free or reduced price lunches, only 39 percent of classrooms had Internet access. In contrast, in those schools where fewer than 11 percent of students were on the subsidized lunch program, 74 percent of classrooms had Internet access (NTIA, 1999).

Furthermore, access to hardware, software, and the Internet in schools is not a static process. New technologies and applications, as well as faster connections, are appearing almost continually, and each advancement provides new possibilities for learning. Consequently, it is important to look more closely at the data, in order to understand what types of computers and other technology are being used and where, as well as the speed of the Internet connections available in the classroom. Many of the published statistics measuring student-to-computer ratios and school Internet access do not differentiate between a ten-year-old computer attached to a 28K modem in a principal's office and a multimedia workstation with a dedicated high-speed broadband Internet connection getting constant use in an active classroom.

This issue of the power of technology is not just of interest to techies; it has major implications for the kinds of teaching and learning that can be accomplished using these tools. The gaps in computing power will only grow more pronounced as new technologies push their way into our lives and schools. For example, in 2001, nine state technology networks linked to the ultrafast Internet2 Abilene Network, and some—but not all—schools in these states are able to take advantage of and explore the pedagogical uses of this powerful technology. Other schools in these states, and schools in the remaining 41 states, will not have such an opportunity until some time in the future. The high-performance networking that Internet2 access will provide enables applications that could provide qualitative leaps beyond what is possible using today's Internet technology (U.S. Department of Education, 2000).

But school access is only one piece in the digital equity puzzle. Access at home is equally important. We know that what happens before, after, and beyond the school day has a significant impact on a student's academic success. Just as the presence of books, magazines, and other reading matter in the home can impact a child's reading readiness and early school reading success, in today's environment the availability of computers and Internet access at home can be important factors for a child's technology literacy readiness.

The Department of Commerce reported that in the year 2000 households with less than $15,000 in income had a 12.7 percent Internet penetration rate, as compared with a 77.7 percent rate for those households with incomes over $75,000 (NTIA, 1999). Most families who purchase computers say they do so for educational reasons (Pew Internet and American Life Project, 2001). These purchases are indeed important for students, as illustrated by the fact that 94 percent of youth ages twelve through seventeen who have Internet access say they use the Internet for school research and 78 percent say they believe the Internet helps them with schoolwork. Even more telling is the fact that 71 percent of online teens say that they used the Internet as the major source for their most recent major school project or report. Although 73 percent of students in this age cohort have Internet access, 11 percent of them cite school as their primary access site (Lenhart, Rainie, & Lewis, 2001).

As noted in the previous chapter, the principle of affordable access to communications was established as a basic tenet of American public policy through the Communications Act of 1934. A few states and districts have set forth policies that make Internet access affordable to all citizens, regardless of location, but, in general, public policy initiatives impacting different rates of home access to technology are far behind those addressing school and library access. Access to computers and the Internet at home is still considered a consumer choice, not a basic educational right.

Barrier 2:   Access to Meaningful, High-Quality, and Culturally Responsive Content and the Opportunity to Contribute to the Knowledge Base Represented in That Content

The availability of meaningful, high-quality, and culturally responsive online content is another critical barrier to digital equity. There is, of course, a large and growing collection of educationally valuable, free content on the Internet. Much of it is provided by federal and state institutions, such as the Library of Congress and the Smithsonian Institution, which are committed to digitizing as much as possible of their vast collections of documents and artifacts. Many museums and other cultural institutions in the United States and around the world are doing the same. A vast quantity of scientific data, maps, and reports from NASA and other government and government-supported institutions is also available for free. Newspapers and other information-related companies are making digitized archives available on the Internet at little or no cost to schools. Nonetheless, high-quality online content remains a barrier to digital equity for a number of reasons.

First, online material is increasingly expensive to create and these costs will skyrocket as technology moves to broadband networks that support video and high-quality audio as well as interactivity. There is a growing trend towards charging for the use of material that was once freely available on the Web. Furthermore, with the demise of many dot.coms, numerous free sites have been unable to remain on the Web. Other sites support their free material with a barrage of distracting ads (Musgrove, 2001). To offer ad-free environments, some sites, such as Encyclopedia Britannica, now charge a monthly subscription fee for full access to their site. Even among commercial publishers of online content, many find it difficult to succeed in a fragmented educational marketplace. As online costs rise, low-income schools and individuals will be less able to afford the best, higher-priced online content available for learning.

Second, because much of the market for online educational content must focus on meeting the demands of state standards and high-stakes testing, online content often mimics the traditional pedagogical approach of emphasis on factual recall and basic skills, with little focus on higher-order learning activities and materials. While there are thousands of lesson plans on the Web, their pedagogical value is mixed at best.

Third and most significantly, much online material fails to address the needs, interests, and concerns of Americans who do not match the narrow demographic profile for which most current Internet content is designed. As a result, the Web's multimedia possibilities have barely been tapped, especially with regards to the effective educational use of such content for a many-cultured society. There is a dearth of content designed for and by people of minority, ethnic, and tribal cultures, as well as for girls and those with disabilities.

In an extensive survey of Web content, the Children's Partnership found that at least 50 million American adults—roughly 20 percent—are potentially underserved because of one or more Internet content barriers related to literacy, language, cultural or content relevance (Lazarus & Lipper, 2000). They found that the majority of content on the Internet is written at an average or advanced literacy level, meaning that 44 million adult Americans (22 percent of our adult population) are unable to benefit from these resources, as are millions of young people whose limited reading skills make much of the content inaccessible to them as well. In addition, 87 percent of Internet content is in English, adding an additional barrier to the 32 million Americans for whom English is not the primary language. Only 2 percent of the sites in their survey were multilingual. Relevant local information— e.g., on jobs, education, and housing opportunities—was either unavailable or difficult to find. The lack of Internet content reflecting cultural diversity, whether generated by ethnic communities themselves or designed around their unique cultural practices and interests, adds an additional barrier (Lazarus & Lipper, 2000). Overall, this shortage of relevant material makes the Web intimidating, irrelevant, or uninviting to countless potential users. Those who find the Web an inhospitable place to visit will be less likely to use it to advance their educational goals.

Some online educational materials are being created to address this inequality. With corporate and foundation funding, an organization called Digital Promise is building support for the creation of a non-profit, non-governmental public agency that would encourage the development of digital information and services for educational, cultural, artistic, and civic activities (Century Foundation, 2001). In the spring of 2001, Lawrence Grossman, a former president of both NBC and the Public Broadcasting Service (PBS), along with Newton Minow, a former chairman of PBS, the Federal Communications Commission, and the Rand Corp, announced a proposal for a new Digital Opportunity Investment Trust (DO IT), a public agency modeled on the National Science Foundation. The Trust would be funded with $10 billion from the anticipated public auctions of telecommunications frequency spectrum to digital wireless companies. According to Grossman: "The federal government has invested billions in wiring schools through its E-rate program. We think it's time to turn our attention to content, which is equally important". (Chapman, 2001, ¶8). By the spring of 2002, this proposal had gained national momentum. Senator Dodd had drafted a bill called "The Digital Opportunity Investment Trust Act" (Century Foundation, 2002).

Another way the online knowledge base can grow and meet the needs of a range of learners is by encouraging and supporting teachers and learners to contribute to the online knowledge base represented by the Web. Presently, many teachers are producing online lessons and sharing their experiences with their colleagues through the Internet, thereby opening the windows of their once isolated classrooms to the world. Even more empowering is the opportunity for students to create, publish, and exchange digital information themselves. Once limited to pen-pal–inspired "key pals" activities in which students and classes shared letters and observations with others around the world, today's student-directed online activities go much farther, for example, participating in projects such as Global Learning and Observations to Benefit the Environment (GLOBE). Students collect scientific information of interest to researchers and contribute this information to a growing online knowledge base. In projects such as ThinkQuest (Thinkquest, 2001), teams of students create their own imaginative, interactive educational websites to address a range of issues that can become a part of other students' learning experiences. Those who have access to these technological opportunities learn in authentic ways, and take for granted that they are contributors and participants in the digital community. Those who do not have access to these same opportunities are marginalized even further. By not participating in the creation of information and resources relevant to their own learning and living, millions of students are at risk of falling further behind in reaping the benefits of the digital age.

Barrier 3:   Access to Educators Who Know How to Use Digital Tools and Resources Effectively

Even if there were 100 percent student and classroom access to the Internet, and even if what is available on the Internet were educationally, culturally, linguistically, and generally of the highest quality, American education would still be faced with a third barrier to digital equity: the expertise of educators. Inadequate teacher professional development is clearly a barrier to advancement of technological change, as noted in a number of reports in the last several years (Office of Technology Assessment, 1995; CEO Forum on Education and Technology, 1999; U.S. Department of Education, 2000; National Association of State Boards of Education, 2001). Few teachers have the time, skill, or commitment to access, analyze, and use the vast array of digital tools and information in the most pedagogically valuable ways with their students. This barrier goes beyond the lack of teachers' technology skills, for skills can be developed with appropriate training. The issue is deeper than one of training, and goes to the heart of teachers' belief about best ways to teach. There is an old expression in education that teachers teach as they were taught; if technology was not in the picture when they were in school, it is difficult for some teachers to appreciate its value as a critical element for enhancing student learning.

Even after many teachers develop some skills with technology, enough for them to feel comfortable using it in the classroom, they adopt technology in ways that support their existing teaching goals and experiences, or that mirror the visions of the leaders and cultures in their schools. Thus, this third set of barriers to digital equity revolves around the varying visions educators have—reflecting their basic pedagogical beliefs and cultures—for technology as a support to student learning. These pedagogical barriers are creating a "didactic divide" that represents inequalities in instructional practice in the ways modern learning technologies are used with different groups of students.

As early as 1990 researchers at the Center for Children and Technology in Education identified the relationship between teachers' educational goals and the ways in which teachers integrate computer-based technologies in their classroom practices. (Honey & Moeller, 1990, p. 13). The researchers' interviews and analyses of 20 teachers (grouped as high-tech and low-tech depending on the extent they used computers) showed that the high-tech teachers used student-centered pedagogical beliefs to facilitate the integration of technology into their curricula. They found more time to work with individual students, took on a more process-oriented teaching style, and used technology to support such educational practices as small-group work and project-oriented activities. In contrast, teachers with more traditional educational beliefs and practices faced complicated barriers for technology integration. "In order to integrate technology into their curricula as the high-tech teachers have done, the very nature of their practices would have to change" (Honey & Moeller, 1990, p. 13). As the study points out, external factors are necessary to support a teacher's shift in perspective to regard technology as a valuable tool for education; this shift in thinking includes a teacher's reconceptualizing of how students learn and develop, and it includes the creation of assessments needed to measure the change.

Since 1990, more attention has been focused on student-centered teaching—the hallmark of the constructivist teaching practice. Not until recently, with a few exceptions discussed below, has there been systematic research on the differences between how technology is used by teachers with traditional teaching beliefs and approaches, and teachers adopting constructivist, student-centered teaching practices. While there has been little analysis of different pedagogies used with students considered at risk versus those used with students who are academically successful, the existing research paints a bleak picture for the future of digital equity if current pedagogical, hiring, and education funding practices continue as they are today.

Based on extensive evaluation of hundreds of videotaped eighth-grade mathematics lessons in classrooms across the United States, Germany, and Japan for the Third International Mathematics, and Science Study (TIMSS), Stigler and Hiebert (1999) conclude that teaching is a deeply embedded cultural activity that one learns to do more by being part of a culture shaped by first participating in fourteen years of schooling, and then by formal training. They describe the American mathematics pedagogy that they observed in more than 80 typical U.S. classrooms as, "learning terms and practicing procedures" (Stigler and & Hiebert, 1999, p. 85).

This pedagogy is so deeply ingrained that many of the teachers observed did not recognize it as such—it is just the way they teach. This finding is important for two reasons. First, teachers whose approach to teaching relegates students to "learning terms and practicing procedures" will see little benefit from using technology, and neither will their students. Secondly, it indicates the difficulty of successfully undertaking pedagogic change. Educators must understand the challenges inherent in changing deeply ingrained cultural practices if they are to successfully change them. Few preservice teacher preparation programs or district in-service professional development programs seem designed to address this barrier to teacher change.

The survey and analysis conducted by Henry Becker and his colleagues at the Center for Research on Information Technology and Organizations also centers on the pedagogical issues (Becker, 2000b, 2001). Becker's Teaching, Learning and Computing survey gathered data on over 4,000 teachers, focusing particularly on the factors influencing teachers' use of information and communications technologies. Teacher respondents completed a 21-page survey booklet about their teaching practice and teaching beliefs (Center for Research on Information Technology and Organizations, 1998). The researchers found that constructivist-oriented teachers use computers professionally in more varied ways, have greater technical expertise in the use of computers, use computers frequently with students, and use them in apparently more powerful ways.

Furthermore, their data indicated that teachers in low-SES schools use computers with students in more traditional ways than do teachers in higher-SES schools. Teachers in low-SES schools are more likely to have students use computers more for routine skills practice (particularly in mathematics) and to learn to work independently, and they are less likely to have students use computers to make presentations, do analytic work, or write. Frequent computer use in math was associated with drilling basic skills to middle school students from economically disadvantaged families, while in science, high computer use was mainly associated with students attending high-SES schools. Becker (2001) suggests that "in science classrooms, access to a sufficient number of computers to make frequent use possible is particularly limited except in economically advantaged schools" (p. 7).

Data collected by the National Center of Educational Statistics confirms this trend: the greater the level of poverty, the more likely it is that computers are used for drills rather than Internet research, graphical presentations, conducting multimedia projects, or other exploratory and problem-solving activities (Donahue, Finnegan, Lutkas, Allen & Campbell, 2000). Reporting on this data in their Year 4 report, the CEO Forum (2001) stated:

> Even when equitable access to education technology exists, students may have unequal learning experiences. Many teachers in poorer schools rely on technology to reinforce basic skills, rather than to support higher-order thinking and the full range of 21st-century skills (p. 29).

State data also shows these patterns. In Maryland, districts completed a survey covering questions on both the level of technology infrastructure present in the schools and the ways the technology is being used. What was particularly striking about the Maryland survey data was the different kinds of student technology use in low-poverty versus high-poverty schools. As recorded within the figures in the Technology Inventory presented in the Maryland State Department of Education report, students in low-poverty schools (defined as those with lower percentages of students receiving free and reduced-price meals) used technology to plan, draft, proofread, revise, and publish text at a higher rate than did the students attending high-poverty schools. Students from low-poverty schools were more likely than their high-poverty counterparts to use computers for gathering information from a variety of technological sources (e.g., the Internet) and to communicate or report information and conclusions or results of investigations. In contrast, students attending high-poverty schools were more likely to use technology for remediation of basic skills.

Part of the reason for this didactic divide may go beyond issues of technology, or teachers' technology skills and beliefs about education, and instead reflect a more basic problem—the inability of high-poverty schools to attract well-qualified teachers. One would argue that these schools need the best teachers available, yet an analysis by the *Chicago Sun-Times* of more than half of the Illinois teachers employed in the fall of 2000 showed that "children in the highest-poverty, highest-minority and lowest-achieving schools are roughly five times more likely to be taught by teachers who failed at least one teacher certification test than children in the lowest-poverty, lowest-minority, highest-achieving schools" (Grossman, Beaupre, & Rossi, 2001, ¶4).

Despite the difficulties, a growing number of teachers are moving beyond traditional knowledge-delivery modes of instruction toward more learner-centered modes by which students become knowledge adaptors and knowledge creators. Students are developing the research, analytical, evaluative, creative, and other high-order thinking skills necessary to utilize the rich Internet content as a catalyst for powerful learning. The conditions necessary for this kind of change to a learner-centered pedagogy exist primarily in wealthy suburban schools, where innovative teachers with smaller classrooms, more resources, and higher salaries have the time, support, and energy to pursue the exploration of rich inquiry-based constructivist pedagogies. Students of such teachers are the ultimate beneficiaries. (See for example the article "Learning to be Wired," about the use of computers at a highly regarded private elementary school in Washington DC [Thompson, 2001].) The challenge of teachers learning technology skills and adopting new pedagogies, and the difficulty of low-income schools in attracting and retaining highly qualified and motivated teachers together perpetuate a pedagogical or didactic divide more insidious and perhaps more difficult to address than the infrastructure components of the digital divide.

Barrier 4: Access to Systems Sustained by Leaders with Vision and Support for Change through Technology

Even the most dedicated, highly trained, visionary teachers face significant barriers of institutional resistance to change, including school structures and schedules that constrain serious focused learning activities. Several characteristics of the current American K–12 educational system make the system itself a major barrier to high-quality student learning in general and digital equity in particular. These characteristics are the system's decentralized and mixed funding, its local citizen-based decision-making structure, its bureaucratic regulatory and certification processes, its underresourced teacher preparation and in-service professional development and support systems, and its strong institutional resistance to change. We do not mean to imply that the American educational system is monolithic or conspiratorial. Nor would we categorize this system as accidental. Belief systems deeply entrenched in American education continue to impede the closing of the digital divide.

This perception—that the system as a whole must first change its thinking about learning and technology in schools—is supported by data collected in a questionnaire distributed at a national educational technology leadership meeting in June, 2001. When asked to list the barriers they believe stand in the way of closing the digital divide in K–12 education, participants' most frequent response was "lack of vision and understanding regarding the link between technology and learning" (Fulton & Sibley, 2001). As one educator put it, "there is not a clear understanding of what can be done with technology and what cannot be done. There is not a clear understanding of how technology can be used to support learning. We talk of new ways of learning, but we never define it so that teachers, administrators, legislators, parents, and community members can understand" (Fulton & Sibley, 2001).

This same educational system has no adequate structure for disseminating educational research findings or innovations to school decision makers or practitioners and no clear path to move successful innovations into supported practice. Boards of elected or appointed citizens who often have little or no pedagogical training or expertise often make curriculum- and pedagogy-related decisions. Serious communication, whether it be between teachers in adjoining classrooms, among students with experts or peers outside their classroom walls, or among academic researchers and practicing teachers, is deemed of minimal value, if not an outright distraction, and is thus minimized.

Complicating the system's ineffectiveness at addressing what technology can offer it, are the schools and colleges that educate the teachers of tomorrow. Many of these education schools merely perpetuate the status quo in teaching. We know that many teacher educators have had limited training or experience in using technology in their own teaching, and even less experience in appreciating how it can be used to enhance learning within PreK–12 school settings (Office of Technology Assessment, 1995). Far too often these institutions are at the caboose of the technology train, rather than acting as the engines of change. Considering the low esteem accorded teacher preparation in the hierarchy of American higher education in general, and the lack of leadership in teacher preparation institutions in directing or adopting educational innovations in the past, these shortcomings might come as no surprise.

Overall, schools have been far more receptive to technology use in traditional ways—that is, in support of basic skills, rather than as a tool for problem solving, higher-order and inventive thinking, high productivity, collaboration, and communication (CEO Forum on Education and Technology, 2001). These 21st-century skills build on and require a strong foundation in the basics of reading, writing, and mathematical abilities. However, they move beyond the basics to focus on skills that make it possible to continue to learn in a continually evolving global economy and interdependent society.

Over the last decade, economists Richard Murnane and Harold Levy have researched the changing nature of the skills required of a 21st-century work force. This research documents the shift toward college-educated workers, and the resulting decrease in the earnings potential of workers without college degrees. Their work also demonstrates that the skills demanded of all workers have shifted measurably over the last 40 years. They provide empirical evidence that:

> computerization is associated with declining relative industry demand for routine manual and cognitive tasks and increased relative demand for non-routine cognitive tasks. . . . [These] changes explain 30 to 40% of the observed relative demand shift favoring college versus non-college labor during 1970 to 1998, with the largest impact felt after 1980" (Murnane, Levy, & Autor, 2001).

The implications of this research go beyond the need to encourage higher levels of college attendance. They speak to the skills all students need to succeed in a challenging and rapidly changing work environment. It is interesting to note that technology has driven this change, as computers have automated more routine manual and cognitive tasks and created opportunities for workers able to perform non-routine cognitive tasks.

When students have access to the technology tools, the content that those tools make available, and to teachers who can guide, encourage, and allow them to use these resources to research serious questions, communicate with other teachers and experts, evaluate and analyze information they have gathered, and finally, to create their own knowledge and to share it with an authentic audience of peers, then students are truly engaged in developing the higher-order academic skills necessary for success in the 21st century. These are the skills that as recently as ten years ago were required only of university graduate students. Today's technologies have provided the resources and tools through which secondary and even middle school students can focus on developing these academic skills. But students without access to the tools, the content, and the teachers needed to teach these skills, will be further and further marginalized and unable to cross the digital divide.

The world is not standing still in its technological requirements of students and their skills. These requirements are at the core of the issue of digital equity. Students who have appropriate technological access have the opportunity to acquire 21st-century learning skills; those that don't have such access do not have equal opportunity to acquire these skills.

Final Thoughts

In the United States, the question is no longer one of access; it includes more specifically, questions of what kind of access, for whom, when, and for what purposes. Students with access to the four critical components needed for digital participation gain significant advantage for future opportunities over those who do not have this access. As this chapter reveals, the barriers to digital participation are complex, but they are certainly not random. Vision is the one feature that influences all four levels of technological access. The engine for pursuing this vision is strong, open-minded leadership, and the fuel for the engine is funding.

We end with a final caveat, stated by one educator in responding to the questionnaire at the 2001 educational technology leadership meeting (Fulton & Sibley, 2001):

> [The greatest barriers to digital equity are] . . . the view held by many that technology offers a "magic wand" to school performance ills, and the lack of patience with technology when they realize that it isn't . . . [as well as] the lack of patience on the part of politicians and policymakers to give reform models opportunities to work.

The American education system, as resistant to change as it may be, *must* change to meet the educational demands of a changing society. Although this is a difficult process, it is already happening in some places and for some children, but not for all. Removal of barriers to digital equity is critical to achieving educational equity. Each of us, as educators, citizens, parents, and learners, has the power and the responsibility to help determine the outcome. Barriers can indeed be removed, but it will take patience, time, effort and vision to get the heavy lifting accomplished.

3

Factors of the Divide

KARIN M. WIBURG

Written with the help of

Rudolfo Chávez-Chávez   **Jeanette Haynes Writer**
Maria Mercado   **Jim O'Donnell**
Elissa Poel   **Paula Wolfe**

FOCUS QUESTIONS

1. Which of the factors discussed in this chapter do you feel are the most important in terms of contributing to this divide?
2. How does the digital divide affect people from different ethnic, language, economic, social backgrounds, and physical ability?
3. What new insights/perspectives may be gained by examining the digital divide from a theoretical perspective?
4. What do the perspectives of technology-using teachers contribute to our understanding of the digital divide?

The purpose of this chapter is to present various factors related to the digital divide and to explore how economic, political, cultural, and pedagogical factors connect to larger issues affecting society and schooling in an electronic age. The contributors to this chapter are scholars who have spent their academic lives studying the roles of culture, class, and power as they relate to education and who have recently begun, as a result of their participation in the Department of Education initiative *Preparing Tomorrow's Teachers Today* (PT3), to connect their academic interests to questions related to technology and equity.

The process for developing this chapter involved qualitative research and computer-based collaboration. The authors work in a Southwest border community and had established as one of the goals of their PT3 grant the need to address the digital divide. They held a statewide symposium on factors related to the digital divide and formed a study and writing group that resulted in this chapter. Their writing process began with a two-hour focus group followed by extensive online collaboration, as well as in-person communication. Each of the faculty-produced mini-papers related to the social, economic, racial, cultural, and political issues that were the subject of their academic research. The authors later added to the richness of the chapter by including the additional viewpoints of technology-using K–12 teachers.

The following chapter is organized around the economic divide, the language divide, special education needs, the divide for Native Americans, border issues, and the pedagogical divide. This is followed by a discussion of the deeper roots that connect all of these factors. The chapter concludes with some suggestions for lessening the divide and moving toward digital equity.

The Economic Divide

Jim O'Donnell is a multicultural education professor and director of the secondary education program at New Mexico State. He was most concerned throughout our writing and discussion with the economic basis for the digital divide. According to O'Donnell, this economic divide manifests itself in a lack of fairness in financing schools, so computers, as well as training, are not equally distributed among districts. The inequalities in school financing (Kozol, 1991; Weinberg, 1977) appear in the material base of schooling (e.g., textbooks, library acquisitions, computer technology) and the physical conditions of the school buildings (e.g., broken windows, desks, and chairs, missing toilet door stalls, and leaking water faucets). These inequalities demonstrate a lack of caring.

It is not, however, the material goods per se that are the most important determinant of the quality of the teaching–learning process. It is when the lack of material goods is coupled with the ideology of "deficit thinking" (e.g., Howe & Edelman, 1985; Valencia, 1999; Valenzuela, 1999) that students are harmed. This sort of thinking assumes that it is the fault of the victim of an inadequate education that she or he is failing, rather than looking at the quality and relevance of the education provided to the student. It also assumes that students who are not succeeding in mainstream schools have a lack of culture—a deficit—rather than a different, but perhaps equally rich, home culture. The pedagogical response by teachers, staff, and administrators who carry within them the low expectations for students who come from a different culture is to offer a mind-numbing routine instruction of rote memorization. This irrelevant curriculum squanders the desire and spirit of poor children to excel. This *pedagogy of poverty* (Haberman, 1991) undermines the educational process. Many teachers who are employed within these poor schools are also victims of this pedagogy of poverty. For the most part, teachers working in poor schools are the least qualified, usually assigned to teach in areas that they are less prepared for and when better opportunities come along they flee the school. They are also the least likely to have opportunities for professional development (Darling-Hammond, 1997).

We asked four teachers with experience in low-income, minority schools to meet with us and discuss their work in addressing the digital divide in the schools in which they had worked. Their remarks were grounded in economic concerns including their common finding that they had had very little technology in their classrooms until new federal grant funds such as the E-rate became available. Elatunbi Adeogba, a teacher for the last ten years in a neighboring border district, explained:

> I was a bilingual teacher for many years. My last assignment was in a very low SES community. I taught first grade and this humble, modest community had very little technology until very recently. It took until my last year in the program to get one computer and a printer for my students. I also had access to a digital camera. Those three elements, the computer, printer, and digital camera revolutionized my teaching practices. It convinced me that technology really, really impacted my students in a very positive way.

While economics was their main concern, the teachers did not consider the main economic problem in their schools to be a shortage of computers. Rather they were more concerned with a lack of network access, technical support, teacher training, and a deficit pedagogical approach that assumes poor and second language students can't use computers for high-end purposes. Linda Pickett, a middle school teacher described how technology first appeared in the district: "Hardware started showing up in libraries, classrooms, public community centers, but there was no access to the Internet. The computers were just there and they were just glorified typewriters for a long time." She continued, "A lot of economically depressed areas do get the equipment. But they have no one to install it, repair it and actually integrate it into the classroom, and that's an economic divide." Shirley Davis, a computer teacher currently working with the border district as a university clinical faculty added:

> It is kind of sad to see all the equipment just sit there. I've visited one school that had lots of equipment and the teacher didn't know what to do with the computers, so the kids were playing with them. I remember seeing students using a simple program [PowerPoint] and I went over and said "Oh no, you do it this way and it will make it go." And one of the kids said, "She knows computers. Let's keep her."

Manual Bustamante, a bilingual teacher from the same district, mentioned the lack of professional development available to teachers in poor districts. "I think that the fact remains that minorities are still using technology less and because of the lack of professional development in these depressed areas, these students are not going to be able to utilize technology in creative ways."

The Language Divide

In the field of bilingual education, issues include an economic divide and also the social and cultural divisions that accompany stratified economic and class lines. Maria Mercado, a bilingual education professor at the university suggested that it is necessary to understand the connections between economic, social, cultural, and linguistic dimensions and how these factors impact children and families living in culturally and linguistically diverse communities—those communities traditionally served by bilingual education.

While Mercado knows that access to computers and the Internet is a necessary condition, it is not sufficient to serve the needs of bilingual students and families. An important factor is how the use of digital tools impacts communities—socially, culturally, and linguistically. In order for cultural and linguistic technological equity to occur, the teacher needs to structure learning situations to support what is known about language acquisition and its roots in a socio-constructivist view of learning. Learning in this manner is more effective than the remedial approaches that utilize skill and drill. Unfortunately, drill-and-practice programs have predominated technology integration strategies with culturally and linguistically diverse children (Butler-Pascoe & Wiburg, 2002; Zehr, 2001).

Sadly for our children, educational institutions have traditionally addressed linguistic and cultural diversity from a deficit perspective rather than from the position of enrichment. Languages other than English have not been valued in schools in the United States, and in fact, historically Mexican-American populations and Indigenous communities in the Southwest have suffered a great deal from such subtractive and ultimately racist policies (Halcon, 2001; Evans, 1995; San Miguel & Valencia, 1998; Sanchez, 1940/1996). This negative view of languages other than English is further limited by the simplistic idea that language can be learned without considering its cultural context.

Language itself is inextricably intertwined with the culture in which it is developed and used, and there is a symbiotic relationship between language and culture that has been documented as an important consideration for the education of language minority children (Au & Jordan, 1981; Gutierrez & Larson, 1995; Heath, 1983; Phillips, 1983). Unfortunately, most federally funded bilingual education programs have typically followed a transitional model, which utilizes the native language as a bridge toward proficiency in English (Bartolome, 1998; Macedo, 2000)—without valuing the native language in context.

To take advantage of the interdependence of language and culture, teachers and schools can make sure to make available computer programs in the children's native languages, where available. Having access to computer programs in native languages, for example, begins to address the aforementioned interdependence, but Mercado's primary concern continues to be how technology can support the developing identity of linguistically and culturally diverse children. Moll (1992) has developed the term *funds of knowledge* to help teachers understand that the child's community should be an inspiration for curriculum development and a source of knowledge for school learning (Moll, Amanti, Neff & Gonzales, 1992). Mercado believes this notion of knowledge within the community can assist us in addressing the digital divide by using technology to demonstrate and value the rich cultural, social, and historical contexts of the communities from which the children come. For example, children can use technology to capture oral histories of their communities, create interactive multimedia related to the origins and travel that have occurred in their extended *familias,* and create their own newsletters about issues of concern to the community—a *funds of knowledge* approach so to speak.

Using computer technology to promote biliteracy has great potential. And although bilingual education is currently under fire, dual language programs offer hope. These programs are increasing and receiving greater attention as a viable approach to dual language learning (Howard & Sugarman, 2001). The integration of computer technology in our classrooms can support the increased interest in biliteracy as a viable alternative to literacy only in English, especially in communities in which English is not the dominant language. In fact, technology can support students in sharing multiple languages and cultures.

Not only are there important cultural differences between two language groups for the Spanish and English Southwest region of the United States, but in increasingly diverse English language learner (ELL) classrooms throughout the country there are also cultural differences among the students, who speak multiple languages and come from many different cultures. Ortmeir (2000) was surprised to find many prejudices within her classroom of diverse English language learners. She first discovered this when she was walking to her classroom with two of her advanced ESL students, one from Thailand and one from Mexico. The boy from Thailand was worried that he would be seen by his father walking with a Mexican since he had been told not to socialize with Mexicans.

As a result of this incident and her increased awareness that students were not only uncomfortable with their new American culture but also with their classmates from other cultures, Ortmeier created the Homeland Project. This Web-based project involved students in finding and combining resources about their homelands into a multimedia presentation for the class. They were also required to use the library's new electronic database to find books about their countries. As students shared interesting information about their homelands, there was increased respect within the class for each other and a sense of community began to emerge. The computer with its network connections to multiple languages and cultural information makes it possible to support diverse students in our classrooms.

The Special Education Divide

The faculty member most sensitive to the needs of special education students was Elissa Poel, who had recently come to the university from the public schools and is now in charge of the special education student teaching program. She believes that the digital divide is a complex issue presenting yet another challenge to individuals with disabilities. The importance of recognizing the needs of over 54 million Americans with disabilities in this country is just the beginning of inclusive practices and bridging the technological gap. According to the National Office for the Information Economy (2000), "access to computers and the Internet, and the ability to effectively use this technology are becoming increasingly important for full participation in economic, political and social life." For individuals with disabilities, this means that accessing and being in command of the Internet highway remains critical to becoming competitive in the work force, achieving a high quality of life, and insuring independence.

Assistive Technology

Assistive Technology devices have been used for centuries (Thorkildsen, 2001). Their availability and capabilities continue to increase through research and government mandates. Assistive devices range from pencil grips and slant boards (low tech) to voice-activated software and Braille writers (high tech). The development and use of Assistive Technology devices has helped individuals with disabilities become independent, participate in more social and academic activities, and be more like their peers who are not disabled.

It certainly would be simple and cost effective if one assistive device or tool could meet the needs of all individuals with disabilities; however, that is not the case. Most often, children are identified early as having a disability—prior to or during their school-age years. Their needs are assessed and reevaluated annually. A team of professionals recommends program development and assistive devices to help students compensate for their disabilities and access the world. Thirteen exceptionalities have been identified and include: Autism, Deaf, Hearing Impaired, Multiple Disabilities, Other Health Impaired,

Speech/Language Impaired, Visually Impaired, Deaf-blind, Emotionally Disturbed, Mental Retardation, Orthopedically Impaired, Specific Learning Disability, and Traumatic Brain Injury (Individuals with Disabilities Education Act, 1997). Each of these exceptionalities identifies specific characteristics. Any one individual identified as having a specific disability can exhibit various combinations of these characteristics making it impossible to implement the concept of *one size fits all.*

Obstacles

An increasing number of people are accessing the Internet, designing Web pages, and taking courses online (U.S. Department of Commerce, 2000). For individuals with disabilities, it is reported that only one in five adults have graduated from high school, over 33 percent live in households with an annual income of less than $15,000, 70 percent are unemployed, and fewer than 10 percent own homes (White House, 2001).

Information involving individuals with disabilities and their access to technology is alarming. A report by the U.S. Department of Commerce (Mineta, 2000) indicates that individuals with disabilities are only half as likely to access the Internet at home as individuals without disabilities. Approximately 60 percent have never even used a computer (compared to 25 percent of those without disabilities), and only 20 percent of individuals with vision impairments have Internet access. Even though there is no one tool to meet the needs of all individuals with all disabilities, general accommodations and modifications to technology and Internet access can be explored, developed, and implemented.

Fairness

Not all individuals with disabilities need adaptive equipment for accessibility, but reasonable accommodations for individuals with visual, hearing, physical, and cognitive or neurological disabilities, as provided for by law, would improve screen reader capabilities, captioning, keyboard alternatives for menu commands, navigation, and illustrative materials (Waddell, 1999; Brewer, 2000).

When exploring the equal access issue for individuals with disabilities, I turn to Rick Lavoie, a leader in the field of learning disabilities. His illustration using the following two scenarios in his video *How Difficult Can This Be?* (1996), puts the equality issue into perspective:

> SCENARIO 1: A child with a learning disability has difficulty copying information from the board. She is expected to do well in the class with no other modifications. The special educator approaches the regular educator requesting that information written on the board for the other children be copied [by the special educator, teacher, or another student] and given to the child at her desk. The regular education teacher replies, "I can't do that; it would not be fair to the others."

> SCENARIO 2: During a lecture, an adult student falls off of her chair. She begins to turn blue. It is thought that she might be having a heart attack. The instructor approaches the woman to say that, "I really would like to help you; however, it would not be fair to the other 30 individuals in the room if I took time out to do so."

The point is that fairness is not necessarily that everyone gets the same; fairness is when everyone gets what he needs to achieve the *same results.*

Laws

Federal laws protect the rights of individuals with disabilities. The Individuals with Disabilities Education Act (IDEA) provides equal access to a free, appropriate public education for all children with disabilities, and for placement in the least restrictive environment available. As inclusion continues to gain acceptance and remains the program of choice in public schools, more students with disabilities are educated in regular education classrooms, exposed to high standards, and encouraged to work to their abilities. Equal access to technology in the classroom is necessary to insure equal access in adult life.

Under Section 508 of the Rehabilitation Act amended by Congress in 1998, accessibility to computers, software, and electronic equipment such as fax machines, copiers, telephones, and other equipment used for transmitting, receiving, using, or storing information in the federal sector will be made available to individuals with disabilities (Waddell, 1999). Major universities and high-tech companies also have committed to expanding research and improving accessibility to individuals with disabilities. In addition, several online sites have been developed to evaluate individual Web pages and online courses for accessibility.

The digital divide is usually defined as the gap in technology ownership and access between those who are affluent and those who are poor or who live in rural areas with limited or no access to the Internet. This ownership and access can depend primarily on three factors: race, geography, and economic status. The future for individuals with disabilities to equal access to technology is bleak as long as there continue to be overrepresentation of racially diverse and poor students in special education classrooms (Gersten & Woodward, 1994), more students with disabilities in rural than nonrural school districts, and more children living in poverty (U.S. Department of Education, 1995). Without serious consideration, commitment, funds, and concrete plans to insure equal access for all, the digital divide will continue to increase and again exclude individuals with disabilities from the mainstream.

As the coordinator of the special education student teaching program at the university, Elissa Poel is charged with training preservice teachers and incorporating technology into the preservice program. As this has not been done before, she asks herself,

> Where do I begin? How do I teach technology in the preservice classroom? How do I prepare new teachers to use technology and assistive technology devices with their students when I do not have the training or access to equipment myself? This situation reminds me of my second year of teaching students with disabilities. At the end of one of our morning faculty meetings, our principal dismissed us with these words: "By the way, we are now an inclusion school, go do it!"

The Divide in Native Communities

Jeanette Haynes Writer is a multicultural education professor and native scholar who is interested in discussing the digital divide in terms of how it affects the Native[1] community.

---

[1]I use the terms *Native American, Native, American Indian, Indigenous, Indian, Native peoples and Indigenous peoples* interchangeably throughout my discussion because there is no universally accepted term among this population or within literature sources. Most Native peoples prefer to use their specific tribal group name rather than any of these collective terms.

As a whole, Native people suffer greatly from poverty. The 1990 U.S. Census reported that the poverty rate for American Indians was 31 percent as compared to 13 percent for the total U.S population (U.S. Department of Commerce, 1993, p. 8). More recently, for 1999, the number of American Indians and Alaska Natives living in poverty was 25.9 percent, while only 7.7 percent of non-Hispanic Whites lived in poverty (U.S. Census Bureau, 2000).

In regard to technology, poverty has certainly affected Native communities through the lack of support infrastructure available. Here the term "support infrastructure" has to be broadened to include not only utility services, but also roads, facilities to house computers, and individuals educated and/or trained to operate or maintain computers (Riley, Nassersharif, & Mullen, 1999).

Recently, federal agencies, such as the Bureau of Indian Affairs and foundations, such as the Bill and Melinda Gates Foundation, have provided funds to increase infrastructure capabilities and access to technology in Native communities. To understand the lack of infrastructure, one must see this as a result of the history of genocide and oppression by the dominant society, which led to the dispossession of lands and the exploitation of natural resources. This is how poverty has become so entrenched within the Native communities. Rather than exterminate us, European Americans found it cheaper to try to educate us to be White farmers, which promoted the dispossession of large areas of tribal/community land for small, individually owned farm parcels (Adams, 1995; Prucha, 1990; Spring, 1996). A dispossession of cultural traditions, which led into another kind of poverty, also came with this federal and social policy.

Finally, the federal government has come to address the linkage of economic well-being in Native communities with technology. In August of 1998, President Clinton announced a plan for improving economic conditions and economic self-determination in tribal communities. This plan included a study of tribal technology infrastructure. In response, Riley, Nassersharif, and Mullen (1999) conducted a study that gave us a clearer picture of the digital divide in Native communities. According to these authors, 94 percent of non-Native rural households have telephone service, whereas, only 39 percent of rural Native households have such service; 12 percent of the Native households also lack electricity. Even if communities have accessibility to phone lines and electricity, economic instability means that an individual may not have money in her or his pocket to keep the electricity on or to keep the computer on—should the individual actually possess one. (In these rural Native households, only 9 percent have personal computers [Riley, Nassersharif, et al., 1999, p. vi].)

Haynes Writer sees the use of technology as very positive in terms of how it can provide a way for individuals and tribes to enhance their economic opportunities. You now see people who live in remote areas having their own Web pages to sell cultural items that they make; they did not have that ability before. They are no longer forced to sell to store owners who pay the artists too little while outrageously marking up the price for their own profit. Tribes now have ways to promote their various business initiatives. The 1999 study by Riley, Nassersharif, and Mullen revealed that 90 percent of the schools in Native rural areas have computers and Internet service (p. vi). This is positive; however, the computers are only available to those students and families affiliated with schools. The high dropout rate of Native students—ranging from 29 percent to 90 percent (Swisher & Hoisch, 1992)—limits access to technology even further because of the numbers of families without access to wired schools. Haynes Writer has also learned that in some Native communities where computers are available, students are not allowed to touch or experiment freely with them because they might break them. The computers become precious items to be protected by the school personnel rather than learning tools accessible to students and the community.

In the area of Native American Education, various groups and organizations are developing their own curriculum and making it available to others, such as with the Alaska Native Knowledge Network (2001) and the Cradleboard Teaching Project (1999). In addition, many people in remote areas have obtained accessibility to education through online courses. Salish Kootenai College (Indian Country Today, 2000) and Fort Peck Community College (Fort Peck, 1999) offer students a wide range of courses through their distance education programs. These are, indeed, positive advances.

Some Indigenous groups are using technology to their cultural advantage through projects such as language preservation. A multimedia dictionary database and multimedia language lessons have been used to help preserve and expand the Arikara, Assiniboine and Pawnee languages (Parks, Kushner, Hooper, Flavin, Yellow Bird, & Ditmar, 1999). Hawaiian Natives have pushed for the recognition of their language in the schools, and now a revitalization effort has been realized. Individuals can learn the Hawaiian language through distance education classes using software (Ka'awa & Hawkins, 1997); however, the authors cited difficulty in providing personal assistance to students and insufficient equipment and training as limitations to this initiative (Ka'awa & Hawkins, 1997).

Although technology has brought about many positive changes, Haynes Writer is concerned that its use may remove social interactions, especially those critical to child socialization. It can inhibit the cross-age interactions that have been common in Native cultures and that are important to teaching of language and other cultural skills. Dr. Lanny Real Bird, a member of Crow Nation and director of the Learning Lodge Institute at Little Big Horn College, mentioned in a presentation at New Mexico State University that the teaching of the Crow language was negatively affected within his community upon the introduction of cable television (Real Bird, 2001). This scholar also has concerns about how technology can negatively influence oral communications and oral traditions of communities. The spoken word is very important in the native culture. Documenting one's words or speaking through a *false means* has negative cultural implications for some individuals. The spoken word has specific value, life, and spirituality in its moment of origin and in its exact social context. To alter this natural context means one's words can be misconstrued or invalidated, and the essence of their totality lost.

As Indigenous people we must be ever cognizant and watchful of misrepresentations and false, even racist, information circulating on the Internet. Recently Haynes Writer was informed by a major textbook company of its website where professors/instructors can view topics and chapters so that they may put together their own course text. On this website was information that was scant, inaccurate, and racist. For example, one chapter described the Pueblo peoples as *primitive*. When she confronted the company's sales representative with her concerns she was passed up the *chain of command* concerning this issue. Ultimately, Haynes Writer was told that she could provide the company with the accurate information; however, she would not be compensated for her research. What is critical here is that this textbook company is viewed as a valid and credible source, yet it is distributing false and racist information. In conclusion this researcher makes the following comment:

For Indigenous people, I see the digital divide as operating within an economic and cultural schism. Whereas technology can be utilized for tribes' and individual's advantage and to support and maintain self-determination and sovereignty as Native people, we must be creative in our use of technology so that we are in control of it rather than having it control us. As members of hundreds of distinct Native communities, we must define the most appropriate ways to use technology so that cultural values and traditions are maintained and respected.

The Border Divide

Rudolfo Chávez-Chávez is a multicultural and critical pedagogy professor at New Mexico State University and our resident scholar on border issues. In this section he elaborates on the role of the U.S./Mexican border in impacting the digital divide. The U.S./Mexican border is a ready-made and potentially rich conversational space between peoples, ideas, cultures, and more; however the conversation that has occurred has not happened on equal footing. In the last decade, popular media represented the border as a line that needs protecting rather than a multicultural opportunity for interaction. We have witnessed the pouring of millions of federal dollars into the Immigration and Naturalization Services' (INS) border operations such as *Operation Hold the Line* and *Operation Gatekeeper.* In the last five years there have been more than 1,300 deaths of undocumented immigrants related to events along the border (Martínez, 1998).

The U.S./Mexican border is a Third World country of around 24 million people. It extends for around 2,000 miles from Tijuana/San Diego to Brownsville/Matamoros, and 800,000 people cross it legally every day (Gibbs, 2001). The border extends for around 100 miles on both sides. According to Gibbs, while the border population is growing at almost twice the national rate of population growth, so are the health problems of the people. Thirty-one percent of all tuberculosis cases are found in the four border states—Texas, New Mexico, Arizona, and California. In these states as well as in Mexico, many people live in *colonias.* Generally, colonias have few or unpaved roads, a scarcity of potable water, and ill-equipped or nonexistent sewer services. Viral diseases per 100,000 colonia residents are found in "poor-world" proportions: hepatitis-A, 43.9 percent; salmonellosis, 21.3 percent; shigellosis, 18.0 percent; and tuberculosis, 28.1 percent (Colonias, 1999).

These border conditions exist at the same time that information about anything and everything continues to grow exponentially because of the World Wide Web. If border issues are included as part of a movement toward digital transformation, one thing is clear—the use of the Web must be connected to the more mundane aspects of equity like clean water, paved streets, working sewer systems, affordable health care, modest housing, a livable wage, and equitable and accessible education.

The question of digital equity then becomes a question of how digital access might help in solving the daily problems of living in the border region. There has been an explosion of people and groups from many walks of life and many places declaring their perspective via the Web. Democracy has, in many ways become richer as a result of these diverse voices, even though the spindly head of totalitarianism also looms. Because we live in the border of things, acting for digital transformation requires rethinking and re-centering what the American paradigm has been, is, and can be. For example, the uses of hardware and software within educational settings (schools, Web pages, etc.) that reflect the so-called superiority of the dominant culture result in diminishing us all. The practice of digital transformation on the border is then a struggle for understanding the potential power of the Internet and how it can serve to further liberate those who work and live on the border. How we envision such a transformation makes a difference.

Digital transformation must be imbedded in what Freire called *"recognitions"* that challenge each of us to respond humbly to human lives and aspirations and to internal, exposed, and lived oppressions—all within the temporality of the everyday and drenched in the contextualized experiences of human beings (Freire, 1992/1998). Teaching and learning with the WWW on the border are inextricable from an ethical understanding of the nature of situated knowledge and the role of race/ethnicity, gender, class, identity, representation, and context in that knowledge (Freire, 1998). To understand such situated knowledge, educators will need to look critically at the content taught (that is, *whose* content is taught) and *how* it is taught. The first context that must be understood is how the border is currently represented in the popular culture and how it could potentially, with the assistance of digital media, be represented differently.

The border is not about Mexico and the United States or about them and us. As actors in digital transformation, we must participate in a discourse that comprehends the widest possible array of contributing cultures and their complex interactions with one another. Let this dialogic/dialectic process support the use of digital media to move beyond the traditional American paradigm in ways that facilitate democratic participation and social justice across the border (Castells, 1997). Digital transformation can help to create infinite new realities full of previously unimaginable images of ourselves, our students, our inquiry, our profession, and those whom we touch and who touch us as well.

The Pedagogical Divide

Paula Wolfe coordinates the reading program at New Mexico State and as a reading scholar has long been concerned with meeting the literacy needs of all children. In the field of reading and literacy, her biggest concern in regard to technology is not the issue of technological access for children of color. Rather, the concern is that technology will more efficiently replicate the current status quo. In other words, in technological reading classrooms, children of color will continue to receive skills in "instructional nonsense" (Edelsky, 1996) rather than real literacy instruction. In the history of reading pedagogy we have seen programs emerge time and again that promise to solve the problem of literacy for minority children. It is Wolfe's contention that use of technology, if it continues to be embedded in a non-theoretical approach will simply replicate the current condition—that in which Anglo middle class children do well in school literacy tasks, and children of color do not. If we, as educators do not examine the underlying purposes of schooling and of school-based technology, access to computers will do little to counter current trends.

Our survival depends, therefore, as C. A. Bowers suggested in *Let Them Eat Data* (2000), on moving beyond technocentric and commodity-oriented uses of computers. We must acknowledge that current school-based reading technology has largely been designed to deliver content more efficiently. As with any tool, technology is by itself neither good nor bad. Rather, one must examine who made the tool (and with what biases) and how the tool is used. The technology itself is perhaps less important than the thoughtful implementation of that technology to enact a more powerful approach to learning.

In order to illustrate this point more fully, Wolfe includes the definition of two learning paradigms, as defined by Lemke (1997): The *curricular learning paradigm* dominates institutions such as schools and universities. The curricular paradigm assumes that someone else will decide what you need to know and will arrange for you to learn it all in a fixed order and on a fixed schedule. In contrast, the *interactive learning paradigm* dominates such institutions as libraries and research centers. It assumes that people determine what they need to know based on their participation in activities where such needs arise and in consultation with knowledgeable specialists; that they learn in the order that suits them, at a comfortable pace, and just in time to make use of what they learn. The interactive learning paradigm is the learning paradigm of the people who created the Internet and cyberspace. It is the paradigm of how people with power and resources choose to learn.

Critical authors in the field of reading have long argued that the traditional curricular paradigm Lemke described is a major contributor to the lack of success of minority children with school based literacy tasks (Altwerger & Saevedra, cited in Edelsky, 1996; Shannon, 1990). These authors argued that in order to address the literacy divide we, as educators, must reconceptualize the role of school in literacy instruction. We must change the school (and the technology) to fit children of color, rather than asking children of color to change in order to fit the school.

Technological Reading Programs

Some of the earliest work done in technology-enhanced reading instruction involved the use of "computer books" or children's books written and designed to be read directly from a computer screen. Anderson and Evans (1996) found, however, that these electronic stories did not contain adequate story grammar. Children negotiate meaning better when narratives are more complex and resemble real children's literature (Greenlee-Moore & Smith, 1996). By far the most widely used reading technology program is Accelerated Reader (AR). AR has been widely implemented in schools, mainly because of statistics showing that the program can significantly boost reading test scores. However, other problematic aspects of AR (aspects that do not show up on tests scores) have been noted. For example Carter (1996) argued that computerized reading management programs have drawbacks such as devaluing reading, diminishing motivation, limiting title choice, restricting materials selection, discouraging independent selection of books, ignoring individual instructional needs, and failing to make the best use of school resources. While there may be positive benefits to computerized reading programs and awards, there may also be serious negative consequences to their use.

The teachers who were interviewed also pointed out issues related to pedagogy and digital equity. Manuel Bustamante suggested:

> It depends on how teachers are using the technology. I know of some schools that use technology, that have a lot of resources and teachers do have some professional development. However, their delivery of content is behaviorist in nature, so maybe the students know facts. Then when it comes to real-life applications, students don't know how to apply technology or even apply the content in a manner that is going to help them create a better life.

The teachers also discussed how even in classrooms with computers, the machines often sat in class unused. Linda Picket added:

> You need teachers who are comfortable with hands-on, diversified activity in the class-room—and a lot of people are not. They want all of the kids doing one thing, everybody doing the same thing. I think a lot of times they feel as though they won't have control because I know that's how I felt when I first started. I didn't have control over my kids. I had twenty kids in there, four of them at the computer working on a book and sixteen of them at various stages of their books . . . and it is a lot of work.

Perhaps nowhere is the digital divide clearer than when viewed in terms of how computers are used for teaching and learning. Technology offers the promise of a curriculum that serves the needs of all students and offers them opportunities to express their cultural background and personal experiences. On the other hand, in the case of reading and other academic content areas, technology has not delivered on that promise. Instead it has been sold as a way to make what we have always done more efficient, even when we have evidence that more drill and practice doesn't usually result in the kinds of higher-level thinking and learning that we need as we enter the 21st century.

Deeper Roots of the Digital Divide

As this chapter evolved, the authors looked critically at the meaning of the terms we had been using and at the deeper themes that tied together the various factors related to digital equity. If it is the point of this chapter and this book to consider how to build digital equity, should we also examine what we mean by *equity*? Among the faculty, deciding what we really meant by equity led to a heated discussion. Chávez-Chávez suggested that it might be best to consider an analogy to food. We are all in need of food, and we should have access to it; but if I am a diabetic and you are not, I need different kinds of food than you do. We both need food that will keep us healthy, but the types of food that would most benefit each of us will be different.

Chávez also suggested that we examine the use of the term *digital divide* itself. Does the use of the divide metaphor assume that we, who have the power, can fill the divide for those who don't have the power? Have we decided we know exactly how to fill it without getting input from the people for whom it is being filled? What if we fill this divide with reading programs that deny the voices of children of color, Internet images that have no meaning for people who live without water or electricity, and the idea that students with disabilities don't need special assistance?

In the Fog

As we worked collaboratively on this chapter, we recognized that many of the popular ideas related to the digital divide and to technology itself—ideas to which some of us reacted critically—might be considered to exist within a kind of fog. It is not clear to many people what are the roots of the digital divide problem. What each of the faculty authors discovered they had in common was a perception that most people seem to see technology as something unrelated to the social, cultural, economic, and political context in which it is used. Our common recommendations called for the development of a deeper understanding of how technology is used, who controls its use, and who is primarily a consumer rather than a producer of digital media.

Along with the many books that praise technology and offer it as a cure for our ills are a growing number of books by writers who take a critical view of our current technological culture. Bowers (2000) has suggested that our survival depends on moving beyond techno-centric and commodity-oriented computing. Another book, *The McDonaldization of Society* by George Ritzer (1996), demonstrated a growing world emphasis on the use of technology for efficiency and greater consumerism. In this book the author talked about going to Finland and meeting a man from Turkey, and how the man from Turkey felt at home in Finland when he saw a McDonald's restaurant. This is an ironic result of corporate globalization, when you can travel to Beijing and feel as if you are in a McDonald's in the United States.

We are concerned that by and large the general public and the popular media present technology in a glaringly positive light, and that Americans have this sense that technology is going to solve the problem; that whenever there comes to be a monumental problem, rather than searching for the fundamental cause of that problem, people think, "Well, technology is going to solve this."

This leads to our fear that educators are not helping students to work to understand the causes of our problems, or even take any moral responsibility for them, because technology (and science) are going to solve them. While considering the pragmatic American approach to problems we were reminded of the old General Electric ads on television that stated, "Progress is our most important product." But what does progress really mean? Who defines progress? Progress for whom? This belief in the inevitable progress promised by technology and science has most recently manifested itself in the current American infatuation with the power of standardized testing for fixing our educational problems. One wonders how continuously taking the temperature of students will help if the underlying need to improve learning and teaching is not supported.

The technology-using teachers we interviewed found it difficult to talk about the problem of the digital divide in terms of underlying social, economic, political, and cultural factors. They talked about the problem in terms of their individual schools—how each of them fought for access to computers or how the support of the principal made a difference. Only one of the four teachers asked questions related to the larger context of our educational system. This teacher suggested that there was a need to provide professional development during the teacher's workday and on a continuous basis but the current structure of schools makes this difficult. This lack of support for teacher professional development as part of their regular work may be a factor in perpetuating the pedagogical divide in the classrooms of poor students.

Teachers are not used to thinking about economics and power. Linda Darling-Hammond (1997) has written about how a larger proportion of the educational dollar is currently spent on administration than on the classroom teacher. How will things change unless more is invested in our classroom teachers? These concerns are echoed Steigler and Hiebert (1999) as they discuss the findings of an international study on student performance in mathematics. They believe educational reform has failed in the United States because too little attention has been paid to teachers and to what happens inside classrooms. In the case of Japan, teachers are supported in doing their own lesson study (a sort of action research) in which they work collaboratively to continuously improve their practice. They are given time to meet, to observe in each others' classrooms, and to discuss how to improve student learning. Steigler and Heibert believe this attention to the professional growth of teachers and to the culture of teaching has been instrumental in the high achievement of Japanese students in mathematics.

Out of the Fog and into New Pedagogy

Paula Wolfe earlier described the current problematic nature of technology-mediated reading programs, but was anxious to share her vision of how technology could be used very differently within an interactive learning paradigm. In this case technology can effectively grant children of color something that traditional schooling has never granted them—control. It is possible, through technologies such as the Internet, for minority students to reject typical school-based literacy opportunities (in which their cultures and experiences often do not appear) and fashion for themselves a more culturally responsive education. It is possible for the voices of children who have not been well represented in mainstream curricula to finally be heard via digital media.

As Mercado suggested earlier in this chapter, we need to articulate more clearly the social, cultural, and political aspects of the digital divide. Language barriers are not often considered as part of the divide, yet in the area of language there is potential for profound technological dividends (Friedman, 2000). Networked computers could provide not only literacy instruction at all levels to people at home but also multilingual and multicultural riches to our schools and homes. It is possible that within each of the digital divides discussed there are also the roots of digital dividends. New advances in assistive technology make possible educational resources for all. Local communities along the border could use technology to help connect people with jobs and community resources. Native Americans can market their own goods for their own good. As you think about each factor in the digital divide consider also how technology itself can help close the divide it helped to create.

All of the teachers agreed that there had to be changes in how teachers teach. Pickett suggested:

> I think that pedagogical change has to be there because, you know, we are so used to that teacher-centered traditional classroom and we should, we need to be, shifting to student-centered, even without computers. It just doesn't make sense that the teacher does all the talking, and we know how little of the information kids get from that if they are not really physically involved.

Out of the Fog—Creating Digital Equity

What we are suggesting to those who are reading this book and are looking for ways to build digital equity is that they look at the deeper issues involved in the many factors that contribute to the digital divide and then consider how these issues can be understood in a way that makes action possible. The problem is complex and for each of the groups we discussed in this chapter—the poor, students with special needs, students learning in a new language, those who go home to homes without water or electricity—the challenges are unique and yet have common underlying roots which lie in the powerlessness of the communities discussed. What is needed for digital equity is to empower individuals and groups within diverse communities to use technology to better meet their own needs.

Teachers who have been successfully working in the trenches to empower kids with technology have some practical strategies. Bustamante talks about how he involved the students in teaching others in the school to use technology,

> There was a time where teachers and the principal and other faculty members found out that I knew a little about technology so anything that would come up, a problem about this or something they would call me, "Can you come take care of [this]? Can you come take care of [that]?" I started giving this training to my students. And I'm talking about third graders or fifth graders, so whenever a teacher or anybody else from the faculty would call me I would send Carmen or I would send Lupe or I would send Joshua or Nathan and they became our school's experts in technology.

The teachers also suggested that schools themselves can be part of the solution for closing the digital divide. They were passionate about opening the schools to become community technology centers. Linda Pickett says:

> I'm willing to stay after school. Kids who don't have access at home can stay and go home on the activity bus. We keep them after school for detention; we could certainly keep them after school for enrichment. You've got to open the doors, you can't just have technology in the school and make it part of the wallpaper. And communities could set up community centers and put libraries and video and music and computers all in a place where everybody can get to it. You don't have to be a certain person. Even grandma can go down there and access it if she wants to and get pictures of her grandkids.

In closing, we were reminded of the 1984 Apple commercial, which was shown once during the Super Bowl. The scene was based on George Orwell's *1984,* a story in which the government used technology to successfully control all human activity. In the beginning of this commercial the people were all sitting around in a sort of fog looking at a screen. A woman came out and threw a hammer into the giant screen and woke the people out of the fog and gave them the idea of their own personal computers. The potential of the personal computer is that all students—from whatever background, economic group, or geographic area—can be authors of their own world and work, and that world can reflect their diversity and humanity.

In order to ensure a level of access that empowers all people and communities, we must work to provide not only hardware and software, but also education and support, equitable content, and the opportunities of digital media for all people. In the discussion of each of the digital divide factors, there were hints of liberatory computer practices that addressed the economic, political, language, and pedagogical divides—bilingual communities using technology to tell and preserve their stories, Native Americans creating their own curriculum, students becoming computer teachers. One may need a conceptual hammer to cut through the fog, to critically examine the seemingly magic technological bullets and the attitudes and practices we bring to using technology, and then to redefine these problems into actions that can transform divides into technology-mediated dividends.

4 Empowering Individuals, Schools, and Communities

JOYCE PITTMAN

FOCUS QUESTIONS

1. What is empowerment?
2. Why is empowerment essential to achieve equity in a democratic society?
3. How does one facilitate educational empowerment in organizations and individuals?

This chapter addresses two broad goals: to connect empowerment to digital equity and to communicate the idea that technology can increase human performance. Access to technology and relevant content allows individuals to further their goals and to learn what they need to know when they need to know it. This freedom empowers people to take charge of their own learning and can lead to changing the way members of society think about the nature of teaching, learning, assessment, and achievement. Finally, efforts to empower schools and communities are discussed, along with the limitations these efforts face.

The Stage Is Set

The National Commission on Excellence in Education's report *A Nation at Risk,* which advocated reform of the entire U.S. education system, started the current era of curriculum reform. This report stimulated and informed fundamental dialogues about the meaning of education and how our nation's work force and citizens would be prepared to meet the demands for new 21st-century skills (U.S. Department of Education, 1983).

Since then, we have come to recognize that achieving digital equity depends on creating new power structures. If empowerment is the key, a useful starting point for discussing it begins with what Delpit (1988) called the "culture of power." In her analysis of what she identified as five rules of power, she concluded, "teachers must teach all students the explicit and implicit rules of power as a first step toward a more just society"(p. 280).

To extend Delpit's reasoning from education in general to digital equity, I propose five key points:

1. **Equitable access:** Issues of power involve insuring that individuals enjoy access to systems, policies, and practices, allowing full participation in a democratic society—in both real and virtual worlds.
2. **Individual responsibility:** The rules of power require people to take responsibility for their own learning and use technology to turn their homes and schools into connected learning communities where education becomes discovery and construction of understandings and knowledge (Solomon, 1992).
3. **Teachers' responsibility:** In new power structures, teachers must take the initiative in reconstructing their roles in the classroom as facilitators and co-discoverers of knowledge in a learner-centered environment.
4. **Leadership's role:** Official and unofficial authorities must take the lead in addressing policies and practices that govern equity in education, building inroads toward digital equity and establishing channels of entry for people who choose to participate in the development of relevant policies and practices.
5. **Governmental responsibilities:** Legislation in education, telecommunications, and labor must clearly state expectations for implementation at the local level. It is in these localities that important links must be forged to build the infrastructure to support technology integration and equity in schools and communities.

Empowerment is a prerequisite for individuals, schools, and communities if they are to achieve equity and fairness in a 21st-century world economy and in society. Toward this goal, education programs must provide their students with relevant theory and skills to leverage any available practical tool, including technology, to help their students. Teachers in the field, since they must understand and use computers and other technology to effectively facilitate computer use, must understand they play a significant role in empowering their students and communities. As important as access and innovative strategies are, fitting literacy and content into the digital divide equation will be equally important (Carvin, 2000, p. 1). Opportunities to acquire knowledge and to practice democratic principles as citizens will require all people to have access to relevant content and the skills to use and produce information effectively.

Defining Empowerment

Empowerment can best be defined as the ability of individuals and local groups to make something happen—to bring positive change to schools, communities, and people's lives. Being empowered facilitates the acquisition of knowledge and can expand the development of attitudes and habits for the effective use of that knowledge; the result is an increase in the individual's capacity for learning. Mere acquisition of information, knowledge, or new technologies alone will not necessarily empower unless that new knowledge is liberating and relevant to users' lives.

Empowerment may mean different things in different environments. In one context it may mean possessing many different types of knowledge. In another, it may mean the capacity to integrate one's knowledge and skills, synthesize multiple perspectives, become sensitized to subtle relationships, and make interconnections in both virtual and real worlds. Gaining an increased awareness of one's own developing point of view, becoming more skilled at expressing it to others, and using it to negotiate solutions for everyday problems permit active participation in democracy to achieve the goals of education reform.

Empowerment: Essential in a Democracy

Empowerment is essential in a democracy because it allows individuals to work in partnership and harmony with schools, community leaders, and policymakers to make decisions. To achieve empowerment in a technological environment, the nature of schooling and the assessment strategies for performance and learning must change. The system must provide the necessary structures to support these sweeping changes in the nature of teaching and learning, and redefine achievement and lifestyles to uphold civil liberties promised in a democratic and technological society.

But these powerful tools cannot effect freedom of speech, open access to information, and increased productivity if so many Americans—especially African Americans, Native Americans, non-English speakers, and others—are simply left behind. One can argue that for the kind of change needed to prevent this tragic loss is for empowerment to become an "ethos," a fundamental value, a new way of life.

What would education look like with this new "ethos" in place? Goals of educational reform in modern democratic societies might focus on the humanistic foundations in the development of the human being as (a) a worker, (b) a citizen, and (c) an individual. Such activities necessarily take place within a predefined set of parameters—groupings of ethnicity, caste, belief, and other local factors that combined we call culture. Technology and access to information must be culturally relevant to support necessary action and lifelong learning.

How technology and information translate into other cultures with regard to education and freedom largely depends on that culture's demands and expectations upon its members. If education is indeed most relevant within its cultural context then educators and policymakers must develop an adequate conception of how new technologies can be used to contribute to understandings in different cultures and contribute within a multicultural democratic society. In supporting the democratic citizen as a worker, access to technology in the learning environment will play a larger role than ever in determining who will get to compete in the world employment market and who will be left behind. In certain communities such as Sioux Falls, South Dakota, the ratio of students to computers is 6 to 1, as reported by Quality Education Data, a Denver research firm. When the question emerges: "Can individuals from traditionally underserved communities compete against graduates of programs like Sioux Falls," the answer about the seriousness of the digital equity divide becomes clear (Hascall, 1996).

Technology also helps empower people in a democracy as citizens. Citizenship demands access to information needed for informed decision making, which in today's world means connectivity. The report *Disconnected, Disadvantaged, and Disenfranchised: Explorations in the Digital Divide* (Cooper, 2000) pinpoints important steps to be taken to overcome the digital divide by examining attitudes toward and experience with Information Age technologies among those who are underserved. What they concluded was that the digital divide is not the result of a failure of those without access to appreciate the importance of technology but the result of simply being unaware and lacking the skills and resources to become aware. The findings indicated that approximately 93 percent of those without access believe that computer skills are vital, 83 percent believe that understanding technology is critical to success, and 84 percent believe that children learn more when they have access to technology.

The report further states that at the same time, those without access have much less confidence in their ability to use these technologies. This lack of confidence was evident by only 21 percent of the "disconnected" considering themselves computer savvy (compared to 57 percent of the "fully connected"). The unawareness was evident in that half say they do not know what the Internet is or how it could help them, compared to one-eighth of the "fully connected." Two-thirds of the disconnected say the Internet is too expensive.

> The Internet is already an important avenue for participation in society. As it becomes the main avenue of commerce and communications, people not connected to the Internet could become a new category of the disenfranchised. Public policy to close the digital divide must give people the skills to use technology, the experience to make them comfortable with it, and the resources to bring it into their homes, where they conduct their personal business (Cooper, 2000, p. 1).

Finally, technology prepares individuals in a democratic society to express their unique talents and fulfill their personal potentials. Much of technology's empowering capacity rests in the natural creative talents of people themselves. Technology simply provides the opportunity for individuals to further enrich their lives by becoming lifelong independent learners (Cooper, 2000).

How can digital technologies empower those left behind in underserved communities and schools to take their place in the front line of the Information Age? How will people get the same sort of access to information in cyberspace that they now enjoy in physical space? What does empowerment have to do with digital equity and the education divides? In a digital age, individuals, schools, and communities are empowered when training and computers provide opportunities to help them access to information than can help them make better decisions about their lives, as well as achieve greater levels of human performance and citizenship through high-quality education.

One example in this chapter that reveals a rich example of how adequate training and access to powerful tools such as computers and the Internet empower traditionally underserved individuals, schools, and communities is the Bell South model.

Empowering Individuals

Technology Empowers Learners

For more than ten years, research has shown how students are benefiting from digital technologies. One study showed that fourth graders advanced two to three grade levels in language skills in one school year while using technology to communicate with students in other states and to prepare their own newspapers (Braun, 1993). Prominent educational technology researchers analyzed the result of 61 studies of technology used with students ranging from preschoolers through college level (Bialo & Sivin, 1990). They reported that children learn more and learn better when they have access to technology in an intelligently designed environment.

Issues in Empowering Individual Learners

It is imperative for bilingual educators to examine and discuss with each other how technology might transform their classrooms and schools into communities where learning is viewed not just as consumption of information but as students and teachers together generating new knowledge, creating literature and art, and acting on social realities. Technology opens up enormous possibilities for validating and expanding the cultural and linguistic experiences that children bring into the classroom (The Center for Language Minority Education & Research [CLMER], 2001).

In this scenario, the speaker clearly expanded the idea of empowerment to include basic communication and production skills. Although access to telecommunications and computers is a key ingredient in the empowerment recipe, cultural and linguistic experience play a role in determining whether equity is achieved when it comes to being able to use the tools to improves one's performance and ability to function independently in society. Technology can address this key issue, a subject that is addressed in more detail in Chapter 5, Defining Literacy for the 21st Century.

Another issue is basic connectivity. A recent report, *Disconnected, Disadvantaged and Disenfranchised,* a study based on 1,900 underserved respondents, revealed that 47 percent them did not have Internet access at home (Cooper, 2000). In addition, even when the technology is available, the content may not be accessible if there are literacy barriers. As a result, the Consumer Federation of America and Consumers Union are calling for a "more relevant focus on connectedness to computer networks when defining the digital divide" when talking about empowering participation in the online world (Cooper, 2000, p. 3). The definition of "connected" in this context must be expanded to include connections to relevant and accessible content to fulfill the principle of equity. Chapter 1, Creating Educational Access, and Chapter 2, Barriers to Equity, further address these problems.

The digital technology industry is producing content created by corporate content developers, who may not be educators, and may not be sensitive to creating content that is culturally relevant to diverse learning. Despite the exponential increase in digital computing power available to the average person, there are still inherent barriers in the human–machine equation that must be acknowledged in a learning environment. Social critic Theodore Roszak, put it this way: "We do not bring the full resources of ourselves to the computer" (Roszak, 1994, p. 71). The structure of empowering learning opportunities is critical so that we can bring the full resources of our rich and diverse student population into the world via electronic connections.

Every child must have a teacher to guide participation in an educational program that empowers and enables him or her to develop into a fully productive, contributing, self-respecting citizen in society. Increasingly in political, business, and personal spheres, the citizens of the future—our youth of today—will be called on to think rather than primarily recall facts. Increasingly, the information available to a child in school or to a teacher in skills-based training may become outmoded, irrelevant, or superseded before it even reaches the classroom. How useful will this static, drilled, and practiced information be to these children when they enter the work force decades later? Learners' continuing effectiveness resides in their ability to solve problems and continue learning, rather than on prior training and the static knowledge acquired in formal traditional schooling—sometimes referred to as the "30 eggs in a crate" model.

How do we know when we are making progress? Learning—and efforts to improve it—should be measured in ways that will lead to clear understanding about educational goals and encourage further efforts to improve outcomes for students. This means educators must create and adopt additional measurements of student achievement and use them in conjunction with standardized tests to assess student success and learning. In addition, we should assess schools, districts, and higher education institutions in part on the value that they add to student learning. Because improvement in student learning takes place over time, it is important for policymakers, administrators, and funding agents to monitor philanthropic investments and grants by articulating interim goals and assessing progress in meeting them.

Technology Empowers Teachers

Solomon (1992) cited research regarding the importance of preparing our teachers to use technology in schools. Solomon reminds us that we cannot continue to shame and blame teachers for their inadequacies when it comes to technology integration in the classroom practice and curriculum, stating:

> We must help teachers learn. We must get teachers' hands on computers by putting the machines in teachers' workrooms, in their classrooms—anywhere they spend their free time . . . and ideally teachers should have computers of their own (pp. 327–330).

Integrating technology is not limited to computers or microcomputer-based laboratories. Everything from low-tech manipulatives to interactive videodiscs, telecommunications devices, and even handheld toys *is* a form of technology. Virtually any technology can be put to appropriate use in a learner-centered environment. At the same time, one must recognize that although technology can empower and change the teacher's role in the classroom, it does not eliminate the need for high-quality, caring teachers.

As educators and policymakers openly examine the portable characteristics of professional development, learning, and teaching models in urban and mainstream environments, expanding support to teachers as individuals in need of professional development in a digital age must be backed by relevant content, strategies, and technical assistance (Solomon, 1992). This preparation must help teachers and learners use technologies to collaboratively engage in developing digital content to transform learning in a more dynamic, demanding, vibrant, and interactive exchange (CEO Forum, 2000). In a community-based public school digital divide study, 100 teachers were asked three questions about their perceptions of technology and how it would affect their learning and teaching. Responses to the questions revealed that teachers may not have reached a clear consensus about their support and training needs because they lack a general understanding of new standards, technology, and what it is they are being asked to do (see Table 4.1).

TABLE 4.1   Teacher Responses to Three Open-Ended Questions

1. **What is the successful use of technology?**

   Will it change the learning setting of teacher education in higher education?

   - Will teacher education continue to have access to the top-quality professors in the field?
   - Will more teacher preparation be online or onsite in professional practice schools?
   - What will it take to motivate and empower teachers to change?

2. **What emerging empowerment trends do you see as a teacher?**

   Education in classroom will be project- and team-based learning. There will be no set of requirements. Learners will take initiative in learning, teacher as facilitator (most frequent response)

   - Teacher as resource person, does not have to know all things, but knows how to get information.
   - Technology allows children to be individual learners.
   - Technology takes into consideration personal interests of learners.
   - Multimedia is helpful to students to learn.
   - Teachers must be trained to address the special needs of individual students and especially girls.
   - College courses must include relevant content and strategies useful in the schools of the future.
   - Districts' efforts must include teachers as decision makers who model the good use of technology to inspire others.
   - Gaining technology must be within the portfolio content in teacher training.
   - Teachers must take training opportunities at schools of education when they need it, rather than when it is required.

3. **What are some helpful solutions to appropriate technology access in schools?**

   - Always ensure the most appropriate equipment and keep updated software.
   - Replace computers in the classroom as they become obsolete.
   - Provide adequate access to a laptop for each student; have satellite or cable TV and digital camera for each grade level (there are plenty of grant opportunities to support the schools' technology needs).
   - Rotate students using four to five computers.
   - Provide a trained teacher in the building to advocate the use of technology. Technology coordinators cannot do that.
   - Mandate teachers to get training, go to training, and show cooperation to learn.
   - Ensure facilities and support for open lab.
   - Provide a more flexible lab schedule and include technology class for students only when large-group activities are required.
   - Require technology teachers to collaborate with classroom teachers in their lesson plans to integrate technology in their curriculum.
   - Provide incentives for teachers to encourage working with instructional and technology coordinators, to improve success in writing grants.

Effective preparation of teachers in urban schools and teacher education programs in new technologies, instructional strategies, and creative learning models are essential. Teachers need training to support equity and empowerment in the use of new technologies and computers more appropriately in the classroom to meet the needs of traditionally underserved learners (Darling-Hammond, 1998; Thompson, Bull, & Willis, 1998).

The increased role of technology in the new dynamic learning model understandably makes many good teachers in the field nervous. We often hear the chant, "Oh, the kids were born with it. There is no way anyone can stop this technology—it is inevitable in schools. Teachers cannot compete with these new learners."

I wholeheartedly agree. Teachers should not compete with students. They should learn from them. One such successful collaboration is Generation Yes, where youth expertise has been harnessed to help teach teachers and students alike. The program, which started with teachers and students in one school district in 1994, has since expanded to 500 schools in 27 states, the District of Columbia and the Virgin Islands (Harper & Generation Yes, 2001). This program was originally developed from federal, state, and private grants to provide a model for integrating technology throughout the curriculum. Students provide the technology training by partnering with a teacher in their school to create lessons that work along with effective uses of technology and national education standards.

Empowering Schools

Our Changing Schools

Telecommunication and collaborations are making alternative education programs a reality for many youth and young urban residents with parenting responsibilities who hope to continue participation in the educational system and improve their potential for a higher quality of life. Virtual high schools and home schooling are now acceptable forms for high school completion in a number of states, for example Florida, Ohio, California, Maryland, and others (National Education Goals Panel, 2001a).

Thirty-nine states and territories showed significant increase in their college enrollment figures since the benchmark was first established in 1992. Figures range from 40 percent of high school graduates entering college in Nevada to 73 percent in Massachusetts. At the same time, the gap in college enrollment between White and African American high school students has closed from 14 percent to 9 percent. According to the *High School Completion Rates Stay Level* report released by the National Education Goals panel members, post-secondary education is becoming increasingly important for young people entering the work force (National Education Goals Panel, 2001a).

These figures bode well for the future competitiveness of the nation with its global neighbors. Of the states and territories that showed increases, the five most improved were the District of Columbia (from 33 percent to 58 percent), California (from 50 percent to 66 percent), South Carolina (from 43 percent to 59 percent), Massachusetts (from 60 percent to 73 percent), and Delaware (from 57 percent to 67 percent) (National Education Goals Panel, 2001a).

A 2001 *Education Week* report, The New Divides: Looking Beneath the Numbers to Reveal Digital Inequities, a report card on the progress of states toward digital equity showed these states and territories being among the leaders in technology use and Internet access in the classroom. Nevertheless, the report affirmed that public education has a long way to go to reach digital empowerment and equity in our schools (Education Week, 2001b).

Major issues in debate over equity in education and technology in schools are emerging in our policy circles, schools, and communities. The goal of equity is to empower all individuals to achieve academic and personal success in order to acquire knowledge and information through the ability to access innovative communication tools. Economic barriers to accessing this knowledge exist. Foundation members are further quoted as saying that inequality of home access places a great burden on organizations like theirs to provide technology resources to individuals with the greatest need (Milone & Salpeter, 1996).

Therefore, it becomes imperative for communities to collaborate with schools and policymakers to overcome these obstacles. Technology provides people expanded and independent learning opportunities when access is equitably distributed. So on the positive side, the anytime-anywhere concept of distance learning could offer a solution to combat the emergence of a new caste system as a barrier to school empowerment. I believe the benefits of equal access to technology empowers schools and learners in six ways:

1. Technology can make education and schools more productive.
2. Technology can make learning more individualized.
3. Technology can give instruction a more scientific base with its extensive research capabilities.
4. Technology can make teaching more powerful.
5. Technology can make learning immediate without dependence on second- or third-hand interpretations.
6. Technology can make access to education equal.

Technology does not have to move people; it can impact people and allow people to impact others via its networks. The limits to improving and empowering teaching and learning through technology are political, parochial, and financial; but the barriers to empowerment and equity are not inherent in technology itself.

Decision makers must enact policies that expand individuals' or children's access to power tools to help them grow and prosper as independent citizens. Schools cannot simply accept inequities. The research shows that if public education does not provide these powerful tools and resources, it will be hurting our children's future.

The gaps between African Americans, Whites, Hispanics, and Native Americans in college entrance rates, reading, science, mathematics, and other traditional measurements of academic success will prevent some individuals in these groups from effectively competing unless they have access to appropriate education and new technologies. A news article highlights the problem of educational equity in Ohio:

> The gap in test scores between black and white students in Ohio is wide, pervasive and persistent. Black students as a group consistently score lower on standardized tests than their white counterparts in wealthy and poor school districts alike, in Ohio and throughout the country. But until this year, Ohioans have largely been unaware of how big the gap is among students in the state. The issue is getting attention in Ohio mainly because Black lawmakers and community leaders demanded the release of the data (Ohlemacher, 2001).

The individuals in America's underserved schools and communities must not be have-nots in terms of access to technology and the academic resources it provides so they can better address their diverse learning needs to compete in society.

One State's Experience in Building a Technological Infrastructure for Equity

American public education is facing a social, educational, and digital technology crisis in urban schools that serve large, traditionally underserved populations, especially African Americans, Native Americans, and non-English speakers. This crisis did not come out of nowhere overnight (Becker & Sterling, 1987). The crisis of inequity in education and our awareness of it grew right along with the reform process, starting in earnest shortly after Congress amended the Educate America: National Education Goals legislation of 1990 to allow local and state governing bodies more local decision making (Stedman & Riddle, 1998; Goals 2000: Educate America Act,1994).

Local school districts in states not participating in the National Education Goals program were allowed to apply for federal Education Department funding when approved by their state educational agency. Twelve states and others took advantage of this opportunity for what they envisioned as more "local control." Among those states was Ohio.

Statewide Collaboration for Equity

I selected Ohio to profile for two reasons: (a) I live in Ohio, and (b) much of my recent research on the digital divide was conducted in the urban communities of Cincinnati. Again the 2001 *Education Week* report, *The New Divides: Looking Beneath the Numbers to Reveal Digital Inequities,* reported on the progress of states in meeting the challenge of digital equities in their states. Below are excerpts from the Ohio report:

> Ohio started spending on school technology in earnest in 1995, and so far, it has funneled some $856 million to Ohio schools. At the center of those efforts are two programs, Ohio SchoolNet and School NetPlus. SchoolNet, a five-year program completed last December, wired every public school classroom in the state to a high-speed network that can support telephone, Internet, and video transmissions. It also delivered one computer per grade—a total of more than 15,000 computers—to the state's poorest schools (p. 97).

Data from two surveys in the Cincinnati area, the Community Access to Technology and Ohio SchoolNet, suggests that the focus must shift beyond the machines to the standards-based curriculum, teacher assessment, and performance in the classroom. Solutions to digital equity and the education divides must target student achievement using enhanced multimedia and portfolio-based assessment to improve learner performance on the Ohio statewide proficiency tests.

Ohio SchoolNet Plus is an empowerment model formed to bring about a 5:1 ratio of students to multimedia computers in kindergarten through fifth grade by fall 2002 with poor districts receiving a higher per-student allocation of funding than wealthier districts. Districts such as Cincinnati Public Schools, which have already met that ratio, can use the state money to buy computers or related services, such as teacher professional development, for sixth through twelfth grades.

The state's next step, SchoolNet Plus Care, which stands for "Continued Aquisition and Repair of Equipment," is to carry out the computer program beyond the fifth grade. According to Sam Orth, the executive director of the Ohio SchoolNet Commission, the Ohio program ". . . has kind of filled in the gaps for poor districts with technology needs not addressed by SchoolNet or SchoolNet Plus" by placing computers in schools demonstrating the greatest need and located in the lowest economic communities (Schnaiburg, 2001, p. 97).

Additionally, collaborative efforts are being focused on some of the poorest districts in the state, both urban and rural. These initiatives, such as computer refurbishing and youth training programs are included in the governor's proposed 2002–03 budget. In the fiscal year 2001, the state distributed $3.3 million to 164 of Ohio's poorest districts in the form of technology equity grants, which districts could use for anything in their technology plans.

> The state also gives teacher technology-training grants to every district, based on enrollment. This year, the grants total $4 million. In addition, the state has put together a voluntary certification program for teachers that aligns curriculum, instruction, and technology and trains teachers in such skills as the use of spreadsheets and networks, multimedia applications, and ways to find the most relevant content. So far, about 40,000 teachers have received "novice" certificates; more than 1,600 have received "practitioner" certificates; and more than 2,500 have become "novice trainers" (Schnaiberg, 2001, p. 97).

Accountability Is Essential to Gauge Equity

As the Ohio example shows, amendments to national policies enacted at state and local levels can provide state leaders, local school superintendents, and principals with added systemic flexibility, control of funding distribution, and spending to meet local needs more appropriately. Thus, pockets of site-based management and local school empowerment models that challenge administrators to take control and responsibility for reform in their communities and schools continue to emerge in states and cities with large populations of traditionally underserved populations.

U.S. data sources continue to report that over the next ten years, across the nation an estimated 2.5 million teachers will remain in need of empowering learning opportunities. These opportunities are necessary if schools are to continuously expand creative and telecommunications technologies and require teachers to learn digital teaching strategies to meet the needs of all learners in their classrooms on an equitable basis.

In a digital divide study, more than 100 teachers from ten inner-city schools in Cincinnati's underserved communities were asked for comments about how they view technology in schools, their role, equity, and empowerment to do their jobs. As stated earlier, Table 4.1 includes some comments teachers made to three open-ended survey questions (Pittman, 2000). These questions were: (1) What is the successful use of technology? (2) What emerging empowerment trends do you see as a teachers? (3) What are some helpful solutions to appropriate technology access in schools? Among the most profound teacher responses were those concerning what it would take for some teachers to change their practice; for example: "Require that teachers apply all relevant standards in practice." This inclusion of standards should include National Educational Technology Standards for students and teachers in their planning and in the classroom. Unless administrators hold teachers accountable, some will never change existing teaching practices in the classroom (National Education Technology Standards for Students and Teachers, 2000).

A strong system of accountability for and information about suitable training and access to technology in these communities is critical for equity to occur. To ensure an appropriate strategy to support adequate educational opportunity and to "leave no child behind," no teacher can be left behind, especially in urban and rural community schools (Bush, 2000; Solomon, 1992). This is especially important in the traditionally disenfranchised communities, where 50 percent of the upcoming teacher shortfall is projected to occur and the need for high-quality teachers is the greatest. As President Bush has said (2000):

> If our country fails in its responsibility to educate every child, we're likely to fail in many other areas. But if we succeed in educating our youth, many other successes will follow throughout our country and in the lives of our citizens (Bush, 2000).

Empowering Communities

Guiding Principles for Creating a Full Community of Learners

Effective education in communities embodies equity; it provides diverse individuals with the means to participate equally in a complex and changing world wherever they are. In a review of support for community-based education and technology centers, the BellSouth initiative emerged as one establishing guidelines for partnerships that can make a difference. The Bell-South Foundation has identified a set of empowering principles that represent the wide spectrum of how educational technology partnerships can create communities that foster total involvement of all learners. BellSouth's core values about education reflect the organizational beliefs that arise from its fundamental commitment to improving learning for all students.

Although many funding agents engage new ideas of active learning in a community of learners, others continue to reproduce workers to meet yesterday's needs. However, the BellSouth's program, Gaining Ground, has created a grant-making program to advocate a different approach to achieve greater impact from collaborating for education and equity that may be useful in creating communities of learning in disenfranchised areas.

Guiding principles of the Gaining Ground BellSouth initiative place emphasis on diversity and equity, learning in different places, strategic uses of technology, and strong leadership (BellSouth, 2001). These principles include:

1. **Learning must be inclusive.** Equity and diversity in all aspects and at all levels of education will promote better outcomes for learners and spur more comprehensive efforts to foster high achievement for all. While real progress has been made toward improving learning, substantial differences in outcomes among students persist. Students from lower-income families, racial minority groups, and immigrant families continue to lag behind their peers. We must make special efforts to ensure that these students do not remain behind. An increasingly globalized and interdependent society requires investments in effective education beyond our own borders.

2. **Learning takes place in many different places.**   Schools are not the only place for students to learn. We must strengthen links between schools/universities and other learning environments in the community. We must reinforce and strengthen the role of parents and other community members as mentors, teachers, and learners themselves.
3. **Learning requires leaders.**   Effective leadership is distributive; it enables adults throughout educational systems, institutions, and communities to take responsibility and have authority for actions that will improve student outcomes. Even where leadership is distributed, district superintendents and higher education presidents play a crucial role for providing a coherent vision, maintaining focus, and setting the tone for what happens in schools. Communities can play a vital leadership role in promoting and supporting effective teaching and learning.
4. **Learning can be fostered through strategic uses of technology.**   Adults in [homes, schools, and community centers] need to embrace, not fear, technology and believe in its transformative power; they must develop new capacities to embed technology in all of their work. We owe [learners] many and varied ways to experience technology's value in the learning process and use it to take charge of their own learning.

Building Educational Technology Partnerships

Clearly, to achieve high standards identified by these guiding principles, private-sector stakeholders must construct partnerships with schools, universities, and government. Partnerships will further ensure that current and future workers have the support to develop essential literacy skills to continue lifelong learning. Without technical and new literacy skills, disadvantaged people are at risk of becoming disenfranchised citizens. Therefore, they may fail to achieve benefits of being fully participating members of 21st-century economy and society.

Colleges of education must internalize and institutionalize the importance of integrating technology into teaching methods and arts and sciences curricula so the teachers of tomorrow, as well as the schools and communities they serve, can take full advantage of the ever-growing digital technology infrastructure.

Almost half a century has passed since the U.S. Supreme Court ruled in *Brown v. Board of Education* in 1954 that differences in access to schooling were unconstitutional. Despite this historical legislation, adequate education in urban schools increasingly falls short of measuring up to school, student, and teacher performance standards. Fortunately, interest and investment in technology as the reform model for education in the 21st century still grows.

Education for Empowerment

Once again, technology poses a challenge. Two questions drive the following section: (a) What are some essential standards for building technological literacy in a democracy to empower underserved groups in disenfranchised communities? and (b) what educational arrangements can effectively and expediently promote their attainment?

Despite the growth of technology in the United States of America, there are still a growing number of deprived urban neighborhoods, with vast number of unskilled workers, poorly educated youth and adults, and limited financial resources, that have been unable to benefit from this growth. The huge disparities in the quality of life among various socio-economic and racial groups remain, and in some cases, become wider as these individuals are unable to reap the economic benefits in the form of jobs or business opportunities. In the meantime, according to Congressmen John P. Murtha (PA) and John B. Larson (CT), America's preeminent global status rests on three pillars for our survival in a technological age: the strength of our economy, the might of our defense, and the quality of our schools (Murtha & Larson, 2000).

While unemployment grows in urban communities, 600,000 high-tech jobs in the United States are going unfilled because there are too few technologically skilled workers. Empowering low-income people through technology is important in addressing one of the underlying causes of the racial unrest in America's overcrowded cities. Access to information and education can help eliminate the feeling of powerlessness. Often the main cause is lack of access to information and training for these new high-tech jobs. This leads many of those who are economically disadvantaged to forego further new opportunities in the digital world.

The Promise: Community Technology Centers Support Learning Anywhere

Proposed plans to open community technology centers in the heart of urban neighborhoods aim to alleviate some of this feeling of powerlessness by providing opportunities for technology education and technical training. Low-income residents would gain the opportunity to develop appropriate skills for better-paying jobs in the expanding information technology sector. These residents could then provide themselves with the social and economic services needed to be self-sufficient. They can begin to take control of their educational, social, and financial interests.

Having a readily available and qualified work force is the best investment we can make as an inclusive community. Though poor neighborhoods and families face daunting challenges, technology deployed in education can help remove inequities between the inner city and the suburbs, between cities and rural districts, and among women, Native Americans, people with disabilities, and members of other minority groups in this country.

Technology can become the force that provides equitable access to educational opportunities for all children regardless of location and social and economic circumstance. This should be the national goal.

The Reality: Divided We Stand

In many communities, numerous organizations are attempting to provide training and access to technology. Many are hamstrung by inadequate budgets and limited technical support. In some cases, the institutions whose programs do well in servicing particular community groups do not fully embrace the empowering nature of technology for the community as a whole.

The Urban League chapter in Cincinnati, Ohio, currently provides programs for both youth and adults. The chapter headquarters building hosts a site for the PowerUp program (PowerUp, 2001) as well as housing an adult development program for Appalachian American and African American men and women called Project SOAR (Urban League of Cincinnati, 2001), where computer training comprises one-third of the program's length.

While both programs use computing power extensively, the two groups of people utilize resources at separate times, precluding the possibility of developing a sense of community. The young adults do not learn computer skills from the children, nor do the children learn valuable life lessons from the adults. Although both programs serve elements of the community, they do not learn together. Barriers are raised, however unintentionally, in the way programs are currently delivered.

Issues to Overcome in E-Learning Initiatives

The problem with some digital age technologies is that many community leaders, workers, businesses, and citizens in underserved communities are unprepared for the growing demands placed upon them for all types of support. Although these initiatives are effective, they are inadequate in number when we consider growing needs.

According to Donahue (2001), individuals, schools, and communities must overcome three problems to be fully empowered to participate in electronic learning environments in homes, schools, and communities. First, there is the problem of rendering traditional content suitable for Web delivery as well as increasing the amount of new culturally responsive content. Second is the challenge of delivering technology to learners anytime, anywhere. Third is ensuring that everyone is optimally involved in the learning process.

The Curtain Closes

At a time when everyone is looking for ways to close the digital equity gap, educators must be careful that the politically and socially popular strategies often written into technology planning initiatives and funding programs do not exacerbate existing inequalities in our homes, schools, and communities. The empowerment model is advanced as a means to ensure that the voices of traditionally underserved communities are heard, so that the needs of these populations are met. The model shown in Figure 4.1 provides essential components for how individuals, schools, and communities must work together for empowerment to happen.

To be empowered, people need training and technical support to master new technologies. Guiding these important competencies are the right products, a process for

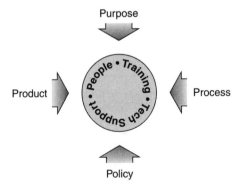

FIGURE 4.1   The Empowerment Model

accessing services and products, appropriate policies to protect users and gauge the effectiveness for achieving the desired purpose.

With access to culturally relevant content and adequate technology resources and support (including learner-centered teachers), youth and adults can act in the spirit of self-determination to close the digital divide in a way consistent with community standards and beliefs. In the process, they can fulfill their rights and duties within our democratic society as fully engaged citizens, responsible workers, and (hopefully) happier individuals.

Many obstacles remain, however. A proliferation of programs, each attacking a particular segment of the population, cannot be expected to coherently address the needs of individuals within the larger framework of a democratic and multicultural society. Teachers and community members will need to find creative methods to overcome institutional and policy barriers that unintentionally atomize communities even as they seek to uplift the individual.

The checklist that follows provides a set of guidelines useful as a tool to reflect on attitude expectations, policies, practices, and standards.

Checklist to Guide Digital Empowerment

The checklist can be used as a tool to reflect on attitudes, expectations, policies, practices, and standards. Place a check after items that could create a more empowered environment in your school, community, or home.

1. View the Internet as an essential skill.
2. View technology as a vehicle for learning.
3. Assess technology performance as a part of academic, school, and program evaluation.
4. Teach individuals how to learn, along with what to learn.
5. Require technology as an essential motivational learning and teaching tool in and out of the classroom.
6. Use technology to support targeted learning to include all genders and special needs of learners.
7. Use technology to promote social, cross-cultural interaction.
8. Require technology as an essential knowledge and skill for all educators.
9. Incorporate technology as a part of educational pedagogy at all levels in all institutions or departments involved in preparing teachers.
10. Provide training and technical support for ongoing implementation.
11. Avoid diverting funds from needed resources to include technology by including it as an essential part of existing resources, not as a discretionary add-on.
12. Provide learner and teacher access to support infrastructure 24/7.
13. Develop infrastructure that ensures classroom access to the Internet.
14. Provide for ongoing commitment to readjust technology and Internet programs, since they are evolving resources that change.
15. Provide local, state, and federal legislation that supports technology in education, schools, and community through categorical funding, as opposed to supplemental appropriations that come and go.
16. Provide grants and loans to individuals and community organizations for technology support.
17. Reduce rates for telecommunications to support universal service programs in homes.
18. Provide implementation, planning, and coordination support through the state's school technology commission or regional consortia dedicated to technology integration.
19. Encourage ongoing technology training for teachers.
20. Support technology standards as a part of school assessments and content expectations to inspire high-quality learning and teaching.

Score 50 percent or higher and you are off to a good start!

5 Defining and Designing Literacy for the 21st Century

KEVIN ROCAP

FOCUS QUESTIONS

1. How do technological changes relate to changing definitions of literacy in the 21st century?
2. In what sense are literacies technologies?
3. What equity issues arise in the context of 21st-century literacies?
4. What kinds of literacy pedagogies are emerging in the 21st century?
5. How might literacies and literacy pedagogies be designed to promote digital equity?

What do you think of when you think of literacy? That generally depends on who you are, where you find yourself on the hierarchies of social status and privilege, the cultural spheres you participate in, and what you do day-to-day. If you were an English-speaking child you might recall singing your ABCs and reading *The Cat in the Hat*. Perhaps for you, literacy evokes images of reading a good novel. Writing a paper. Or doing either of these in a language other than English. What about filling out a job or a welfare application? Being literate might mean having the skills to create a financial spreadsheet, compose a symphony or write a computer program. It might mean carrying out a conversation in American Sign Language or writing a note to put on the refrigerator telling family members when you'll be home and that you love them.

Literacy might be tied to the communal study of a religious text—the *Bible, Torah, Koran,* or *Upanishads*. It may involve pictographic, non-Roman, non-phonetic characters and reading up and down or right to left. Perhaps for you, it includes sending out invitations to your daughter's *quinceniera*. Or it may involve reading and passing down to your children the treaties that define the formal relationship between your Indian nation and the U.S. government. In the 21st century, typing on your computer keyboard in order to chat in an online forum about your favorite television show; or, better, to participate in an online educational "virtual world," is a digital literacy act. You might also include, in your literacy definition, watching and making sense of the news, or any other television program, where speech, image, video, and text merge as "media." Media authoring, not merely watching or surfing, is also key to interactive multimedia environments and the World Wide Web. If you have privileged access to digital technologies and educational opportunities, literacy may involve the multimedia rendering of 3-D visualizations of molecular structures, crafted, shared, and manipulated in simulations over networked digital computers. Or, perhaps, you have opportunities to create digital videos that express your point of view and then to stream them over the Internet.

Literacy acts are diverse, personal as well as public, multicultural, multilingual, and multi-modal (involving print, books, images, video, computers, gesture, smoke signals, art, etc.); they pervade forms of communication and social participation, coordinate activities and social purposes, and occur in diverse, situated contexts (Cope & Kalantzis, 2000; Engestrom, Miettinen, & Punamaki, 1999; Lankshear, with Gee, Knobel, & Searle, 1997; Lave & Wenger, 1991; Vygotsky, 1978). This may not be news. However, some of the literacy opportunities mentioned above would not have been possible for nearly all of us only 30 or so years ago, with many emerging broadly only since the mid-1990s—and are still not available to most people in the world.

How do new digital technologies relate to changing notions of literacy in the 21st century? This chapter will discuss some ways in which information and communication technologies are intimately involved in enhancements and transformations of traditional literacy, as well as how current and potential uses of digital technologies create not only new possibilities, but new requirements and, at times, obstacles for participation in social, economic, and political life. We'll consider, as well, the roles of public education and other public spheres in working towards equity in a digital age.

Literacy Considered

Literacy and literacy pedagogies are vast topics. This chapter is not meant to be a review of literacy research or even literacy and technology research (such topics are covered extensively in other places; see chapters on technology in the *Handbook of Reading Research Volume III* or the *Handbook of Literacy and Technology,* 1998, as two possible starting points). This chapter will raise critical issues and questions about larger issues regarding the social construction of literacy. The defining and designing of literacies in the 21st century is a social process that, through ethical human agency, might be turned toward equitable democratic purposes (or might exacerbate current inequities).

When thinking about literacy new opportunities may come to mind, but literacy can also be used to erect barriers, as was the case with discriminatory literacy testing requirements in the U.S. South. So-called *literacy laws* were designed to bar African Americans from voting, even after the right to vote had ostensibly been secured through Civil Rights legislation. Robert P. Moses, the founder of the Algebra Project and advocate for mathematics literacy, worked as a civil rights worker in the South during the 1960s and describes the literacy laws in effect at the time. He notes that what African Americans were asked to read were often obscure constitutional passages that could not have been comprehended by the ruling Whites, who were not required to read them. In fact, during slavery, literacy itself was outlawed, making it illegal for slaves to learn to read and write and underscoring how literacy facilitates social action that may run counter to *official* purposes. As a present day example, high-stakes standardized tests also serve a gatekeeping function and raise issues of cultural, racial and class biases, raising questions about who defines literacy and who is positively or negatively impacted (Moses & Cobb, 2001).

The Expansion of Literacy

Whatever the situation, you may reasonably associate literacy predominantly with visual artifacts—handwritten script, print text, and images, some might say the manipulation and interpretation of signs and symbols generally—as opposed to the strictly oral and aural experiences of speaking and listening. But even these distinctions can blur depending on your community, your values, or the technologies available to you. Digital technologies, for instance, facilitate the convergence of sound, text, and image, which can all be equally well encoded in the bits and bytes format of digital files. Literacy definitions that traditionally include descriptions of material processes of encoding and decoding meaning (usually alphabetic or other character rendering on paper), increasingly need to accommodate and make sense of digital rendering on digital media as well (e.g., digital data on floppy disks, CD-ROMs, and DVDs.). These new media generate new enactments of literacy, and new social practices; consider, for example, computer-supported collaborative learning: collective and shared engagement with disciplinary content, databases, and varieties of information and communication technologies, usually over networked computers in the context of sociocultural learning theories and practices (Koschmann, 1996). Or, more prosaically, think of online karaoke.

If you speak into a microphone attached to a computer, speech-recognition software will "transcribe" (digitally convert) your words into text that displays on the screen. You can then store your text as a digital word processor file. In turn the word processor can "read" the text back to you through your computer's speaker. In this example, as you work, are you speaking or writing, are you reading or listening, or both? What are the implications for literacy pedagogies? Both hardware and software mediate your literacy activities—a software program processes your keyboard input and is responsible as well for displaying the digital information which would be otherwise inaccessible were you simply handed the physical hard drive on which the digital data is inscribed.

E-mail, also, is a kind of hybrid of speech and writing, straddling, as it were, the technologies of letter writing and the telephone. Again by virtue of software (Internet protocols written in unspoken languages, another new form of literacy), e-mail is able to be distributed easily to multiple, even multitudinous participants worldwide, for multi-way communication. In another vein, understanding the contributing effects of audio (e.g., music and tone of voice) in television news show, alongside interpretations of visual text and images, is critical to media literacy. The use of diverse media may influence emotion and meaning, creating another challenge to strictly alphabetic or print notions of literacy.

Digital technologies increasingly shift text literacy from page to screen, creating, for example, new reading requirements (as well as new *writing* or, in the case of Web pages and multimedia, programming or *authoring* requirements) that include understanding how to navigate and make meaning of nonlinear text. Hypertext and hypermedia documents, where any text, image, or video may have embedded links to other text images and video, can be read, and in fact benefit by being read, in a nonlinear fashion. Clicking on a text or image link and jumping from one screen to another involves active reader choice in deciding which links to follow. This affects the experience of what text is viewed in what order, and the meaning-making process. Warschauer (2000) provides this summary of related skills for reading online:

- Finding the information to read in the first place (Internet searches, etc.)
- Rapidly evaluating the source, credibility, and timeliness of information once it has been located
- Rapidly making decisions as to whether to read the current page of information, pursue links internal or external to the page, or revert back to further searching
- Making on-the-spot decisions about ways to save or catalogue part of the information on the page or the computer page itself
- Organizing and keeping track of electronic information that has been saved

Further, Warschauer (2000) notes the need for new writing/authoring skills:

- Integrating texts, graphics, and audiovisual material into a multimedia presentation
- Writing effectively in hypertext genres
- Using internal and external links to communicate a message well
- Writing for a particular audience when the audience is unknown readers on the World Wide Web
- Using effective pragmatic strategies in various circumstances of computer-mediated communications (e-mail, e-mail discussion lists, and various forms of synchronous real-time communication).

Beyond and aside from their language basis, emerging literacies are tied as well to visual image manipulation, sound integration, and the material resources and technologies available to a community, such as networked computers and the Internet and World Wide Web. Different material and technological resources in a community (as well as different values, aspirations, and activities) connote different literacies at work in that community. Digital equity is not simply an issue of equitable distribution of computers and connectivity, but, significantly, of the education, resources, and opportunities that support meaningful participation in the definition, design, and use of these technologies for self- and community-defined purposes.

It is useful to remember that what we currently know about social engagement with information and communication technologies derives largely from practices of and research on those with privileged access to the media (users are predominantly White, well-educated, and from families with relatively high incomes). At a recent conference on the design of online agents (in this case, animated talking heads in one corner of the computer screen able to interact in somewhat intelligent ways with online learners), I was struck that all of the animations I saw had White, European features. The researchers were interested in how learners might interact with these agents, but seemed not to give much thought to the variables of skin color, facial features, language, or accented speech as relevant factors that might affect different learners interactions differently. This experience underscores the reality that researchers often work within biases that favor dominant group members' perspectives, another face on the digital divide.

Official Literacies

Literacies are composed of diverse values and technologies. Consider, for the moment, whether you would agree that oral cultures and diverse cultural modes of expression and communication, including the use of art and visual images prominent in Aboriginal culture or the historical practice of sending smoke signals, for example, are as significant and worthy of privileged status as any dominant Western print-based literacy practices. What does it mean to value (or not) these divergent forms of expression in a digital age (or in any age)? What makes a type of literacy official or unofficial? How do literacies acquired in school relate to literacies acquired outside of school? Do literacies become official only insofar as they are associated with formal institutions, like schools? Are so-called unofficial literacies ever important to individual, family, and community well-being? If so, how and when, and what are the implications for public education?

Economically and politically, dominant or *official* literacies can and often do marginalize groups that engage in culturally diverse practices of communication and with non-dominant content. Digital technologies, democratically deployed, might support these varieties of cultural expressions and practices. Paul (2000) for example, sees rap and hip-hop generally as a site of critical inquiry, susceptible to media literacy strategies, engaging and didactically powerful for urban youth and able to provide a potential bridge between racially and culturally different teachers and students. She teaches critical media approaches to rap to preservice teachers as a way of addressing cultural barriers. Such an approach lends itself as well to critical multimedia authoring possibilities. In spite of such promising approaches, certain official forms of digital content still dominate most of our interactions with computers, e.g., corporate mass media, financial and business uses of largely office technologies, and standardized, top-down networked systems. This is not surprising since a key metaphor for our interface with computers has been the *desktop* (Johnson, 1997). Cultural and economic values are often implicitly, if not explicitly, embedded in the metaphors and designs of information and communication technologies. Likewise, the defining and designing of literacy (digital or otherwise), involves political decisions about what kinds of literacy count.

The International Adult Literacy Survey

Changing notions of literacy are reflected in international initiatives to understand literacy in various settings. The International Adult Literacy Survey (IALS), carried out by members of the Organization of Economic Co-operation and Development (OECD), was a 22-country initiative involving the survey of over 75,000 representative adults between 1994 and 1998, the largest international adult literacy study to date. The purpose of the comparative study is to "understand the nature and magnitude of the literacy issues faced by nations and to investigate the factors that influence the development of adult literacy skills in various settings—at home, at work and across countries" (Tuijnman, 2000, p. 9).

The study defines literacy as *the ability to understand and employ printed information in daily activities, at home, at work and in the community—to achieve one's goals, and to develop one's knowledge and potential* (Tuijnman, 2000, p. 9). This definition stays within a fairly traditional print literacy perspective, in contrast to prior discussion in this chapter, but does provide some expansion in terms of linking print information to how it is used in the pursuit of individual goals and purposes. One might wonder, for instance, what occurs when individual goals or purposes diverge from dominant or even standards-based literacy notions?

Of note in the current testing-dominated K–12 climate is the instrumentation used in this adult literacy study. Literacy skills were evaluated along a multidimensional continuum (Tuijnman, 2000, p. 5). This highlights important concerns regarding literacy in the United States, as many *literate* members of U.S. society (based on testing) have trouble performing in ways that meet work and life demands. Literacy in this study is measured operationally across three domains, quoted from the study, below:

- **Prose literacy**—the knowledge and skills needed to understand and use information from texts including editorials, news stories, poems and fiction
- **Document literacy**—the knowledge and skills required to locate and use information contained in various formats, including job applications, payroll forms, transportation schedules, maps, tables and charts
- **Quantitative literacy**—the knowledge and skills required to apply arithmetic operations, either alone or sequentially, to numbers embedded in printed materials, such as balancing an account, figuring out a tip, completing an order form or determining the amount of interest on a loan from an advertisement (Tuijnman, 2000, p. 10).

Although promoting access to information and communication technologies (ICTs) is one of ten policy imperatives cited in the study, explicit reference to ICTs is scant. Further, the potential role of these and emerging technologies in addressing the other nine policy objectives is not explored. This is consistent with literacy definitions that stay at a basic adult literacy level (where literacy is thought of more as a minimum, than a high standard). However, the IALS study does raise the bar on the meaning of *basic* literacy. Notably the role of searching, finding, authenticating, and utilizing various types of documents is a highlighted literacy domain that brings fundamental information literacy skills into even basic conceptualizations of adult literacy. Information literacy is an arena in which digital technologies play an increasingly significant role (e.g., digital libraries) with regard to the organization, classification, analysis, and use of documents, including the use of metadata to digitally tag content (like a digital version of the information in a library card catalogue) and related data mining activities in the context of diverse human, organizational, and social practices. While the IALS definition and domains help in part to demonstrate that the knowledge economy and new information and communication possibilities are changing notions of basic adult literacy; they arguably do not go far enough in terms of the role of digital technologies in a new society.

Changing Work in the New Economy

The construction of official literacies and the setting of standards in education is generally a backward planning process. Hypotheses regarding the roles and functions of future citizens or workers become the basis of determining what adults should know and be able to do. Certain views of the future often gain prevalence over others. Key ideas about changes in corporate capitalist work, for instance, affect the setting of standards.

Changes associated with information and communication technologies (ICTs), taken together with other social, scientific, and technological changes—such as the unraveling of genetic code, the rise of biotechnologies, improvements in transportation modes, and new economic structures and relations associated with globalization—contribute to the 21st century notion of global "knowledge workers" or "symbolic workers." These ideas of what it means to be symbolic workers influences our sense of the literacies required to fulfill these roles. In 1993, business expert Peter Drucker proclaimed, "Knowledge is now fast becoming the *one* factor of production, sidelining both capital and labor. It may be premature (and certainly would be presumptuous) to call ours a 'knowledge society'—so far we only have a knowledge economy. But our society is surely 'post-capitalist'" (Drucker, 1998, p. 15). Drucker further states that human capital in the form of knowledge, talent, social networks, and the ability to learn and contribute to innovation and performance in the high-skills, service-oriented, information-based global economy may matter more than traditional forms of financial/material capital or labor. Gee (2000) views this as "people as portfolios" (p. 61). From a learning perspective, two cognitive psychologists active in the development of K–12 computer-supported collaborative learning environments contend that people must become expert at becoming experts (Bereiter & Scardamalia, 1993).

In the new economy corporate hierarchies are replaced by transnational partnerships, teamwork, and fluid, entrepreneurial enterprises, with a commensurate rise in jobs for consultants, part-time workers, and temporary workers. Further, calling someone a symbolic worker refers not only to the ability to understand and manipulate symbols through and within diverse media in order to accomplish complex tasks, but to recognize that the very marketing and dissemination of products and services in the 21st century involves understanding the role that these goods and services play as symbols in consumers' lives. Thus, 21st-century literacies involve the manipulation of symbols by "symbolic workers," in ways that relate fundamentally to issues of identity, community, consumer engagement, and economic participation. Becoming a knowledgeable citizen, as opposed to a knowledge worker, then, may entail developing the savvy to avoid being manipulated by symbolic practices related to increasing consumerism. While Drucker proclaims a "post-capitalist" world, Jeremy Rifkin (2000) and others characterize it somewhat differently as a *hyper*-capitalist world, what Rifkin terms an "age of access," where the equivalent of subscription, licensed or fee-based access to key products and services, or even to lived, cultural experiences, is superceding traditional forms of ownership, property, and experience. These authors suggest that actual ownership may reside in fewer and fewer hands (we, most of us, pay to use someone else's things, rather than for the things themselves; think of Blockbuster or Time-Share vacation condos, for relatively mundane examples).

From an equity perspective these changes in our work environment represent both new possibilities and new threats. The social construction of future work seems to require a simultaneous devaluing of the skills, knowledge, and by association the contributions of agricultural, industrial, and so-called low-level service workers, or of artists and other forms of cultural workers, even when these workers arguably still provide the day-to-day backbone to both local and global economies. Thus, a wider range of diverse personal and cultural aspirations is not always included as we envision the new global world. Yet how the future is conceived determines the K–12 literacy standards we develop.

The Social Construction of Literacy in K–12 Education

To define something that *every* child should know and be able to do is to socially construct what it means to be *literate,* in some key sense of that term. I should explain here that *social construction,* in this instance, refers to the very concrete practice of experts (of whatever ilk) sitting around the proverbial table deciding and documenting what all children need to know and to be able to do usually at each grade level of their schooling in a given content domain (e.g., math, science, social studies, language arts). Standards setting can involve many people, sometimes thousands over a significant length of time, or only a relative few. Yet there is process of standards development, so it seems appropriate to describe as a process of *social construction,* with the understanding that the fact that it is *social* does not necessarily translate into it being either a particularly democratic or participatory.

Whether and when such standards-setting processes should be participatory is also an open question. Certainly relying on expert guidance in specific subject matter domains makes sense; mathematicians are well situated to identify important math concepts and knowledge. Yet questions and concerns arise. Consider E. D. Hirsch's educational series based on his original book *Cultural Literacy: What Every American Needs to Know,* which sets out to describe what it means to be *culturally literate* in the United States in the 21st century. While this cultural literacy is presented as everything an American needs to know, it omits key histories, contributions, cultures, and values of the racially and ethnically diverse learners and their families least well-represented in the U.S. K–12 system, as well as those histories and perspectives that might inform an understanding of the United States place and role internationally. (Since September 11, 2001, this seems a particularly poignant omission, educational blinders as it were, codified as standards.). When considering digital content and digital technologies it is important as well to critically examine whose cultural values, representations, and expressions are given privileged status and whose are omitted or negated.

What is "official" literacy other than the range of practices, institutions, events, artifacts, and socially defined and valued competencies or enactments that come to be associated with dominant uses of the term? I had this in mind in posing the question that opened this chapter: *What do you think of when you think of literacy?* It is a pertinent question and any individual's or group's answer may or may not align with institutionally supported, official literacy definitions and further, will likely be determined in large part by the technologies with which one is comfortable and familiar. What are the implications in a democratic society of both differing views of literacy and technology-constrained literacy aspirations? Arguably educators need to understand and support the aspirations, values, and future visions of their learners' diverse families and communities, as well as promote principled democratic participation in the wider society, including facilitating access to materials and technologies that might broaden learners' and families' notions of what is possible for them.

This chapter, and this book as well, suggest that it is in the scope of human ethical agency to proactively design learning that promotes equity in a digital age. Yet the social construction of literacy is multidimensional and as readily marked by conflict, contestation, and unequal power relations as by consensus, agreement, and participatory practices. Promoting equity involves ensuring that key stakeholders from traditionally underserved or oppressed groups are active participants in the processes of envisioning and designing social futures, in setting K–12 standards, and in designing quality learning activities. Further it is important that the aspirations and goals of traditionally underserved learners are routinely and formatively assessed and addressed in learning environments (see Ramirez, Chapter 14 of this volume).

Multiple Intelligences

Changes in theories of learning also influence literacy notions and practices. In education Gardner's theory of multiple intelligences, for example, provides a framework for transforming teaching, learning, and assessment in ways that are still not widespread in U.S. classrooms. Gardner (1993) and his colleagues examined data from sources that include studies of normal child development as well as studies of exceptional individuals. They describe seven intelligences. The seven identified intelligences are: linguistic intelligence, logical-mathematical intelligence (most rewarded in school learning, along with linguistic intelligence, though in the United States with a rather strict English language bias), spatial intelligence, musical intelligence, bodily-kinesthetic intelligence, interpersonal intelligence (the ability to interact well with others), and intrapersonal intelligence (the ability to know yourself well enough to operate effectively in life). Each of these diverse intelligences might be reflected in different types of *literacy enactments* that can be associated with a given intelligence. These are not intended to be hard and fast categorizations of intelligence, but rather to point the way towards embracing a wider variety of literate performances and pedagogical approaches.

Gardner writes that the identification of these intelligences represent a "critique of a universalistic view of mind . . . [and supports] . . . the notion of an individual-centered school, one geared to optimal understanding and development of each student's cognitive profile. This vision stands in direct contrast to that of the uniform school. . . ." (1993, p. 9–10). People generally exhibit a spectrum of these intelligences, according to the theory, each of them on a continuum, with certain intelligences more or less pronounced in different individuals. The intelligences often work together in problem solving and, of course, in learning environments these intelligences will arise in diverse types of situated learning activities (bodily-kinesthetic intelligence will likely go unnoticed during a paper-and-pencil test, for instance). This facet of multiple intelligences creates some convergence with other theories of language and sociocultural learning that see linguistic competence and learning as situated in specific circumstances and activities that give them context and meaning (Koschmann, 1996; Lave & Wenger, 1991; Vygotsky, 1978). Theories of multiple intelligences also open the door for an expanded notion of the literacies associated with diverse type of intelligence.

Literacies as Technologies

In the United States, common usage of the term literacy often exceeds the type of definition employed in the International Adult Literacy Study, and refers not only to basic literacy or functional literacy, or even only to print literacy, but also to higher-order skills, like media literacy, information literacy, bi-literacy (literacy in two languages), and some of the other literacies mentioned throughout this chapter. Literacy may even refer to performance competencies such as those identified in the 1991 Secretary's Commission on Achieving Necessary Skills (SCANS) Report. These work-related SCANS skills include initiative, teamwork, ability to work with diverse co-workers, systems-thinking, appropriate technology use, and problem solving (all, arguably, deemed *functional* for participation in the 21st-century workplace). In a more recent report, the CEO Forum, a forum made up predominantly of computer, media, and telecommunications executives, also embraces these workplace and computer technology "use" competencies as building blocks for student achievement, recommending these as fundamental to the schooling of a 21st-century citizenry and work force. Literacies, then, tend to carry a connotation of being fundamentals, building blocks, things that ultimately undergird competence for participation in diverse aspects of society.

U.S. educators and policymakers likewise define literacy at times as "basic skills," while at other times redefining literacies across content areas in order to raise the bar of expectations for *what every child should know and be able to do.* These determinations are then codified as (hopefully) challenging content standards. Literacy, in this case, connotes any fundamental learning expectation we have for all K–12 learners, exceeding the simple coding and decoding of text to include, for instance, academic literacy in content domains. Thus literacy toggles between being a floor and a raised bar. To not end up on the floor, one needs to aim for the bar. For many children this may mean exploring alternative paths of learning and literacy. With regard to the exploration of these alternative paths, literacy may also be conceived potently as *critical literacy* with a focus on empowerment, critique, democratic participation, and social transformation (Freire, 1982; Menkart, Lee, & Okazawa-Rey, 1998; Nieto, 1996; Sleeter, 1996). Critical literacies interrogate existing power inequities in society. They help to raise the voices of and improve life chances for traditionally underserved or oppressed individuals and groups, as well as to promote education that supports social justice broadly.

Plainly the word *literacy* is over-determined and may even support contradictory connotations, or as Lemke (cited in Reinking, McKenna, Labbo, & Kieffer, 1998) describes it "literacies are legion" and adds "that literacies are themselves technologies, and they give us the keys to using broader technologies. They also provide a key link between self and society: the means through which we act on, participate in, and become shaped by larger 'ecosocial' systems and networks" (Lemke, in Reinking, et al., 1998, p. 283). In the 21st century, and certainly throughout its history, literacy is and has been a moving target.

Oral Cultures, Literacy, and Digital Technologies

Societies without an alphabet or similar sign system of writing are often referred to as *pre-literate,* privileging, rightly or wrongly, alphabetic or written sign-based literacy as an inevitable trajectory for all societies. Imagine the Greece of Homer and standing in a crowd listening to Homer recount the tale of the *Iliad.* How do you remember and recall the story when Homer is not there? Social gatherings, conversation, retelling of the story, architectural spaces, visual works of art, such as religious and hero-worshipping art, sculpture, crafts, all provide not only an aesthetic, practical, or social role, but serve importantly as mnemonic devices for sharing the stories and histories of communities and entire civilizations.

We do not have to limit ourselves to Western history and culture nor turn to Homeric Greece, for instance, for evidence of oral cultures today. Present-day nations and ethnic communities also live without written systems of signs, whether traditionally or due to language losses associated with colonialism and related forms of conquest and oppression.

Some of these groups are even turning to digital means to document and rejuvenate their oral languages, cultures, and stories, or to revitalize or develop a written form of their language. Considering an example of a present day "preliterate" group provides some insight into the interactions of literacy, schooling and the wider society and the ways in which technologies mediate values as well as skills and knowledge.

The Nomadic Rabaris

In their ethnographic study of the Rabari nomads, a non-literate group, from Gujarat in the west of India, Dyer and Choksi (2001) consider the interactions of literacy, schooling, and development alongside the goals of the World Conference on Education for All. They note that underpinning the notion of basic education is a view of "neutral and universal" literacy, and go on to point out the assumptions surrounding many so-called neutral literacy education practices including the presumption of a settled, rather than mobile population, that is, a population available to attend sedentary classes. Such assumptions can put the state and the nomads at odds, with the nomads potentially perceived as difficult to control or belligerent, because their continuous movement is perceived as "a sort of offence to the requirements of any modern state" (Klute, quoted in Dyer & Choksi, 2001, p. 27). The state's requirement to educate and develop literacy as it has defined literacy practices, on its own terms, can create the conditions for viewing the nomads as "problems."

Migrant Education

Many traditionally underserved learners in a U.S. context are also often labeled as problems. This can be indicative, as in the experience of the Rabaris, of a mismatch in the literacy purposes and practices of schools and those of learners and their communities. Yet in some instances digital technologies are being implemented in ways designed to address the needs of diverse learners. Migrant students' experiences reflect complex issues of mobility, race, culture, and class. Project Estrella developed with federal Technology Challenge Grant funding involves the use of satellite-television–transmitted educational programming and a laptop-lending program that migrant students use for their schoolwork and to connect to the Internet. They make use of online resources and interact with distant teachers via e-mail and other available forms of telecommunication. With this approach, participating migrant students attain a continuity in their educational program as they travel, and they develop sustained relationships with participating teachers over satellite and via telecommunications. Innovative program designs, supportive policies, funding, resources, appropriate educational personnel, and the involvement of learners, parents, and other community members are critical to projects like Estrella. We might call such approaches to learning "equitable education by design."

Equitable Literacy

In conceptualizing a framework for equitable literacy in the digital age we should highlight important considerations. First, digital equity in education should not entail the devaluing or denigrating of oral cultures or other cultural technologies and practices that are not digital. In the K–12 context we should find ways to help learners become technologically literate in ways that go beyond conventional uses of that term. We need to help students understand that technologies arise from, serve, and transform social purposes in situated contexts, reflect diverse experiences and histories, and may either reinforce or help transform an inequitable status quo. The identities, ways of being, knowledge, and, in some cases, wisdom of diverse communities are embedded in equally diverse varieties of art, architecture, storytelling, sculpture, fashion, language, technologies, and literacies. An equity perspective seeks to reduce inequities in decision-making power in order to help ensure that technology designs and uses do not disadvantage certain groups and communities while advantaging others, thereby increasing gaps and inequities. A good example, as shown in Project Estrella, is to set out with the explicit purpose of designing human and technology approaches that improve the participation and learning opportunities of traditionally underserved learners.

Toward Multiliteracies

In the 21st century, modes of literacy and opportunities for becoming literate through the use of digital technologies are purportedly multiple—so-called learn anytime, anywhere, technology-enhanced learning opportunities continue to increase in number and expand their reach. Groups like the U.S. Department of Education (2000) urge legislators to realize and facilitate the beneficial shift from narrow-band to broadband connectivity, from single mode (text) to multi-modal, rich connectivity (text, sound, images, video), from tethered (wired) access to untethered (wireless), and from the status quo of users adapting to the technology to an imperative of technology adapting to the users. Yet amidst these digital prescriptions education and opportunity divides persist based on familiar indices that include race, class, gender, language status, immigrant status, migrant status, and special needs. And as Don Tapscott (1999) warns in *Growing Up Digital,* the threat of "information apartheid" for those who are growing up without meaningful access to digital information and communication opportunities is very real.

An international group of literacy educators gathered in New London, New Hampshire, in 1994 to grapple with historic literacy issues, emerging literacy trends, and the future of literacy teaching. Now known as the New London Group, they have published jointly and individually and have coined their own conceptualization of *multiliteracies,* which is relevant to the discussion of literacies in this chapter:

> Multiliteracies engage with the multiplicity of communication channels and media: and with the increasing salience of cultural and linguistic diversity. Mere literacy remains centered on language only. A pedagogy of multiliteracies, by contrast, focuses on modes of representation much broader than language alone. In some cultural contexts—in an Aboriginal community or in a multimedia environment, for instance, the visual mode of representation may be much more powerful. Multiliteracies also create a different kind of pedagogy: one in which language and other modes of meaning are dynamic representational resources, constantly being remade by their users as they work to achieve their various cultural purposes (Cope & Kalantzis, 2000, p. 5).

What does it mean for languages and other modes of meaning to become *dynamic representational resources*? The key evidently is for the resources to be in the hands of their users, *for their own purposes.* Resnik, Rusk, and Cooke (1999) of the MIT Media Lab, for example, make a related point in describing what they call technological fluency:

Technological fluency means much more than the ability to use technological tools; that would be equivalent to understanding a few common phrases in a language. To become truly fluent in a language (like English or French), one must be able to articulate a complex idea or tell an engaging story—that is, be able to "make things" with language . . . A technologically fluent person should be able to go from the germ of an intuitive idea to the implementation of a technological project. (Resnick, Rusk, & Cooke, 1999, p. 266)

Resnik, Rusk, & Cooke (1999) describe the design and experience of Computer Clubhouses, as places that promote learning, play, and use of advanced technologies in low-income communities. Children, youth, and adults come together in Computer Clubhouses and "mess around," working on projects of their own devising. Children are as likely to coach adults in using new technologies as adults are to mentor children. Learning in the Clubhouses involves different members emerging as experts at different times, to assist or collaborate in learner-defined projects. This informal learning environment also provides a paradigm for one way to rethink traditional literacy practices.

Critical literacies may be especially needed in designing future literacy practices that promote digital equity. One might want to explore, for example, the kinds of literacies that would permit U.S. K–12 learners not merely to plug into already established or articulated institutions and social relations but might also point the way to collectively constructed alternate and equitable futures; multiple futures, perhaps, not yet imagined. Paulo Freire's was a strong voice for such critical and transformative literacy.

Freire and Transformative Literacy

Twentieth-century Brazilian educator Paulo Freire advocated for and worked to develop critical, liberatory, and transformative literacies not merely of reading (interpreting) and problem solving, but of writing (acting) and problem posing. Otherwise one may become "literate" only in order to read about someone else's reality and to solve someone else's problems. Freire (1982) describes literacy simply, but profoundly as both "reading and writing the world" and "reading and writing the word." Thus, he broadens fundamentally our view of literacy to include ways of "reading" (understanding and interpreting) the world in order to "write" (act in and transform) the world, with the reading and writing of texts, nevertheless, being instrumental to these broader endeavors. Further, by proposing that humans always "read and write the world," whether or not they can yet "read and write the word," Freire liberates us from the notion that we must set up such strict dichotomies between those who are "literate" and those who are not, underscoring that learners generally bring to literacy learning abilities and skills that are too often untapped in narrow approaches to literacy development.

For Freire (1982), literate adults benefit from engaging in spiraling cycles of action, reflection, and dialogue, called *praxis,* learning through experience, thought, and social interaction to discern both what is natural (and perhaps objective and immutable in the world) and what is cultural or historical (human-made, designed, and susceptible to change) in order to then participate in social action and processes of change for individual and communal well-being. Culture and history are exclusively human domains; and full humanity, for Freire, is measured significantly by the ability to be an active subject, a critically conscious *shaper* of culture and history. Oppression is the condition of being a human object, rather than a subject, at best adapting to historical and cultural realities imposed by others; schools facilitate these kinds of objectifying impositions, sometimes in the guise of ostensibly benevolent goals of "assimilation" or "mainstreaming." Critical education, which becomes requisite for equitable education and equitable literacy, in Freire's sense, is incomplete unless it includes analyses of power. Who decides in literacy learning environments which cultural and educational norms to impart? Who is positively or adversely impacted? Who imposes meaning and structure? Who lives as subject and who as object? Why? How can oppression be transformed into liberation? Literacy that empowers (and not all self-described literacy practices do) is a key.

21st-Century Literacies, Equity, and the Telling of Stories

In the 21st-century "knowledge society," with its vastness of data contributing too often to information smog and information overload, storytelling is acknowledged to be a critical organizer of human knowledge, potentially combining multiple perspectives, moral values, mental images, affect and propositional knowledge to facilitate human understanding and communication and to inform and coordinate purposive human action. What follows are brief stories from current K–12 contexts that provide suggestive examples of how digital technologies may help to shape equitable literacies and learning.

Project Fresa

In Oxnard, California third- and fifth-grade Spanish/English bilingual students, children of strawberry farmworkers, use a variety of technologies—tape recorders, video cameras, digital still cameras, scanners, computer software, and the Internet—for in-depth exploration of their own community as well as for collaborative inquiry into the lives of other farmworker communities nationally. Project Fresa participants (*fresa* is the Spanish word for strawberry) develop bilingual interview and research questions to find out, among other things, how long members of their families have worked in the fields, how much they make per box of strawberries picked, and why many suffer from headaches and back pain. They use spreadsheets to create pie charts and bar graphs of interview responses, and publish these on the World Wide Web.

The students create art that is then digitized, develop biliteracy through the writing of poetry and journal entries (using word processors and Web page publishing software), and carry out geography and social studies research on the Internet regarding strawberry production nationally and internationally, using of off-line resources as well—books, journals, and newspapers. They also become aware of and research the dangers to their parents of fertilizer and pesticide use in the fields and mount e-mail and letter writing efforts to express their concern and to call for appropriate safety measures. Further, as part of an e-mail–based learning network project they connect with the children of coffee farmworkers in Puerto Rico in order to collect and share similar data and stories and to discuss and analyze the similarities and differences of their lives and struggles in diverse, low-income agricultural communities. These Oxnard students have these new literacy and learning opportunities in significant part due to the vision, expertise, and technology-use competencies of their bilingual teachers. They still have only limited access to digital technologies but have many ideas for what they could do with greater access.

Southeast Asian Educators and Students

A group of conference attendees sits at individual computers in a conference "hands-on" session. If you look over their shoulders you'll see that they are making painstaking progress using a basic paint program to draw what to untrained eyes look simply like beautiful designs—some intricate, some made up of simple strokes of black. This is not a technology conference. This is the conference of the California Association of Bilingual Educators (CABE) and the participants in this hands-on session provided by the Center for Language Minority Education and Research (CLMER) include educators of Cambodian, Vietnamese, Chinese, Laotian or Hmong descent, as well as a few white European American educators fluent in the languages of these ethnic groups, who also teach in K–12 bilingual education programs. This is not a session on technology and the arts. The attendees are learning from their colleagues the strategies, tricks, and tips they have devised for creating Web pages that can include the character scripts of the languages of their students and of their own Southeast Asian American communities.

The American Standard Code for Information Interchange (ASCII) which has dominated computer technologies for decades makes use of a 7-bit code space and its 8-bit extension to represent Roman characters, specifically A–Z and a–z. In short, ASCII does not support the non-Roman characters of participants' languages. The newer Unicode Standard allows for virtually any extant character within world languages, yet is not fully implemented in all software programs, especially not in the dated software most readily available in high-poverty K–12 classrooms. The ASCII Standard reminds us that exclusion from certain literacy practices can take place at the level of what might seem to be innocent or neutral technical standards that, in reality, reflect and reinforce the values and purposes of those who designed them.

Native Americans/American Indians

Baldwin (1995) notes that the rapid evolution of communication technologies played a role in the European invasion of the "New World" (at that time, changes in print distribution and transportation technologies), that TV and radio came late to reservations, with relevant cultural content coming even later, while simple telephone service is still far from universal today. Internet use and participation in cyberspace remains an elusive goal on many reservations, though participation is growing. Implementation of new communication technologies also involves the complex cultural responses of diverse tribes with as much concern about the threats of new technologies as there may be hopes for its potential. For example, Baldwin writes, "Indian people who use the public data networks are now asking, 'How do we implement the principles of *tribal sovereignty* and *self-determination* online?' (Baldwin, 1995, p. 143).

One nation, the Oneida Nation, early-adopters of Internet technologies, created an online Treaties Project, to educate their children and others about their tribe's treaties with the U.S. government. Yet besides creating new kinds of literacy acts (digital publishing) and modes of communication, cyberspace creates new challenges to cultural identity, according to Baldwin (1995). Internet aficionados often extol the virtues of being able to assume different identities and to role-play in the relative anonymity of cyberspace. Yet such fluid forms of identity can pose a threat to tribes to identify who can speak for the tribe, a right they would like to see carried over into cyberspace. And the stereotypes of archaic Indians need to be dismantled, according to Baldwin (1995):

> This stereotype clashes with the reality of the tribal councilmen who are now considering the use of reservation lands as a storage site for nuclear and medical waste. Or the tribal council that must choose which subcontractors should design software that will integrate casino and bingo operations with overall tribal budgets. Or the tribal planner utilizing a Geographic Information System to track development of tribal roads and industry, a satellite network of Indian-owned and -operated radio stations, or a national satellite video network of Indian colleges (p. 140).

Issues of physical infrastructure and access are, perhaps more than ever, critical to Native American/American Indian participation in new forms of literacy and communication; additionally, a wider range of sociocultural issues is implicated in ensuring digital equity, the maintenance of treaty rights and tribal sovereignty.

Kansas Collaborative Research Network (KANCRN)

K–12 participants in this online community of scientific inquiry follow guided processes that include generating research questions, engaging in field and online research, hypotheses development and testing, data collection, use of collectively populated databases, analysis and development of online software-supported Geographic Information Systems (GIS) visualizations, and database-driven maps based on students' own collected data as well as public and private data sets. K–12 participants collaborate with peers online—sharing data, visualizations, and analysis, and writing or co-writing research papers. Through KANCRN, participants also collaborate with adult experts and scientists, often at a distance. One young participant identified a new species of a studied animal and co-presented a paper at a conference in Northern Europe with an internationally known expert. Through KANCRN, scientific and social science literacies, database manipulation, and use of visualization and data modeling are integrated into new information and communication technology-enhanced forms of teaching and learning for those teachers, learners, and communities privileged with the capacities to participate digitally.

Community Technology Centers

During the 1992 "disturbances," or uprisings, in South-Central Los Angeles one African American community leader, Joseph Loeb, watched his community literally go up in flames fueled by anger and historical patterns of neglect. Joseph decided he had to do what he could to make a difference. He quit his job, sold his car, and cleared out his garage to set up a makeshift computer lab to start teaching computer skills to inner-city children and youth, as a way of providing new skills and hope for an economically brighter future. Joseph and many more committed members of the community then opened two or three small community technology centers before the newly formed Break Away Technologies found a home in a 15,000 square foot facility near Jefferson and Crenshaw in Los Angeles. Break Away Technologies became an after-school and weekend center for inner-city children, youth, and adults. It became a point of training and access for community-based arts, nonprofit, and economic development organizations, and, among many other programs, initiated a successful CyberSeniors program, with many seniors developing high-tech entrepreneurial skills and becoming mentors to neighborhood children and youth. Further, Break Away Technologies, through high-speed connections to an Internet gateway at University of Southern California, became an Internet Service Provider, providing access to online services as well as to training, support, computer recycling programs, and networking services for community organizations and inner-city schools.

In collaboration with the Center for Language Minority Education and Research (CLMER), Break Away became a community site for the "Computers in Our Future" (CIOF) Initiative of The California Wellness Foundation. Over four years Break Away collaborated with ten similar sites statewide to develop new operational visions for community-based and -managed open access, education, training, and support centers where underserved youth and adults can gain access to and develop competencies in using, building, and maintaining computer and network technologies—including using computers and the Internet for personal, academic, and job-related learning activities, engaging in Web page development as well as in multimedia, animation, and graphic design activities, and developing work readiness. Break Away and CLMER also collaborate on a federally funded Community Technology Centers project that supports Break Away's ongoing vision and operations. Further, Break Away Technologies with assistance from CLMER and in collaboration with a variety of private and public partners has helped to bring computers and network technologies to over 200 community-based organizations and schools through its "200 by 2000" initiative.

Yet community-based movers and shakers are not deluded. They recognize that computers and the Internet are not panaceas, but are most useful when addressing specific learning issues and social purposes in the context of appropriate additional resources, expertise, and community goals. They also understand that donated computers, better than none at all, become quickly outdated for running new software programs, installing memory-hungry new versions of operating systems, or for addressing evolving network requirements. Yet savvy members of low-income and economically distressed communities who recognize the value of 21st-century literacies are helping themselves and each other to the benefits of networked and relevant digital literacy opportunities, even when steady and stable streams of appropriate public funding, resources, and professional development support that would ensure meaningful participation for their communities are not otherwise available.

Literacy Transformations at All Grade Levels

Leu (2000) sees technology changes as creating rapidly and continuously changing literacies in K–12 contexts at all grade levels. Literacy practices one day may change the next, with, for instance, the introduction of handheld digital assistants and scientific probes. He invites us to consider some classrooms at all grade levels that already make use of networked technologies in ways that are likely still novel in too many classrooms and especially in the classrooms of traditionally underserved learners. For example, children in K–2 classrooms in Portland, Oregon, have kept a pet gerbil in a terrarium; they have also had in the past a GerbilCam, a 24-hour Internet camera, allowing the children to make observations of the gerbil's behaviors and habits over the Internet from home or from other places in the school or community. Children's artwork and writing about their gerbil observations and projects have become part of online digital electronic portfolios. This kind of use of computer technologies for learning is motivating. With appropriate facilitation by teachers, students might also develop nascent ethical sensibilities about scientific and surveillance uses of video, which may inform dialogues at various grade levels around issues of privacy rights for humans or the ethical treatment of animals in scientific experiments.

A video vignette developed by the North Central Regional Education Laboratory (NCREL) depicts upper elementary and middle school students participating with other classrooms in a Windmill Project facilitated over the Internet by the Franklin Institute in Philadelphia, Pennsylvania. Students design and build windmills of various shapes and materials, sharing their design choices with collaborative classroom partners at a distance using CUSeeMe Internet videoconferencing software (preferably over high-bandwidth connections). By sharing their budding theories of aerodynamics and receiving peer feedback at a distance, students develop speaking and presenting abilities, may share written plans and drawings as well, and come to experience processes of peer review and iterative design that mirror experiences of adult engineers, inventors, and designers.

The students depicted in the Windmill Project are predominantly white, English-only students in a multiple computer classroom with extensive hands-on materials for their Windmill construction project. On the one hand, that they are well-resourced helps us at least to get some glimpse of the potential of information and communication technologies in education; on the other, similarly resourced schools with high numbers of linguistically, racially, and culturally diverse underserved learners might lead to yet other innovative project ideas, like a higher-tech Project Fresa focused on issues of agriculture and agricultural workers, or the First Peoples global learning network project linking indigenous children internationally in sharing powerful, digitized artwork and stories about their diverse indigenous communities.

Towards Digital Equity

In the 21st century, new gaps open in and around "reading and writing the word" and "reading and writing the world," within which newly acknowledged intelligences along with literacies and technologies, like those discussed in this chapter, proliferate. Manuel Castells (2000) in his book *The Rise of the Network Society* draws upon Melvin Kranzberg's first law of technology, which is that "technology is neither good nor bad, nor is it neutral." (Castells, 2000, p. 76). Expanding on this notion I'd like to suggest that literacy practices and other associated educational practices are also neither inherently bad nor good, nor are they neutral, but are always already embedded political endeavors with human agency and historical conditions interacting to shape those practices and their outcomes. If, as Leu suggests, literacies change with technologies and material resources (and especially rapidly in a digital age), and if equitable public education in a democracy is ostensibly based on equitable literacy opportunities for all learners, a failure to provide equitable material and technological resources to all learners is tantamount to denying access not merely to those specific materials and technologies, but more importantly to the literacies that are not possible without them. The struggle of human agents who care about equity is to marshal educational practices and technology uses to equitable ends.

6 Connections across Culture, Demography, and New Technologies

HENRY T. INGLE

FOCUS QUESTIONS

1. What role has technology played in the erosion or loss of culture?
2. How do cultural perspectives affect the use or appropriation of digital technologies?
3. What are the implications of the demographic changes on issues of digital equity

> The urgency that many feel is afoot in the digital divide discourse to play catch up with the array of rapidly evolving communication and information technologies tied to the use of the WWW and the Internet, has in many instances overshadowed the need to sufficiently assess the risks, or detrimental effects, these technologies pose to long-term sustainable social and human development. [These] challenges underscore the need to first and foremost examine the socioeconomic and cultural dimensions of the different populations groups seeking to use the technologies, followed by a careful analysis of the local environments that facilitate or mitigate against successful application and use of technology by these groups. There are those who share this view who contend that the most pressing . . . issue in this regard is not the introduction of these technologies from the point of view of the technical infrastructure and diffusion and adoption cycle, but rather from the point of view of the multi-faceted access, control, content and equity factors that can arise from their use in a given social setting without undermining local and time-honored cultures and traditions . . . as people work against the tide of mainstream Western values and attitudes often introduced by the technologies (Morales-Gómez & Melesse, 1998, p. 11).

In today's context of dramatic communication technology breakthroughs and a growing concern for cross-cultural communication amidst changing student population demography, the ideas expressed above by Morales-Gómez and Melesse might well apply to the business of education. Increasingly the interplay across the teaching–learning process has come under both public and professional scrutiny, and the methods of instruction have been judged by many as out of sync with the cultural antecedents of those students most in need of schooling. In the case of education, the concern is on *who* is or is not learning, *what* is being taught, *where* the learning is taking place, *why* learning does or does not occur, and *how* the learning is delivered. It is an underlying argument of the so-called "digital divide" that it is imperative to focus the benefits of the new digital technologies of communications on the needs of changing student demography, while in the process, preserve and integrate the cross-cultural antecedents of those students. As the chapter on access notes, discussions about the digital divide must move away from a focus on installing computer hardware and toward a focus on developing appropriate and culturally relevant content. Such content reflects the diversity of underrepresented communities and links, in a culturally appropriate manner, the use of these digital and Web-based technologies to the diverse challenges these communities are facing. Educational practitioners and scholars are ". . . calling for greater investment in online content that meets the needs of . . . those who may not feel that the Internet is for them . . . so that society can share in the benefits of having as many voices and perspectives as possible in cyberspace" (Young, 2001).

The questions of access to digital media need to be framed within the broader context of understanding the impact of technology on culture and of culture on technology. Digital divide challenges can no longer be characterized as being only technological in nature. Access to hardware alone will not by itself empower those communities most in need of the benefits digital technologies can provide in terms of communication and the exchange of knowledge. We need to focus attention on the development of content that is relevant to particular communities and on training and developing educators who are proficient in the subtleties of cross-cultural differences. These educators need to be enabled to work with diverse student groups, to teach information literacy, and to build on the rich traditions of both minority and majority group engagement with new technologies and technological innovation. Within this broader context, we need to also be cognizant of how new technologies are situated, how we can facilitate access to them, and how we can structure policies and practices that foster greater diversity in content and more broad-based, culturally relevant access. Of equal importance is the need to have educators and students who are savvy technology users, and who see themselves as both consumers and producers of content on the Internet.

Throughout history, technological innovation has had adverse effects on cultural diversity, resulting in the homogenization of culture and the communication of attitudes and behaviors that fail to know, honor, and revitalize the valuable societal aspects of cultural diversity; however, as DeVillar, Faltis, and Cummins (1994) pointed out, "in order to make use of the power of the computer as a cross-cultural communication and discovery tool, students must have some non-trivial reasons for communicating with others and motivation to search out and interpret particular forms of information, as well as [knowledge of] how to cooperate with others in seeking solutions to common problems" (p. ii). This is particularly important now when "across North America . . . demographic changes are occurring that make the *culturally and linguistically heterogeneous* classrooms increasingly the norm" (DeVillar & Faltis, 1991). They indicate that the refocusing of the interplay between technology and culture can be markedly enhanced by equitable and appropriate forms of new digital technologies (p. iii).

These twin concerns of technology and cultural diversity have become more prevalent given the fact that the United States is currently experiencing a radical demographic shift that is changing the color and the cultures of its citizenry and, in particular, the student demography in our classrooms. According to recent statistics from the U.S. Census Bureau (*Newsweek*, 2000), one American in four currently defines himself or herself as non-White. By the year 2010, because of higher birth rates and immigration trends, non-Whites are expected to constitute more than one third of the American people, and upwards of 50 percent of its school age population. By the year 2050, the average U.S. resident will trace his or her cultural antecedents either to Africa, Asia, Central and South America, Mexico and other Hispanic/Latino regions of the world, the Pacific Islands, the Middle East, and almost anywhere but Europe. As this cultural diversity increases in our nation's schools, teachers, administrators, and other education personnel will be challenged to become more knowledgeable about the assumptions, attributes, and norms of a range of cultures, languages, and traditions. The challenges will occur in every dimension of school life and the classroom, beginning with the curriculum and extending to the instructional tools that are used, as well as the communication that occurs between students and teachers in classrooms and cyberspace. As a result, the issue of the interplay between technology and cultural diversity will, by necessity, have to be more forcefully taken into account if effective education is to be a reality in our nation's schools (Lindsey, Robbins, & Terrell, 1999). In addition, there is a long-standing concern from minority group scholars (Ingle, 1998) about the social effects of technology on people and cultures. Cultural groups are becoming increasingly concerned about the intrusion of technology into the traditional lifestyles of their communities and the possible destruction of their culture and way of life. At this juncture in history, it is not clear whether the benefits of technological innovations outweigh these perceived negative effects.

Framing the Context for Discussion and Analysis

This chapter seeks to profile the cultural factors that are necessary to help America's diverse cultural groups deploy advanced telecommunications and digital technologies in ways that can better facilitate information sharing, cross-communication exchanges, and culturally relevant teaching and learning for population groups that historically have been underserved in these arenas. The chapter also addresses the changing levels of student access to computer-based technologies across America's diverse cultural groups and the socioeconomic imperative of educational institutions to better meet the learning needs of culturally diverse minority populations. This means, in educational terms, that educators must work to assure that every student—regardless of socioeconomic status, language, race, geographical or physical restrictions, cultural background, gender, or other attribute historically associated with inequities—has equitable access to advanced technological communication and information resources and the learning experiences they provide.

Information tools, such as the personal computer and the access it affords to the World Wide Web and the Internet, are increasingly critical to economic success and personal advancement; yet, while more Americans than ever have access to telephones, computers, and the Internet, there is still a significant divide separating America's information haves and have-nots in terms of having access to these new communication tools from an equipment standpoint, as well as from the dual roles of consumers and generators of a more culturally diverse knowledge base that mirrors the changing population demography the new digital media delivery systems seek to attract. At the moment, regardless of the data sets brought forth for analysis, it is clear that individuals of middle- and upper-class White Anglo-Saxon background are more likely to have access to the Internet than Blacks, Hispanic, and Native American groups from any location—be it in schools, at work, at home, or in community centers.

Inequality.org is a current website that speaks to these issues and concerns. Created and maintained by a network of journalists, writers, and researchers, this website features news and analysis of both the economic and cultural ramifications of the growing digital divide and the ways the new technological developments in information and communication technologies will affect different segments of society. Increasingly, the more miniaturized, sophisticated, affordable, and easier-to-use technologies are thought to be having the same type of impact on our society that the pencil had on writing (Ingle, 1998). Most experts agree that the new information technology is not a passing fad; it, with all of its ramifications, is here to stay.

Interest in the social and cultural effects of electronic communication technologies—going back to the introduction of the telephone, followed by radio, television, and the VCR—historically has been derived from a sense of their newness and our need to become comfortable and familiar with them (Meyrowitz, 1995). Hindsight, which comes with use and familiarity, rather than foresight, has helped us to understand the principal effects of each succeeding communication medium on a particular population group and in a given situation. This hindsight has sensitized researchers and policy analysts to what futurist Christopher Dede (1985) has called the *parking lot syndrome*—that is, concentrating not on the particular gadget or hardware, but rather on what happens to us because of the gadget. For example, on the upside of the equation, the automobile has promoted modernization and social change; and on the downside, the automobile has produced highway traffic congestion and the game of hunting for a place to park the car.

Today, new communication media and technology, and the concomitant considerations of policies and the effects on society that surround their use, are not unlike Dede's automobile analogy (1985). Although electronic and telecommunication media are becoming commonplace in the workplace, the classroom, and indeed, the home (Greene, 2001; Meyrowitz, 1995; Paisley, 1984; Zorkocy, 1982), the knowledge base of the effects of these innovations on quality of life and cultural preservation is still evolving.

Some believe that an individual's chances in life, and eventual social and economic well-being, are directly linked to the ability to use the new information technology. Consequently, people express concerns that our society is becoming stratified along the lines of electronic access to knowledge and the new technological information resources. The terms *information rich* and *information poor* have been coined to describe this new equity and access debate.

Two questions, which are the recurrent themes of this chapter, are of particular importance to the debate (Golding & Murdock, 1986):

1. How will developments in the new digital communications technologies, and their patterns of use for cultural, educational, business, and information services, affect patterns of social inequality?
2. How can we use the new communication technologies to ease current and future socioeconomic disparities between the so-called information rich and information poor?

Of particular concern to this debate is that segment of the U.S. population generally identified as the information poor. They are primarily the nation's low-income ethnic, language, and cultural minority groups: Hispanics, African Americans, and Native Americans.

Coming to Grips with the Digital Divide and America's Information Poor

As noted in the previous chapters, the term digital divide has become a catchall concept in the media, referencing a variety of marginalized conditions associated with having access to, proficiency with, and benefit from the use of new information technologies and the knowledge resources and learning experiences they provide. The very first writings on the topic of information access surfaced in the late 1960s, when Childers and Post (1975) began looking at America's library resources. Childers and Post were concerned about the people in America who were not getting access to libraries. They included women, blacks, immigrant groups, and individuals with disabilities—some of the very same population groups we are targeting today in terms of the digital divide. In brief, Childers and Post's description of the problems of access to information reads as if it were written just yesterday. Clearly, the concern surrounding the digital divide did not surface with the advent of the desktop computer (Skerry, 2002). It has been with us for generations operating in the historical context of the changing demography of the country and issues of access to information resources. It is important therefore to understand the realignment of the digital divide in terms of the interplay across demography, technology, and the challenges our nation faces in working with diversity and cultural proficiency. It is also important that in our queries about the digital divide, we not perceive the situation as a crisis, but as a generational stage of development coming to grips with technology and its impact on different groups. It is important to remember that the Web is less than ten years old, and during this period there has been exponential development and use of Web-based resources. Currently, there are about nine billion people using the Web and this number also continues to grow exponentially. The lack of access to this technological tool remains closely related to race, socioeconomic status (SES), geographical location, and other factors that we must seek to better understand. As noted in Education Week (2001),

> The challenge is no longer just getting machines into schools—that's happening as prices go down and philanthropic and private sector partnerships grow. Rather, it is a people issue tied to very specific reasons why individuals from diverse backgrounds either avoid or seek out opportunities to use these new digital and computer-based technologies and what happens to them as a result of this use or non-use pattern.

Thus, attempts at either bridging or closing the digital divide require us now to reach for deeper understanding and more culturally relevant and integrated solutions. Tinkering with only one side of the complicated equation will not resolve the other, and for these reasons, many school districts are not using educational technology as wisely or as effectively as they could. We will need to be more proactive and comprehensive in advancing and implementing solutions that are based on far deeper levels of understanding of the reciprocal effects of technology on culture and culture on the use of technology.

Changing Cultural Perspectives about Technological Change and Innovation

Technology innovations have cycles of peaks and valleys, or highs and lows, and no technology is forever. It generally has a beginning, middle and an ending stage (Innis, 1951; McLuhan, 1960; Rogers, 1986). Pinpointing the various stages of a technology's development cycle across different groups, however, is a challenge. Indeed, assessing the impact or effects of a particular technological innovation on a given population group requires keen hindsight and reflective thinking which hinges on one's ability to look at broad areas of interrelated human and cultural behaviors, attitudes, and thoughts, as well as economic, political, technological, and demographic trends afoot in society at any given time. Cross-cultural communication specialists suggest that where there is overlap in our understanding of the characteristics of a particular communication medium with the characteristics and behaviors of the users, the content being delivered over the medium, and the environment for its use, we tend to get the best and most widespread use of the technology; but to reach this stage requires careful planning and orchestration. It cannot be left to chance. For these reasons, the challenges of the digital divide suggest that technology, culture, and demography are now working together as drivers for change. A large shift in student demography is taking place that we have not been very good at surveying, monitoring, and understanding. At the same time, the operative conditions for learning are changing because of the technology and lifestyle conditions where you do not necessarily have to go someplace to access information and knowledge; rather, it comes to you via online interactive media. This underscores the importance of these changing conditions for learning that will move us away from strict adherence to content and a greater appreciation for the cultural context in which different groups use and develop new knowledge. It suggests that it is not what you know that will be important, but rather knowing how to use what you know in particular contexts and knowing how to seek and create information for those contexts that are unfamiliar to you.

Population Groups in Transition—Redefining Minority and Majority Status Groups

The face of American society already has dramatically changed. Demographic projections of the student population at the turn of the century suggest that in California and in several other key states undergoing demographic population transformation—such as Texas, New York, Florida and New Jersey—minority students already outnumber the traditional majority White Anglo population. The nearly epidemic high dropout rate among minority students at present, however, suggests that should current trends continue, American society will, by the year 2010, be even more separate and unequal. Statistics abound on the subject, and personal reflections reinforce the fact that many students from diverse cultural backgrounds fail to graduate from our educational institutions. They leave sadder but wiser, convinced that they cannot compete effectively in the academic marketplace or any other sector of the society.

Obviously, to avoid this pathetic scenario, we need new and more effective efforts to retain and graduate these new majority populations that will soon mirror the multiethnic face of society. Failure to do so risks the sobering prospects of a more uneven society of haves and have-nots (Pemberton, 1993). Educators need to look more critically at culture to try to find new approaches and solutions. Illustrative examples of this type of analysis can be found in *uni-cultural* groups, where technology offers the potential of exposing students to trans-cultural and multicultural settings. There are also opportunities for bilingual and dual language education and multiple language immersion programs that respond culturally to language minority groups; and, of course, there are cultural storytelling patterns for teaching and learning that characterize many traditional communities.

Carefully undertaken, such instructional analysis and intervention with technology can promote cross-cultural understanding and raise the level of consciousness about the diversity that is represented within the United States. In the process, educators can develop practical insights and guidelines that can help them work in new ways with this changing student demography to master the increasingly higher levels of technological skills and knowledge that will be required of them as key players in America's future workforce. As stated so pointedly by Louis Uchitelle (1997):

> . . . for all the creative powers of a booming U.S. economy that we have all expected to be forever, the overflowing prosperity of the past decade in America has failed to raise the "second class" incomes of the one-third of Americans who have not gone beyond high school.

Part of the difficulty in responding to the current implications of technology on the changing demography is the fact that the research base and consequently the policies and practices that have shaped and guided America's behavior toward culturally diverse and minority populations were developed several decades ago. Economic conditions were strikingly different at the time. The need to be informed about and understand international, ethnic minority, and cross-cultural issues seemed to be less important, and certainly, society viewed women, minorities and individuals with learning challenges and special education needs as a significantly less important segment of the work force and of society in general.

A first step in this analysis, therefore, requires that each of us undertake what James Cummins calls a process of personal redefinition to reconcile outmoded and often grossly erroneous and stereotypical frameworks that have shaped the way many in the U.S. majority population think about America's diverse population clusters (Cummins, 1986). Any attempt to characterize America's diverse population in general, global terms is a difficult task because of the interplay of both the homogeneity (language background and cultural ancestral roots) and the diversity (levels of educational attainment, immigration histories) represented in the population subgroups that the umbrella term *diversity* encompasses. We must always consider carefully when we generalize about the diversity of the total population, or we run the risk of stereotyping and misrepresenting the important *contradictory realities* of significant population groups in America.

Nonetheless, the characterization of America's diverse population groups, in general terms of their antecedents, present realities, and likely future evolution, is an important first step toward understanding the changing socioeconomic circumstances in America and their relationship to issues of technology and culture. This analysis is important in the pursuit of necessary changes in current policies and practices that affect education and the integration of new technologies that can facilitate new teaching–learning opportunities. Furthermore, some generalizations of diverse populations are valid and can serve as a springboard for intervention and change.

Illustrative of these generalizations are the research data that suggest that minority population groups in the United States are predominately young and will become the majority in the 21st century because of the extraordinary increase in birth rates and immigration. With a median age of 23.7 years for minorities versus 32.6 years for non-minorities, nearly 35 percent of the nation's population is today under 18 years of age. Minority participation in the work force, however, is lower than comparable figures for non-minorities, and tends to be concentrated in low-skill, low-paid positions, which results in a median family income 65 percent lower than for mainstream population groups. Education, most experts suggest, continues to be the key determinant of employment opportunities, and success in the future for these culturally diverse groups depends on schools working to improve their critical thinking skills while also valuing and building upon their cultural background.

Digital Media Access: Profiles of America's Minority Communities

Across the country, educators are proposing that the new digital technologies be put to more significant use in academic settings with culturally divergent student population groups. These new technological tools, for example, allow for the design and implementation of instructional approaches that can engage the culturally diverse class with its unique set of learning styles and array of instructional learning needs. Among the relevant questions that the teaching–learning agenda needs to answer are: Which targeted solutions will contribute to the knowledge base of best practices for using technology in the classroom in a culturally relevant and sensitive manner? How realistic is it to expect that governmental agencies, educational institutions, and corporate America will assume responsibility for resolving current digital media and cultural group performance discrepancies, and if so, which specific intervention roles should each of these three sectors play across underserved communities?

Digital Media and America's Hispanic Communities

At present, the appropriation of digital technology by Hispanic communities represents a complex picture that we must examine carefully. Today, two U.S. residents in ten are of Hispanic ancestry. By the year 2010, three out of every eight U.S. residents will be of Hispanic ancestry. According to the U.S. Department of Labor, many of the 6.5 million new jobs that Hispanics will fill between now and 2005 (93 percent in the service-sector) will require high levels of education and training, as well as literacy with new technologies.

Data from a 1998 U.S. Department of Commerce (NTIA, 1998) study found that less than 13 percent of Latino households had Internet access, compared with 30 percent for Anglos. In the past three years, however, the gap has narrowed as increasing numbers of upwardly mobile Latinos rush to get online.

There are a number of innovative efforts to accelerate home access to technology resources. One example is Quepasa.com, a Phoenix online firm that is distributing two million computer disks to attract more Latinos to its bilingual website. The site, a sort of Latino version of AOL, offers an array of news and information both in English and Spanish as well as chat rooms, links, and a search engine to help guide viewers around the Internet. Quepasa's chief operating officer has said that while the decision to offer free Internet access is primarily market driven, the company also wants to help close the information-technology gap between Latinos and Anglos: "The Internet is the only venue that establishes the opportunity for our community members to be competitive, productive citizens, who both consume and contribute to information on the Net."

A challenge facing a website like Quepasa's is to provide content that is relevant to a broad range of interests and backgrounds given the fact that the Latino community is rich in diversity. These differences, such as country of origin, length of time in the U.S., education, and literacy levels, affect Internet usage.

An illustrative website that has developed relevant and culturally sensitive digital content both in English and Spanish for the Hispanic population along the U.S. Mexico border region is The Borderland Encyclopedia: A Digital Repository of Educational Resources on The U.S./Mexico Region 9, which was developed by faculty and students at the University of Texas at El Paso (Ingle, 1998).

While the media have, at times, created a stereotype in which the Hispanics in the United States are not active in the computer revolution, the data suggest the contrary. As a result, the business community has become more aware of demographic trends and are increasingly more culturally sensitive in marketing approaches used with Hispanic and other cultural groups. The education sector needs to do likewise.

Educators seeking to stay abreast of the evolving information on the interplay of culture, technology, and the Hispanic community in the United States are encouraged to visit the Spanish language site LaBrechaDigital.org (The Digital Divide). It lists spokespersons who are instrumental in defining technology within the context of multicultural population groups and provides information on diverse learning styles, cultural background, and lifestyle conditions that interact with media content and educational information across America's changing demography.

The following recommendations represent ways to create realignment in technology access within the U.S. Hispanic community, as well as other marginalized minority groups:

- Telecommunications reform should reaffirm commitment to reasonable and affordable rates for all essential platforms of services that will encompass a new definition of universal access for all population groups.
- The information technology sector should begin to recognize the significance of the growing shift of the nation's population from minority to majority status in terms of consumer markets, which *do not* currently purchase technology goods or find themselves, as a rule, on the development side of content for the Web.
- Technology infrastructure development in the schools should consider the need for quality technology access for all learners so that they are adequately prepared for the technology-based jobs of the future and that their cultural voices find a place on the Net both in the more mundane applications, as well as those integrating advanced technological literacy skills.
- Multi-language campaigns highlighting the importance of computer literacy to the community should be undertaken which address the cultural dynamics of technology for communities speaking languages other than English, such as is now happening in Hispanic print and electronic media campaigns.

African Americans and Technology

The Black community in America mirrors the larger segment of other minority and poor populations who are disproportionately at a disadvantage in terms of access to computers, the Internet, and other telecommunications services. National aggregated statistics reflect this situation, as do the qualitative observations of key spokespersons such as William H. Gray, President and CEO of the United Negro College Fund:

> There is a digital divide. If you look at African Americans as a group, we are still lower-middle income to working class and poor. And as lower-middle income, working poor and underclass people, we do not have access and ownership of computers even when compared with white counterparts in the same economic class. Every study, private and public, has documented this regrettable situation (Gray, quoted in Roach, 2001).

Ramon Harris, director of the Technology Transfer Project for the Washington-based Executive Leadership Foundation offers cultural observations related to the technology adoption practices in the African American community.

"Most of us are still thinking that the digital divide is about computers, but it's not just about computers," Harris says. "It's about information technology and long-standing cultural perspectives one holds about technology—who has access to it, who owns it, who can exploit its full potential, who profits from it, whether educationally or economically. Money is an issue—but it's not the only issue." It will be incumbent on the African American community to take stock of its educational and cultural challenges and really nurture where we want to go (Harris, quoted in Roach, 2001).

Roscoe Giles, executive director of IAAEC and computer science professor at Boston University, suggests that in working with the issues of technology and culture, " . . . special attention will need to be paid to helping African Americans develop new innovative ways to think about and use information technology since the language of IT often presents cultural barriers for them (Giles, quoted in Roach, 2001). Clark (quoted in Roach, 2001) observes that

. . . the notion of "surfing the Net" is a metaphor that doesn't come out of the Black community . . . even the term "desktop" as in "desktop computing" since it implies that everyone either works in an office or has a desk at home with a computer to work. As a result, a more holistic approach to understanding the socio-economics and cultural dynamics of Black family life in needed (often headed by one parent, a women, or elderly grandparents of very modest economic means).

Giles, Gilbert, and Clark (quoted in Roach, 2001) note that the real challenge ". . . will be building an E-culture for the African American community that makes IT an integrated part of our lives." Thus, in terms of the linkages across technology and culture, the African American history with communication technology—e.g., oral and written language, printing, photography, telegraphy, radio, television, the VCR and now computers and digital media—have caused tremendous changes in culture as one technology has supplanted another in terms of totally new social structures, conceptions of truth, knowledge and reality. For example, Postman (1992) cites the oral language traditions and musical and chanting communication traditions of the Native American and African communities in which an individual's thoughts and judgments are shaped by sayings and proverbs, as opposed to print-based cultures, where something is most likely accepted as truth if it has been "documented," that is, someone has marshaled knowledge and information attesting to its truth by writing it down. Communication scholars, agree with Postman that ". . . a particular form of expression will relentlessly shape the thoughts of its user in much the way language influences thought. Also, a form of expression may have limitations that make certain thoughts, feelings or habits of thought, difficult or impossible" (Postman, 1992).

We can agree with Postman's observations, ". . . that adopting a new technology such as the new digital media whose entertainment attraction have taken center stage across cultural groups worldwide, and the global world view that comes with it, always involves what he calls a Faustian bargain. Something is gained, but something else is lost, and sometimes the bargain is, we belatedly realize, a bad one."

The problem today in terms of culture and technology and, amidst the Internet and Web-based culture, is the overabundance of information available instantaneously and the need to better educate students of all cultural backgrounds to determine the value of such information both in their consumer and knowledge-generator roles.

Andrea Gooden (1996) in *Computers in the Classrooms: How Teachers and Students are Using Technology to Transform Learning* profiles a decade of Apple Computer-funded projects, in both public and private schools, in which digital media is creatively used by educators to integrate cultural and demographic concerns into exciting and challenging learning that crosses traditional curricular boundaries and actively involves and excites students of all cultural backgrounds. Among these efforts are profiles of promising technology projects in the African American, Hispanic, and Native American communities that are framed within the context of more appropriately linking technology to the evolving cultural dynamics of the nation. The lesson emanating from these projects, according to Gooden (1996), is one of

> . . . educators focusing attention on a holistic approach to solving important social, cultural, pedagogical and economic problems that confront students today. And there is no one recipe for success; what works for one school . . . may not work for another, and as a result, the interconnections across the environment, resources, culture, media and people need to be better orchestrated to contribute to new and unique blends of opportunities and circumstances that can help guide vision and implementation (pp. 155–156).

Technology and Native American, Alaskan, and Hawaiian Communities

When one examines promising directions within the context of the new digital technologies for education, the concept of multiculturalism, and its relationship to technology and cultural differences, must be analyzed in at least three dimensions: as an idea or concept, as an educational reform movement, and as a teaching–learning process. Multicultural education, therefore, incorporates the idea that all students—regardless of their gender or social class or their ethnic, racial, or cultural characteristics—should have an equal opportunity to learn in school (Banks, 1994). Technology needs to be viewed within this context, for it allows student ownership of the learning so that the culture of that student fits into the learning experience in relevant ways.

Education in the 21st century needs to give significant attention to these challenges of the changing student demography and how to make the future better for students of diverse backgrounds. Along with the Hispanic and African American communities, Native Americans, Alaskans, and Hawaiians form part of a diverse group of students who are the most overlooked in terms of these concerns in the United States. However, Alaskan, Native American, and Hawaiian groups are beginning to set an example to follow in appropriating technology to address their unique cultural and educational challenges and needs. Native American tribes and other indigenous communities have their own language, culture, history and resident knowledge, which is rarely reflected in adopted textbooks. It is easy for these children reading a textbook on American or European history to conclude that their people have no history. Native American communities are now developing their own curriculum resources using technology. For example, the Hannahville Tribe and others are using the new multimedia technologies to help their students learn their native language, to capture oral histories from elders, and to develop other curriculum resources that honor and value the resident knowledge, history, and culture of the community.

Websites such as that of the Four Directions Project, directed by the Laguna Pueblo Department of Education, provide a rich array of technology-based curriculum resources developed by Native American schools, as well as professional development materials and other resources to enable schools to create or share culturally responsive curriculum and instructional practices for Native American children.

The new digital technologies are also, for the first time, providing an opportunity for Native American voices to be heard globally. Up to the present, much of what has been said about Native American communities has often come from non-Native voices outside the community. The Internet and other digital technologies are now enabling Native American communities to share their culture, history, and resident knowledge from their own perspectives and in their own voices.

Digital technology also represents an important tool for local economic development. The Northern Ute Tribe, seeking to enhance economic opportunities, paid cable companies to install hundreds of miles of high-speed optical cable through the mountainous terrain of the 4.5 million-acre Uintah and Ouray Reservation. High tech could strongly influence the future of this tribe, which suffers unemployment rates of 65 percent or more. Now Uinta River Technology (URT) is one of a handful of Native American IT outsourcing companies that have sprung up in recent years. Native Americans have been traditionally underserved by information technology. But tribes like the Northern Ute and the Cheyenne River Sioux are hoping that new technologies will help bridge economic and information divides.

At the national level, the U. S. Department of Interior recently completed a five-year effort to provide network infrastructure and connectivity to all federally supported Native American schools. The connectivity enables classrooms to access global information resources and to share cultural and learning resources with other schools.

In Alaska, important investments have been made to teach children and their parents how to use the Internet and connect to other parts of the world. For example, the rural community of Galena, Alaska, through a NTIA/TIIAP grant from the U.S. Department of Commerce, enabled students to take home computers. Both they and their parents were able to explore the new technologies and resources through the home-school connection. Currently, there are several radio stations that air only Native programming via satellite.

The American Indian Higher Education Consortium (AIHEC), comprised of 29 tribal colleges in twelve states, is developing a satellite-based system to share instructional resources between the colleges. When fully implemented, the AIHEC network will assist the colleges in the development of local telecommunications infrastructure (U.S. Office of Technology Assessment, 1995). In addition, Native American organizations are working with universities to develop leadership programs in telecommunications.

Clearly, the innovations taking place in Native American and Alaskan communities are expanding various levels of access in schools, tribal colleges, and communities, providing opportunities to use technology for local economic development, to produce culturally responsive curriculum and to create a Native American voice and presence on the Net. Although media and technology have been factors in the loss of native culture and language, the new generation of digital technologies is now empowering native communities to use these tools for educational, cultural, and economic revitalization.

Culture and Technology Implications

The new digital technologies provide both opportunities and challenges to design learning environments that encompass the varied learning backgrounds, cultural antecedents, and other diversity requirements of today's diverse students. Such environments will be characterized by:

- Different voices and perspectives in all classroom activities—be they in cyberspace or in the confines of four walls
- Different sources of ideas and evidence about the issues, concerns, and content presented
- Different conditions or contexts to practice and gain proficiency in the prescribed classroom goals and objectives that make use of the new technological tools for learning
- Access to rich culturally responsive curriculum
- Students prepared at an early age as both consumers and developers of content for technology-based information systems

The accomplishment of such a goal is not an easy task. Current differentiated instructional research literature and educational practice (Lindsey, Robbins, & Terrell, 1999; Tomlinson, 1999 and 2001), note that the following factors will need to be considered in designing technology-supported culturally responsive learning environments:

1. Different communication styles across different student groups
2. Different attitudes toward conflict and resolution of differences
3. Different approaches to completing tasks
4. Different decision-making and information processing styles
5. Different attitudes toward disclosure and collaboration
6. Different approaches to what knowledge is important and to knowing across diverse students

These are all areas of inquiry that are evolving and informing the knowledge base for promoting effective cross-cultural communication practices in schools and, as a result, the use of the Internet with the changing student demography.

Finally, it is most important for educators and policymakers to recognize that those who control and direct the tools of instruction and the content may well control both what has happened in the past and what can happen in the future. Commentary from Rodney Bobiwash, a member of the Aneshnabek Nation near Lake Huron, Canada, and John Afele from Africa provides an appropriate summary.

> The rapid advances in information technology and telecommunications are relevant to all cultures and economies. What is essential is the ingenuity of local champions of the Internet to contemplate the unique ways in which this technology can be adapted to local situations and cultures. The various cultures of the world could, for the first time, be visible to all who have access to the Internet. There are no technological barriers to deployment of information technology anywhere in the world today; it is political will and imagination of these institutions that will determine how much a culture benefits from the Internet. On the other hand, there is a greater concern within . . . [different cultural groups] . . . that the same forces that brought them useful technologies have also brought Coca-Cola, Nike, and other innovations [whose intent, planned or unplanned] has often been the undermining of local culture, language, and tradition. Indigenous elders realize too well that the one who controls the narrative—that is, who tells the stories—controls both the cultural future and the past (Bobiwash & Afele, 2001, pp. 5, 6).

7 Technology and Native America: A Double-Edged Sword

VIVIAN DELGADO

FOCUS QUESTIONS

1. What are some of the philosophical and ethical issues concerning technology that may occur for someone with a Native American worldview?
2. In what ways is the adoption of advanced technologies a double-edged sword for Native American people?
3. What are some of the special educational needs of Native American students that technology can address?
4. What are some exemplary projects and promising practices related to the use of technology with Native American students?

Some of this book's chapters, especially those that deal with culture, curriculum, and language, point out that students from different cultures have different learning needs and strengths and that those needs and strengths need to be addressed for the realization of the potentials of those students. This chapter explores a deeper, subtler interaction between pedagogy and culture, one that stems directly from worldview. Worldview is "the . . . subconscious, fundamental organization of the mind; the assumptions upon which decisions are made in a culture" (Cobern, 1991). For cultures whose worldview elements—such as epistemology, teleology, and ethics—are not of Western European derivation, the adoption of technology can be very problematic. This chapter, written from the Native American perspective, is an example of such a worldview struggle. Although the specific points of conflict may well be culture-specific, readers of many cultural backgrounds may recognize and understand the problems discussed in this chapter.

Native American Worldview

Many Native American cultures have a worldview that identifies balance and harmony with the environment and includes a reverence for nature and the natural world of human beings.

Digital knowledge has a new place in this integrated and harmonious world, a place that has yet to be defined. Where do these new advances fit in the time/space continuum?

Time/space is a sacred concept for Native people. Its nature cannot be articulated; time/space just *is*. Movement in the smallest life force has as much respect among Native people as any other life force, and for that reason, digital activity must be considered a life force. What we see with digital knowledge is therefore an activity in time/space that has yet to be defined by Native intellect, but even more so by Native spirit. For these reasons, technology is not as yet totally accepted by Native peoples.

The opportunities for Native people to advance is never a given; it is a door that opens briefly and sporadically. With all of the advances in technology and access to information, Native people still struggle not only to keep up with the latest innovations, but with increasing economic, political, social, and spiritual crises that seem to plague the heart of the people. Time for reflection is secondary to survival; for that reason we must prepare for an alternative voice that considers both survival and reflection in technology.

Digital Equity and Native America

The ideas of respect and sharing must be a part of technology for Native people. We must be creative in finding various and multidimensional ways that these values can be reflected in the digital world. Native people must determine a strategy for using these new tools, a strategy that will provide opportunity for our future without robbing us of our past. Historically, the introduction of digital tools has resulted in a relinquishing of privacy; it should instead be a means to open other doors. In the past, the most profound Native teachings took place verbally and experientially, and those who taught always considered consequences: "Be careful when you draw on the ground in the dirt because you are opening doors" (O. Gillette, Mandan-Hidatsa, personal communication, March 30, 2001).

The long-term effects that digital equity will have on Native people are not known. "Prophecies say we will experience technical-energy failure" (H. Mann, Cheyenne, personal communication, March 26, 2001). The elders have warned that whatever we learn in a digital sense must first be learned in a cognitive sense. In many tribal cultures, languages and values have never been printed; yet the Western world has now moved past the printed word to include the digitized word. What we have not acquired in the printed world obviously cannot be found in the digital. Understanding must proceed expression. Although it is the hope of many Native cultures to work with both the printed and the digital, "that place that Indians talk about" will never be reached by either source (Cajete, 1994, pp. 42–43).

I can remember the first time I heard the phrase, "That's the place Indians talk about." Acoma Pueblo poet Simon Ortiz said it in a wonderful story about the spiritual connections Indian people feel to the special places in their lands and their lives. By talking about those special places, they connected their spirit to them through their words, thoughts, and feelings. I remember thinking how beautifully simple, yet how profound, this metaphor was. It still illustrates the special quality and power the spirit has to orient us through the breath of its manifestation in language, song, prayer, and thought (Ortiz, personal communication).

In an academic sense, technology is a tool that will promote the tangibles in Indian education, law, medicine, and other areas that maintain contemporary survival, but where is its *place*? How do we become oriented to it so that the spirit may regenerate us? The power for both technological and creative advancement, like any other resource, will cease to reproduce unless replenished.

Inventions and the Sacred

Native people have always given careful attention to the most sacred parts of ourselves, our mind. Even in the making of sacred objects such as drums, pipes, paddles, and songs, Native people acknowledge that it is the thought of the creator of such objects that makes the object sacred. We therefore should consider the implications of Western technology, of a lifestyle where one lives surrounded by the products of technology. For many those products include televisions, computers, microwaves, cars, cameras, and every new technological invention. Keep in mind that technological inventions are a product of the corporate Western mind; we do not know that the sacred was part of the thought processes that produced these objects. For some Native people this concept—being surrounded by the non-sacred—goes against the very basic tenets of Native life and thought.

As Jerry Mander wrote:

With each new generation of technology, and with each stage of technological expansion into pristine environments, human beings have fewer alternatives and become more deeply immersed within technological consciousness. We [Western thinkers] have a harder time seeing our way out. Living constantly inside an environment of our own invention, reacting solely to things we ourselves have created, we are essentially living inside our own minds. Where evolution was once an interactive process between human beings and a natural, unmediated world, evolution is now an interaction between human beings and our own artifacts (1991, p. 32).

Native consciousness has been excluded from digital invention and advancement (like many other inventions), and, although we, like the earth, are silent, we are not without thought or logic. There is a sense of timelessness in Native teachings, and even when action and consequence become connected with time, it is for the purpose of nourishing the knowledge necessary for prophecy. A Native person could not even hope to achieve living inside one's technological mind at a conscious or subconscious level because there are boundaries of the mind that are determined only by spirit.

Influence and Complexities

Critics of technological invention refer to an invisible influence that some Native people regard as the *presence* of what is not visible to the eye. Space—which can be any place and which is often referred to as the center of the universe—has sacred meaning that is quite different than what is considered invisible. It includes all that is intangible. For example, space includes the degree of complexity that technology has created for simple tasks, such as the process of applying and looking for a job. If you are not able to complete this process via the Internet, then the paper process becomes lengthy and time-consuming and possibly punitive; thus, those without technology skills—and this absence may be by choice—are disenfranchised. Another complex issue is the attitude that once you have worked success-fully using technology, it is impossible to work without it. You will find a need to use tech-nology, especially if your work involves multi-tasks, immediate response, convenience, and access to instant information. Correspondingly, for those who are not able to communicate digitally, there is a sense of guilt generated by peer pressure. Although it should not be, many of those who cannot join the digital connection feel inferior.

The Challenges of Digital Storytelling

In storytelling, it is important to Native people to preserve the moral essence of the story. Digital memory has created challenges that are difficult to resolve. For instance, for most Native people, storytelling is a spiritual and holistic encapsulation of what is happening with the storyteller. There is no right or wrong way to tell a story, and typically a story is never told exactly the same way twice. Therefore, the linear and precise orientation that is present in computer-generated word processing would not be applicable to traditional sto-rytelling methods. This way of instruction—storytelling—is very old and is just as power-ful today as it ever was. There are qualities—even gifts—that have been passed down from generation to generation by word of mouth that have no place in the digital world.

Native people have always prided themselves in their ability to recall or remember events, history, songs, language, prayers, stories, families, and people. It remains a healthy and natural practice to depend on your mental capacity for this type of information. Rarely were Native people of the past, including many of our present elders, hindered by dementia and other forms of memory and mental illness—and certainly not to the extent that they are today.

There is a price that we will pay for digital convenience. Among the present and past generations who have endured without electricity—and in many cases running water as well—the experience of inner and outer dialogue and communication was highly devel-oped. Those who have lived simply can attest to knowing and appreciating their own thoughts and feelings quite well. This in part is due to minimal exposure and influence from others. Individuals developed ways of knowing and imaging by being able to see loved ones in the mind's eye and learned to cherish their relationships using highly developed memory and instinct. In traditional Native ways, the heart and mind were never separated and affec-tion for the culture and the people was always at the center.

Psychological Implications

I have found that many Native people, when given the option to access digital communica-tion, decline the opportunity. In part this is due to the lack of skills and knowledge needed to have a successful experience, the lack of mentors and technical support, and the physical disequilibrium that is generated by viewing the screen for long periods of time. Many times technicians are few in lower socioeconomic communities, and when they are present they spread themselves too thinly to be effective. The coming of age for the technological gen-eration is a foreign concept for some Native people, who identify it with assimilation and acceptance of the values of the dominant (Western) world. Dependence on instinct, dreams, face-to-face interaction, common knowledge, common sense, rationalization, and observation are still preferred as ways of knowing and communication for many Native people (Banks & Banks, 1997).

The Digital Voice

There is, of course, a positive side to the information age. Ethnographers and anthropologists have expended considerable time and resources on research to determine to what extent Native culture does or does not exist. Although their efforts are appreciated, members of each Native group should determine the extent to which their culture is or is not assimilated. Digital access, rather than print-based academic publication, can serve as a means for some Native women and men to have their voices heard. In the past, only those who had attained of key leadership positions in government, institutions, and organizations typically had publication privileges. Now, however, once people have secured the skills for Web page development, e-mail, and listservs—and have sufficient material and financial support to go online—they can share their voices across public digital lines. Digital access is a way to create representation in educational and intellectual discussions and curriculum. It eliminates the political struggle of discrimination and unfair employment practices found among people of color in higher education, education, and educational policymaking.

Unless the Native voice is heard, educational leaders, researchers, and political representatives will continue to incorrectly define discrimination as conservatism and educational programs such as Chapter I and other Title programs as agents of social services. These programs should be considered educational support partnership programs. Digital equity may have a bigger part to play among Native people in the political arena than in any other area that can bring justice to the long identified problems of inequality.

Deliberated Economics and Digital Access

In President Clinton's last year in office, he visited several Indian reservations in an attempt to support technological advancement. At that time a program called Link-Up was developed with Qwest (formerly known as US West). Link-Up was designed to offer digital access for low-income families who qualified, using Food Stamps, Medicare/Medicaid, Disability, and Aid to Dependent Families as criteria. The irony of this attempt to bridge the gap is that those who qualified as low-income could not afford computers and the support programs that went along with them, and therefore had no use for digital access. On the other hand, the families who could afford computers and their support programs did not qualify for Link-Up services because they were not eligible for low-income programs. This left nearly entire Indian populations in the same position as prior to the special Link-Up programs. I do not believe that the general population has any idea what challenges the Native peoples of this country face in order to achieve basic digital service.

One could see this as a misdirected attempt by the government that resulted in continued oppression and acts to silence the voice of an almost forgotten people. On the other hand, some Native people could view this as the inevitability of the spiritual environment buffering the Native people from something that will inevitably add to their existing complex political condition.

Digital Tools and Native Philosophy

Even given the traditional Native philosophical mindset to digital advancement, some Native people have found a way to work with it. "If your work comes from your heart it can be transferred. We are evolving; we have to evolve with technology in order to feel what is happening" (J. Roderick, Nooksak Nation, personal communication, April 20, 2001). It would be safe to say that feelings that are generated by the senses can be expressed through technology, but the spirit of each Native individual ultimately belongs to the earth and will protect itself from unnatural and foreign intervention, much like the earth does. With all of science and modern invention, there are aspects of the human being and the earth creation that can never be changed. This is good because it protects us from what has the potential to do irreversible harm.

I believe that it is this topic—the relationship of the spirit with technology—that needs investigation. I believe that that all people, not just Native people, need to be informed about how they are being affected by technology beyond the Western scientific standard. I believe that though many use technology with the utmost integrity, the heart-to-heart interaction between human beings remains missing.

Perhaps, when we consider the problems associated with access to and acceptance of digital technologies, there is a place for Native philosophy. Perhaps it will give the practitioner of technology the much-needed perimeters and ethical criteria necessary to advance with the least amount of risk of harm and intrusion to self and to others. O'Meara and West (1996) offer valuable words of wisdom in their work on Native philosophy and the justification for Native people to share their worldviews via the written, digital, and artistic.

> The distinct views and worlds that are the intellectual property of indigenous peoples can be shared through storytelling and conversation, but not through the aggressive curiosity that exemplifies traditional academic pursuits . . . (p. 8).

> Native American thought should not be approached as an archaic form, which sheds light on contemporary humans of European descent. It should be approached as a complete, alternative explanation for the world and for human nature (p. 15).

> It is only when Native American scholars begin to address the deeper philosophical issues underlying the familiar surface stories compiled by anthropologists and folklorists that there will be such a thing as "Native American Philosophy" (pp. 17–18).

The Teachings

Many of the Native teachings do not manifest themselves in an "instant" or automatic sense. Native people have always considered time and patience essential for understanding many of the teachings concerned with human development. We must think back to some of those teachings and reflect on how they eventually created deep and purposeful meanings. "I have lived in a time where skyscrapers and the eagle landing [man landing on the moon] were not considered. That [technology] is not part of who I am; I will go [pass on] before then. The new ways of modern man will destroy him" (L. Santistevan, Tewa, personal communication). It is common knowledge that man could easily destroy himself and the earth with the technology that has been developed. Native people, as many other people, are concerned about the possibilities of global ecological destruction. Native people also recognize that the spiritual, emotional, psychological, and physical development of humans is often ignored with technological advancement and that ignoring these aspects can lead to a more immediate form of destruction. When you consider the human mind to be the most sacred part of the human being, then you must consider who is teaching your children and the part that technology plays in today's educational system.

The Double Edge

Addressing digital equity includes not only addressing the disparities among the haves and have-nots; it also means identifying and explaining the effects of machines that are consuming, complex, powerful, and socially accepted without consideration of the consequences. Many Native people have considered *the dark side* of technology, the invasion of privacy, digital public domain used for personal gain, the misuse of control (who has the freedom to use or not use digital communication in the work force), and manipulation. The double edge that promotes both good and bad is challenging and needs ethical attention.

Technological influence has permeated Native America. Some Native people have received more credibility in both worlds through the use of technology. This is not to say that many elders and others from older generations have become comfortable with technology; some of them remain uninformed about technology out of their own choice. Not only is dealing with remote-controlled machines, microwaves, and computers difficult, but there is a part in their own consciousness that puts up a wall and prevents them from attempting these tasks. Our elders cherish simplicity; they are more concerned with human interaction than with the artificial substitute for it that technology provides. Most Native people have been taught that the natural order of living and the simple things in life are what keep our people sane. I do not know to what extent the Western personality can appreciate this mindset; what is obvious is that some have assumed that a slowness to adopt technology reflects a lack of Native ambition and have not recognized the ancient, ecological logic that goes with it.

Native Students

No matter how quickly or how completely young Native students adopt technology, we must remember that time, energy, movement, and space continue to be part of the unknown and thus sacred. Young people become prey to technology's animation and amusement, never really knowing how to define its purpose in relationship to their basic human survival, identity, and education. It may well be that when we come to understand these dimensions more completely, technology can help realize the goal so many hold for it—to reverse the academic underachievement of Native students.

The responsibility to educate the Native youth is a profound concept that lies at the heart of preserving America's original identity, the original teachings, and the original spirit of this country. This is not a selfish statement aimed to only support Native peoples, it is an opportunity for all Americans to develop their patriotism and belonging by protecting the ancient and unique indigenous heartbeat of our great country (Cajete, 1994).

The Need for Indigenous Approaches to Education

Alienation of Indian students from mainstream approaches to education has been constant. Most attempts at addressing these issues have revolved around refitting the problematic Indian student to the system that caused their alienation. Too often, the Indian student is viewed as the problem, rather than the unquestioned approaches, attitudes, and curricula of the educational system. The knowledge, values, skills, and interests that Indian students possess are largely ignored in the favor of strategies aimed at enticing them to conform to mainstream education. Few comprehensive attempts have been made to create a body of content and teaching models that are founded on American Indian educational philosophy. The inherent worth and creative potential of Indian students and Indian perspectives of education have not been given serious consideration by mainstream education. As a result, many of the brightest and most creative Indian students continue to be alienated from modern education and drift about in a malaise of apathy and self-abuse.

The alienation of Indian students from education and the resulting loss of their potentially positive service to their communities need not continue if we revitalize our own deep heritage of education. Indigenous approaches to education can work if we are open to their creative message. We must apply our collective creative energy to revitalize and reintroduce their universal processes of teaching and learning. Indigenous educational principles are viable whether one is learning leadership skills through community service, learning about one's cultural roots through creating a photographic exhibit, or learning from nature by exploring its concentric rings of relationship.

Educational principles in regard to technology need to be added to the list of Indigenous approaches to modern education. The direction of digital media needs broader attention and research. It offers educators the opportunity to promote creative innovation that will attract, retain, and challenge Native students. It is my belief that a multidisciplinary approach that addresses the Native cultures in the framework of the curriculum will open the doors to technology in a way that is appropriate and progressive to Native peoples without disrespecting the inherited way of knowing.

CD-ROM Curriculum

If the sacred is generated by the mind, then technology has the potential to deplete parts of this treasured resource if we are not careful to evaluate its use. Technology in all of its forms has everything to do with the mind; one does not know to what extent we can implement the Native mindset in technology in such a way that would benefit Native people. Though spirit is not visible to the eye, it can be felt in the heart and mind.

CD-ROM technology has offered some promising results in addressing the needs of Native American students in ways that honor the spirit. Creatively and most sincerely, artists and educators such as Dr. Buffy Sainte Marie have produced software focused on Native cultures in science and social studies. Her Cradleboard Project has proved to be an effective tool for educating children and educators from all backgrounds and in helping them to understand Native ways and the Native mindset. It is not a replacement however, of the living cultures; it is a tool. One knows that values can be *supported* digitally, but they cannot be taught that way. Native values must continue to be taught at home, prior to digital access and development. It is in this way that the Native mindset will survive. Native people have moved to new frontiers where survival is not only a human need based on physical power and dominance, but now involves spiritual stamina and definition.

Other CD-ROM projects also serve as examples of appropriate use of technology. For example, Ted Jojola has developed a CD-ROM that he has made available to only Tewa students, generally in the Albuquerque area. Tewa is a language that is not publically sharable, according to the cultural values of the Tewa-speaking tribes. The language, however, under the pressures of modern society, has become somewhat endangered. Allowing the community to produce such a product for use in the community addresses both of these needs, to preserve and teach the language and to protect the privacy of the language.

Four Directions, a Technology Challenge Grant project directed by the Laguna Department of Education, has also been instrumental in helping communities use software such as Hyperstudio™ and Fontographer™ to create community-based CD-ROMs that reflect language and culture. One example of such projects is a CD-ROM created by students from schools in New Mexico and Arizona in collaboration with the Heard Museum. It documents the history of education in their communities (Allen, Christal, & Resta, 2002). Another project of that program that has received international attention is the online virtual museum that Potowatami and Santa Clara students created for the National Museum of the American Indian (Allen, Christal, & Resta, 2002). This project enabled communities to experience a kind of virtual repatriation, so that artifacts that had been taken from local communities throughout our nation's history could again be viewed and appreciated not only by people globally, but more importantly, by the people to whom the artifacts belonged historically, people who would never travel to New York or Washington, D.C., to the major museums of our nation.

The Internet has also offered an opportunity for community-based publishing; for example, the Oneida Nation now has their treaties and other curriculum available online. Several tribes, whose languages are sharable, have used RealAudio® technology to provide language instruction online (Allen, et al., 1999).

Even with the minimal advancements that we see, it must be made clear to Internet users that they should not confuse accessing Native (commercial/consumer) markets with academic intellectual contributions towards digital equity in education. What should happen is the establishment of a clearinghouse board or virtual faculty to ensure that the material that is reaching Native communities and students and presented to a worldwide audience is authentic and represents the constituency that it has identified, that the histories are accurate and complete, and that there is a deliberate attempt not to leave any stakeholders out. Digital educational curriculum has the potential to model the Native world with a degree of accuracy that has never been done so before—but only if Native people are central to the development and dissemination of such materials. Rapidly, we are engaging in a whole new world of digital knowing; this path, like others in our lives, must not be taken lightly or without thought. We must speak to its energy, ensure that the route that it takes is visible to our eyes, and reflect on the time and space that it demands and the good that can come of it.

Summary and Implications

In considering the pros and cons of the use of technology by Native people, we must also consider the deeper philosophical inquiries that rest in the consequences of using technology. Will the long-range consequences benefit Native and all people? The irony is that the digital discrepancies that exist between technology and spirit have come at a time in this country when Native people find themselves in a period of redefinition of culture after years of disenfranchisement.

In order to take real leadership in this regard, I feel moved to say that although the biggest contribution Native people can give to humankind is the voice that comes from the Native perspective of the earth in all its beauty and balance and its teachings directed to becoming a whole human being, ultimately attaining peace before death. The call of the day is dictating equality and leveraging every opportunity to move underrepresented minorities forward. Native people are calling for justice as well as equity, but justice for Native people involves correcting, and in some cases punishing, the wrong that has been done. The fact remains that obtaining equity and justice often does not provide the inner peace we desire and deserve.

There are choices. Foremost is the question: Do Native people want to pursue digital equity? If so, on whose terms do they acquire this equity? What attitudes, beliefs, and behaviors are not inclusive or politically correct, or even traditionally accepted? Exploring oppression has been an underlying theme for Native learners, with and without technology. Will Native people be allowed to go beyond this? Who ultimately makes this decision? What about the diversity among Native peoples that continues to plague solidarity? Does the public understand that there is a broad continuum of Native peoples from the traditional to the acculturated to the assimilated? There are also the extensive differences between the Native population on the reservation and those who reside in our nation's cites to be considered. There are also hard questions about who is and who is not Native and how to include those of mixed bloodlines. Does it matter? Finally, we have Native people who have inherited identities, but know little or nothing about their history, culture, and language. How do we address their needs as we address the needs of Native people as a whole?

It is fair to say that at the very minimum, you will find technology and digital access on most reservations, either in their schools and/or governments. They, too, are questioning the consequences of moving forward in technology adoption. I believe if tribal members and others who represent their communities receive training in using digital technologies in culturally appropriate and culturally supportive ways there will be more success in the adoption of technology. There is a real and pressing need in Indian country to control what power is accessed with technology.

Self-empowerment is a reality when there are choices, access, and training. This is the direction that most Native people want to take. Tribes want to be able to develop their own digital products, at their own speed, in their own time, under their own conditions, using their own knowledge and judgment that defines equity/equality. Through their expressions, we will all learn the real issues that they face and in that process learn that digital equity has layers and dimensions that have not been discovered or addressed. Opportunity is at the heart of equity; all people need the opportunity to succeed or fail at what they do. Without opportunity there is no risk taking and in most cases no growth.

What is secret is sacred and what is sacred is secret. Let there be boundaries and limits to what is made available with technology. I believe the deeper meanings and teachings are only effective under certain conditions. I believe that progress of any sort should not influence the ancient ways of knowing; they are unique because they have changed little throughout time. Native people need to defend and teach why these values are so important. The survival of one is the survival of all.

Briefly, we have discussed the issues raised by the elders of Native communities. They are our cultural leaders and have years of expertise in what it is that makes us who we are. Technology has little or no place in their teachings and ways of knowing. We need to make every effort to ensure that their gifts are respected and to understand that under no circumstances should their knowledge be threatened. We need to stress that we can take what is good from the oral and from digital information, understand that each is valid under different circumstances, and remember that " . . . when individuals choose not to contribute their talents to a social system because they are demoralized or angry, or when they are actively prevented by racist institutions from fully contributing their talents, society as a whole loses" (Delgado & Stefancic, 2001, p. 134).

In closing, I would like to offer my rationale for writing and speaking to the heart of the readers. Many disparities and battles that Natives face in academia are not necessarily battles that they would personally choose. Many times the struggles find the most well-intended and emotionally strong, who confront the issues for the principle of the matter and with future—and past—generations in mind.

> The Native people . . . are not allowed a valid interpretation of their history, because the conquered do not write their own history. They must endure a history that shames them, destroys their confidence, and causes them to reject their heritage. Those in power command the present and shape the future by controlling the past, particularly for the Natives. A fact of imperialism is that it systematically denies Native people a dignified history (Adams, cited in Deloria, 1971, p. 28).

Technology offers a means for Native people to interpret their own histories and shape their own futures. We must ensure that this promise is fulfilled.

These are not battles that Native people alone face. Many historically disenfranchised groups will hear echoes of their own voices in my words.

8 Building Learning Communities

AMY STAPLES

JOYCE PITTMAN

FOCUS QUESTIONS

1. What does the law say about educational equity for students with disabilities?
2. What is an inclusive learning community?
3. What conditions exist in public education classrooms that may exacerbate the problem of educational equity for all students?
4. In what ways can technology empower teachers to work with all students, especially those with disabilities in the general education classroom?

A dominant theme throughout this text is the unique role technology can play in creating a more equitable educational experience for all children. In this chapter, we focus on students with disabilities. It has been less than 30 years since federal legislation guaranteed students with disabilities a free appropriate public education alongside their nondisabled peers in general education classrooms. Students with disabilities have been marginalized with respect to education both philosophically and physically. For years people thought these children, because of their physical, cognitive, language, behavioral, or emotional characteristics, were not candidates for the public education system. While the law has granted students physical access and emphasized the need for cognitive access as well, we will learn that much work is yet to be done to ensure students with disabilities a *free appropriate public education* (FAPE).

This chapter provides an introduction regarding the evolution of law as it relates to educating students with disabilities, discusses growing concerns related to equity in education for students with disabilities, shares the powerful role technology can play with regard to leveling the academic playing field for students with disabilities, and examines the implications of research and field experience about equity and technology in teacher education programs and K–12 classrooms. Special attention is given to strategies for restructuring preservice and graduate teacher education that will support programs that prepare teachers to provide free and appropriate education opportunities for all students in their classrooms.

Technology: A Lifeline to Learning

While many of the authors have discussed how technology can transform education, for a large number of students with disabilities, technology sometimes serves as the lifeline to even the most basic education. Students with disabilities use special technology called assistive technology to communicate, participate in lessons, complete schoolwork, learn, and move about their school. Without ready access to these technologies, the students would have no way to relay opinions, ask questions, write down their thoughts, or reread text to clarify meaning. Technology offers physical access for individuals with motor impairments stemming from disabilities such as cerebral palsy or sensory impairments such as blindness. A child might type text by operating a keyboard via a stick placed in her mouth or explore the pyramids in Egypt through an Internet-based virtual tour controlled by a special switch. A student who is blind can use a traditional keyboard and screen-reading software to read books and newspapers, or to take tests. Special text-to-speech and speech-to-text software programs can offer cognitive access for students with language or learning disabilities by enabling them to reread text to increase their comprehension or assist their composition skills by typing what they speak. All these tools encourage independence and foster self-esteem by building feelings of self-efficacy, which can in turn enable academic advancement to proceed at a more rapid pace. Research has demonstrated that students with disabilities who use appropriate technology improve academic and communication skills (Higgins & Raskind, 2000; Lewis, 1998; MacArthur, 2000; Mirenda, Wilk, & Carson, 2000), spend more time engaged prosocially in learning (Castellani, 2000), and show a greater motivation for learning.

However, while assistive and educational technologies have long been used with some students with severe and multiple disabilities in educational settings, not all students have had ready access to the technologies they needed to receive a free appropriate public education. It has only been in the past decade or so that technology such as word processors, talking word processors, word prediction, the Internet, and special content area applications have been used broadly with students with high incidence disabilities such as learning disabilities and attention deficit hyperactivity disorder (Lewis, 1998; MacArthur, 2000). Further, many teachers, in both special and general education settings, who are just now seeing how assistive, educational, and instructional technologies can equalize learning opportunities lack the technology expertise to use these technologies well, not only with students with special needs, but also with other students. As a result, students with disabilities are often silent bystanders to the education of their nondisabled peers. The student with cerebral palsy, a disability that sometimes results in an inability of the individual to walk, talk, or control physical movements, must watch her peers dissect a frog in biology class, hoping her visual field is not disrupted by the other students hovering around the dissection area. This same student could be actively involved in the dissection of a frog by using assistive technology to access an Internet site such as The Interactive Frog Dissection at the University of Virginia which would enable her to direct the computer's dissection of the frog. Her "virtual" dissection could be just as informative as the "hands-on" dissection. The class could be split so that half the students completed the dissection using traditional techniques and half completed it virtually. Afterwards, the students could compare their experiences and summarize what they learned.

The student with learning disabilities, a condition that makes it difficult for some children to read, write, or perform other academic tasks as well as their peers, may listen to a peer read *My Escape from Slavery* by Frederick Douglass to him, relying heavily on his listening skills to support later discussion and assignments about the text. If his teacher had used the Internet to download this book from one of the many repositories of public domain texts, such as the University of Virginia's Ebook Library or the Afro American Almanac this same student could be reading the text more independently using a computer software program that reads the text out loud at the pace the student determines, while highlighting each word as it is read. If this student could control his own reading, he could do what other students do—reread text that doesn't make sense, read some portions more slowly or quickly than others, search through a selection for answers to end-of-chapter comprehension questions, and so on. The student could even access one of the many sites devoted to this author such as those listed at the Frederick Douglass Museum and Cultural Center to help him understand the context of the story, given the author's life. This sort of assistance empowers all students in the class, not only the students with disabilities.

In each of these examples, when technology is used it places the student in an active learning role, offers a more robust and memorable experience, and likely leads to greater understanding and retention of material. Perhaps equally important is the empowerment it provides the students and the clarity it offers teachers regarding the students' skills. Students with disabilities often experience feelings of low self-esteem, helplessness, and dependence on others. When technology is used to help them access content and related materials, they take control of their learning. Similarly, teachers who are used to seeing students sit passively in class may construct a different, more positive view of students when they see what the students can learn and retain when given the proper tools. These examples highlight how combining assistive and educational technologies with Internet resources can lead to more successful inclusion and a more equitable learning experience for individuals with disabilities.

The 1997 amendments to the Individuals with Disabilities Education Act (IDEA) legislation adds a new challenge to technology integration and educational reform efforts. This new challenge relates to equal access to learning opportunities in general education for all students. The reauthorized legislation focuses especially on students who experience overt personal disjunction in the general education classroom, commonly referred to as students with special needs. Why is this legislation necessary? How many students have disabilities? Who are these people and how big of a problem is equitable education? The next section addresses these questions.

Equity and the Growing Concerns about Learners with Special Needs

Students with disabilities, comprising 10 percent to 12 percent of the nation's student population, are those individuals who evidence a developmental delay in one or more of the following areas: physical development, cognitive development, social or emotional development, communication development, or adaptive development (IDEA, 1997). In the 1999–2000 academic year, roughly 5.6 million children received services under the auspices of the Individuals with Disabilities Education Act (IDEA) (IdeaData.org, 2001). Disability does not discriminate based on gender, race, culture, or socioeconomic status. However, the population of students identified as having disabilities does not mirror the characteristics of our nation's population. More boys than girls as well as a disproportionately large number of students of color are identified as having disabilities in need of attention (Wenger, Kaye, & LaPlante, 1996). Similarly, children below the poverty line are more likely to be identified as having disabilities than students whose family income is above the poverty line. These statistics are of concern because disability might be assigned based on diversity rather than actual presence. An example of this overrepresentation can be seen in African American students. Although they comprise 14.8 percent of the student population, African American students make up 20.2 percent of students identified as having disabilities. Overrepresentation also exists relative to disability type. Of students with disabilities, 8.4 percent are identified as having behavioral problems. However, 26.4 percent of those students are African American, more than three times the number it should be given the percentage of those students in the general student population (U.S. Dept. of Education, 2000). Many experts in the field of special education believe overrepresentation of disabilities within race or culture have more to do with testing bias and school climate than an in-child condition (Osher, Woodruff, & Sims, 2000; Oswald, Coutinho, & Best, 2000).

With regard to type of disability, more than 70 percent of students with disabilities have learning or language-based disabilities as their primary diagnosis (U.S. Dept. of Education, 2000). The remaining population is comprised of students with cognitive, emotional, visual, hearing, orthopedic, other health impairments and other low-incidence disabilities (U.S. Dept. of Education, 2000). More than half of all these children are educated in regular classrooms, learning the general curriculum. Although this news is encouraging from a legal and perhaps even moral standpoint, it speaks to the educational or administrative process, not student outcomes.

These students are present but their education is not as wholly successful as for students without disabilities. Reading and writing skills for students with disabilities are dramatically poorer than those of their nondisabled peers (Graham, Berninger, Abbott, Abbott, & Whitaker, 1997; Graham, Harris, MacArthur, & Schwartz, 1991; Koppenhaver & Yoder, 1992), and oftentimes physical or learning disabilities prevent them from accessing text and other educational materials independently. Similarly, teachers often feel ill equipped to respond to the education needs of these students (Edyburn, 2000). They do not have training in specific disabilities or support technologies. Many teacher education programs require just one introductory course in exceptional child development. Even special education certification programs, while providing ample training on modifications or specialized instruction, do not always require their students to learn how educational or assistive technologies can support student learning.

Years of difficulty and feelings of failure lead many students with learning or behavioral disabilities to leave school before graduation. For example, national diploma graduation rates hover at 75 percent for students without disabilities, but students with disabilities are more likely to drop out, with only 25.5 percent earning a high school diploma. Education certainly impacts employability. In recent years, many states have reported unemployment rates in the low single digits for nondisabled citizens yet roughly 70 percent of adults with disabilities are unemployed (National Council on Disability, 2001; U.S. Dept. of Education, 2000). Not surprisingly, as many as 40 percent of African Americans and 27 percent of Euro-Americans with disabilities are arrested within three years of dropping out of school (Oswald, Coutinho, & Best, 2000). Overall, 70 percent of prisoners performed at a first- or second-grade reading level. Although minorities make up 24 percent of the general population, 65 percent of the prison population is minorities (Haigler, Harlow, O'Connor, & Campbell, 1994). These statistics speak to disparity.

There is growing evidence that students with disabilities experience a different kind of education than their peers without disabilities. They engage in fewer higher-level learning activities, spend more time in transition from one specialist to another, are excluded from many school activities, and are often viewed as separate and unequal. Most of these students, with the needed or appropriate technology, could receive an education more commensurate to their peers. While some of the technology may be specialized, providing students with an equitable education may often require little more than the technology now available in many schools. More than ever, technology may serve that lifeline role in education.

Technology—educational, instructional, and assistive—can support students with disabilities in their efforts to learn information, communicate their knowledge and opinions verbally and in text, and participate in classroom activities. However, as mentioned previously, technology is not always available, despite the existence of laws that say technology must be considered and where appropriate provided free of charge to students with disabilities so that they may receive a free appropriate public education.

On a national scale, just 24 percent of people with disabilities own a computer and just 10 percent uses the Internet (Kaye, 2000). While this statistic refers to adults with disabilities, the news remains disturbing and is likely mirrored in public schools. Individuals with disabilities may require the computer to acquire and maintain a job, control their environment (turning on/off a television, opening a door, dialing the telephone, etc.), and access text (via screen readers). Do schools take care to ensure that their technology is accessible to children with disabilities? As they acquire newer and better machines and install high-speed hookups to the Internet in their classrooms, are they taking care to ensure that a proportionate number of those computers is physically and cognitively accessible to students with disabilities, either through touch screen monitors, special keyboards, scanning software, or screen readers? Technology has the power to narrow the equity gap in education for children with disabilities. Are schools capitalizing on this resource? Just as new construction in the United States must adhere to the Americans with Disabilities Act (1990) and have accessible entrances and bathroom facilities, just as employers must make reasonable accommodations so that customers, visitors, and employees with disabilities have full range of access, are schools adopting a universal design philosophy when acquiring new materials and technology, when hiring new teachers, and when considering staff development opportunities for current employees?

Historically, children with disabilities were not expected to attend public school, nor were they required to. With the enactment of Public Law 94-142 in 1975, children first gained access to school buildings, then regular education classrooms, and now finally to the curriculum. The laws have become stronger, demanding that children with disabilities receive a more rigorous education and more aggressive services. However, the world too is changing rapidly. The information age threatens to force students with disabilities, the majority of whom are not conventionally literate, to compete with their nondisabled peers for the shrinking work force of food service and manual labor. As a result, we cannot work to provide students with disabilities the education of yesterday but must be working to provide them with the education of today and tomorrow.

The state of education for children with disabilities is not entirely bleak, however. Thousands of teachers across the nation dedicate themselves to providing an exemplary education to their pupils. Researchers study how children with disabilities learn best, collaborate with teachers and publishers to develop materials to support teachers in the field, and share these materials and methods. In the next section, ways technology has and can be used to support the learning of students with disabilities are shared. A model for thoughtful consideration of appropriate technology acquisition and use is suggested.

Policies and Practices: Assistive, Educational, and Instructional Technology

Education is a civil rights issue. If we believe it is a right of every citizen to receive an education, it follows that every student should be treated to whatever professional, physical, and material resources are needed to receive an equitable educational experience. *Equitable,* however, does not mean *the same.* Different students need different experiences and materials to truly make their education equitable. Technology may provide students who don't perform well in traditional pencil-and-paper, didactic teaching environments the medium they need to receive a more equitable education. Using computers with graphics and sound, using the Internet to learn more about their own culture, using special technologies to access print or simulated activities may improve academic performance, motivation, and engagement and result in a reduction of behavior problems and referrals to special education. In fact, several research studies have made this very determination (Bryant & Bryant, 1998; Bryant, Bryant, & Raskind, 1998; Castellani, 2000; Howell, Erickson, Stanger, & Wheaton, 2000; Kraus, 1998; Lewis, 1998; MacArthur, 2000; Mirenda, Wilk, & Carson, 2000). In this section different technologies and their uses are presented.

Assistive Technology

What do we mean when we say *assistive technology* (AT)? Isn't all technology assistive? Some, especially novice users, would argue against this notion. However, while most technology can be considered assistive—computers make it more efficient for us to write, edit, and complete written documents; eyeglasses make it easier for us to see; stools make it easier for us to reach places normally out of our reach—assistive technology is technology typically developed for and marketed to individuals with disabilities and includes familiar devices such as wheelchairs as well as highly specialized and not often seen devices such as communication devices that enable nonspeaking individuals to communicate auditorally or wireless switch interfaces that allow an individual to control the computer or common household items by blinking, staring, or speaking. It is technology that can provide physical access, serve as a sensory prosthetic, or help learners circumvent their disability.

Augmentative and alternative communication (AAC) refers to the means used by one person, other than speech, to send a message to another person. It is important to note that AAC is not meant to replace existing communication skills but rather to enhance them. AAC can include natural communication techniques such as gestures, vocalizations, or speech (Tanchak & Sawyer, 1995); today we largely mean graphic or manual signs, and communication aids. In terms of technology, we concern ourselves primarily with communication aids. These aids might include picture communication symbols arranged on a paper or computer display, an electronic device that enables the user to sequence selections to construct a message, or a computer that incorporates a picture and text-based system to support communication.

Case in Point—Technology for Communication.   Kayla is a seven-year-old with cerebral palsy. She is unable to speak or walk and has poor fine motor control. She uses an electronic wheelchair to move around in her school. She uses an augmentative and alternative communication (AAC) device to speak. By pressing a series of pictures and/or icons, Kayla constructs a message and then when she finishes her message, she tells the device to speak.

As the message is constructed it appears in an LCD display window so she can monitor her message. Having this device enables Kayla to make comments while reading a book with her teacher, call to children in the classroom, compose text, and participate actively in instruction. Without this device, many adults might incorrectly presume that Kayla is not intelligent, has little to say, or does not belong in a regular classroom.

With the device, it is easy for even novice observers to see that Kayla is an intellectually gifted young girl with much on her mind. If Kayla did not have a way to interrupt, ask questions, or make comments in class, the quality of her educational experience would be significantly reduced.

The term *special needs* refers to a much larger and more inclusive group of students than ever before. The accommodation of students with special needs may include, but is not limited to instructional and assistive technology, technical support, and other necessary services. However, it is important to note that assistive technology is not intended to instruct or teach. This is a primary distinction between AT and *instructional technology* (IT). Assistive technology is used to increase access to instruction—while instructional technology enables learning to take place in a variety of ways (such as computer-assisted instruction).

Because physical barriers to education have been addressed in an earlier chapter, we will give mobility little attention here. However, children with disabilities miss out on a number of activities and experiences because of mobility issues. In terms of mobility, students need to be where the education is. For most of our student population, this is not an issue. For students with physical disabilities, access to the art room, gym, nature trail, field trip, or even the playground might be a problem. Imagine a teacher in an early elementary classroom leading a reading lesson. The children are gathered around her on the floor, with the exception of a child with physical disabilities, who is sitting in a special chair at the fringe of the group. As the teacher reads the text, children without disabilities can speak out of turn, get up and point to items in the book, and engage the teacher in a spontaneous way as they react to the story presented them. The child with disabilities may have the same thoughts, questions, and excitement as her peers, but without a means for getting to the front of the class and pointing to the group or speaking out of turn, her education experience is very different. A wheelchair or walker might give her more independence. For some people, devices such as seats and wheelchairs might just seem a physical issue. If a child is not supported properly though, he may develop cramping and spasms that make it difficult to focus on lessons. The child may cry out or sleep to escape discomfort. Teachers may erroneously conclude the child is not able to follow or is not interested in a lesson rather than that the child is in discomfort.

Assistive technology for individuals with sensory impairments includes such equipment as braillers (devices that create Braille text), magnification systems that enlarge text for students with low vision, computer screen readers that read any text on the computer screen out loud to a user, and amplification systems for students who are hard of hearing. Screen readers can be a terrific help to teachers and students in terms of providing timely information to students. By using a screen reader and the World Wide Web, students with visual impairments can access varied and timely information. There is no time delay, whereas a text or newspaper is brailled or books on tape are ordered from the Recordings for the Blind. However, because of the highly graphical nature of the Internet, many websites may be difficult for a student with physical or sensory disabilities to access (Clyde, 2001; Lazzaro, 2000). Pointing and clicking on pictures or text is convenient for most users. For people with vision impairments, it is impossible to see where to point or click. To be in compliance with the Americans with Disabilities Act (1990), websites should be accessible to all individuals, including those with disabilities. A text-only version of the site should be available to facilitate screen reading. Guidelines for constructing accessible websites, referred to as "Bobby Approved," are available through the Center for Applied Special Technology (www.cast.org). Recently, a number of schools have outfitted their classrooms with speakers and a microphone for teachers. The speakers amplify the teachers voice so it is the primary thing a student hears. It helps reduce the din of the classroom and keeps children's attention. Initially this system was devised for children with hearing impairments, but the practice now supports students with attention problems as well.

Assistive technology for school system administration or personnel may include programs that allow personnel to make modifications or supplements to typical instructional materials to maximize student participation. For example, Boardmaker, a symbol library by Mayer-Johnson, Incorporated, enables speech-language therapists and regular and special education teachers to pair symbols with text to construct more universally accessible class schedules, story vocabulary, directions, appropriate student responses to a lesson, etc. These symbols can be printed out in a range of sizes and arrangements, depending on the needs of the user. By pointing to or giving the picture communication symbol to the teacher or a peer, the student can communicate more effectively.

Assistive technology applications and strategies for students include packaged software and materials but also the unique methods teachers use to promote participation of their students. Often these applications can be categorized into content areas such as reading, writing, or math. Talking word processors read text out loud to a student, and the better ones highlight the text as it is read. These programs enable students to monitor their text as they compose or access text they might otherwise be unable to read. Students can write more quickly, more conventionally, and for longer periods of time without fatiguing by using word prediction software that guesses the words students want to write as the students type individual letters (Lewis, 1998)

Case in Point—Technology for Writing.   Brian is nine years old and attends third grade. His language and learning disabilities make written expression particularly difficult for him. He has stories in his head but his writing skills make it difficult for him to write even a sentence that would be readable to others.

To illustrate the impact technology has on his ability to express himself through print, he was asked to write a story to a picture prompt. When provided with pencil and paper, after 20 minutes of saying his sentences aloud, trying to sound out words, and writing, this is what he wrote:

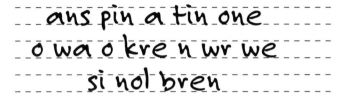

FIGURE 8.1   Student Writing without Word Processor

When provided with the same photograph prompt and a word processor, after 20 minutes of similar behavior, this is what he wrote:

I lik The Brn the Kin
tie kio of the Brn

FIGURE 8.2   Student Writing with Word Processor

When provided with the photograph and a word prediction program (a program that predicts words based on grammar, recency, and frequency as the student types each letter), after 20 minutes this is what he wrote:

Once upon a time
were a girls. She
asks her mom if she
could buy a bunny.
The bunny turned
five in February.
The bunny is cute.

FIGURE 8.3   Student Writing Using Word Prediction Program

Finally, when allowed to dictate his story to an adult so that there were no barriers to expression, after five minutes this is what he wrote:

The girl playing with her bunny. And her bunny running around in the living room. Then the bunny had to eat and go to bed and when she got back from school she played with her bunny. She ate snack and watched tv and her rabbit laid beside her. And then the bunny ate and her parents ate and then the bunny had her birthday and she was six months old. And she got a little toy to play with. It was a ball. She was brown and white and cute. Everybody liked the bunny rabbit. The girl name was Cinderella. The End.

FIGURE 8.4   Student Story Dictation to Adult

The difference between these samples is striking. It is clear that Brian has much more to say than he is capable of expressing with pencil and paper. After completing his first writing sample, even he was unable to read it. As the sample looked more conventional, he was able to read it. When the goal of a teacher is for a child to compose a story, technology may be a critical support. Technology enables Brian to continue to develop his language and composition skills without relying on an adult or another child to work. Even though Brian works with a reading specialist to continue to develop his skills, the technology makes it possible for him to participate with his peers.

Educational Technology

While assistive technology is often necessary for students with disabilities, many students can participate more fully, actively, and meaningfully in their education by using educational technology common to most schools and classrooms. Computers and typical educational or productivity software programs provide a rich interface through which students can learn and share information across content areas such as reading, math, social studies, science, and the like. Tape recorders make it possible for students to listen to books and directions, or compose text. VCRs or DVDs can be utilized to offer students another way to experience a story or learn about mammals, different countries, and cultures.

The power of educational technology is great. To be an effective and efficient tool, technology must be used often and well. Many teachers use these types of technology during center time, inside recess, or as a reward. A recent survey of three urban schools indicated that, even in classrooms rich in computer technology (five to six computers per room plus a computer lab), the technology was underutilized (Staples & Pugach, 2000). Teachers reported having students work primarily on drill programs or use the computer to make a neat copy of a composition. The participants in this survey appreciated the important role technology can play in education but recognized they were not as skilled as they wished in terms of integrating that technology effectively into their teaching. Lack of time to learn the software programs and consider how best to use them with their students was the reason most often cited for not using computers more often or more effectively (Staples & Pugach, 2000). When teachers have not had the time or the inclination to make technology a priority for their typically developing students, it seems unlikely that ways to use such technology to support learning for students with disabilities would spring to mind.

Instructional Technology

One of the most powerful ways teachers can foster a more inclusive environment for students with disabilities is to integrate technology into their instruction. The students don't simply use technology as a pencil or book substitute, they use technology to construct meaning. They use technology to learn more about themselves, the community, and the world. Thus far, discussion of the Internet and software applications has been restricted to their consideration as an assistive tool that allows students access to relevant content. However, the Internet, with its ever-expanding content, its format of text supported by rich graphics and sound, its generally user-friendly interface, and its allure can be a powerful instructional support. Educational software can also serve this purpose.

Even young children can benefit from Internet resources. Electronic texts such as those from TumbleBooks (www.tumblebooks.com), PBS (www.pbs.org), or the Internet Public Library (www.ipl.org) provide the user with not only text that can be read aloud to the student, but also offer animation and digitized rather than synthesized speech. The animation and graphics ease comprehension for young children. Virtual sites, such as whale watches (www.whalewatch.ca), egg hatchings (www.ext.vt.edu/resources/4h/virtualfarm/poultry/poultry_incubation.html#), museum tours (www.louvre.fr), and the like provide students with a more visceral learning experience, and thus, maximize learning.

Careful selection of educational software, which is accessible to all students and promotes careful, developmentally appropriate, research-based skill development, can be powerful. For example, rather than assign young students the task of completing a drill-oriented reading program, having them use a program like Edmark's Bailey's Bookhouse might be a better choice. It exposes the children to letters, sounds, rhymes, and story construction activities in a child-directed manner, is accessible to even students with the most serious physical disabilities due to its built in scanning feature (a large cursor appears on the screen and moves in a counter clockwise fashion on the screen over the possible choices, enabling the student to make selections by pressing a switch), and all the activities lead to real reading. Teachers can use the program as a lesson centerpiece and discuss story structure or rhyming and they can make it a choice for students to revisit during independent work time.

For older students, software programs like Learning Company's Bodyworks, an anatomy and physiology program, supports content-area learning for *all* students. By clicking on various body systems, students might see the screen change from a skeletal to circulatory view, and then clicking on a speaker will result in the program reading pertinent information aloud. The speak-aloud feature is available to all students and is native to the program. This is an example of how educational technology can be both assistive and instructive, thus creating a more inclusive, equitable learning environment for the students.

Evolution of the Law

A series of laws over the past 30 years has supported the education of students with disabilities. Section 504 of the Rehabilitation Act of 1973 prohibited discrimination on the basis of disability in any programs receiving federal financial aid. This opened the door to public schools for students with disabilities. Public Law 94-142, passed in 1975, stipulated that students with disabilities were required to receive a free appropriate public education. The assumption was the student would attend his or her neighborhood school but no expectation for inclusion and no provisions for academic content were made. Students were simply expected to work on individual education goals. IDEA, passed in 1990, more specifically addressed academic aspects of educational experience and the reauthorization of this act in 1997 stipulated that students be educated to the greatest extent possible in the regular education setting, that they receive assistive technology supports as needed, free of charge, and that they learn the general curriculum. It marked a shift to improving teaching and learning. It effectively raised the stakes. It was no longer enough for students to be physically present. Simply mandating that schools seek out, evaluate, and provide needed special education services to children with disabilities did not guarantee that teachers or schools felt equipped to meet the needs of these unique students. Additional funding promised by the federal government to support start-up and ongoing efforts (an additional 40 percent of average per pupil expenditures) enabled schools to hire staff and purchase a variety of materials.

Challenges and Solutions to Educational Equity

The physical presence of students with disabilities in America's schools represents an improvement from decades past, but more work needs to be done to effectively include these children in typical instructional activities. The skills and tools we use to include these children will no doubt improve the quality of the educational experience for all children. Instructional, educational, and assistive technologies may be the key to active participation in school and the work force.

Considering the needs of all of their students and how technology might maximize student learning and engagement should be standard practice when teachers plan lessons to teach certain concepts or skills. If teachers are unfamiliar with technology or disabilities, this type of consideration can be difficult. Working collaboratively with other grade-level teachers, the instructional technology specialist and a special education teacher or related service provider—such as an assistive technology specialist, a physical therapist, or a speech-language pathologist—will likely yield the maximum benefit for the learning community. For these technologies to be effective, however, they must be considered, teachers must be skilled in using them, and resources must be available to acquire them for all the students who need them.

A systematic plan of consideration can facilitate this process as well. For example, if a teacher is planning a unit on weather, each person on the planning team could offer different pieces of valuable information. The technology specialist could make the team aware of software programs or Internet sites that allow students to develop maps, track weather systems, and see different examples of storms. The assistive technology specialist might

Lesson Plan				
Title:		Subject Area:		
Objectives:				
Materials Needed:				
Procedures:	Instructional Setting:	Interaction Type:	Technology:	Adaptations Modifications
1. 2. 3. 4. 5.				

FIGURE 8.5   Lesson Plan Format

know how to access a Web browser application that reads all text or a magnification program that will enlarge the text and images on the screen so all the students can see them. The other specialists might focus on access or interaction concerns that are particular to the student with a disability. A chart like the one shown in Figure 8.5 might ease planning.

Objectives and procedures help determine instructional setting (whole group, small group, students in pairs or alone, etc.). Knowing the objectives, instructional setting, and materials can help determine the best procedure and communication needs of all students. Knowing these things helps consideration of appropriate technologies to employ and any modifications the students might need. Selecting the appropriate technology and instructional setting might reduce the number of modifications a student might need. As planning becomes more automatic, this process will be less laborious and may not require a written plan. This process can help create a more inclusive learning community.

Educator Preparedness

The research shows a trend in State Departments of Education (SDE) to support professional development programs for educators and teacher education programs that focus efforts on adapting the entire curriculum using multiple technologies (Cormier, Folland, & Skau, 1998). Several states (Vermont, Maryland, Kentucky, Arizona, Connecticut, New Mexico, Wisconsin, and others) have incorporated provisions for assistive technology for general education in their technology plans to meet teacher training and the learning needs of special needs students.

Methany (1997) describes how a single book can be adapted using thematic activities supported by technology. He believes that one of the most difficult challenges faced by teachers is educating students who have special needs to achieve outcomes or standards expected of all students. He emphasizes that the strong push for higher standards of learning poses a challenge to states and schools to implement these standards to ensure that they include all students.

Another observation is the emphasis being placed on software for special needs students that are designed to provide a wide range of options. Many of these options allow hardware/software to be tailored to meet student's needs (Hurley & Shumway, 1997). Teacher education programs are showing interest in integrating assistive technology with emerging instructional technology programs as they revamp their programs to meet not only IDEA requirements, but also NCATE technology and diversity standards (Bohren, 1999).

Mead (1994/1995) advocated that teacher education programs must place more emphasis on principles of effective instruction to appropriately use technology. The effective strategies include demonstration-prompt-practice, pace, wait time, and coaching. She added now that computers are used in education, a new challenge facing teachers is to select appropriate software to match both curriculum goals and the student's stage of learning.

To meet the growing need for training and professional development the use of telecommunications (Internet) is establishing virtual learning communities for educators and administrators to acquire more just-in-time learning opportunities. An interview conducted by the Research Institute of Assistive and Training Technologies discusses distance-learning training modules being prepared for preservice teachers in early childhood education. The modules will focus on infusing technology into the early childhood curriculum (Benton, 1997). Despite the best intentions of many efforts, recent studies reveal that a very small percentage of teachers feel comfortable working with special need students in the general classroom (Riley, 1998).

Implications for Program Development in Teacher Education

The implications for program development and restructuring of technology infusion components of teacher education programs will be presented and discussed in this section.

Professional Development in Inclusion for All Educators

This is significant because teachers will not only be required to learn and integrate new computer technologies, but must now be prepared to create inclusive learning environments. This will only be possible through the help of assistive technologies. This means teachers will need new levels of knowledge and awareness, as well as instructional and technical skills to meet these new challenges and standards.

Teacher Perceptions and AT, Teaching, and Learner Needs

These new challenges are incorporated into the new high-quality teaching standards that will require teachers to demonstrate their ability to teach all children in ways that improve their achievement levels. Without adequate access to effective professional development for educators and administrators, the efforts of IDEA and other reform measures aimed at improving the quality of teaching will be thwarted.

Discussion

In order for teachers and schools to support students with disabilities and ensure digital and educational equity, both proactive and responsive activities must occur. Schools of Education must commit themselves to educating all preservice teachers, whether enrolled in special or regular education programs, about students with disabilities. This education must include the law and it must include assistive technology. While it may be unrealistic for general education programs to graduate students who are expert in assistive technology, these students should have a general knowledge of typical assistive technologies available to their future students with disabilities. They should be required to determine what assistive technologies are present in their field placements and who the building or district experts are with regard to AT. These students, as part of their technology coursework, should learn to evaluate educational software and hardware not only as it relates to appropriateness of content and culture but also as to whether those materials and equipment are inherently accessible and/or flexible enough to meet the cognitive and accessibility needs of students with disabilities. Institutions of higher education which graduate special education teachers and related service personnel should require their students to not only be proficient users of typical educational and instructional technology (because much of this technology can be used to more effectively include students with disabilities), but also to be familiar with features of typical assistive technology such as computer programs, portable computers, calculators, touch screens, screen readers, books on tape, scanning devices, switches, and simple augmentative communication devices. Special education teachers should be able to integrate these technologies into their lessons and should be able to provide consultative services to general education teachers on how to use technologies to include students with disabilities more actively and meaningfully in all classroom activities.

School administrators must put assistive technology and inclusion on the agenda. Each year schools schedule staff development on topics ranging from blood-borne pathogens and employee benefits to literacy to behavior management. Until school leaders require all staff members to have at least a common core of knowledge of the law and accommodations for students with disabilities, including AT, systemic change will not occur. School districts typically have a technology committee or work group that plans and makes policy decisions regarding system-wide technology acquisition and use. Every district should include someone with expertise in AT on this team to help ensure that the needs of all students are considered during policy decisions. Similarly, principals and other district leaders must support the ongoing education needs of their personnel with regard to AT. Special education teachers or assistive technology team members should have opportunities to attend state and/or national technology conferences that specialize in the use of assistive technology with students with disabilities. If a core group of professionals at the elementary, middle, and high school level has current age-appropriate knowledge regarding

AT use, this information can be more readily transmitted to special and regular education teachers. Some school systems have an AT committee or department that regularly offers workshops or shares information regarding new practices and information.

Schools and school systems must develop policies for evaluating the assistive technology needs of students, acquiring appropriate technologies, and providing training to support the implementation of those technologies. QIAT (which letters stand for "quality indicators for assistive technology"), a consortium of leaders in the area of assistive technology, has developed recommendations regarding evaluation, acquisition, and implementation of AT. Every school building should have this document and refer to it when considering the needs of students with disabilities. When schools become proactive, services and equipment will be provided in a more timely, effective manner and students with disabilities will be better able to benefit from a quality education.

Summary

At the outset of this chapter, the following four questions were posed for consideration:

1. What does the law say about educational equity for students with disabilities?
2. What is an inclusive learning community?
3. What conditions exist in public education classrooms that may exacerbate the problem of educational equity for all students?
4. In what ways can technology empower teachers to work with all students, especially those with disabilities in the general education classroom?

The law says that disabilities are within the continuum of normal life experience. As such, students with disabilities deserve a free appropriate public education. They are expected to attend their neighborhood schools, and receive the same education in the same classrooms as their nondisabled peers, to the greatest extent appropriate given their unique needs. In order to receive a free appropriate public education, students with disabilities may require, and should have provided to them, assistive technology and/or related services. An inclusive learning community is one in which students with disabilities are legitimate, valued, visible members of the community.

Lack of funds, trained personnel, and appropriate assistive technology may exacerbate the problem of education equity for students with disabilities. As much as statistics point to the paucity of resources and differing instruction for students in rural or urban areas, this problem is worse for students with disabilities. Technology can provide a window to a truer picture of a student's skills and abilities. Students with disabilities who have no access to technology to communicate may be perceived as cognitively disabled, or without literacy skills. Technology can empower teachers to raise their expectations—expectations for themselves and their students.

9 Gender Issues and Considerations

LYNNE SCHRUM

SANDRA GEISLER

FOCUS QUESTIONS

1. Do you believe your perspectives and usage of technology are influenced by your gender? If you answered affirmatively, in what ways did your gender influence you?
2. Do you believe that girls and boys use technology in different ways?
3. Can cultural stereotypes impact the perspectives and uses of technology by girls and boys? Are you aware of their impact on you and your choices regarding technology?

Setting the Stage

Sugar and spice and everything nice! Imagine a time when girls heard that all the time, and boys learned that they were supposed to get into trouble, take things apart, and be active. Does this type of thinking influence girls and boys as they relate to technology? A recent anthology began in this way:

> [Girls] are relegated to an inferior place in American society because of the strength of the cultural stereotype that girls and their culture are insipid and insignificant, unworthy of close attention. Even in Toyland, who gets to deal with serious issues, G. I. Joe or Barbie? G. I. Joe confronts his enemies with a hand grenade; Barbie, presumably, whips out her blow dryer (Inness, 1998, p. 1).

Discussions about a gender divide have been around for several decades, and many experts have offered suggestions for improving existing discrepancies. Despite growing attention to this issue, however, a significant gender divide continues to exist in our lives. This reality has been documented by recent reports (AAUW, 2000). The Bureau of Labor Statistics reported that as of 2000, women now earn an average of 76 percent of the amount of their male counterparts, although that is up from the first available statistics in 1979, when women earned an average of 63 percent of what men earned (Bureau of Labor Statistics, 2000).

We know that girls represent only 15 percent of those taking the Advanced Placement exam for computer science (Gehring, 2001). In 1984 women received 27 percent of the computer science undergraduate degrees, a downward trend from the 37 percent in 1984, and girls represent only 23 percent of those students enrolled in computer programming classes in high school, and only 6 percent of those in Business and Artificial Intelligence (U.S. Department of Education, cited in AAUW, 2000). The percentage of women in IT occupations in the United States also appears to have steadily declined over the past fifteen years, moving from 40.2 percent in 1986 to 28.9 percent in 1999 (Bernstein, 2000). This decline is in sharp contrast to the increased need and opportunities available in the technology field.

The National Council for Research on Women (Thom, 2001) released a study of women's careers and found that women had made significant progress in the sciences over the last two years; however, in computer science and engineering gains noted previously have been stopped or even reversed. The goal of this chapter is to focus on the discrepancy found in women's and girls' use of technology and in technology as a career choice. It will present research that documents some of the causes of this situation, present descriptions of programs and projects that have attempted to change the current conditions, and provide recommendations and strategies to educators and parents for altering the circumstances. This discussion will also be focused on gender issues in mathematics and science, as the three subjects are so closely connected.

Framing the Gender Discussion

Each of us begins life in a variety of cultures and is socialized through the lenses of those who parent, teach, entertain, and befriend us. Culture has an impact on many of the decisions we make in our lives, and our society perpetuates attitudes that suggest that girls cannot become scientists, mathematicians, or engineers, and that computers are for boys. Culture may be defined as the "integrated pattern of human knowledge, belief, and behavior that depends upon one's capacity for learning and transmitting knowledge to succeeding generations" (Merriam Webster Dictionary, 2000), and the patterns that influence our daughters, sisters, and mothers have been around for a very long time.

It is useful to examine the influences within the current culture to gain an understanding of the ways that individuals are socialized because no one develops in a vacuum. As Byrne (1993) put it:

> If a plant fails to flourish, to grow or even to survive in our human-constructed garden, we do not blame the plant. . . . We accept that it is we who have created an inappropriate ecological environment and that we must adjust the environment if plants, other than the indigenous hardy ones, are to survive and flourish. Yet we refuse to accept a parallel responsibility for the learning environment we create (p. 49).

Media

In today's world, more than in previous times, the electronic and visual media play a large role in shaping our identities, and part of this is differentiated if we are boys or girls. When we think about the messages carried in our images, moving pictures, auditory material, and the like, it is obvious that the most common stereotypes still exist. Skeele (1993) suggested that computer software packages support male learning styles by including "competitiveness, assertiveness, noisy sound effects, stereotyped vocabulary, and biased graphics" (p. 15). Conversely, software designed for women and girls often focus on very different attributes. One ad suggested, "Become a princess on a romantic quest, run your own pet shop, dress a paper doll." As another example, Barbie Storymaker allows girls to create an animated Barbie doll show, complete with multiple characters, outfits, scenes, and action. In a recent examination of software designed for girls the authors found the following:

- "Let's Talk About Me" presents a multimedia version of a teen magazine, including a scheduler, diary, and scrapbook.
- "Madeline European Vacation" is an interactive problem-solving program, based on the popular Madeline book and video series.
- "McKenzie & Co." is an interactive role-playing program that allows the user to select an alter ego, and a guy she would like to know.
- "American Girls Dress Designer" provides girls with the opportunity to design and dress models.
- "Barbie Riding Club" in which participants choose a horse to care for.

On the other hand, software does exist that can encourage all children to engage in creative uses of computer programming skills. Stagecast Creator is one such program. It allows students, parents, and teachers to create interactive games, simulations, stories, models, and lessons. It is easy enough for early elementary students to use, as it employs a visual interface to create "rules" for objects to follow.

Visual media may also reflect and support gender stereotypes. Binns and Branch (1995) for example, reported a significant discrepancy in the ways men and women and boys and girls are depicted in clip art. They found that men were predominately shown in "positions of authority and leadership, whereas women are generally shown in subordinate roles often serving or assisting others" (p. 315). Brownell (1993) found a similar result in investigating clip art, and reported that 52.2 percent of the images were of men, while only 25.3 percent were of women. Television commercials also depict differential perspectives. Boys' commercials were found to be fast-paced, outdoors and rugged, with upbeat music and camera angles that place boys in a dominant position. On the other hand, girls' commercials were found slower-paced, indoors, and frequently show tender and caring events (Knupfer, 1999). Knupfer (1997) reported:

> Furthermore, current advertising in the mass media perpetuates women and men using computers in different ways. A cursory look at a range of popular magazines reveals consistently that women are depicted in supportive or sex-charged situations, using computers to do routine tasks, but not necessarily gaining any advantage from doing so. On the other hand, the advertising typically depicts men in superior situations, using the computer to advance their careers, "work smarter," and gain status (p. 34).

In addition, our daily exposure through media

> ... affect[s] our child-rearing practices, choices of products and activities, fashion design, attitudes, value systems, aspirations, self-concepts, opportunities, access to information, social contacts, and wage earning potential. The stereotypes are so deeply ingrained into our society that even when people recognize the discriminations, they accept them as the way things are (Knupfer, 1999, p. 22).

Education

Wilder (1996) investigated a wide variety of studies that sought to understand the often reported differences between males and females in cognitive abilities, particularly in mathematics, science, and technology. She looked at the research of biological differences and found that certainly genetic, hormonal, and perhaps brain-functional differences exist. However, the biological factors interact substantially with the social environment, and she concluded:

> Some of the observed differences in the behaviors of men and women ... are caused by differential expectations and treatment which, in turn, shape further differences in expectations and treatment. Of major importance to the issue of gender differences in cognitive functioning are the dissimilar educational experiences of boys and girls (p. 20).

Thus the biological differences—which do actually exist—are amplified by the stereotypical treatment. These stereotypes are pervasive throughout our educational materials and school system. A glance back to the not so distant past will place education in context. For generations education belonged exclusively to males. Once females were able to attend school, they found unequal treatment and differential opportunities, including less challenging curriculum, hefty fees, and school at off-peak times (Sadker & Sadker, 1997). It was after all not until the 1970s and 1980s that women were admitted to Ivy League colleges.

Technology course materials used in schools show a significant amount of gender stereotyping. Not only are women pictured less often than men in computer science materials, but often when women are pictured they are shown in traditional roles, for example secretaries, clerical workers, and data entry personnel (Schofield, 1995, p. 172).

While educators would most certainly claim that they treat boys and girls equally, research studies demonstrate otherwise (Knupfer, 1997; Sadker & Sadker, 1986; Sadker, Sadker, & Klein, 1991). Overwhelmingly, teachers reprimand boys more frequently and punished them more harshly, but they also "talk to them more, listen to them more, and give them more active teaching attention" (Sadker & Sadker, 1997, p. 462). If we are to achieve equity in achievement, then it is obvious that the situation of inequitable treatment by gender in classrooms must change and perhaps this change is most essential in the area of technology use, comfort, experience, and support. Morritt (1997) conducted in-depth research with nine computer-using female educators, and they related their experiences and difficulties learning about and using technology. In a similar study Smith (1999) investigated the lives of twelve women working in areas of technology, math or science. Six of these twelve women had broken barriers to forge their careers in male-dominated areas. Both of these studies concluded that girls and young women needed role models, mentors, and supportive families and friends to overcome the pervasive stereotypes found throughout society. The studies also concluded that with proper support, women are able to move beyond the stereotypes they have been assigned.

It is important to differentiate the stereotypes that permeate our media, experience, and cultural patterns, which are invalid and limiting, from real, observable differences between boys and girls, which must be accounted for in well-designed instruction. Additionally, whether the differences are biological or cultural in origin, they cannot be allowed to exclude girls from participating fully in technology. Over the years, perceptive educators have noticed that boys and girls respond differently to almost all kinds of technology.

A series of studies conducted about gender differences around attitudes and approaches to technology indicates that girls are more ambivalent about technology than boys, who are more positive. Boys tend to be more excited about their experiences with technology, particularly video games, while girls like video (i.e., stories) and tend to get put off by bad technology experiences. Girls are also less likely than boys to attempt to fix a broken piece of technology (AAUW, 2000; Cassell, 1998; Schofield, 1995). Girls, unlike boys, are not expected to know about technological matters, and are often encouraged to be merely consumers and users of technology (Berber, 1984; Carter & Kirkup, 1990; Cockburn, 1988). In part this orientation to technology in general is due to the dearth of early informal and formal learning experiences that build on girls' interests and draw them into exploring and inventing technologies on their own terms (Mcilwee & Robinson, 1992; Whiting & Edwards, 1988). Several researchers have found that girls are less interested in technology for technology's sake, but are more often drawn to science and technical courses that emphasize how such subjects apply to social and everyday problems (Caleb, 2000; Rosser, 1990; Turkle, 1984; Turkle & Papert, 1990).

Boys, on the other hand, appear to be drawn to computers by the sense of challenge it represents. Consistent with Turkle and Papert (1990), boys "appeared to be attracted to computers by the enjoyment and sense of mastery and accomplishment they got from exploring them as well as from using them in a way that let the boys test themselves against others or against the computer . . ." (Schofield, 1995, p. 160). The focus on programming as a set of decontextualized computer skills is likely to hold little interest for many young women. Perhaps more importantly, women's desire for communication, collaboration, and integration are not central to a more masculine technological worldview which emphasizes the importance of speed, power, and the inner workings of machines (Brunner, 1991). Unfortunately, this view continues to dominate as a mindset for structuring technology experiences in school.

Examples exist in which girls and boys learn programming skills in order to solve authentic problems, thus targeting one of the most common reasons girls give for not engaging in computer activities—they have no real purpose or authentic goals. One project focused on "less tinkering, more problem solving" to draw females into computer programming classes. Dubbed TeachScheme, this project is located at Rice University and was designed to address the concerns identified by the AAUW (2000) study. Computing is taught as a systematic activity that helps with all the other subjects, such as science, journalism, debate, and even poetry. Other projects have reported encouraging programming for creating sculptures, animating designs, building scientific instruments and gathering data, and inventing machines to solve real problems.

Experience at Home

Boys' and girls' experience at home is worth special attention, as it is particularly important in the context of very young children. Schall and Skeele (1995) identified subtle differential treatment and messages to boys and girls in their access to and use of home computers. Armitage (1993) supported the perspective that parents may unintentionally contribute to the problem by more frequently locating computers in boys' rooms.

An extensive research study (AAUW, 2000) reported that girls are particularly critical of the current computer culture. Girls were clearly not computer phobics, but rather described themselves as more interested in collaborative activities, games with simulation, strategy, and interaction than in playing games that are designed for competition and that focus on death and destruction. Koch reported "feelings of incompetence and alienation from technology start or are reinforced in school. How girls and women relate to technology and the value that they bring to it are often ignored or devalued in education" (1994, p. 14). Unfortunately, girls often receive messages that denigrate their perspectives.

The impact of home use of technology has a greater impact on boys in school than girls. Boys tend to spend more time on computers at home than girls, and this use remains level with age for boys but declines for girls. The home computers were used primarily for games rather than for educational activities, and unfortunately, the children studied viewed educational software as "boring." Where educational software was used in the home, a high level of parental involvement became the determining factor in children's willingness to use it at all. Parents spent time choosing appropriate software, coached the child on its use, worked with the child at the keyboard, and provided constructive feedback. Unfortunately, this level of parental involvement was the exception, not the rule (Mumtaz, 2001).

Exploring Differences: Research on Gender and Technology

The research on gender and technology presents a fascinating glimpse into the lives of our children and teens, and by reflection, a view of our schools and our homes. The studies presented come from a variety of countries and circumstances, thus demonstrating that the concern about the issues under investigation is not confined to the United States.

In a study of a typical high school in Israel (grades seven through twelve), a well-connected country, Nachmias, Mioduser, and Shemla (2001) investigated boys' and girls' uses of technology, including comfort levels and preferences. They found that far more boys use technology extensively than girls. Further, they found that with the exception of word processing, significant differences existed in the types of usage between boys and girls. Interestingly, boys saw themselves as more technologically proficient (40.9 percent to 15.9 percent respectively), and 14.2 percent of the boys identified themselves as highly competent while none of the girls did so.

Kafai and Sutton (1999) conducted a study of computer use among families in a university laboratory school, where 89 percent of the families reported at least one computer in the home. The research sought to identify the types of activities that students engaged in on their computers. Boys were significantly more likely to use the computer for games and for educational software, while girls were more likely to use the computers for word processing and creativity software. Similarly, when asked about their use of the Internet, boys used it for more net surfing and information retrieval than girls.

One might expect as computers become more prevalent, that all students would become more comfortable using them. Unfortunately, a recent study did not find this to be true. In a study of entering university students from 1992–1998, Todman (2000) found that the degree of computer anxiety (CA) among psychology students decreased significantly over the time period; however, "it became clear that, whereas average male CA had undergone a substantial and highly significant reduction, average CA among the females had not changed significantly during the period (p. 33). He concluded that the reduction in CA was based almost entirely on the reduction of the number of men who exhibit CA, rather than the overall reduction of individuals, and that the gap between males and females with CA had widened significantly. He suggested that "it looks as though some aspect of girls' experiences with computers during secondary education may be less than satisfactory" (p. 34).

Similar studies reported results that support these findings. In a study of 1,730 high school boys and girls, Shashaani (1994) found significant gender differences in computer experience, computer class selections, amount of computer usage, and computer ownership. In a later study (Shashaani, 1997), she found "male college students were more interested in computers than were females, and had more self-confidence in working with computers" (p. 47). Interestingly, women, even those not personally self-confident about computers, did not hold stereotypical views about women in general as computer users. Males also did not appear to hold a gender-biased view of computer users. Students who had had more computer experience and greater access to computers were also more interested in computers, thus supporting the notion that lack of exposure to computers may exacerbate individuals' fear and dislike of computers.

Crombie and Armstrong (1999) compared learning experiences in three computer science classes, one that was all female and two were mixed-gender. Females in the all-female class reported significantly higher perceived teacher support than both males and females from the mixed-gender classes. Females in the all-female class and males reported similar levels of computer confidence, but females in the mixed gender classes reported lower confidence. Additionally, the females from the all-female class reported less stereotypical attitudes about the appropriateness of computer science for females than did the males.

In an effort to understand the ways boys and girls use computers and to determine how gender may or may not play a role, Upitis (1998) undertook an intensive study of one class of seventh- and eighth-grade students where computers were integrated throughout the class curriculum. The students used technology in interdisciplinary classroom assignments and during their free time. She conducted interviews and made observations for most of one school year, tracking home use as well as classroom use of technology. Through her observations, 'computer personalities' emerged: "hackers, game players, game creators, reluctant users, luddites, eager users and sporadic users" (p. 293). Ultimately she concluded that girls took part in almost all of the types of uses of computers (for tools, game playing, game creating), but more of them were reluctant users and were less comfortable solving problems. Further, none of the girls fell into the "hacker" category, and although one of the girls had all the skills and talents of the hacker boys, she never identified herself as really fitting into that category.

It appears that the time period between the fifth through the eighth grade is the most critical time to firmly introduce computers to children, especially girls. Studies have found that in the seventh grade, boys increase their knowledge of the computer as compared to girls. By the eighth grade, attitudes about computers are strongly established. Other studies indicate that the earlier computers are introduced to girls, the better (Butler, 2000; Sadker & Sadker, 1997).

An unpublished evaluation study of an after-school computer program also supports the importance of early introduction to technology (Schrum, Geisler, & Wise, 2000). The program was designed to help girls in grades five through eight to gain skills and knowledge in a variety of computer programs, make progress in their attitude toward technology, and strengthen their academic skills within an after-school program at local Boys and Girls Clubs. The curriculum was designed to engage the participants in active investigation as travel agents, with a goal to design four possible itineraries for clients. They created logos for their travel agency, investigated locations, possible activities, and costs. Unfortunately, those girls at the upper range of the grade range were strongly influenced by peer groups and attitudes that had already been established, while the younger participants were much more interested in the activities. While the parents were eager to sign up their daughters, many of the programs could not get a sufficient number of participants to sign up. The recommendations from this study included a strong need to target similar projects and course materials for the younger age groups, and beginning the activities as part of school curriculum.

De Jean, Upitis, Kock, and Young (1999) presented a case study of six girls. The girls spent time on an adventure game, Phoenix Quest, designed to make mathematics appealing to girls from ages nine to fourteen by incorporating game and activity elements that girls find interesting, important and challenging. Phoenix Quest is a 65-chapter story written by an award-winning author. Presented in a nonlinear format, the story contains a female protagonist actively involved in an adventure game. Reading, writing, math, and problem-solving activities are included throughout the storyline, requiring interaction with the story's characters instead of fast action and violence. The findings compared the responses of the six girls to those of 41 boys and 57 girls to the same game. Interestingly, most of the girls in the larger study did not realize there was math embedded into the storyline. This connection to real-world uses of mathematics was missed due to a lack of needed teacher involvement. Overall the study found it was important to the girls that they have a strong and adventurous female protagonist, one with whom they could personally identify. Also, contrary to popular beliefs, the study found that the female protagonist was accepted by the boys who enjoyed playing the game. Cooperative play and group problem solving engaged all the participants while the female protagonist specifically attracted the girls.

It is important to note that not everyone agrees that a gender discrepancy exists. Kleinfeld (1998) examined the data from a variety of sources and determined that African American males are much more at risk than all females, and that they are kept away from good careers and given fewer opportunities than females, findings that specifically contradicted the AAUW (2000) study. She quoted statistics showing that women earn more doctorates than in the past. Her work, however, does still demonstrate that a discrepancy remained noteworthy in computer science, engineering, mathematics, and physical sciences, as women earned only 18 percent, 15 percent, 24 percent, and 22 percent of the total number of those degrees, respectively.

It is worth noting a different aspect to this discussion, specifically that biological and other factors play a role in career choices. In his research that examined women's occupational decision-making process, Henwood (1998) was at odds with the WISE (Women into Science and Engineering) discourse of gender and equal opportunity. The WISE solution was that women are in need of more "information about the work and changing images of engineering and technology from masculine to more feminine ones" (p. 36). Henwood found instead that women have the information they need to make occupational choices and yet they were choosing fields other than computer science and engineering. Women's knowledge gave them both positive and negative feelings towards traditionally male occupations. This view will be examined more fully as research on these topics is presented.

Projects That Make a Difference

It does appear that differential treatment still exists and actually sustains and exacerbates the gender divide. Schools and other organizations have devised a variety of projects and activities to change the status quo in the media, educational communities, and at home. This section will report on several of the most visible and successful.

At Carnegie Mellon University, women's share in first-year computing classes rose from 8 percent to 40 percent over a five-year period in response to an aggressive campaign to keep them involved. Rensselaer Polytechnic Institute greatly improved its retention rate of women in engineering and technical majors. Women's institutions—such as Smith College in Northampton, Massachusetts, and Spelman College in Atlanta—have been successful in recruiting women into engineering and other technological majors. Other projects are described below.

Girls As Designers

The Educational Development Corporation (EDC) has had significant experience working on efforts to promote girls' and women's' use of technology for innovative activities. The promise of digital equity requires that diverse groups be invited to act as designers capable of building dynamic applications and setting innovative directions for the future development and implementation of emerging technologies.

The EDC's Center for Children and Technology (CCT) researchers interviewed and documented the work of high school students in an innovative mechanical engineering program. Interviews with girls participating in the program confirmed that girls need opportunities to express ideas for invention and innovation that build on their different ways of approaching and interpreting the artifacts, systems, and environments that constitute the designed world that we identify as technology (Bennett & Bruner, in press). Young women revealed that they were interested in designing devices that had social significance while the curriculum required students to design catapults and other devices not related to social utility. Many of the girls openly complained that their more socially oriented perspective was excluded from activities and discussions.

The CCT team focused its efforts on creating *Imagine,* a prototype computer program where girls mapped out and illustrated their ideas for imaginative inventions or "fantasy machines." Pilot research revealed that Imagine was effective in serving as a "conceptual tinkering" environment. This led to the creation of the "Designing for Equity" project to create and test an integrated set of design-based curricular materials to accompany the software program (Honey, Brunner, Bennett, Meade, & Tsen, 1994). Curriculum activities and software were designed and modified to encourage girls to create, reflect on, research, and revise designs, and, when appropriate, to access information to expand knowledge. This research demonstrated that girls responded well to activities that allowed them to explore relationships among familiar technologies (e.g., different communications devices such as telephones and telegraphs) and activities that enabled them to investigate how technological design is related to the design process of artists, scientists, and other professionals. In addition, girls were very interested in creating devices to solve problems that were personally relevant to them, such as creating multifunctional devices that helped them finish chores more efficiently. It was also clear that girls benefited greatly from sharing their design ideas and concerns about technological decisions with peers and adults who could help facilitate such discussions (Honey et al., 1994).

Imagine evolved into Imagination Place!, a continuation using the latest Internet technologies, offering children an opportunity to participate in an interactive online design environment. Imagination Place! makes use of online animation tools, graphics, and sound as well as accompanying off-line activities to encourage girls to:

- Consider technological design in a larger social and societal context
- Construct their own imaginative ideas for devices and inventions that are personally relevant to them
- Engage in collaboration and discussion around design projects with their peers and other adults serving as facilitators.

Such an opportunity for collaboration, sharing, and discussion set the stage for a design process that is typically found in schools or in specialized technology/design classrooms (Bennett, 2000).

Institute for Women in Trades, Technology, and Science (IWITTS)

This organization, with funding from the National Science Foundation and Cisco Systems, Inc., designed a variety of initiatives to increase the number of women in technology careers. They promote recruitment activities, and provide electronic publications, and mentoring relationships to retain women once they become involved in these careers.

Their recruiting efforts were designed to disseminate information about diverse female roles, as well as offer suggestions for making math and science courses user-friendly to women and minorities. These activities might be as simple as providing a women's technology page for course catalogues or supporting a "Women in Technology Expo" and hands-on demonstrations. They reported significant growth in the number of women entering educational programs for technology careers, and substantial retention of these women in their programs.

Gipson (1997) reported on a project that looked at "girls only" after-school activities in a Young Women Scholars' Early Initiative Program. The project was formed by a collaborative between Wayne State University, school districts in southeastern Michigan, and industry. An advisory committee selected 40 young women from primarily disadvantaged backgrounds from over 350 applicants. The program ran for five weeks during one summer and met for 20 sessions during the fall and winter months. Mathematics, science, and technology projects were developed, and female role models mentored the girls. Attitudes, perceptions, and skills were strongly influenced by this program, and their goals and plans were changed by this project.

Techbridge: Encouraging Girls in Technology

Techbridge is a technology program designed for girls. Funded by the National Science Foundation for three years, Techbridge seeks to support girls in middle and high schools by teaching them technical skills and preparing them for possible careers in a variety of technical fields.

Five middle schools and four high schools in Oakland, CA, participated in the Techbridge program. Primarily meeting as after-school clubs, the groups worked on various projects in the fields of science and technology. The participants' interests ranged from real-world problems at school and in their community, to designing products such as a girls' magazine, to taking field trips and meeting influential female role models in technology.

Techbridge also provided development opportunities and resources for teachers and school counselors, helping them engage girls (and boys) in technology in their schools. Recognizing the value of technology support in the home, Techbridge also offers assistance and ideas for parents.

Eyes to the Future: Middle School Girls Envisioning Science and Technology in High School and Beyond

This project was funded by the National Science Foundation (NSF) and Arthur D. Little and is based at TERC, Inc. in Cambridge, Massachusetts. After two successful pilots in 1997 and 1998, the program received full funding from NSF for three years. Terc's Web page states,

> "Eyes to the Future" is a multi-age mentoring program that supports middle-school girls as they make the transition to high school and make informed choices about the opportunities available to them in high school and beyond. "Eyes to the Future" uses the Web to link middle-school girls with high-school girls in their school districts who have stayed interested in math and science and with women who use science, math, and technology in their careers (TERC, 2000, np).

This program is based on studies showing that girls' self-confidence with math and science can be greatly improved through mentoring. The project not only matches middle school girls with female mentors working in the math and science field, it also matches them with girls currently in math tracks in high school. The object was not only to inspire young girls toward long-term math, science, and technology careers, but also to inspire them towards these goals in their immediate future.

The results of the pilot have shown that this type of mentorship can "provide important content and motivation in math, science, and technology (MST) for middle-school girls." The pilot also "suggested important complementary roles for high school and adult mentors in the program" (TERC, 2000, np).

Single-Sex Classrooms

Many after-school projects are focused entirely on girls or young women, and in some areas of the country this has also led to investigation of single-sex schools or classrooms. The results of these efforts are mixed. Haag (2000) reported that several studies contradicted each other on the question of single-sex schools increasing self-esteem in boys and girls. In terms of attitudes toward academic subjects, she found that studies indicated that girls' preferences for math, science, and other stereotypical "masculine" subjects increased in single-sex schools.

Haag (2000) also found that studies may show increased achievement for girls in single-sex schools; however, once those scores were adjusted for socioeconomic or ability variables, the differences diminished. One outcome that appeared to be stable was that girls in single-sex schools had less stereotypical views of gender roles than girls in coeducational schools.

Yet it is difficult to ignore the reports of specific research projects that did investigate the use of single-sex classrooms. Murray (1995) describes his schools' use of such classes specifically for math and science. After two years, Murray declared:

> Observations by the math, science, and computer teachers who work with sixth grade have been broadly consistent over the two years. The girls' groups have been a lot noisier than the boys'. The girls are much more animated and lively than they ever were, and are, in coed classes. The girls really like the comradely feeling of working with other girls and they are highly supportive of each other (p. 2).

In a report on this topic by the American Association of University Women (1998), the authors concluded that there was no evidence that single-sex education worked or was better than coeducation. The report suggested that good education was the most reliable characteristic needed, and that this would include small classes and equitable teaching methods, as well as curriculum that was focused on academic achievement. At a minimum, we can look to single-sex classrooms for strategies that work in support of girls and technology. These classrooms of necessity must focus on girls' interests and perspectives.

Insights for Practice

As researchers begin to study ways in which women and girls make use of the new information technologies and how women's values shape the design of information technologies, there is a shared understanding that providing access to equipment and programs is not enough. Rather, a consideration of the social context of use, the kinds of technology-based projects children are engaged in, and the use of digital technology as a tool for design is vital to supporting women and girls in becoming critical designers as well as users of the new information technologies.

Insights for Practice in Schools

As an educational community it is important to insure that the feminine perspective on technology is as much a part of the policymaking process about technology integration in education as the masculine one is. The following suggestions may assist educators encourage girls and young women in developing positive attitudes about the use of and possibilities for technology in their lives.

- **Technology in context, not just for technology's sake.** The feminine attitude toward technology looks right through the machine to its social function, while the masculine view is more focused on the machine itself. One implication of this difference might be that presenting technology as an end in itself—a special subject of study (as in a programming class), is less likely to appeal to young women than to young men. If the technology is introduced as a means to an end, however, as a tool for in-depth research or for making a multimedia presentation, in the arts and humanities as well as in the sciences, young women are as likely to take to it with an enthusiasm comparable to young men. Projects that include technology in music, history, or the sciences are more likely to encourage girls and young women to explore.
- **Technology to solve genuine problems.** Young women tend to be more engaged when a a greater emphasis is placed on the impact of a new technology. Does the technology solve a genuine social problem or merely speed up a process? The Science, Technology, and Society movement among educators, which integrates science and social studies into a curriculum that considers the impact of science and technology on society, addresses these kinds of issues and is likely to make young women feel invited into a discussion of technology.
- **Information technology for communication not just information.** The Internet, particularly the World Wide Web, is as likely to appeal to young women as it is to young men. The ability to communicate with others, to share ideas, stories, news, and advice, corresponds to feminine notions. The ability to send and receive information instantly from vast resource archives and to publish one's own ideas to the world at large, corresponds to the masculine fantasies (Bennett, 2000). If Internet access is used to allow students to communicate with each other and with mentors, it will appeal to girls as well as to boys.
- **Technology for design not just consumption.** Girls' access to full participation in software design or other design activities is important not so much because they learn particular computer skills, but rather because participation affords girls a way to connect with the male-dominated practice of technological design. Previous intervention models such as science and technology after-school programs and summer camps that reach out to females in high schools and colleges, while important, may take place too late in development, considering that girls form many beliefs about themselves and their relationship to science and technology at a much younger age. For that reason, it is necessary to provide younger girls with opportunities to interact with advanced technologies and design in substantial ways.

Insights for Practice at Home

Research has shown that computer use in the home can have a positive impact on a child's success in school (Armitage, 1993; Schall & Skeele, 1995; Skeele, 1993). Home use influences a child's comfort with and use of technology in school. Even after controlling for family income and for social and cultural capital, it has been shown that computer use in the home improves test scores in math and reading (Mumtaz, 2001).

The importance of parental involvement cannot be overemphasized. Encouragement, support, and mentoring of girls must begin at home. Parents also need to take an active role in school to help insure equal opportunities and a positive environment are available to their daughters as well as their sons. The following suggestions have been provided to assist parents and caregivers in providing more equitable perspectives and experiences for girls:

- Raise your own awareness about inequitable patterns of computer use.
- Encourage exploration of new computer software on their own.
- Involve girls in software purchases.
- Be a positive role model.
- Ask your daughter for help.
- Look for activities you can do with your daughter, for example exploring the World Wide Web.
- Introduce girls to women in technical careers. (Furger, 1998)

Conclusion

This chapter provided an introduction and overview of the gender digital divide. By reviewing the current status and past research, it has offered a glimpse at a systemic and persistent dilemma that is found in homes, schools, universities, and throughout technological and other employment venues. Despite years of effort to remedy these situations the problems have remained and even grown.

This chapter also provided a wide variety of current projects that are making an effort to overcome the gender digital divide, and suggestions to improve the current situation with respect to the females in our communities, schools, and lives.

There have been and continue to be a number of technology projects designed to encourage girls to use and enjoy technology for a variety of reasons. However, these programs only begin to touch the number of girls in our country impacted by gender issues. These programs appear to have provided the type of activities needed to rectify some of the imbalance between the genders, but the solutions will require significant changes in our homes, schools, and the larger society, including the media. In presenting these, and additionally offering suggestions for educators and parents, it is hoped that all individuals who interact with girls and boys and young adults will make an effort to be more inclusive of all exploration and perspectives. This is particularly true when we consider teacher preparation programs. Moreover, it is also going to require that all parents encourage software companies to invest in programs that appeal to girls as well as boys, and perhaps it is now time for every parent, educator, and citizen to pay close attention to the subtle messages that surround us, and respond accordingly.

10 Refocusing Curricula

LYNNE SCHRUM

BONNIE BRACEY

FOCUS QUESTIONS

1. In what ways has technology exacerbated the differences in educational opportunity among different student populations?
2. What role does curriculum play in addressing equity issues?
3. How can technology-enhanced curriculum support the goal of greater equity?

The Current Challenge

Imagine a classroom in which all students are actively engaged in investigations about the historical roots of the conflict in the Middle East. Students find resources in their native languages, discuss their theories with local and distant partners, interview students living in areas of conflict, and then create a multimedia presentation to explain their newfound knowledge to family and friends. For many educators this is the realization of their goal of appropriate and relevant uses of technology—to support a challenging curriculum that allows each individual to develop and learn appropriately. Unfortunately, the current challenge of creating such classroom practice is often exacerbated by a lack of equity in the use, access, skills, and experience that is found in some classrooms, schools, and communities. This challenge derives from a recognized gap in access to information technology that is clearly more significant for certain schools and communities, specifically schools whose student population is either minority, rural, physically or mentally challenged, culturally or linguistically different, of low socioeconomic status, or female. The case has been made for more equitable access to technology in other chapters in this book; however, the challenges go far beyond just getting the boxes and wires into all classrooms.

This issue is complex and reflects the conundrum found throughout our society. Clearly a consideration of school curricula mirrors that complexity. Moursund (2001) stated, "Rather than simply focusing on access as the quick fix for the Digital Divide, we need to concentrate on information technology integration and training" (p. 5). This chapter will look extensively at the current ways in which teachers and students use information technologies in our schools, particularly in schools with high percentages of minority or poverty students. Next, it will discuss ways in which curricular resources may exacerbate the problem of differential opportunities. Finally, this chapter will explore possibilities in which curricula and activities, specifically using technology, may offer opportunities for emancipation for all our students.

It is important to situate this chapter within the context of learning in general. Discussion of equal opportunity in learning must consider curriculum and the ways in which the thoughtful use of technology may contribute to the curriculum goals. Educators, researchers, and policymakers have expended significant energy to determine the potential for using technology as one aspect of a radical reform of our educational system. They "have argued that technology needs to be an integral part of a well-planned pedagogy for students and that programs need to be designed so as to ensure equitable and substantial access" (Hess & Leal, 1999, p. 544). In addition, this chapter focuses on the development of curriculum that is inclusive and respectful of all cultures and encouraging of multiple perspectives. One definition of this type of curriculum, offered by Gollnick and Chinn (1986), summarized the broad objectives:

> Multicultural education is the educational strategy in which the student's cultural background is viewed as positive and essential in developing classroom instruction and a desirable school environment. It is designed to support and extend the concepts of culture, cultural pluralism, and equity into the formal school setting (p. 5).

In addition, this curriculum must include a deliberate educational attempt to incorporate students' ethnic roots. Further, multiculturalism is designed to empower students by assisting them in becoming self-directed learners "who take an active role in improving the quality of the various communities they inhabit (classrooms, school, local, national, and world) and learning how to work independently and interdependently to accomplish these tasks" (Kim, in Davidman & Davidman, 1994, p. 5). Further, this must be done within a collaborative relationship among parents, teachers, students, and the larger community, especially in communities that have a history of "disempowerment" due to racism or impoverished economic conditions (Comer, 1988).

Differential Technology Use

We've seen in other chapters that educators may not be making the most of the technology they have in their schools. In addition to Cuban's estimate that less than 10 percent of teachers' instructional time incorporates technology, he said that only about 5 percent of teachers use computers in imaginative ways (2001). McAdoo (2000) asks fundamental questions about the digital divide:

> The issue of equity now centers not on equality of equipment but on quality of use. The computers are there, yes, but what is the real extent of access? What kind of software is avail-

able? How much computer training are teachers getting? And are schools able to raise not just students' level of technical proficiency, but also their level of inquiry, as advanced use of technology demands? (p. 143–44)

A recent survey, the Education Week/Market Data Retrieval/Harris Interactive Poll of Students and Technology provided a more global look at the use of technology in the classroom. In summary, according to the student respondents to the poll, "it seems educators may be making more progress in providing access to technology than in figuring out how to use it as a learning tool" (Doherty & Orlofsky, 2001, p. 45). Roughly half of the student respondents spend about one hour or less per week using school computers, but even more disturbing is where and how they are being used.

Thirty-nine percent of the students reported that most of their computer use takes place in computer labs, and 35 percent said they most often use them in libraries, while only 24 percent reported they most often use school computers in the classroom. Many technology experts argue that classroom use is important because it allows students to use computers more regularly and seamlessly—rather than just for typically short, disjointed experiences in computer labs (Doherty & Orlofsky, 2001, p. 47).

Thirty-five percent of the students reported that their teachers "often" or "sometimes" let computers serve as a reward for good behavior in class. It may be worth asking then, which students are most likely to earn those rewards?

It is also necessary to consider other factors that have an impact on a school or a single classroom's ability to effectively employ technology in the curriculum. Experience has shown that technology coordinators provide valuable assistance for classroom educators through a variety of curriculum-related activities, including giving demonstration lessons, finding appropriate software, and engaging in collaborative planning. Yet full-time technology coordinators are less likely to be found in schools with high percentages of students qualifying for free or reduced lunch, whereas parents in wealthier schools are more likely to volunteer and supply extra funding for technology and support as well as having a greater ability to get corporate sponsors. These factors affect access, of course, but they also affect the manner in which the technology is used for educational goals.

It is important to look carefully at the ways in which the technology in predominately minority classrooms is actually being used. Burnett (1994) suggested that

the methods and purposes of computer use often differ radically from school to school and from district to district: Sometimes computer use enhances learning for all students and sometimes it simply confers a new technology sheen on the low-level programs that have long been a staple of education in the United States (np).

Additionally, if students only perform drill-and-practice and remediation activities with the computer, they miss the opportunity to explore the synthesis, analysis, hypothesis testing, and problem-solving activities that lead to higher-order thinking. Furthermore, they are not exposed to opportunities for creative and imaginative uses of technology. Herbert Kohl, a well-known educational researcher, visited many inner-city schools looking at how computers are used and believes that "covert" racism limits the types of activities that children of color can accomplish on the computer. He stated, ". . . students in schools with predominately minority enrollments are more likely to use their state of the art technology for drill, practice and test-taking skills. Meanwhile, white students in more affluent communities are creating Web sites and multimedia presentations" (Kohl, cited in Reid, 2001, p. 16). Wenglinsky (1998) also reported that African American children were especially likely to use computers for "drill-n-skill" purposes, unfortunately with the effects of lowering their math scores on the National Assessment of Educational Progress (NAEP), a test given to a sample of fourth-, eighth-, and twelfth-grade students. These individual reports are reinforced in more widely ranging studies. Maryland conducted a study of students' use of technology. Seventy-two percent of classrooms were connected to the Internet, a substantial increase from the 58 percent found in 1999. Unfortunately, the study also found that, "Maryland students in wealthier districts are more than twice as likely as their peers in poorer communities to use technology to gather, organize, and store information. They are also three times more likely to use technology to perform measurements and collect data" (Maryland State Department of Education, 2001, np).

Nationally, the U.S. Department of Education found a similar story (National Center for Education Statistics, 1999). Schools with a high percentage of students living in poverty have access to fewer computers with multimedia capabilities and Internet connections. Without these capabilities, it is again likely that computers will be used for drill and practice as opposed to productivity, investigation, problem solving, or problem generation.

Schools with high poverty rates and those in rural areas that have access to the Internet typically have slower connections to the Internet (NTIA, 2000). In fact, this research reported that rural areas in particular currently lag far behind urban areas in broadband availability. This can have a significant impact on the types of activities that students are able to accomplish. For example, let's imagine that an educator wanted to download the first one hundred hours of the Holocaust survivors' personal accounts to include in a unit on World War II. It would take approximately 9.5 minutes when using Internet 2, about 11 days when connected via a T-1 line (available on most university campuses), and an astonishing 1.5 years on a traditional dial-up phone line (U.S. Department of Education, 2000, p. 38). Even if an educator wished to use these primary resources it is doubtful that he/she would spend the time to offer the full richness of this valuable resource if it were to take such an inordinate amount of time to download.

It is also worth noting that students with limited English proficiency (ESL) are also at a disadvantage in using computers for creative and problem-solving activities. Many times equipment is not available to ESL programs, but even if the hardware exists, software and websites are primarily in English (Zehr, 2001). Equally disturbing, schools face a serious shortage of educators who know how to use technology effectively and also have skills and training in ESL. These factors lead to less use of technology, and more importantly, when technology is used, it is more likely to be used in mundane ways.

Similarly, a gender divide remains firmly entrenched in our schools. For example, the College Board reported that only 15 percent of those taking the Advanced Placement exam for computer science were girls (Gehring, 2001). Further, women received 27 percent of the computer science undergraduate degrees, a downward trend from the 37 percent in 1984; girls only represent 23 percent of those students enrolled in computer programming classes in high school, and only 6 percent of those in Business and Artificial Intelligence (U.S. Department of Education, as cited in AAUW, 2000). Without these basic courses it is unlikely that women will be prepared for, or even recognize, the potential careers that offer exceptional opportunities.

The problem is more than one of access; it is rather a problem in the ways computers are used and the messages given to girls as they reach middle school. Many studies have discussed girls and women in schools and the ways in which they may be disadvantaged by subtle and even unknowing behavior on the part of educators, councilors, and administrators (Sadker & Sadker, 1994). These messages lead to what Koch found as, "feelings of incompetence and alienation from technology start or are reinforced in school. How girls and women relate to technology and the value that they bring to it are often ignored or devalued in education" (1994, p. 14). Girls often get messages that denigrate their perspectives, as Bigelow (1995) found in an examination of Oregon Trail, one of the most popular computer software programs. He reported that, although girls and women are in almost every scene, they only live the experience from the perspective of a male adventurer.

In extensive research reported in *Tech Savvy* (AAUW, 2000), evidence surfaced that girls are critical of the focus and perspective of the current computer culture. Girls are not computer-phobic, but rather are more interested in collaborative activities than in playing games that are designed for competition and that focus on death and destruction. They were more interested in games that feature simulation, employ extensive strategies, and focus on interaction. Similarly, Hanor (1998) spent time investigating what girls deem important and meaningful about computers. She found that girls' sense of the importance of interpersonal relations significantly contributed to their enjoyment of working with technology. Hanor explained, "While games were remembered with great detail and were considered top priority, they were described as being 'not that funny' if you played them alone. Playing them with someone else made them 'funnier' " (1998, p. 66).

This section has focused on the differential curricular uses of information technology in schools with high minority or poverty populations, and also has looked at specific difficulties faced by students for whom English is not their first language and for girls and women. It also provides evidence that learners in rural areas may face challenges in access to high-speed connections. Now it is worthwhile to look at the ways in which resources such as textbooks and software have had an impact on the curriculum and activities of learners.

Examining Educational Resources

If we share the goal of educating all our learners in culturally appropriate and respectful ways, and hope to encourage a thoughtful and informed citizenry, then it is important to look carefully at the design and construction of all the curriculum materials that confront learners in the classroom. According to De Vaney (1998),

> Film, video, and computer software construct an imaginary student by the manner in which they address, instruct, and understand their target audience. For these media to communicate clearly, they have to address a student of a certain culture, age, and gender (p. 3).

It would be comforting to believe that each classroom and the educational materials found within it are completely without biases, and further, always represent "truth." However, that would be a naïve view of the world. It is worthwhile to return to Habermas's (1971) view that one role of education should be to serve students' emancipatory interests. If what he proposed, "undistorted domination-free communication," actually could exist, then concerns about educational materials might disappear. Unfortunately, the world does not work that way, as individuals with specific views, histories, and biases write educational materials, and, as Heidegger (1962) reminded us, language is significantly important because of its ability to hide within it one's way of understanding the world.

Thus, it is not surprising that all curricular media, textbooks or software, arrive on our doorsteps with built-in biases. It is worth asking whose perspectives are built into those words and images. It is also important to question whose voices have been ignored, and whose worldviews are honored or ridiculed. Educational specialists have long thought about curriculum as a multilayered experience, and recognize that an official curriculum (the accepted doctrine), an operational curriculum (what and how educators actually teach), and a hidden curriculum exist together. The hidden curriculum is described as "issues of gender, class and race, authority, and school knowledge, among others. The lessons that the hidden curriculum teaches include lessons about sex roles, . . . distinction between work and play, and which children can succeed at various kinds of tasks . . ." (Posner, 1992, p. 11). This section will look at the perspectives found in textbooks and software as examples of the ways in which seemingly simple teaching resources exacerbate the challenge to educational equity.

Textbooks

Educators have traditionally depended heavily on textbooks, but it is essential to consider who has written them and which lenses the authors have used to filter the ideas, words, and pictures found in those textbooks. Historically, a monocultural perspective has dominated our history books, due to European-influenced history of the United States and other Western nations. We can easily remember the debates and discussion generated when E. D. Hirsch (1987) published his *Cultural Literacy: What Every American Needs to Know.* His notion that a set of important works from a Western perspective could be identified for every person in this country, and that his list ignored authors of color and multicultural themes was completely abhorrent to many educators.

This "back to basics movement" has had a profound effect, and this is particularly true in urban or inner-city schools. Kohn (1999) reported that such inner-city schools are particularly vulnerable to this direct instruction or programs that stress memorization. "Minority children are also more likely than their peers to spend time taking multiple-choice standardized tests and to be taught a low-level curriculum designed around those tests" (p. 9). Equally important, the textbooks and materials may be designed to ignore these students' cultural background. In an interview, Elizabeth Martinez, a Chicana writer, activist, and teacher, remarked, "A lot of educators do not mind promoting tamales in the cafeteria on Cinco De Mayo. But they do not talk about how the Mexican war was started or on what pretext" (Madigan, 1993, p. 171). David Bleich, in a thoughtful analysis of textbooks, stated, "the language of the text as well as the messages become part of a movement in which mercantile interests overrule pedagogical needs" (cited in Gale & Gale, 1999, p. 5).

Software

As we consider current software, it is important to first describe the various types of software that schools commonly use. Means and Olson (1995) presented four ways in which technology can expand learning opportunities. They identified:

- Tutorial uses (where the technology does the teaching)
- Exploratory uses (where the student wanders through the information, perhaps encouraging a discovery approach)
- Tool uses (where the curriculum does not reside in the software but rather in the instructional activities)
- Communication uses (where students and teachers are able to access human and non-human resources)

We can consider these possibilities within the context of specific types of software. One type of software is considered drill, or skills software. These may be valuable for practicing new learning or for reinforcing basic skills. For example, software may teach sounds and letters, reinforce multiplication facts, or test specific comprehension questions. Sometimes these types of software come packaged together in Instructional Learning Systems (ILS), which also provide tracking software so that a teacher might know how far each student progressed on specific tasks.

Other software packages can be considered exploratory or collaborative. These might provide students with problem-solving activities, simulations, or higher-order thinking tasks. For example, these might present real-world problems in a context in which the students may have control to solve the problems. Two examples, both of which have been around for a long time, represent this category well. The first established the students as owners of a lemonade stand, and individually or in small groups they had to purchase supplies and attempt to make a profit. The second created a scenario in which the deer population of a small town was becoming a problem. Groups of students represented various stakeholder groups (town council, home owners, animal rights activists). They had to create various policies, and then respond to the results over several trials.

The last common group of software is tool software. This includes word processing, spreadsheets, databases, drawing programs, and telecommunications packages. These tools are open-ended, and allow students to use them in myriad ways to accomplish creative and problem-solving activities. Each type of software has its place in the total use of technology in the classroom.

It may not be difficult to find evidence of bias in textbooks, but software often appears to be completely neutral. After all, students just play a game or create a story with a computer. But in reality, technology is little different from textbooks. Multiple media are now firmly entrenched in the classroom, and all these media together convey a perspective that must be addressed. Metaphors arrive on the doorstep, or the desktop, within any prepared educational material, and this needs to be addressed by the educator (Bowers, 1988, 2000; Hanor, 1998). "Within computer applications, greater opportunities need to be provided for students to interact on a personal level, as themselves, rather than as previously defined and limited characters" (Hanor, 1998, p. 69). For example, "A knowledge of the educational uses of computers . . . should also involve an understanding of how this new technology alters the cultural ecology of the classroom as well as influences the larger culture" (Bowers, 1988, p. 2). Significantly, Roszak (1994) suggested that when students sit in front of the computer, the relationship to consider is not that between the computer and learner, nor is it between the instructor and the learner. Rather it is between the mind of the student and the mind of the people who created the computer and wrote the software. The impact the authors of software have had goes far beyond an individual student and a single computer. Bowers (2000) stated,

The failure of cyberspace proponents to understand how computers have effected a cultural transformation that causes us to overshoot the sustaining capacity of our natural systems and undermine culturally unique modes of knowledge points to educational shortcomings we urgently need to address (p. 11).

Bowers (2000) also stressed a serious concern for the ways in which language in software continuously influences the students. He explained that software misses the "appreciation of differences in cultural ways of knowing, an understanding of metaphorical language and cultural intelligence, or even the cultural mediating characteristics of print-based technologies such as computers" (p. 125). The software may reflect a specific perspective. Bowers (2000) identified the hidden messages in software for "competitive decision making, extreme subjectivity, and consumer tendencies" (p. 124). For example, in the two examples that opened this section we might recognize a Western or capitalist perspective, as one goal was to make money and the other was to "control" animal populations.

As each software program is explored, educators should ask a variety of questions such as:

- What assumptions are embedded in the program's goals?
- Whose perspectives dominate the program?
- Whose voices are left out of the dialogue and program?
- What messages are promoted?

After reconsidering the educational materials in the classroom, it is worthwhile to look carefully at the types of activities that are designed to acknowledge the challenges and move forward to meet the goals of equity for all students.

Revising the Curriculum with Technology

If classrooms do face challenges with traditional textbooks and software programs, then what options exist for educators and students? One answer may be to effectively use information technologies to change the curriculum in dramatic ways. Everyone has no doubt heard the saying that technology will help change the teacher from the "sage on the stage to the guide on the side." That is not enough of a reason to radically change teaching, unless the outcomes of these changes have credibility. Certainly the use of technology might strive to go beyond the contention of Cummings and Sayers (1995) where they suggested that learning to use the Internet would lead to a more innovative and productive work force who would be able to effectively deal with information.

Muir (1994) said, "We know that students learn by constructing their own knowledge through using information in meaningful ways. This new knowledge must be built directly on what each student already knows, and the student must see the connection between the new ideas and their own world" (p. 30). Peters and Lankshear (1996) expand this notion by commenting, "This participatory and interactive medium potentially offers new accessibility to the power to inform and be informed: not as a commodity or fixed possession bought and sold under the logic of exchange value" (p. 64).

Torrez (2000) suggested that "multimedia and computer technologies provide the capacity for presentations with dazzling graphics and engaging interactivity" to overcome the stereotypical negative images and non-native language materials still found in most classrooms (p. 5). She also stated that the mix of these media can "enhance the drive to learn, provide students with access to a rich diversity of information and ideas, and enable them to reach across community and cultural borders" (p. 6). Technology also offers the possibility of using current events in creative ways. "An article appearing in yesterday's newspaper or an online news service can spark today's discussion of the possibility of life on other planets or the impact of a Supreme Court ruling" (Brinkley, 1999, p. 1).

Empowering Activities

Technology has enormous potential to increase students' ability to perform complex tasks, enhance motivation and self-esteem, spark collaboration, and encourage coaching and advisory roles for educators. The reality is that active learning is rarely a neat process. Students engaged in such activities often create busy, noisy, and messy classrooms. It's important to recognize that this kind of learning takes practice for both teacher and students. Activities and learning environments must be carefully guided and structured, so learners are fully engaged. In exploratory instruction, the structure of the classroom seems informal—perhaps even disorganized—but student learning is still taking place, as the teacher has carefully created the environment. Educators must recognize that if students are investigating and asking questions, writing about what they're learning, and doing those things within an authentic context, then they are additionally learning to read and write and think. In such a classroom,

- Students don't "learn" technology; technology provides the tools for authentic learning.
- Students are active, rather than passive.
- Educators encourage a diversity of outcomes. Educators evaluate learning in multiple ways, rather than traditional paper-and-pencil tests.
- Educators and students move from individual efforts to being part of learning teams, which may include students from all over the world.

Educators have spent considerable time and energy to overcome the negative effects of textbooks and software, as well as to create new models of curricular activities that infuse technology in pedagogically sound ways, specifically those that strive to overcome the traditional discrepancies that have plagued some of our students. Some of the projects and activities presented here are research based and others are reports of experiences, but all are worthy of examination. Overall they represent efforts at bringing digital equity to the classroom and individual students.

Hickenbotham and Schamber (2001) described a project in which students on a Native American reservation learned about their own Lakota culture and connected with students in Australia to explore other cultures, all within a math and science curricular context. The authors reported, "The Internet allows Native American children to communicate, share their culture, and gain a voice for themselves. . . . Once teachers truly understood the Lakota culture, they were able to use technology to help students understand cultures beyond the reservation" (p. 23). They summarized their experiences by stating, "With access to the world through technology, the Native American students were finally equal participants in learning despite their isolation." (p. 27).

In other projects, rural and geographically isolated students also were able to learn about their own cultural roots:

> Students in the Kake, Alaska school district (located on Kupreanof Island, 95 air miles from Juneau and not connected by road to any other community) are reviving their Tlingit language and culture using the Internet. Students at Bullard High School in the farming valley of Fresno, California are using the Web to study the immigrant experience, Hispanic culture, and John Steinbeck's novels (Katz & Serventi, 2001, p. 37).

Cifuentes and Murphy (2000) conducted a study of two educators and their students in an effort to investigate the results of cross-cultural collaboration. The educators developed curricular activities and multicultural activities. The students, one class predominately Hispanic and the other predominately Caucasian, engaged in a year-long set of activities through teleconferencing, multimedia development, and electronic communications. The results demonstrated that the educators developed "empowering multicultural relationships while their students developed multicultural understanding and positive self-concept" (p. 69).

Students whose native language is not English often face particular challenges in most classrooms. Researchers have demonstrated some promising results regarding this challenge. Gonzalez-Bueno (1998) discovered that students learning Spanish who used e-mail assignments employed a greater amount of language, used a greater variety of topics and language functions, demonstrated a higher level of language accuracy, had more student-initiated interactions, and used more personal and expressive language. Similarly, Sayers (1995) investigated activities that supported intercultural and multilingual activities through telecommunications. He found that these activities have great potential to support second language learning and offer insights into many cultural and familial resources.

Other projects have tackled the difficulties that students have when they have limited English proficiency and also travel from school to school within migrant experiences. Knox and Anderson-Inman (2001) reported on the first three years of one federally funded program. This program, Project In Time, identified its goal as providing wireless note taking in traditional classrooms in Oregon secondary schools for migrant students. This stemmed from the challenge to secondary students who frequently arrive with little English, and most of what they do know is the informal language useful outside of classrooms. The academic vocabulary may be extremely difficult, and thus the students fall further and further behind. The results of the project demonstrated that participants had higher grades and appropriate academic work, access to academic enrichment, confidence in first and second languages, and that they had gained skills in appropriate, student-centered technology.

A similar project was investigated by *ESTRELLA (Encouraging Students through Technology to Reach High Expectations in Learning, Lifeskills, and Achievement). *ESTRELLA is a laptop computer project designed for secondary school migrant farm worker students (Kinser, Pessin, & Meyertholen, 2001). Students have the opportunity to continue their education and work on essential skills while they are traveling, and they are able to use the modems to keep in touch with educators and other students. Although the primary goal of this project was to improve test taking, it also provided students with other opportunities to use the technology for more creative activities.

In many classrooms educators use a technique called collaborative learning. This instructional model uses small groups of students as a way to achieve academic goals. The students support each other's learning, accomplish tasks that may not be possible individually, and learn how to cooperate in ways that replicate the work of adults in many occupations. Proponents of collaborative learning believe that students benefit from exchanging ideas and also are able to achieve critical thinking beyond the skills of one person. In a classroom setting collaborative learning may encourage more participation by minority and female students, as well as provide opportunities for students to use their own unique perspectives into these project-based learning experiences. In creating situations using technology, this type of learning may further enhance the goals of equitable use of the tools, as well as provide individuals with the chance to develop their own abilities and self-esteem.

Harris (1998) described many types of curricular activities that use technology to create, support, and communicate, many of which employ collaborative learning in project-based situations. She provided a framework with which to identify and understand them. This framework divides possible learning projects into three dominant types of learning acts with eighteen individual structures subdivided from those three:

- **Interpersonal exchanges**—keypals, global classrooms, electronic appearances, telementoring, question-and-answer activities, impersonations
- **Information collection and analysis**—information exchanges, database creation, electronic publishing, telefieldtrips, pooled data analysis
- **Problem solving**—information searches, peer feedback activities, parallel problem solving, sequential creations, telepresent problem solving, simulations, social action projects

Individual educators may desire to participate in the type of collaborative projects described above, yet may be uncertain as to how to establish the connections to accomplish such a project on their own. Several organizations have created projects for educators and students, around every imaginable topic, subject, or educational goal. Thinkquest, for example, promotes youth-centered learning on the Internet. Students work together in teams and use the Internet to investigate a topic they have chosen in science, mathematics, literature, the social sciences, or the arts. They then create a website for their peers in classrooms around the world. These projects allow the learners to interact with educators, parents, and other interested adults, but they take responsibility for defining, managing, and implementing the project, as well as for publishing the results on the Web. These projects afford groups the opportunity to design, create, and develop in ways that encourage individuals to participate and grow. They also encourage classrooms and teachers to partner with community support organizations.

Another project, The International Education and Resource Network (I*EARN) has provided connections and opportunities for classrooms around the world to engage in meaningful educational projects. It offers structured environments, primarily focused on collaborative service-learning projects, and provides interaction within a culturally diverse community. Students and educators communicate electronically and share their activities and personal stories, as well as discuss the impact of their projects on the planet. This type of organization allows all students to participate at their own levels, and to contribute their personal perspective, as well as to learn in authentic activities. This represents one more way that technology can be used for innovative and equitable projects.

These two projects represent different types of activities in their goals and expectations. Also, participation in Thinkquest is free, while I*EARN charges a small yearly fee. In light of the goal to reach digital equity, it is worth considering which schools may have discretionary funds to pay participation fees, regardless of how reasonable they may be. On the other hand, it is always possible to request reduced fees, or to use this activity as a way to communicate with the community for partnerships. Additionally, it is worth noting that many other projects and organizations do exist, and these are merely two examples.

Special Needs Students

Students with special needs have always faced significant challenges. Curriculum activities have most often focused on the basic skills and ignored more creative and innovative issues (Donlevy, 2000). However, the use of technology has changed this in significant ways. In one study, Lewis (1997) compared the use of technology and software from 1987 to 1994 in California schools. She found that students with disabilities used computers with special education teachers, with peers in general education, and in a computer lab. In 1987 educators reported that the primary software packages in use were math drills, but by 1994 tool software (that is, software that does not contain curriculum within it, such as word processing software) was more common.

This study also reported dramatic changes in the effects for students with disabilities. In 1994 educators reported that students with physical or sensory impairments and communication disorders were able to use technology to compensate for their learning challenges (Lewis, 1997). Further, respondents reported that technology allowed students to participate more fully in general education activities.

Bottge and Hasselbring (1999) used a multimedia approach based on the Jasper series (Cognition and Technology Group at Vanderbilt, 1997) to teach mathematics to secondary school students with learning disabilities. These students solved complex problems by working as members of a team using a variety of technology support systems. In a research project focused on writing skills, Zhang (2000) worked with students with learning disabilities and written language deficits using a specially designed program as a writing tool. The students showed positive gains in their writing behaviors and written products, as well as their attitudes towards themselves as writers.

Technology Projects and Gender Issues

As mentioned previously, girls and women are significantly underrepresented in the field of technology and in technology-related classes. Educators and researchers are making strides, however, to reverse these trends. One project, Eyes to the Future: Middle School Girls Envisioning Science and Technology in High School and Beyond, uses a website that links middle school girls of all abilities with female high school role models and with women professionals in science and technology fields. This project, described in more detail in Chapter 9 of this book, supports middle school girls as they meet in after-school clubs to explore issues of gender; communicate electronically with high school and adult role models; engage in science activities related to adult mentors' careers; and create an online magazine to tell other middle school girls about science and technology.

Another project, Techbridge (also discussed in Chapter 9), provides a student-centered approach to technology, math, and science for middle school girls. Techbridge supports girls by teaching them technology skills, helping them make the transition to high school, and helping them plan for the next steps to college and careers.

In summary, this section presented a variety of projects and research studies that are making a difference for all students. Essentially, equality in technology-enhanced education provides opportunities for all students, regardless of historically limiting characteristics, to use technology in creative ways that value and include their personal backgrounds. It is of note that these experiences can lead to higher academic achievement for all students. The evidence suggests that positive steps do make a difference, and reinforces the notion that digital equity is an essential goal for our schools to achieve.

Avoiding Bias In Educational Materials

Educators have a responsibility to thoughtfully analyze and evaluate the materials that are used in their classrooms. Organizations and groups have created checklists of questions to ask when choosing or evaluating materials. The authors have adapted one of the best of the checklists, and it is presented here as a way to heighten awareness of the subtle ways that materials may send unwanted messages or reinforce stereotypes.

Ten Quick Ways to Analyze Children's Books for Racism and Sexism

The Council on Interracial Books for Children has provided this list of tips on examining published material for children. Try this list in your examination of one or more children's titles and other media. Compare your notes with those of others.

1. Check the Illustrations
   A. Look for Stereotypes
      You might find an extreme case, such as illustrations with captions denoting the "naked savage" or "primitive brave and his squaw." You might find variations of these stereotypes, such as the "naked savage with sombrero."
   B. Look for Tokenism
      Do native or other ethnically diverse people look like brown Anglos? Do all faces look the same? Or, are people of each race portrayed as having unique features?
   C. Who's Doing What?
      Are non-White peoples always in subservient roles? Are females inactive— in the background?
2. Check the Story Line
   A. Standard for Success
      Does only the acculturated Native person succeed? To gain acceptance, does a Native person have to be extraordinary? What are friendships like between

Native and non-Native people? Does the Native person do most of the teaching, forgiving, and understanding?

B. Resolution of Problems

How are problems presented? Conceived? Resolved? Are people of color or Native origin considered the problem? Are poverty and social problems seen as inevitable or are their reasons explained? Does a White person resolve all the problems?

C. Role of Women

Are women depicted as intelligent, strong? Do they succeed only through their relationships with men or through their physical appearance? Could the same story be told if the gender roles were reversed?

3. Look at Lifestyles

Is being Native or non-White depicted as negative?

4. Weigh the Relationships between People

Are Whites the leaders or those who make the important decisions? How are family relationships depicted? Who is in charge? Why?

5. Note the Heroes

If there is a native person as a hero or heroine, what factors cause them to be so designated?

6. Consider the Effects on a Child's Self-Image

Would a child's self-image be affected? Would a child's aspirations be limited?

7. Consider the Author's or Illustrator's Background

Do they have backgrounds that would prepare them to work on this subject?

8. Check out the Author's Perspective

No one is totally objective.

9. Watch for Loaded Words

This also includes sexist words.

10. Look at Copyright Date

Checking the copyright date may alert you to bias common in that time period.

Source: Adapted from The Council on Interracial Books for Children, 1841 Broadway, New York, New York, 10023

Steps Forward and the Larger Context

The information in this chapter has identified some serious concerns in the area of pedagogy and equity in education, particularly in schools with a high percentage of minority or poverty students. The problems are exacerbated when educators do not recognize the disparity that exists and use technology in ways that may, in fact, increase that disparity. Although it is true that the projects presented are noteworthy and significant, they only affect a small number of students. The problem is widespread, and thus requires systemic and sweeping solutions. What steps can be taken to change the current situation? Linda Darling-Hammond (1999b) noted, "Educational outcomes for minority children are much more a function of their unequal access to key educational resources, including skilled teachers and quality curriculum, than they are a function of race" (p. 28). The evidence presented here confirms her opinion. Unfortunately, teachers in poor inner-city and rural schools meet more challenges in integrating technology into their classrooms, first because the infrastructure and technological support have been much less available, but also because they have had significantly less training than teachers in wealthier schools (Kleiman, 2000).

Further, teacher's professional development in technology and the use of computers to teach higher-order thinking skills were both directly and positively related to academic achievement in mathematics and the social environment of the school, according to Wenglinsky's research for ETS (1998). He analyzed a national database of student test scores and classroom computer use. A major conclusion was that students whose teachers had technology-related professional development experiences outperformed students whose teachers did not. In addition, students who used the technology for problem posing and solving gained in mathematics test scores, while those who used the technology for drill and practice saw no rise in their achievement scores. Swain and Pearson (2001) summarized this by stating,

> We must educate all teachers and students to use the computer as a productivity tool as well as a tool for learning, research, networking, collaboration, telecommunications, and problem solving. Always using drill-and-practice software does not allow students to participate in meaningful and engaging learning environments (p. 12).

Teachers understanding how to use technology, and how to use it effectively, are not enough. Hanor (1998), based on her research, suggested,

> Observation of students at work at computers must go beyond the superficiality of observing opportunities for choices that spring from within the software and educational applications. Additional strategies are needed to ascertain how students are making choices, making sense, and creating meaning (p. 70).

Closing Thoughts

This chapter examined the use of curriculum in our schools, and in particular, the differential uses of technology in schools. The evidence is overwhelming that schools with primarily minority or poverty students do not have equal opportunities to explore the potential of technology to add relevant, authentic, and exploratory curriculum. Next it explored the ways in which traditional textbooks and educational software promote a uniform and frequently monocultural perspective. Last, this chapter presented research results and testimonials on the ways in which technology supports emancipatory curriculum, in particular with minority, special needs, or other students who may have been left out of the adoption of technology. It is important to also consider the differential professional development that educators get in various types of schools.

Educators have a responsibility to offer curricular opportunities to all learners, but the educational community has a responsibility to provide the essential conditions that support and encourage those activities. It is important that we identify the problems, and then begin to tackle them so that each learner can make the most of his or her future.

11 Professional Development for Change

CARMEN L. GONZALES

STEVEN A. SÁNCHEZ

FOCUS QUESTIONS

1. What technology and integrative capabilities do educators need and what kinds of professional experiences will lead to the acquisition of these capabilities?

2. What policies ensure that all students have equitable access to technology and to teachers who know how to integrate appropriate technologies in a meaningful way?

3. How can engagement with digital age tools narrow the gap between the "haves" and "have-nots"?

4. When developing professional development programs, what strategies should be included to address the needs of diverse groups?

This chapter explores professional development as a critical component in the complex puzzle of educational reform. While a technological revolution has fundamentally transformed society, many students and teachers continue to be left behind. Minority and rural students continue to be the "have-nots" in this emerging digital world, enlarging an already significant learning divide. New models of sustained professional development for teachers and administrators can serve as powerful forces to bridge this learning divide. Skilled educators who are well prepared to use available technologies as part of an engaging curriculum can ensure that all learners, regardless of circumstances, have the opportunity to develop essential competencies, fulfill their potentials, and ultimately, secure and maintain productive employment in the twenty-first century.

As has been pointed out in previous chapters, surveys tracking the growth of computer connections in homes and schools have provided a picture of what the U.S. Department of Commerce calls a growing trend for digital inclusion (Mineta, 2000). Consequently, the digital divide may appear to be closing. However, not all teachers and students have access to the same equipment and network connections. In addition, many educators lack the technological skills that would allow them to use these digital tools to their fullest potential. Because the classroom remains the sole access point to technology for many learners, a well-conceived professional development model that addresses these issues is critical to achieving our nation's educational goals.

The literature suggests that sustained, lasting change in teaching performance is most likely to occur when teachers participate in a support network with partners. Building communities of learners that allow educators to share ideas and resources with their peers can open the isolated classroom and support new models of teaching (Fullan, 1993, 1999; Means & Olson, 1995). In this chapter, we will examine the impact of school reform and professional development experiences on the ability of teachers to incorporate new technologies that change teaching and learning. We will also share our interpretations of why these changes are important in addressing the learning divide and how best to sustain them. In addition, we will discuss policy issues, funded initiatives, and quality professional development opportunities that focus on ensuring equity. Finally, we will provide examples of exemplary practice in the areas of professional development and technology that explicitly address equity issues.

Technical and Human Infrastructure

> *"History does not suggest that equitable access to and use of the newest technologies will happen automatically or even easily"* (Neuman, 1990)

As had been pointed out in previous chapters, surveys tracking the growth of computer connections in homes and schools have provided a picture of what the U.S. Department of Commerce calls a growing trend for digital inclusion (Mineta, 2000). However, these statistics continue to suggest that minority groups and the poor still lack adequate access to information and communications technologies. Blacks (23.5 percent) and Hispanics (23.6 percent) lag behind their White (46.1 percent) counterparts, and 12.7 percent of households earning less than $15,000, as compared to 86.3 percent of households with an annual income of at least $75,000, are connected. In the fall of 1999, 95 percent of U.S. public schools reported connectivity to the Internet, up from 35 percent in 1994. However, in schools with high levels of poverty, only 39 percent of instructional rooms had Internet access, compared to 62–74 percent of instructional rooms in schools with lower levels of poverty. In addition, statistics continue to show that the nation's poorest schools are least likely to report use of the Internet by both educators and students. These numbers point out the continuing inequity for a significant number of students and sound an alarm for schools that remain the only access point for many students.

While we have seen considerable changes to the technical infrastructure in schools, we have not seen analogous changes to the human infrastructure. In a 1995 comprehensive nationwide study, the U.S. Office of Technology Assessment (OTA) indicated that teachers, who are perhaps the most valuable part of the education equation, are often overlooked during the acquisition of school technology (OTA, 1995). On average, districts devoted no more than 15 percent of technology budgets to professional development. The OTA report suggested that this figure should be closer to 30 percent. Yet, in many schools and districts across the nation, the figure spent on professional development is only 3 percent (Carvin,

2000b). Employing technology to best effect in the classroom requires that educators understand and use these tools themselves. Thus, not only must the funding for the technology infrastructure be in place, but also for the human infrastructure.

Despite having increased access to technology in schools, a substantial number of teachers report that they do not use computers and other technologies regularly for instruction (Smerdon et al., 2000), with usage being lowest in minority schools. In the same study, the authors confirmed earlier findings that teachers in high-minority and/or high-poverty schools were less likely to use computers and the Internet than their counterparts in low-minority and/or low-poverty schools. For example, in schools with 50 percent or more minority enrollments, only 41 percent of teachers used computers or the Internet for research, compared with 57 percent in schools with less than 6 percent minority enrollments.

Studies on learning technologies have typically focused on access in schools, with much less research available on technology use in the classroom. The research that does exist suggests that as availability has grown, so has the number of teachers and students using technology (Levin, Stephens, Kirshstein, & Birman, 1998). However, even with the availability of computers and the Internet in schools, teaching and learning has not changed dramatically. Chris Dede (1998) suggested, "As educators, our task is to prepare our children to function in a future civilization created by the biggest leap in technology since the Industrial Revolution two centuries ago" (p. vi). To successfully achieve this goal, we need a sustained professional development initiative that prepares educators to integrate twenty-first century tools into their classrooms.

Professional Development: Building Learning Communities

> *"What teachers really need is in-depth, sustained assistance as they work to integrate computer use into the curriculum and confront the tension between traditional methods of instruction and new pedagogic methods that make extensive use of technology"*
> (CEO Forum, 1999)

Background—Reform Efforts

Traditionally, the role of education has been to impart information to students to enable them to obtain gainful employment. Teaching, based on behaviorism and the scientific management ideas of Frederick Taylor, viewed the student as an empty vessel to be filled with knowledge. Teachers were viewed as technicians who delivered a pre-developed curriculum with little deviation from the plan. During the last 50 years researchers such as Piaget, Dewey, and Vygotsky have tried to steer us from the notion of teaching as merely imparting information to a more inclusive pedagogy that views learning as an active process.

The realization that our educational system needed to change drastically came about with reports such as *A Nation at Risk* (National Commission, 1983). As a result, educators and policymakers rallied around the notion of school reform and the economic and social implications of the report's findings. Increasing emphasis on accountability and restructuring of schools continues to focus on improving student achievement. However, growing evidence suggests that the single most important factor in increasing student achievement is the quality of the teacher in the classroom (Archer, 2000; Darling-Hammond, 1999a;

Sparks, 2000; Sullivan, 1999). While schools and students have changed, teachers are still the driving force of instruction, and we must provide teachers with ongoing opportunities to reflect on and adapt their practice to an increasingly diverse student population.

In 1994, the Information Infrastructure Task Force concluded that American methods of teaching, learning, transmitting, and accessing information had remained largely unchanged from a century ago. The task force found the following conditions in American education, which persist today:

- The textbook is the basic unit of instruction. Absorption of its contents tends to be the educational goal.
- Instructors use "chalk and talk" to convey information. Students are often recipients of instruction rather than active participants in learning.
- Teachers work largely in isolation from their peers. They interact with colleagues for only a few moments each day. Most other professionals collaborate, exchange information, and develop new skills on a daily basis.
- While computers are a frequent sight in America's classrooms and training sites, they are usually used as electronic workbooks. Interactive, high-performance uses of technology, such as networked teams collaborating to solve real-world problems, retrieving information from electronic libraries, and performing scientific experiments in simulated environments, are all too uncommon.
- The U.S. education system is a conservative institution that slowly adopts new practices and technologies. Highly regulated and financed from a limited revenue base, schools are subject to local consent and serve many educational and social purposes.
- Computer technology, with its demands on physical space, teacher professional development, instructional time, and the budget, has slowly found a place in classroom practice and school organization.

Halley and Valli (1999) found that "an almost unprecedented consensus is emerging among researchers, professional development specialists, and key policymakers on ways to increase the knowledge and skills of educators substantially" (p. 127). There is agreement that meaningful reform will not occur until teachers are recognized as full partners in leading, defining, and implementing school improvement efforts (Boe & Gilford, 1992; Darling-Hammond, 1998; Fessler & Ungaretti, 1994). However, Mary Howard Futrell (1994), a former president of the National Education Association, found evidence that most reform initiatives have excluded professional educators from the development process, and instead have been developed by policymakers with little or no educational experience.

In response to ongoing concerns about education, Americans have attempted to reform the public schools many times. In fact, as Fullan (1993) noted, "the greatest problem faced by school districts and schools is not resistance to innovation, but the fragmentation, overload, and incoherence resulting from the uncritical acceptance of too many different innovations" (p. 197). Complicating the issue further are the politics of accountability, one of the major components of any reform initiative, which is often driven by factors outside the realm of education (Ginsberg & Berry, 1997). If teaching and learning existed as strictly technical, skill-driven tasks, easily regulated through bureaucratized policies and simple prescriptions, quick-fix practices would have resolved the many pressing challenges confronting the

American educational system. However, quick fixes and simple solutions that have attempted to circumvent the classroom teacher as the essential unit of change for school improvement have led to disappointing results (Berliner & Biddle, 1995).

As fundamental changes occur in the characteristics, conditions, and learning needs of students, knowledge about teaching and learning is also expanding dramatically. Thus, schools will continue to face ongoing pressures for accountability and reform (Berliner & Biddle, 1995; Smylie & Conyers, 1991). This rapidly shifting landscape of education has created an unprecedented need for the development of teachers' knowledge and skills. "It is critical that [learning organizations] develop appropriate curricula and instructional approaches to deal with student differences" (Knapp & Glenn, 1996, p. 215), systemic inequities, and the effect of technology in the classroom. Nonetheless, teachers are often cast into a system of "one-shot" professional development seminars, with no thought given to continuity between workshops, follow-up, or to whether this system meets the needs of either teachers or students (Bullough & Baughman, 1997; Kennedy, 1992; Little, 1993; Sparks & Hirsch, 1997). Loosely defined goals and traditional methods of implementation have often left teachers to return to classrooms without the capacity to apply new tools to change classroom practice.

The Potential of Technology

"Technology builds a bridge between our individual potentials and our ability to act on and influence our world" (Norton & Wiburg, 1998, p. 2), and can provide a path for American educational reform to close the learning divide. This reform continues to gain momentum, as teachers, school administrators, and policymakers abandon old paradigms and develop greater understanding of the inherent power of technology to radically transform teaching and learning.

However, the transformation processes without an accompanying focus on changing traditional attitudes about teaching and learning through quality professional development may never be realized. The President's Committee of Advisors on Science and Technology (1997), in its *Report to the President on the Use of Technology to Strengthen K–12 Education in the United States,* recommended that technology be used to support the current pedagogical shift in education toward a constructivist paradigm. While constructivism was a prominent methodology used by educators in the 1930s and 1940s (Rice & Wilson, 1999), renewed interest in this instructional practice may have grown due to the fact that sophisticated technological capabilities have caused educators to reconceptualize the teaching and learning process.

The move away from traditional methods of instruction is based on the premise that one can learn with, not from or about, technology, allowing computer-based technologies to become important tools in a constructivist learning environment (Boethel & Dimock, 1999). Classroom environments that support constructivist ideals require that learners have access to a wealth of materials, experts, and peers outside of the classroom walls. Educational technologies offer powerful ways to access these resources and engage the learner in authentic inquiry, thereby, promoting acquisition of higher-order thinking and problem-solving skills. In order to create such environments for students, according to Boethel and Dimock (1999), teachers need to experience learning in constructivist environments. As a result, teachers will learn new skills, will be able to apply confidently a new pedagogy to the teaching and learning process, and will recognize the limitations inherent in accepted practice.

Learning in the twenty-first century is a critical survival skill for all students. While mastering the basics of reading, writing, and arithmetic is still important, educational success can no longer be measured in isolation of essential information age competencies. Literacy must not be narrowly defined, but rather understood as a complex process where all learners emerge as:

- Information seekers, analyzers, and evaluators
- Problem solvers and decision makers
- Productive and creative users of technology tools
- Communicators, collaborators, publishers, and producers
- Informed, responsible, and involved citizens (New Mexico Department of Education, 1999).

It is essential that educational communities recognize the need to transform professional development opportunities for teachers, and especially those in high-minority and low-income schools. Guided by sound learning theory and clear program goals, professional development experiences can expand the capacity of teachers to translate theory into practice. Extensive training for teachers and administrators will have a direct impact on the educational lives of their students. Educators who are helped and encouraged to understand the medium will use its currency and authenticity to their advantage (Adams & Burns, 1999; McKenzie, 1999) and the advantage of those in their classrooms.

Thus, there must be a vital connection between technology and the professional preparation and continued development of teachers and educational leaders. In addition, it is essential to establish a robust technological infrastructure that allows the learner, both teacher and student, to transcend the traditional barriers of most classrooms so learning is not confined by location or circumstance. Norton and Wiburg (1998) noted that "designing learning opportunities that meet today's technological challenges while simultaneously using technology, as part of the solution, is one of today's most pressing demands" (p. 13). It is also one of our most important opportunities.

Engaging a Community of Learners

Is professional development a catalyst for change in classroom practice? It is, according to a U.S. Department of Education study, *Does Professional Development Change Teaching Practice?* This three-year study examined professional development programs developed to educate teachers to use specific instructional strategies. The report stated that those who participated in such programs increased their usage of modeled strategies in their own classrooms (Porter, Garet, Desimone, Yoon, & Burman, 2000). By exposing teachers to effective methods for the integration of technology, and by giving them time to learn and adapt those strategies, professional development experiences impact classroom practices. Teachers begin to use what they learn in the workshops, adapt it to their specific needs, and change their instructional procedures to better facilitate student learning. They then create similar settings for their students, such as collaborative work and student-initiated activity, as those experienced in the workshops (Becker & Reil, 2000). In addition, U.S. Department of Education reported that there is "a substantial benefit when teachers from the same school, department, or grade level participate together in technology-related professional development" (Porter et al, 2000).

It is time for education leaders and policymakers to focus not only on the technology divide, but also on emerging social and learning divides. There are no easy ways to eliminate social disparities, but without question, technology could do far more to help. New technologies, applied in targeted ways by knowledgeable educators, could make efforts to narrow the learning divide much more effective than they currently are. However, this will come only with substantial cost. Money spent on technology without investments in organizational change and professional development is essentially wasted (Morino Institute, 2001).

The Policy Arena

States and public school districts are beginning to recognize the need to transform the professional development experience for teachers and administrators. A series of national and state reports, written between 1993 and 1995, agreed that what teachers are expected to know and do has increased in amount and complexity (Abdal-Haqq, 1996). Additionally, "reform efforts place demands on teachers to improve their subject-matter knowledge and pedagogical skills; understand cultural and psychological facts that affect student learning; and assume greater responsibilities for curriculum, assessment, outreach, governance, and interagency collaboration" (Corcoran, as quoted in Abdal-Haqq, p. 1). In this context, teacher professional development practice extends beyond mere acquisition of new skills or knowledge; it also requires that teachers reflect critically on their practices, and fashion new knowledge and beliefs about content, pedagogy, and learning.

A State Perspective

A review of recent New Mexico educational initiatives provides a rich case study of the evolution of state supported or mandated professional development plans. Between 1985 and 1989, the New Mexico State Department of Education (NM SDE) and the New Mexico State Board of Education (NM SBE) developed both a Leadership Initiative and an Educator Support Plan. Their goals were to enhance the skills of teachers and administrators and to provide support and assistance to both experienced and new educators. Between 1991 and 1992, the Legislature became involved, enacting three initiatives relevant to professional development and systemic reform. The first of these, the Teacher's Opportunity Study, concluded that while effective professional development is crucial to their professional growth, teachers received far too few professional development opportunities, most of which were inappropriate to their work. Thereafter, the NM SBE organized the Systemic Change in Education Advisory Committee (SCEAC) task force to examine professional development.

In 1994, the NM SDE conducted a random survey of 1,100 teachers, principals, superintendents, and directors of instruction to identify the most critical professional development needs in the state. As a result, a Blue Ribbon Panel released a planning guide to assist schools and districts in the design and implementation of their educational and professional development plans. Between 1995 and 1999, the Legislature introduced additional bills to fund professional development days for teachers, with a Professional Development Act finally passing in 1999. In that year, the Legislature appropriated an additional $3 million into the

State Equalization Guarantee (SEG) and passed Senate Bill 110, requiring school districts to develop specific plans for professional development. In collaboration with external experts, the NM SBE developed a framework according to criteria developed by prior committees. Finally, districts submitted plans for approval before the release of their state funding.

National Policy

On the national front, the Technology Innovation Challenge Grant program, the Technology Literacy Challenge Fund program, and the E-rate program have supplied states and school districts with federal moneys for both technical and human infrastructure. Each of these programs has given states an opportunity to provide school districts—especially those with high poverty rates—with funds to help meet their most important technology needs.

The Technology Innovation Challenge Grants provide five-year funding for school districts in partnership with business, institutions of higher education, community organizations, and educational researchers. Since its inception it has funded more than 100 programs, several of which are now self-sustaining. In 1998, the focus of the funded projects was professional development, especially for schools and/or states serving large numbers of under-represented students, and students living in low-income communities. Twenty school district partnerships in seventeen states were awarded grants totaling $30 million, which provided them with the means to support and prepare new teachers to use technology effectively.

The Technology Literacy Challenge Fund (TLCF) and the E-rate program were both established in 1996. The former provided five years of funding to the states, with a focus on President Clinton's four goals to ensure that every student in every school would become technologically literate in the twenty-first century. The E-rate program's major objective was to make services, Internet access, and internal connections available to schools and libraries at discounted rates based on student income level and geographic location. As of February 28, 2001, $5.8 billion had been committed to E-rate applicants throughout the United States. Funds from these programs are disproportionately awarded to low-income and high-minority school districts; thus, they have helped to limit potential increases in social inequities caused by the digital divide (Puma, Chaplin, & Pape, 2000).

Model Programs

It has become clear that teachers do not need to be told what to do, but rather become active designers and participants in their professional development. Teachers need time to reflect on carefully researched models of good practice that support multiple strategies for integrating technology into the learning process. However, moving beyond the quick-fix mentality requires the implementers of any promising model to carefully examine the critical conditions that allow for the replication of a model under varying circumstances. Without this critical reflection, achieving similar results may not be possible if the capacity of the learning organization differs significantly from the local setting where the original model was successfully implemented.

This section highlights three professional development programs from three states: New Mexico, (statewide model), Texas (district/university collaboration), and New Jersey (district model). Each of the initiatives serves communities that have high-minority and low-income populations.

Model Program—New Mexico

In New Mexico, a minority-majority state, the Regional Educational Technology (RETA) program, operational since 1995, has emerged as a powerful initiative. RETA provides "professional development opportunities for teachers and administrators to improve teaching performance, educational leadership, and student learning through increased understanding and use of learning technologies" (Gonzales, Pickett, Hupert, & Martin, 2001, p. 1). This project, a collaborative effort between local districts, the New Mexico Department of Education, and New Mexico State University, serves as a model for constructive engagement. It employs digital age tools to enhance the capacity of individual teachers to acquire the critical technology literacy competencies as outlined in New Mexico's Educational Technology Plan (New Mexico Dept. of Education, 1999). Since its inception, the RETA program has addressed the digital divide, making a concerted effort to reach those schools earmarked as in need of improvement or in rural and high-poverty districts.

The RETA program has five goals, but its main goal is the professional development of teachers, administrators, and higher education faculty in the meaningful use of technology to improve content learning. To accomplish this goal, the RETA project provides weekend workshops offered throughout the state to help educators meet the challenges of implementing technology within established classroom traditions. The workshops use the model of teachers teaching teachers. They have been designed to provide opportunities for educators to experience excellent models of technology integration and to think systematically about the translation of those models into their districts. Each workshop focuses on a specific curricular area, and while exploring this sphere, teachers experience both a technological and a pedagogical model that they can adapt to their own classrooms.

RETA has also enhanced the learning potential of teachers through the creation of an online professional community. This online community not only addresses the ongoing learning needs of its participants, but also combats the problem of rural isolation. Further, the creation of regional support centers in institutions of higher education throughout the state has provided direct support for school administrators and teachers ready to capitalize on the opportunities provided by the emerging technologies. Access to exemplary curriculum models is available at http://reta.nmsu.edu.

Many RETA participants have remarked that one of the most useful aspects of the program has been sharing with others; thereby, being introduced to new ideas and instructional resources. Teaching can often be an isolating profession. The RETA workshops offer teachers the chance to meet with other teachers who share their concerns about and interest in technology. They also have time to talk with other teachers, discuss lesson plans, make contacts, and establish a support network.

The creation of support networks is especially important for successful technology integration because a teacher's ability to use these tools is often dependent upon numerous factors over which she has little or no control. These include her access to equipment, software, the Internet, and technology-enhanced curriculum that is appropriate for her grade level and subject matter; the support of her administration for experimenting with new teaching techniques; the expectations she is required to meet in terms of standards and content; the technical support available at her school, and her own technical abilities. Often, teachers need to work with other teachers who share similar challenges in order to get a practical sense of how to overcome these obstacles. One new RETA instructor noted that in her workshops the participants shared what they did in their classes. One thing she remembered enjoying as a participant was having that time to share and collaborate with colleagues. They would plan and develop curriculum together; it was a cohesive factor.

Not only is the RETA project helping to educate New Mexico teachers in the use of technology, it is also helping to establish a cadre of technology leaders throughout the state. Teachers who participate in RETA become active in their school and district technology committees, help the districts make decisions about technology purchases, help write grant proposals to acquire equipment and networking services, and provide technology instruction to their colleagues, to administrators, and to parents. These efforts are especially valuable in schools and communities in remote areas of the state (serving large-minority and low-income students), where technical expertise and leadership are sorely lacking.

Model Program—Texas

The University of Texas and the Austin Independent School District (AISD) faculty collaborated on the development of a scalable model for technology-infused educational preparation of middle and high school mathematics and science teachers. Funded by the U.S. Department of Education's Preparing Tomorrow's Teachers to Use Technology (PT3) program, the initiative allows cooperating teachers to reexamine their own practice as they provide modeling and mentoring to preservice teachers and other teachers in their schools. The project has three goals:

- To intensify, extend, and enrich the use of technology as an institutional and collaborative tool in the early courses in the majors of mathematics and science
- To institutionalize and fully implement the integration of technology in the three mathematics and science education professional development courses and in the conduct of student teaching
- To establish an intensive collaborative Technology Leadership–Learning Community among all teacher–educators in the UTeach program, to plan for technology infusion, to establish an integrated program, and to share expertise.

The project supports the University's UTeach Program for science and mathematics educators and facilitates collaboration between College of Education faculty, College of Natural Science faculty, and the cooperating teachers in the Austin Independent School District (AISD). Preservice teachers enrolled in this program receive a technology-rich experience, with technology integrated into their education methods courses, natural science content courses, and in the classrooms of their AISD cooperating teachers. Activities of this learning initiative include setting technology requirements and standards for the students' portfolios, supervising graduate students who assist faculty with technology integration, and coordinating necessary professional development experiences for cooperating teachers in the use of technology.

Twenty-eight skilled mathematics and science teachers were chosen to be PT3 Fellows. These teachers serve as cooperating teachers for the UTeach student teachers during the 2001–2002 school year and act as technology mentors to other teachers in their schools. AISD has provided each Fellow with a Dell notebook computer, a Palm Pilot, and an LCD projector for the department, as well as unlimited technical support throughout the school year. Fellows are compensated for their successful completion of a four-day technology training seminar provided by UT faculty and students and AISD instructional technology experts. The project has a website that acts as the hub of the emerging cybercommunity and provides a space where members can share expertise and access relevant science, mathematics, and technology education news.

Model Program—New Jersey

In February of 1996, Union City, New Jersey, a predominately Latino, inner-city community, received national recognition when President Clinton and Vice President Gore acknowledged the extraordinary accomplishments of this urban/minority school district. The unique blending of comprehensive school reform, technological innovation, and corporate sponsorship was cited by the President as a national inspiration and a model for educational excellence. In 1990, the district implemented a five-year plan that included a variety of reform efforts to bring about substantive changes in their educational system. Three main objectives were central to the district's plan: to create a print-rich environment; to recognize and promote reading and writing as integral to all content areas; and to encourage teachers and students to explore new ways of teaching and learning. One of their main goals was to create a curriculum that emphasized the development of thinking, reasoning, and collaborative skills throughout the content areas, rather than utilizing rote learning and whole-group/lecture modes of teaching. Teachers came together during the summer to develop the curriculum, which focused on students learning by doing. In 1995, they received NSF funding to continue their efforts with the Union City Online Project (Honey, Carrigg, & Hawkins, 1999).

In order to accomplish the needed reforms, they established effective professional development for integrating technology to support new models of teaching and learning. Honey, Carrigg, and Hawkins (1999) indicated that the professional development provided the teachers at Union City was a process, not an event, and focused on five stages:

- **Awareness**—broad and/or new concepts, such as whole language and cooperative learning techniques introduced in large groups
- **Practice**—a commonly used approach for technology integration
- **Sharing**—a time for teachers to discuss their experiences, both successful and less so, when integrating the new approaches (including technology)
- **Peer coaching**—experienced teachers open their classrooms to coach and team-teach with colleagues working with these new approaches
- **Mentoring**—a mentor is partnered with up to three protégés for a period of time

The district has implemented several successful teacher-to-teacher and teacher-to-student mentoring programs.

Common Elements of Model Programs

Some important aspects of these model programs can serve as a basis for others who are seeking to implement similar initiatives. These include:

- **Key parties working together:** Support from district leaders, administrators, and school boards enables teachers to engage in the program's activities. Teachers, who

share with other teachers the challenges of integrating technology, often find support
and knowledge that assists them in overcoming obstacles.

- **Respecting teachers as professionals:**   In order to create a network of knowledgeable education professionals who are willing to assume leadership and advocacy
responsibilities, a professional development program needs to treat the participating
teachers like the professionals they are.
- **Responding to feedback:**   Respecting teachers as professionals includes listening
to feedback and making changes in the program in response to that feedback. In this
way, the participants learn to see themselves as integral and respected members of the
program community.
- **Tailoring instruction and adapting content to meet the needs of diverse groups:**
Programs that seek to educate a diverse array of teachers must design professional
development that is flexible enough for instruction and content to be adapted to the
needs, interests, and experiences of the participants.
- **Close connections between curriculum and technology:**   Successful professional
development initiatives emphasize curriculum goals and integration over technological mechanics and mastery of software. In addition, teachers must engage in a re-
examination of their own practices and how to change them.

Conclusions and Recommendations

Educators who are provided with quality professional development are able to better integrate the ideas they have acquired into their schools and classrooms, affecting the teaching
and learning of countless children and narrowing the digital divide. Well-planned initiatives
encourage the development of networks of teachers who rely on one another in acquiring
technological skills, and who are more likely to model this collaborative approach in the
education of their students. "Research confirms that meaningful technology experiences
often elude academically struggling students" (Manzo, 2001, p. 22). We must ensure that
professional development models do not keep teachers captive to the same phenomenon or
further contribute to the learning divide.

Effective and ongoing professional development programs must become the norm.
Moving beyond the traditional quick fix will require the careful collection and analysis of
relevant data to determine best practices. This will ensure that professional development
focuses on important topics unique to the community of learners and challenges traditional
beliefs that impede reform and equity. Such practices can serve as a realistic driver for sustainable reform. The role that technology plays in this critical endeavor is unquestionable.

If our schools are going to succeed in meeting the educational demands of the twenty-
first century, policymakers and school administrators must understand the impact of technology on teaching and learning. However, inequities exist, not merely in access to computers
and the Internet, but also in the way teachers use computers to educate children (Johnston,
2001). Therefore, we must reflect deeply about which professional development models
can help educators to bridge the technology divide that currently exists in our schools and
universities. The challenge will be for reformers to create programs that are equitable, affordable, sustainable, and scalable, and that capture the opportunities offered by emerging
technologies.

12 Leadership for a Changing World

NANCY J. ALLEN

LINDA WING

FOCUS QUESTIONS

1. What characteristics are common to leaders whose institutions are making significant progress toward achieving digital equity?

2. What leadership models promote innovation in solving digital equity issues?

3. How can individuals and institutions foster the development of future leaders who will be effective in achieving digital equity?

The American Dream of Educational Equity and Excellence

Enabling every child in the United States to achieve at high academic levels is the American Dream. The American Dilemma lies in the glacial pace at which the dream is being fulfilled.

The dream calls for educators to recognize and address each child's unique interests and needs while at the same time teaching all children to be able to use their minds well and to contribute to the common good. In classrooms and schools scattered around the country, teachers and principals have made great strides in helping their students realize this dream; however, we have far to go to fulfill the dream for all students. We know, for example, that children must read well in order to access knowledge and skills across the curriculum, yet two-thirds of the nation's fourth-grade students scored below the proficient level of reading on the latest National Assessment of Education Progress (Donahue, Finnegan, Lutkus, Allen, & Campbell, 2001). Only 14 percent of children in poverty demonstrated reading proficiency, compared to 41 percent of other children. While African American and Hispanic fourth graders did not, on average, improve their reading achievement, white and Asian students did. The single most important dilemma facing educators today is how to close disturbing achievement gaps like these while simultaneously developing the capacity of more and more children to learn at increasingly high levels.

A potentially powerful tool for envisioning and implementing effective efforts to realize the dream and solve the dilemma is technology. Yet as this book indicates, our use of technology has yet to conceptually and materially alter how and to what standard we teach all our nation's students. Instead we have reproduced historical gaps in children's opportunities to achieve at high levels by creating a divide between those who have access to advanced digital learning experiences and those who do not have such access.

To reverse this trend, we must bring about continuous improvements in high-standards teaching and learning for every child. We must appropriately incorporate the advantages of technology into our instructional strategies with special attention given to enriching and accelerating the learning of children least well served by current practices. In accomplishing these goals, we would go far toward addressing the dream, the dilemma, and the divide. Continuous instructional improvements that address the unique and shared needs and possibilities of children are possible if public education is systematically and systemically transformed. The purpose of leadership is to create and foster environments in which these changes can occur.

The Role of Leadership in Creating a Culture of Change

There is consensus among business leaders, educators, policymakers and parents that our current traditional practices are not delivering the skills our students will need to thrive in the twenty-first century. As part of our efforts at school reform, we should apply technology's resources to develop the full academic abilities of all our students (CEO Forum, 2001).

Leadership is a key element in creating the systemic, sustained transformation of learning communities required to meet the challenges that face education today. Among these challenges is understanding how technology can help all students to realize their academic potential—excellence through equity. Other chapters in this book emphasize the importance of reconceptualizing the meanings of terms such as access, literacy, empowerment, and curriculum to reflect twenty-first-century realities and the needs of all students. They describe the changes in organizational structure and professional development that must come about to allow fruition of these ideas. Yet all of these necessary changes will remain ideals without the leadership of responsible, committed individuals willing to take the risks that always accompany change. Individuals in decision-making positions must not only be able to visualize an entirely new kind of learning, but must also provide the planning, commitment of resources, staff development, and reward systems necessary for the realization of these visions (National Technology Education Standards, 2001; Milken, 1999).

It is not easy to bring about change, and the use of technology in the powerful and equitable ways this book encourages requires a total revisualization of education. Tom Carroll, former director of the Preparing Tomorrow's Teachers in Technology Grant Program, describes this process within a sociocultural model. Schools are cultural in nature and, like all cultures, are highly resistant to change. When innovation occurs, existing cultures resist redesign by assimilating change to reinforce traditional roles, rules, relationships, and tools.

To introduce change, one can adaptively modify these cultural elements, but to truly transform an organization—which is what must occur if technology is to fulfill its promise—the organization must invent new roles, rules, relationships, and tools (Carroll, 2001). Technology is just such a tool, one that can help us reinvent education to meet the challenges of the twenty-first century for all students; but visionary, sustained leadership is essential if this change is to occur. It is not just the speed of innovation that is the issue, but also the direction and scope. All students must be included in this brave new world. "As the nation moves forward in digital learning environments, it is imperative that technology be used to remove existing barriers [between students because of race, ethnicity, gender, geographic location or economic status] and avoid creating new ones" (CEO Forum, 2001, p. 29).

Equity in Educational Opportunity: A Moral Imperative

Even if one considers equity issues based on self-interest alone, it is clearly in the interest of all Americans to provide all students with the education they need to contribute to the economy. To be competitive in today's economy, students leaving our schools must be literate in computer and information technology. Sixty percent of jobs today require skills with technology (Irving, 1999), and of the fifty-four jobs expected to experience the most significant growth in the next four years, only eight do not require technological fluency (U.S. Department of Education, 2000a).

We, the authors, believe, however, that most educators go beyond issues of economic self-interest and consider educational issues from a perspective of morality, which requires an even deeper commitment. As Beck (1994) writes, "We [school administrators] must wrestle with what it means to be moral leaders of school systems, individuals who embody justice and caring and demonstrate a genuine concern for the development of others and their communities . . ." (p. 8).

Access to and appropriate use of technology, as other chapters in this book have outlined, are clearly high-stakes and complex moral issues, requiring commitment that leads to thoughtful action. Thus, either from self-interest or from a sincere commitment to social justice, it is imperative that educational leaders consider and act on issues related to technology.

Defining Excellence in Leadership

A New View

Anderson and Becker (2001), in interpreting data from a study involving almost 900 schools across the nation, proposed that traditional views of leadership, focusing on personal charisma and strength, were inadequate for today's challenges. They identified three characteristics common to effective leadership for the twenty-first century: "interrelationships among distributed participants (Neuman & Simmons, 2000; Schultz, 2000), a leader's ability to cope with complex change (Fullan & Stieglbauer, 1991), and . . . [the establishment of] a culture of continuous learning (Senge, 1990)" (p. 2). They further suggested that such non-traditional leadership is essential; first, to foster technology integration in schools and second, to ensure that the instructional program that results accommodates the needs of diverse groups, including at-risk students of all types.

> For instance, a stated policy that the school is committed to equal access to technology could result in reduction of access discrimination. A more potent policy would specify details of different types of access and specifically mention the digital divide with respect to income, race, gender, ability, and disability (p. 4).

It is the responsibility of leadership not only to establish potent and equitable policies, but also to ensure that those policies are realized. In our review of research and our search for examples of effective leadership we identified six characteristics associated with effective leadership that leads to equity. These characteristics are vision, collaboration, informed reflection, creative resource management, courage, and perseverance.

The characteristics we identified are not inconsistent with those of Anderson and Becker; they are rather a different set of terms for explaining similarly observed phenomena. We are, so to speak, using different levels of magnification.

Vision

Effective leaders share certain identifiable characteristics and management styles. First in time, and perhaps in importance, is that effective leaders are visionary. "The only kind of leadership worth following is based on vision" (Depree, 1989, p. 133). Although it is common today for schools to articulate vision statements, this process in itself is not enough. True vision occurs when one believes in a cause larger than oneself (a characteristic listed by Hoyle, 1995, as imperative for leadership).

A leader's vision cannot be simply a dream; rather, it is "centered on the enduring beliefs and values that motivate individuals to strive for the highest ideals and performance" (Hoyle, English, & Steffy, 1998, p. 1). It is congruent with community values and priorities and developed collaboratively with all stakeholders (R. Wallace, 1995; Short & Greer, 1997). Such vision results in clear goals, articulated and integrated strategies for implementation, measurable outcomes, and a schedule of expected progress (Milken, 1999). Research shows that co-workers of visionary leaders are loyal (Hoyle, 1995), trusting of their colleagues and their leaders, like their jobs, work longer hours without complaint, and have higher performance ratings than staff working with non-visionary leaders (Conger, 1989). In other words, people like to work for visionary leaders, and they work hard.

William Mehojah is such a leader. Mehojah is an American Indian, a member of the Kanza tribe, and Director of the Bureau of Indian Affairs Office of Education Projects (BIA-OIEP). The BIA has 185 tribal schools across the nation in its educational network, serving 51,000 children in 23 states on 63 different reservations. The location of these schools spans the continent—from Maine to Florida, from Washington State to California. They are located in some of the most geographically isolated and remote areas of the nation, and some of the most economically depressed. Students often do not have English as a first language or, if they do, their language patterns are non-standard, having been derived from other linguistic traditions. They are culturally and ethnically different from the main stream and from each other, representing over 250 separate tribes (personal communication, March 21, 2001). They have historically experienced the highest dropout rates and the greatest academic underachievement of any cultural group in the United States (Tharp & Yamauchi, 1994). They have also had the least access to communication and information technologies. Historically, they have studied from materials that did not represent their culture, their language, or their traditional values (Allen & Crawley, 1998; Matthews & Smith, 1994). They clearly represent the other side of the divide.

Mehojah's vision was to increase achievement for American Indian students through culturally relevant curriculum mediated by technology. He, and others who shared his vision, believed that technology was a means through which classrooms could be changed from teacher-centered environments—in which content and learning models are derived from the dominant culture only—to student-centered environments, in which the history, values, prior knowledge, and learning styles of American Indian students are valued. As early as 1985, Mehojah, Paul Resta, and other dedicated individuals began experimenting with connecting tribal schools—by modem—for the purpose of professional development and sharing of resources. As the technology progressed, they continuously looked for ways to strengthen the network. By 2001, all 185 schools and 14 tribal colleges were on the network. To date it is the third largest network in the Department of the Interior, the oldest national network serving Indian schools and communities.

Perseverance

The effort to provide meaningful access for American Indian students also illustrates a second characteristic of effective leadership: perseverance. Leaders must have he commitment to persist under the most difficult circumstances if vision is to be realized (Anderson & Dexter, 2000; Hoyle, 1995). Networking BIA schools involved incredible perseverance and dedication by numerous individuals. That the goal was accomplished in spite of all these challenges is a tribute to BIA-OIEP leadership.

A recent BIA-OIEP briefing paper summed this process up as follows:

> By joining forces to foster community solutions, BIA, academia, and industry are readying American Indian schools and children for a 21st Century education without sacrificing closely-held values and traditions. So, what at first seemed almost impossible is about to be achieved—almost a quantum leap out of isolation into the 21st Century. And what's the worth of it? To look into the eyes of these children is to see the future of the American Indian people (Grover, 2001).

Collaboration

Effective leaders collaborate within their institutions, their communities, and with private, corporate, and other educational institutions. Collaboration within institutions involves sharing leadership roles and establishing and supporting horizontal organizational structures (Lambert, 1998). Effective leaders are no longer "power brokers" (Wheatley, 1992, p. 12), but rather they seek to develop relationship among all stakeholders, including staff, students, parents, and other community members.

Leadership in an effective educational system is not an individual quality. Many successful organizations have leadership teams composed of individuals who have formed leadership relationships, have staff who share mutual commitment of purpose, and achieve goals through common action (Donaldson & Sanderson, 1996; Fullan, 1993). Skills in shared decision making and in creating a supportive school and district climate that accommodates racial and ethnic differences are critical to community building, according to Lachman and Taylor (1995). In supporting this diffused model of power, effective leaders foster the development of leadership qualities among their staff, especially among those staff members from historically underrepresented groups.

Effective leaders collaborate within their communities and form strong partnerships with parents. Such shared leadership is especially important in relation to digital equity because the acquisition and integration of technology requires significant change, and thus requires strong community support for success. In addition, students learn more when parents are involved in their education (Horn & Chen, 1998). Parents of minority children, however, may not have a history of having been included in the education of their children (Allen & Crawley, 1998) and may require significant encouragement before they feel secure in fully participating in a leadership role.

Effective leaders actively seek partnerships with private and corporate partners and other educational institutions. Such partnerships are crucial in maximizing the impact of resources. The activities of Huston-Tillitson College (HTC) Department of Education may serve as a model for the kind of collaboration and distributed leadership that fosters digital equity. HTC has a long history in leadership in equity issues. When the school opened the doors of Allen Hall in January 1881, the building was " . . . the first building in the State of Texas for the higher education of Negroes, and also the first of its kind west of the Mississippi" (Huston-Tillitson, 1999, p. 15). It was also the first public education of any kind for people of color in Austin, Texas. Today, HTC supports its students with extensive technology, including distance learning facilities, wireless network capabilities in the residence halls and in other areas most utilized by students, computer labs in the majority of academic buildings, electronic blackboards and projection systems in classrooms, extensive distance learning opportunities, virtual museums, and individualized testing systems. It was recently designated by the 77th Legislature of Texas as the "Most Wired Historically Black Institution in Texas," the "lead institution in the state for high-tech applications and classroom instruction at private historically black colleges and universities" (Huston-Tillitson, 2001, Texas Technology Funds Awarded, ¶1). More importantly, HTC uses this technology to enhance a teacher education program that experiences very high success rates, as measured by percentage of students passing the state certification exam, by the success of teacher–graduates in the classroom, and by the retention rates of teacher–graduates (Loredo, personal communication, September 8, 2001).

A key factor in this success is the spirit of collaboration that permeates HTC. Dr. Judith Loredo, Dean of Academic Affairs and Chair of the Department of Education at HTC, and Dr. Larry Earvin, President of the College, work closely together and with the staff members to not only create a sense of being a team with the college of education, but also to foster interdepartmental exchange so that the advances in the Department of Education are shared throughout the college. A collaborative team spirit such as this is vital to the success of an institution if it is to surmount the barriers of the digital divide.

HTC also reaches out to the community. Among their technology-supported outreach efforts are shared courses via distance learning with other Historically Black Colleges and Universities in Texas, so that those institutions with fewer resources may benefit from HTC's resources. They provide teacher support and mentoring via distance learning to neighborhood elementary and junior high schools with high minority populations and have recently expanded a community program through which unemployed or underemployed individuals can enhance their computer skills in free classes sponsored by the college.

HTC could not have achieved this level of success without strong collaborations with state agencies and corporate partners. The Texas Higher Education Coordinating Board and the State Board for Educator Preparation have been a major funding source for technology the college, as have the SMARTer Kids Foundation, the Telecommunications Infrastructure Fund, Microsoft Corporation, Dell, and IBM. It is through collaboration—within the institution, among institutions, with the community, and with state and corporate partners—that HTC is able to produce teachers who can provide high-quality educational experiences through technology for their students because they have experienced such education themselves.

Informed Reflection

Effective leaders participate in informed reflection (Lambert, 1998). They are, in modern jargon, *data-driven*. Hoy and Tarter (1995) note that many school administrators fail to really consider the consequences of their strategic decisions and merely "muddle through" without a system of benchmarking their activities and goal accomplishments (p. 12). It is the ineffectiveness of such muddling through that has led to the current focus on benchmarks and standards in all areas, including technology integration. The CEO Forum, a group of business and education leaders committed to assessing and monitoring progress toward integrating technology in America's schools, suggests that schools measure and evaluate outcomes against standards and adjust accordingly. "Schools need to utilize clear standards, benchmarking and regular data-driven evaluations of educational improvements to evaluate performance and target areas for improvement and readjustment" (CEO Forum, 2001, p. 17).

The Community Capacity Project, developed by Lois Cohen at Portland State University (PSU) is an example of using informed reflection as a means to bridge the digital divide. Cohen, director of a PT3 project, realized that colleges of education were not the only entities using technology with students. Schools, libraries, community centers, after-school programs, and youth clubs often provide computer access and various levels of technology-supported learning. Corporate entities are also supporting community access, such as Intel's Computer Clubhouse initiative. Even supermarkets and malls have made Internet access available in some cities.

Cohen realized that gaps and redundancies in the geographic distribution of resources could result in inequity. She enlisted the help of teacher educators at PSU and their students in developing a database of information, so that all providers in the Portland area could make data-driven decisions regarding technology services. PSU is planning to extend the project by hosting meetings at which providers can find ways to collaborate and share resources, by offering free or low-cost courses in educational technology to providers, and by expanding the project into other geographic regions through working with partners such as Texas A&M University and the Benton Foundation.

Creative Resource Management

The process though which schools are funded in America tends to result in significant underfunding for underrepresented groups (Renchler, 1993; Riddle & White, 1994). Poverty, the criterion which researches have most closely and consistently correlated with underachievement, simply does not produce the local taxes needed to fund technology initiatives. Many states are trying to mitigate this effect by allocating additional resources to school districts based on their enrollments of students who are in poverty, who are English language learners, and/or who are physically or learning disabled (see Abbott v. Burke, 1998), or through requiring sharing of resources among school districts, as exemplified by the Robin Hood laws of Texas (Abbott v. NJ, 1998). These efforts are only beginning to have effect in schools. In addition, small or underfunded schools often do not have the expertise available to seek outside funding. Leaders who have been most successful in achieving digital equity have been aggressive and creative in identifying, obtaining, and leveraging funds from a variety of public and private resources. Each of the organizations we selected as examples have obtained funding from diverse sources in order to achieve their goals.

The Kids as Agents of Change Project provides such a model. Rogers and Hollard Independent School Districts, rural farming communities located in central Texas, rank in the bottom ten percent of wealth in the state. Six years ago the schools had almost no computer or information technology in the classrooms. What they did have was economic hardship, widespread health problems (ranking as one of the counties in the state as having the highest number of health risks), traditional pedagogy—and new, dynamic leadership. Today the teachers and students in these two districts present an outstanding model of systemic change through technology.

Dr. Carol Ann Bonds, a principal in Holland ISD, and other school leaders in the two-district consortium, decided that the first priority was meeting the health needs of the students to bring them up to a physical standard for academic excellence. They envisioned having clinics on site, but at that time they did not even have school nurses. They wrote a grant together and obtained funding for the clinics, but it soon became clear that they needed more frequent interaction with professional partners at larger hospitals. The next step was to compete for and win an Eisenhower grant, which allowed them to put in local area networks (LANs) and wide-area networks (WANs) for both districts to facilitate this interaction. As the Eisenhower grant neared completion, Bonds and her staff decided to build on this infrastructure to totally reconceptualize schooling in the districts. Their new vision, Kids as Agents of Change, focused on students as researchers and creators of knowledge through technology. Collaborative grant writing led to increases in technology infrastructure, hardware, software, and professional development, including money for both students and teacher to attend and to present at national and international conferences. Teachers used the increased technology resources "invisibly," integrating them into student-centered instruction (Bonds, as quoted in TCET, 1998).

The new instructional approach is centered in project-based efforts, in which students and teachers work collaboratively with online mentors in authentic scientific research and sophisticated data analysis related to real-life problems.

As a result of the changes initiated by Ms. Bonds and other leaders in this rural, poverty-ridden area students are becoming self-confident individuals, capable researchers, independent thinkers, and self-motivated learners. Scores on standardized tests rose after the program was institutionalized and have continued to stay high. Teachers have adopted more effective, more student-centered pedagogies and have become more interested in their own development as professionals (TCET, 1998). The schools are catalysts for change within the community. Such efforts spotlight the potential of technology to not only to enhance education, but also to empower students and the communities in which they live.

Courage

It takes courage to be a change-agent leader. Because such leaders are venturing into largely uncharted territory, success is not guaranteed. One must believe strongly enough in the vision to choose it as a priority, to commit resources—both human and material—that might have been expended toward other goals. There is always risk.

There is, for example, political risk. William Janklow is an example of a politician who was willing to take this risk to provide digital equity for students who often experience disenfranchisement because of geographic remoteness. During the mid-1990s, as governor of South Dakota, Janklow visualized distance learning as a way to bring quality education to even the smallest and most remote schools in a state. He led a campaign to wire every school in the state with T-1 lines and to provide the professional development for teachers crucial to effective change.

To provide the funding for this immense undertaking, Janklow obtained corporate donations, especially from the telephone and computer companies. In addition to wiring the schools, the state offered a month's immersion technology training to teachers in the summer, with the state paying for room and board, giving teachers $1,000 stipend, and sending another $1,000 to the home district of each participant for use as the administrator so determined.

The project was extremely visionary, but it has been rewarded with significant success. Nearly 3,700 South Dakota teachers have taken advantage of the training opportunity, about 41 percent of the state's teaching staff (Newsweek, 2001). In 2000 and again in 2001, South Dakota was named by the Center for Digital Government as the number one state in the nation for school technology (South Dakota Department of Education, 2001).

Corporate entities must also demonstrate courage if they are to be on the forefront of change for equity. Intel® Corporation showed such courage when they elected to fund a training center dedicated to the American Indian community in their innovative Teach to the Future initiative. This multi-million-dollar program is an effort by Intel®, with support from Microsoft Corporation, to prepare teachers and students globally to effectively use technology (Intel, 2001). The program has been very successful; however, in 2001, individuals from the American Indian community approached Intel officials with concerns that the program, as structured, would not be effective for Indian communities. The group asked Intel to consider funding a training center that was specifically designed to meet the special needs of this population. To do so was a political and financial risk by the Intel staff that supported this move, but after a year of planning, during which numerous adjustments had to be made, the Center for Education Technology in Indian America was established. To date training sessions operate at full capacity with a waiting list of teachers wanting to be trained. The courage Intel staff showed in funding this center has resulted in increased digital equity for this underserved population.

A Vision of Tomorrow's Leaders

We see the leaders of tomorrow as individuals who will follow in the path of the most effective leaders of today. They will exhibit vision, perseverance, collaboration, informed reflection, creative resource management, and courage in the pursuit of equity and excellence. At the same time, the leaders of tomorrow will need to break new ground in order to be effective, because standards-based reform calls upon future leaders to do what no other generation of leaders has done before.

Excellence in an era of standards-based reform is a moving target. The bar is constantly being raised. What is more, all students, irrespective of their poverty, race, language, or other demographic characteristics, are expected to excel, and it is the public schools that are held responsible. Standards-based reform thus converges with the social justice agenda to empower children through a rigorous education that challenges their minds, engages their hearts, personalizes the curriculum, and supports them in multiple ways to acquire the knowledge and skills they need to fulfill their hopes and dreams and those of their communities. This convergence presents future leaders with nothing less than the challenge and opportunity to transform public schools so that they finally make good on their promise—to insure equity and excellence for all our children. To rise to this challenge and to seize this opportunity, leaders of tomorrow will need to know and be able to do more than their predecessors in at least three ways.

First, the leaders of tomorrow must demonstrate understanding and mastery of the science and art of learning and instruction. They will need deep knowledge of the pedagogical implications of research findings on issues such as the relationship between a child's bilingualism and learning in the content areas and the interplay between racial identity formation and academic identity formation. They must understand the instructional techniques associated with fostering metacognitive development of children from diverse backgrounds by drawing upon their sociocultural capital and the analytical strategies involved in reflecting upon one's teaching in order to make changes in lessons that will more effectively engage students across a spectrum of learning needs.

Second, tomorrow's leaders must focus their work on bringing about teaching and learning improvements that are systemic and continuous. It will no be longer sufficient for leaders of the future to concentrate on merely removing barriers to quality educational opportunities. Tomorrow's leaders must support existing quality learning opportunities while developing and sustaining new opportunities.

The good news is that we now have evidence that quality teachers and quality teaching lead to quality learning opportunities. A substantial body of studies indicates that teacher quality is a stronger influence on children's achievement than poverty, race, or language (Darling-Hammond, 1999a). Additionally, an emerging body of work is adding to our understanding of the teaching strategies that constitute best practices (Kaplan & Owings, 2001). Given grossly inadequate numbers of good teachers across the country—in California alone, 42,000 teachers do not meet minimum quality standards, as indicated by their lack of preliminary teacher credentials (Bell, 2001)—the job of future leaders will very much be defined as the *lead teacher of teachers.*

Third, the leaders of the future must be effective in creating a new form of organizational culture—a culture of "distributed leadership" that concentrates on the ongoing improvement of teaching and learning at scale (Elmore, 2000, p. 11). That is, new leaders must shape, support, and sustain clusters of close working relationships among teachers, principals, and themselves such that each member of the cluster takes leadership responsibility, complementary to that of others, to improve instruction (Spillane, Halverson, & Diamond, 1999). The intended cumulative effect of these clusters, which all together will involve every teacher and every principal, will be to continuously raise the achievement of every single child in the school district.

Unlike other forms of shared leadership, such as school site councils that involve individuals in episodic meetings, distributed leadership will be part of the fabric of everyday work. All teachers and principals will be involved, whereas other collaborations, including school-based instructional leadership teams, are generally exclusive in membership. In addressing the core interests of teachers and principals to meet the learning needs of their students, distributed leadership has a deeper purpose than shared decision making around governance and management issues. Future leaders, in engendering and engaging in distributed instructional leadership, will not so much share power as expand it.

Fundamentally, we are, in Carroll's terms (2001), inventing a new sociocultural model of leadership as an essential component of our revisualization of education. In our view, the improvement of instruction must become the *sine qua non* of every new leader's work. Until leaders concentrate their efforts on astutely and systemically transforming teaching in concert with principals and teachers themselves, equity and excellence will remain elusive goals.

What does this new model of leadership mean for technology? As Honey has observed, teachers generally use technology to do "the basic work they are already doing" (2002, p. 27). If teachers mainly expect their students to do rote exercises, and there are many teachers who do, then providing more access to technology is very likely to result in their expecting students to do rote exercises using technology. If the digital divide were to be eliminated in terms of students' material access to technology resources, the more fundamental divide in students' access to quality teaching and learning would persist. Some students would still have quality teachers and quality teaching and other students—far too many—would not.

A more sanguine view is based on a different theory. If leaders support and reward teachers in working together towards instructional improvement with the goal of enabling all students to learn at high levels, then teachers would be engaged in developing their expertise in knowledge and use of best practices and in seeking to incorporate tools that would enable them to achieve their goals. This theory suggests that the divide in access to quality instruction and the divide in access to technologies will disappear, hand in hand, with technology always in service to the more fundamental goal. It is this perspective that informs our model of tomorrow's leaders.

The Challenges of Developing Tomorrow's Leaders

Our new model of leadership necessitates a new model of leadership development. Historically schools of education have prepared individuals to be educational administrators. Administrators work to ensure the efficient operation of structures and systems on behalf of the organization. Their job is conservative in purpose, to manage the status quo. The leaders we envision in this chapter work to dramatically improve teaching and learning, especially on behalf of children least well served by current practices. Their job is transformative in purpose. They are change agents who shape the future. While leadership with the purpose and the power we propose encompasses the knowledge, skills, and strategies of administration, the reverse is not true.

Moving from longstanding programs of educational administration to new programs of leadership development will present challenges to schools of education. Change is nearly always difficult. Moreover the market demand for educators who will head schools, school systems, and other learning organizations provides little incentive for schools of education to change how they conceptualize and develop leadership. We will look at the American superintendency as a case in point (Blumberg, 1985; Johnson, 1996; Murphy, 1991; Scott, 1980).

The first superintendents in the early nineteenth century acted primarily as clerks. They worked under the supervision of school boards, consisting of laypersons who not only had governing authority for the schools, but also made decisions about their day-to-day operations. In this era, school boards sought no special expertise in superintendents and superintendents needed no particular preparation for the job.

When the scientific management notions of F. W. Taylor and others took root in business in the early twentieth century, the demand for superintendents who had expertise in administration followed. School boards decided to cede their functional responsibilities to superintendents, while maintaining their power to hire employees, set policy, and raise revenue. Boards sought to hire superintendents who possessed technical knowledge and skills obtained through the study of business organization and business administration. The demand for superintendents who are managers has been dominant ever since this time (Cuban, 1976; Cuban, 1988). Schools of education have met this demand by providing programs where individuals study administration applied to the context of education.

An alternative concept of the superintendency emerged during the 1960s. Out of the civil rights movement came the hope for superintendents who not only looked like the children in the inner cities, but who were also committed to, and capable of, desegregating schools and ameliorating the effects of poverty and racism through the provision of equitable educational opportunities. Urban school boards in particular began to consider equity issues when seeking to hire superintendents; and people of color, women, and activists began to enter the superintendency because they saw education as the means by which they could promote social justice for children. These new entrants to the superintendency were more likely than others to prepare themselves for the job by honing their skills and knowledge as teachers, by working to meet the needs of children by developing innovative programs and instructional approaches, by looking to research on the empowerment of disenfranchised children, families, and communities for lessons to be applied to education, and by holding themselves to the highest standard of professional learning—earning doctorates in education. However, the demand for superintendents distinguished by their commitment to equity combined with excellence has never been large. Indicators of the small demand lie in the demographics of the superintendency. Only 13 percent of the nation's superintendents are women and an even smaller number—5 percent—are people of color (Glass, Bjork, & Brunner, 2000).

The recent spate of appointments of superintendents with backgrounds in business, politics, and the military by school boards in New York, Los Angeles, New Orleans, and a number of other cities (Matthews, 2001) confirms the longstanding demand for superintendents who are managers. These superintendents, while new figures in education, have the organizational and administrative expertise historically valued by school boards and have degrees in fields such as business, law, and economics. Some have the title of chief executive officer to underscore the corporate-style management their school boards believe their school districts require. In view of these school boards' emphasis on the business of education, schools of education emphasize programs which prepare educational administrators in the business mode.

It is our position that educational leaders, in addition to business managers, are critically needed if our country is to dramatically accelerate its progress towards achieving educational equity. To promote demand for the leaders we envision in this chapter and to provide incentives to schools of education to prepare such leaders, we look more closely at the comparative advantages of management and leadership. For the purposes of this discussion we will call the former the *black-box* model of management and the latter the *change-agent* model of leadership.

Black Boxes Versus Change Agents

In our model of management, we take the term *black box* from business, specifically economics. Economists describe market forces that are ill understood as being inside a *black box,* as if invisible to observation. We know what goes into the black box (inputs) and we know what comes out of the black box (outputs), but we cannot define the process that ties the two together.

In the case under discussion, teaching and learning interactions, because they fall outside the scope of the superintendent's management expertise, are considered inside the black box—occurring behind closed classroom doors. The inputs are the strategies that superintendents use to support teachers. The outputs are the educational outcomes considered important by the superintendent. These invariably include student test scores.

A black-box superintendent's main objectives are to obtain and manage resources, to insure the efficient operation of the infrastructure, and to hold schools accountable for student achievement. The resources are capital investments—political capital, financial capital, and human capital. The superintendent's efficiency efforts typically include reorganizing the central administration and rationalizing payroll and human resources systems. Accountability policies specify the expected student achievement results as well as the rewards and sanctions for schools' meeting or failing to meet the targets.

Management strategies of a black-box superintendent stabilize the organization and make its operational processes efficient and reliable. There is clarity as to how the organization measures success—via test scores. However, there is a fundamental problem with the black-box model of management: the superintendent essentially accepts the status quo in teaching and learning. The strategies used by a black-box superintendent with respect to resources, operations, and accountability are primarily supports for, and pressures on, teachers to do more of the same. Yet cataclysmic improvements in the quality of interactions between teachers and students are necessary if the public schools are to raise the achievement of all students to unprecedented levels, eliminate the underachievement of minority students, and truly close the divide in access to advanced digital learning opportunities.

The use of information technology by black-box superintendents as the centerpieces of their accountability strategies illustrates our point. Information technology makes it fast, easy, and cost effective to collect, analyze, and display large amounts of test score and other outcome data. Depending on the results of the data analysis, black-box superintendents reward and sanction schools. There is no evidence, however, of a relationship between accountability policies imposed upon a school and the improvement of instruction by the school's teachers (Newmann, King, & Rigdon, 1996). Yet lacking knowledge and understanding of the classroom realities the data represent, black-box superintendents are not in a position to go beyond doling out carrots and sticks in attempting to influence teachers. Without guidance and support for learning how to do things differently, teachers do more of the same. More of the same does not yield substantially different results in student learning.

The black-box model of management stands in sharp contrast to the change-agent model of leadership. The change-agent leader has a strong, clear vision of the potential of children to fulfill their dreams and make significant contributions to the world if they are superbly and equitably educated. In an effort to realize this vision, the change-agent superintendent seeks to transform teaching and learning in the classroom. Her fundamental position is that learning depends upon teaching, that achievement cannot be raised without attention to the improvement of instruction. The change-agent leader takes teaching and learning out of the black box so that the relationship is visible.

The change-agent leader is convinced that the primary purpose of her leadership is to improve teaching and learning and that she has the capacity to bring about the same focus among stakeholders throughout her organization. "The more focused the superintendent is on teaching and learning, the more focused the district will be on teaching and learning" observes Negroni (2000, p. 2). The change-agent leader works to make instructional leadership not only the shared focus of everyone in the organization, but also a shared expertise and a shared responsibility. The shared expertise is based upon current knowledge of research and effective practices. The shared responsibility directly and substantively connects the work of the superintendent and principals with the work of teachers and students and calls on all to exercise leadership in complementary ways. Distributed leadership with a continuous, laserlike focus on bringing about dramatic improvements in teaching and learning comes to life. In this environment, the cultural norms and the means are in place to reach the goals of leaving no child out when it comes to rigorous and engaging learning experiences, and leaving no child behind when it comes to achievement at high levels.

The change-agent leaders focus on the organization-wide transformation of teaching and learning positions teachers and students to take full advantage of digital technologies. Technology is effective in proportion to its alignment with proven educational strategies— i.e., good technology-supported teaching promotes student achievement, poor technology-supported teaching does not (Milken, 1999; Wenglinsky, 1998). As good instruction becomes ubiquitous throughout the change-agent organization, more and more teachers will seek the value that technology can add to their efforts to engage students in intellectually challenging work and to enable them to demonstrate their learning in creative and meaningful ways.

Moreover we foresee teachers in change-agent organizations doing research on topics important to their learning and of value to the profession in ways parallel to what they expect and teach their students to do. Work by Stigler and Hiebert (1999) suggests that teachers intent on honing their instructional skills and knowledge will assess the classroom performance of their students in order to identify specific learning needs that require different instructional approaches and then engage in a research and design process to develop, test, and refine new lessons accordingly. In a change-agent organization, the learning needs teachers prioritize will be those of children least well served by traditional pedagogical approaches, and teachers will use computer and information technologies to increase their professional knowledge base.

In addition, the change-agent leader will go beyond efficiency as a goal. When attending to managerial strategies and decisions, she will be guided by the question, "What difference will this make for continuous improvements in teaching and learning for each and every child?" (Payzant, 1995). We will consider and implement answers to this question that are enhanced or made possible by technology. We foresee the change-agent leader giving particular priority to next-generation information technologies that can be used to capture a wide range of performance data that informs the improvement of instructional practices in addition to accountability policies.

In these examples we see how the public schools can close the achievement gap and the digital divide if improvements in teaching and learning—student-centered and sustained over time—are the shared value, shared expertise, and shared work of everyone in the organization. There are clear and compelling gains in educational equity and excellence in the organization led by the change-agent leader we envision.

However, the black-box model of management, dominant throughout the history of public education (Elmore, 2000), is deeply entrenched. It is a model in which individuals who choose to become school administrators "are de facto choosing to de-emphasize teaching and learning in their careers." (Resnick & Fink, 2001, p. 599). Altering the model will require a resounding societal demand for change-agent leadership of the public schools, and innovation upon the part of schools of education to prepare individuals committed to connecting their leadership work to the essential work of teachers and students. We have so far in this chapter provided some of the basic elements of the demand argument. We next suggest guiding principles for schools of education in creating programs to prepare individuals to exercise change-agent leadership.

Standards for Developing Change-Agent Leaders

How can institutions prepare individuals for change-agent leadership? We suggest eight standards that pertain to essential dimensions of change-agent leadership development programs. Taken together, they comprise a normative framework for program design, development, and assessment. While we do not provide a map for program development, for each standard, we give a specific suggestion or example as a means of giving direction.

1. Practice-based and research-based knowledge and skills.   The course of study of a program of change-agent leadership should be based upon the documented best professional practices of educational leaders and the best thinking of academic researchers who focus their work on teaching, learning, and leadership. To enable their students to study comprehensively the processes and benefits of linking practice and research, programs of leadership development will find it important to identify living examples in the public schools known to be associated with improvements in teaching and learning. In addition to learning from these living examples through in-class study, students of leadership will find it invaluable to do on-site visits to the field where they can observe teachers, students, and principals in action and interview them for their reflections on their work.

The Knowledge Forum, formerly known as the Computer-Supported Intentional Learning Environment (CSILE), offers one important living example of combined research and practice work in leadership (Koschmann, 1996). Students of leadership will find it instructive to study articles and other publications by CSILE that describe and discuss the findings of these examinations.

2. Expert practitioners and expert investigators of leadership.   Change-agent leadership development programs should include well-conceived and well-structured opportunities for students to learn how to improve teaching and learning in school district contexts under the guidance of expert practitioners and in university contexts under the guidance of expert researchers. In each setting, the experts act as mentors to the students, shaping their learning experiences to address their developmental needs and potentials. Throughout these experiences, the mentors coach the students, give them feedback, and help the students identify the professional and personal lessons to be learned.

3. Learning to achieve academic and professional excellence at all levels.   Achieving equity for every child in a school district requires a change-agent leader to identify pockets of excellence that exist in individual schools and work to take that excellence to scale, transforming all schools into a connected system of excellence. An example of this is the examination by the Center for Children & Technology of district-wide improvements made in teaching and learning by educators and community members in Union City, New Jersey (Chang, Honey, Light, Moeller, & Ross, 1998; Education Development Center, 2000). Bilingual educators in Union City, a mainly Cuban immigrant community with a large proportion of Spanish-speaking children, took the lead in organizing teachers and parents to revisualize a low-performing school system. The core vision and coherent strategies used by Union City can inform students of change-agent leadership as to how an entire system can be improved at scale, as evidenced by many indicators, including increases in student test scores, with the use of technology as one important tool of change.

4. Inclusion of non-traditional educators from diverse backgrounds in leadership programs.   By non-traditional, we refer to teachers and other practitioners who, while lacking the formal authority of administrative titles and positions, have made a difference—not only by taking individual responsibility for the teaching and learning of students, but also by drawing upon the force of their commitment, knowledge, and skills to persuade others in schools and/or school districts to change their practices and/or policies on behalf of children's achievement. Such individuals, given the conservative, hierarchical culture of most schools and school systems, have demonstrated real authority and thus real leadership potential. This is especially the case if they are women and people of color who have historically not been perceived as leaders, as indicated by their persistently low numbers among sitting administrators. Only 13 percent of the nation's superintendents are women, despite the fact that about 75 percent of the nation's teachers are women.

Programs of change-agent leadership must go beyond defining candidates as most competitive by use of traditional standards. Effective recruitment calls for programs to be explicit in stating their vision of equity and excellence in education and explaining their model of change-agent leadership. Further programs must cast a wide geographic net and access areas, such as highly rural locations, that have historically been underrepresented.

5. Collaboration as a hallmark of leadership.   In a program of change-agent leadership development, the faculty see themselves as learning as much from the students as the students learn from them, and they expect and support the students in taking responsibility to teach and learn from each other. The learners with non-traditional and diverse backgrounds represent a rich array of perspectives and experiences, in terms of the contexts of their professional work, the populations of children and youth whom they have served, the kinds of issues they have faced, and the range of expertise they have developed, and thus they have much to teach to and learn from others.

Furthermore, we know that the work of a change-agent leader is purposefully done with, through, and for others. Her primary goal is to enable teachers, principals, and other educators throughout the system to learn how to work in concert in exercising thoughtful and effective leadership to improve instruction. Learners of change-agent leadership must therefore learn how to engage in and lead collaborative work around teaching and learning issues as an integral part of their course of study.

6. High standards of teaching and learning.   Programs of change-agent leadership must exemplify the kinds of teaching and learning environments that they envision for children and adults in the public schools. Learners of leadership need to see examples of well-considered, high-performing systems and structures whose purpose is to support teaching and learning. This means teaching and learning in a change-agent leadership program are supported by advanced digital technologies. In exchange for learners meeting the many demands and high expectations a program of change-agent leadership development places upon them, the program must provide the learners with multiple forms of financial and academic support. There must be reciprocal accountability.

7. Ongoing program development.   Inquiry, scholarship, and research in all dimensions, most especially the experiences of learners and the views of graduates, should be the basis for a program's continuous self-improvement efforts. Ongoing program development based upon analysis and creativity is needed to keep pace with the demand for new leaders whose work will represent significant progress in raising student achievement to high levels. Self-study is additionally a program's means of contributing to knowledge about the learning of leadership.

8. Forward-looking change-agent leadership development programs.   Programs of change-agent leadership must constantly scan the horizon to identify new leadership roles, rules, relationships, and tools (Carroll, 2001). The focus of this book is on the promise of digital technologies to support advances in teaching and learning for every child. In the future, other catalysts and supports for transforming education may take on different forms. Change-agent leadership development programs prepare leaders to welcome and respond to new challenges in creative and innovative ways.

Essential Questions for Change-Agent Leadership Study

The following six sets of questions are intended to guide the aspiring change-agent leader in thoughtfully and rigorously considering who she is as a learner and a leader and in engaging actively and intensively in a 360-degree exploration of research- and practice-based knowledge about teaching, learning, technology, and leadership for instructional improvement. The questions provide scaffolding for learners to think about, to read, write, and to talk about, and to engage in research on and to try out practices leading to instructional improvement.

1. What are my core values and beliefs? What is my vision as an educator? During her preparation for leadership, the learner should make her core values and beliefs explicit, enabling her to critically examine the set of basic tenets and non-negotiables that motivate her as an educator and define her integrity. An aspiring leader must develop also a cogent and compelling vision of the future. She needs to know where she is heading and why in order to gain the public's trust in her to exercise responsible leadership on behalf of children and to persuade others to join her in achieving the common goal of continuously improving teaching and learning improvement.

2. What do I know and what can I do? This question is intended to help the learner set capacity-building goals. Surfacing assumptions is an essential means of checking on the validity of what you think you know. Identifying as an assumption what was heretofore implicitly considered an immutable fact sets the stage for the learner of change-agent leadership to see teaching, learning, technology, and leadership interactions with more clarity and to be open to new knowledge about how to change those interactions through leadership.

3. What are my strengths as a learner? What is my evidence? How can I build upon my strengths? If an aspiring leader has unspoken doubts about her ability to learn, given opportunities and supports to learn at high levels, then she is likely to have the same doubts about children's ability to learn. These doubts—which can be self-fulfilling low expectations—need to be addressed and resolved. Individuals who believe that high-level learning is outside their own capacity and that of all children should think about a career outside education.

4. How do I develop the capacity of principals, subject matter experts, and others to collaboratively exercise leadership to enable and support good teaching and learning? This question has to do with how the learner thinks about her leadership for the improvement of teaching and learning. A future leader needs to develop and test the rigor of several working models so as to construct her own understandings of how she could effectively exercise leadership to have impact upon specific and essential elements of the system of teaching and learning in a learning organization. The learner can begin to create working models by critically reading, thoughtfully discussing, and writing analyses of the implications of the research literature.

5. What do I know about teaching and learning with technology? The "special challenges and opportunities" presented by technology must be specifically and intentionally addressed if the digital divide is to be bridged (Dede, 1998, p. 200). Well-known challenges are associated with the costs of maintaining and upgrading technology. A major opportunity is found in work suggesting that digital teaching and learning innovations might be scaled up through "reflective adaptation" (p. 298). Reflective adaptation takes place when originators of the effective practice and implementers of the effective practice in a new context engage in ongoing conversations which lead to jointly made modifications in the practice and in the context in order to arrive at a goodness of fit.

6. What do I know about insuring social justice for children in terms of their learning opportunities and outcomes? The learner of leadership needs to acquire comprehensive knowledge of longstanding and emerging inequities in education. Of most importance, she needs to conduct an exhaustive investigation of the means by which the learning of underachieving children can be accelerated while the learning of all children at ever-higher levels is simultaneously made possible. The knowledge base for this investigation includes work done by the Benton Foundation and others that focuses on the identification, analysis, and remedy of societal inequities exacerbated or associated with digital technologies.

Change-Agent Leadership: A Theory of Action for Equity

The six essential questions call for the learner of change-agent leadership to engage in rigorous self-reflection and critical inquiry. The eight standards call for programs of change-agent leadership development to create environments and infrastructures to support and guide the learner's self-reflection and to challenge and assist the learner to engage in critical inquiry. The questions and the principles complement each other and are consistent with the concept of change-agent leadership.

What will the graduate of a change-agent leadership development program know and be able to do? As we see it, the budding change-agent leader will have in place a personal theory of action that represents salient aspects of what she knows and can and will do. Her portfolio consists of working models pertaining to what she considers most essential to realizing her vision of leadership to bring about good teaching and learning for every child. The working models are strategies, derived from existing knowledge and tested in practice, which the future leader has reason to believe will contribute to her effectiveness.

In effect, the personal theory signifies the future change-agent leader's power and legitimacy to exercise new and effective leadership. It is the representation of her demonstrated capacity to lead for the purpose of equitably achieving the American Dream of enabling every child to achieve at high academic standards.

Summary

Strong leadership is essential in the quest for digital equity. We can observe excellence in leadership and infer from these observations the qualities we are seeking. These qualities include vision, collaboration, informed reflection, creative resource management, courage, and perseverance. Leaders for today and tomorrow must focus their work directly on instruction to insure that all children have equitable access to the high-quality learning experiences associated with advanced technology. They must reflect the diversity and rich cultural matrix of our nation. They must be change agents who are willing to take risks and create new rules, roles, and responsibilities in response to emerging issues and trends. It is only through such brave innovation that America will ever achieve its dream of enabling every child to fulfill his or her academic potential.

13 Building Meaningful Organizational Change

KAREN M. KEENAN

JOAN M. KARP

FOCUS QUESTIONS

1. What advantages do digital learning environments provide for education organizations?
2. How does digital equity change the culture of educational organizations?
3. What processes help educational organizations move toward digital equity?
4. What technology integration and equity practices can organizations easily adopt?
5. Which models provide direction for successful systems change?

A system, or organization, is created when a group of people work together toward common goals. The processes, procedures, and structures they develop are the organizational foundation of their relationships. System change is the organization's response to dynamic events, actions, and new innovations (Senge, 1999; Senge et al., 2000; Wheatley, 1999). While systems change theory applies to any organization, the systems of interest in this chapter are those school organizations that serve students of low-income urban and rural communities and from traditionally underrepresented populations. The following conversation illustrates the complexities that technology integration creates when a school district incorporates it into teaching and learning for all students.

Superintendent Don Riverson from Beaver Lake, a small rural community arrives at my office on the University of Minnesota Duluth campus. He wants to talk about how our project, the Arrowhead Preparing Tomorrow's Teachers to Use Technology, assists undergraduate education students, preschool through high school teachers, and university faculty in integrating technology into teaching and learning.

"Don," I inquire, "I understand you want to talk about what we're doing here at the university. Before we get to that, would you tell me about what you and your organization at Beaver Lake are doing?"

"We're in the midst of applying for a technology grant from the state. I've been at Beaver Lake for two years now. In that time we moved our computers from the lab to the classrooms so that our teachers can integrate technology into their teaching," replies Don.

"That's a progressive move for your organization, Don. Are the students in your schools pretty tech-savvy?" I inquire.

"A few are," Don says. "I'm not sure about how much technology is available for them in their homes, but a few seem to be quite advanced. With the prison in our community, we have many students who move in and out frequently, almost like a migrant population. The students' basic needs are met at home, but most families don't have extra money for computers. The bigger problem is Beaver Lake teachers don't feel comfortable using the computer, the Internet, and other technologies for teaching and learning. They mostly use computers for word processing. Next year our school district is going to have more bandwidth than any other surrounding district. We have so much technology potential, but it's not being used to the degree possible. Consequently, our students are not learning how to achieve in today's digital world. How do I help people within my educational organization change so that they integrate effective learning theories and technologies to the best advantage?"

Superintendent Riverson asks one of the most provocative questions being articulated by educational professionals in today's schools: how do educational organizations re-create themselves to provide digitally equitable learning environments for their students, teachers, and communities? His organization has access to sufficient technology, but the issue is how to build digital equity through technical support and professional and community development. In other districts, the primary concern is how to gain access to the up-to-date hardware, software, and servers needed to seed the organization with sufficient equipment while building technical support. Is there hope for finding answers to these extremely valuable questions? Yes, there is. Don and I continue to talk about possible strategies that, if applied, will help his organization transform from a traditional twentieth-century modern age educational system into one that prepares Beaver Lake students for equal footing in the digital age. This chapter describes the foundational theories and practical applications we discussed.

A Scaffold for Meaningful Change

When asked why technology is not pervasively used today for teaching and learning, Larry Cuban, Stanford University education professor, says that it's something about how schools are organized. "For fundamental changes [such as digital equity] in teaching and learning to occur there [needs] to be widespread and deep reform in schools' organizational, political, social, and technological contexts" (2001, p. 195). We believe the fundamental changes suggested by Cuban can happen when educational organizations consider and take actions with regard to the five factors that influence change and help diffuse innovation (Rogers, 1995). The change factors are: relative advantage, cultural compatibility, complexity, trial-ability, and observe-ability. Table 13.1 outlines Roger's five factors in the context of creating digital equity.

TABLE 13.1   Factors That Influence Change

Factor	Influence	Digital Equity Context
Relative advantage	What will the change do?	What advantages do digital learning environments provide for education organizations that serve traditionally underrepresented and/or low-income populations?
Cultural compatibility	What will the change do for the organization's culture?	How does changing the culture of educational organizations lead to digital equity?
Complexity	How easily can the change be used?	What processes help educational organizations move toward digital equity?
Trial-ability	What are some small-scale practices that could easily be tried?	What technology integration practices can organizations easily adopt to increase digital equity?
Observe-ability	Where can people see a demonstration of the change?	What models provide direction for successful system change that promotes digital equity?

Adapted from *Diffusion of Innovating,* by E. M. Rogers, 1995, New York: The Free Press.

What Advantages Do Digital Learning Environments Provide for Education Organizations That Serve Traditionally Underrepresented and/or Low-Income Populations?

This question addresses the factor of relative advantage, "the degree to which an innovation is perceived as being better than the idea it supersedes" (Rogers, 1995, p. 212). Early adopters of technology are quick to point out obvious technology advantages. For example, valuable time is created when teachers let software and hardware tools collect, analyze, and communicate student information (Dexter & Seashore, 2001). According to the work of Bransford, Brown, and Cocking (editors) and the Committee on Developments in the Science of Learning in their book *How People Learn* (1999), technology supports individualization of instruction, enhances group learning, nurtures distance collaboration, and promotes avenues for community building. Further, technologies make it easier for students to learn through active engagement, to receive valuable feedback about their progress, and to build upon their developmental knowledge. Simulation software helps students visualize; consequently they are better able to conceptualize new knowledge. Additionally, technology is helping professionals to learn that concepts previously thought to be too difficult for some students are, in fact, easier to comprehend at earlier ages with the assistance technology provides. Finally, technologies provide varied information through access to people and digital libraries. The vast Internet archive and communication techniques provide an endless learning opportunity for all learners to practice lifelong learning. Students, parents, teachers, administrators, and community members alike can realize these benefits.

Research on the effects of using technology for teaching and learning has not yet shown consistently positive effects on student's learning, but there is growing evidence that students learning in technology-rich environments are learning better and are learning better content (Roschelle, Rob, Hoadley, Gordin, & Means, 2000). Computer technology enhances student learning in four key areas: active participation, group learning, increased interaction and timely feedback, and through links with real-life contexts (Roschelle et al., 2000). For example, one study has shown that middle school students who use the "Micro-computer-Based Laboratory" software, an immediate graphic feedback data collection and analysis tool, to conduct experiments in science labs gain of 81 percent in their ability to interpret and use graphs (Mokros & Tinker, 1987). "Positive effects are especially strong for students categorized as low or middle achievers" (Roschelle et al., 2000 p. 81). Another study, in which students used Computer Supported Intentional Learning Environments (CSILE) to build knowledge and communicate ideas in the areas of science, history, and social studies, demonstrates that collaboration technology helps students perform better on standardized tests. The students develop abilities to create more in-depth explanations than students who do not use the technology (Scardamilia & Bereiter, 1999).

Technology is a useful feedback tool. It can provide students with rapid interaction and immediate response. It can capture individual or small-group student attention for extended periods of time, and it can, in some instances, analyze student performance in a timely manner. These digital feedback tools help students to achieve. For example, Carnegie Mellon University researchers using Practical Algebra Tutor with urban high school students found that students made small gains on standardized math tests such as the Scholastic Aptitude Test (SAT), but more than doubled their achievement in complex problem solving compared to students not using this technology (Koedinger, Anderson, & Hadley, 1997).

Technology advances as described in the previous paragraphs are certainly appealing. However, a key question remains: If students are learning better with technology and the skills technology provides are central for a literate citizenry, then how can all schools change to effectively take advantage of these beneficial tools? Taking a look at the full reality of the current change climate is important.

How Does Changing the Culture of Educational Organizations Lead to Digital Equity?

Cultural compatibility is "the degree to which an innovation is perceived as consistent with the existing values, past experiences, and needs of" potential adopters in the organization (Rogers, 1995, p. 224). To the observer, the culture of education in this rapidly changing world is transforming at a snail's pace. In fact, schools born out of the industrial culture continue to maintain their hundred-year-old practices. The education of our parents and their parents is similar in content, social structure, and organization as was for us and is for our children. There is little fundamental change. However, the world culture outside of school, public or private, is changing vastly. People working, living, and learning in today's increasingly collaborative society are, as Peter Vaill, professor of human systems says, living in a state of "permanent whitewater" in which we "are all confronted constantly with new methods and technologies" (1996, p. 6). This discrepancy between our present school culture and our ever-increasingly digitally savvy society is the paramount digital divide. This is a major contributing force behind the call for educational systemic change.

Think about a school system or district organization. This system is "built" by internal policies and procedures that create the learning culture, or "how we do things around here." However, the internal system, in addition to being continually influenced by its members, is also influenced by external systems and individuals, such as state and federal laws, cultural trends, its community environment, and technical advancements like digital technology. When one internal or external system or individual influences the established system, a disturbance is created that may trigger change. Learning happens during the process of change. In this manner, "The organization (system) doesn't just do something new; it builds its capacity for doing things in a new way—indeed, it builds capacity for ongoing change" (Senge et al., 2000, p. 15). Today's technology has the potential to trigger a significant cultural disturbance in all schools.

Our foundational assumptions for this chapter reflect the importance building a collaborative culture in which inclusive processes welcome the voices of all the partners in the change at the personal, community, and organizational levels. Previous chapters show that it is easier to gain access to technology than it is to use it meaningfully in educational settings and, because there is so much emphasis on the economic benefits of technology's integration into learning environments, the civic and social aspects of developing meaningful technology-integrated applications for teaching and learning are not being effectively addressed (Cuban, 2001). Consequently, while technology shows an increasing benefit in our ability to provide a world-class education for each and every American public school student, teachers by and large do not place technology integration as a top priority. Until teachers, the key gatekeepers of what really happens in the classroom, become key cultural players in the organizational, political, and social changes necessary to create an environment where students can experience digital equity in our American schools, we predict that there will be little change. Decision makers "must understand teacher expertise and perspectives on classroom work and engage teachers fully in the deliberations, design, deployment, and implementation of technology plans" (Cuban, 2001, p. 183).

As a model, we look at:

> Business organizations, in particular, have found that the pressures of global competition and the technological advances posed by the computer have reshaped the way that the most successful among them conduct and organize themselves. Flattened hierarchies, decentralized decision making, shared power and renegotiated relationships between management and other employees have become the norm in companies that are on the frontiers of their industries. (Waddock, 1995, p. 7).

We see similar transformations happening in schools. If teachers, parents, and community members are actively involved in the decision making with school administrators, the complex challenges created by technology integration followed by the planning and implementing that takes place will result in more effective systems for the organization as a whole. They can work from a shared understanding of the issues and challenges being faced by the school system, they share a common vision of the community's future, and they can share resources to achieve the vision. This participative approach leads to sustained organization development and cultural transformation because people develop a commitment for the change and willingness to work toward it. The following steps outlined by Friere and Hooks and also in the leadership chapter of this book can assist school systems to examine their culture.

Freire, in *Pedagogy of the Oppressed* ([1970] 1994), presents a critical philosophical and practical model that calls for first examining and identifying the dehumanizing conditions and mutual relationships between the oppressed and oppressor, thus raising the consciousness of each. He then posits establishing a problem-posing praxis as an instrument for liberation. The action and reflection considered by the oppressed and oppressors are mutually undertaken in a dialogue that leads to resolution and understanding. This process, begun by Freire in South America, is a model of community-based organization development at its best. It has been applied throughout the world and has led to liberation for many oppressed peoples.

Hooks (1984, 1990, 1994) applies critical pedagogy, multicultural, and feminist theories to African American students and women's issues. She argues that to overcome the racist, sexist, and classist biases perpetuated in educational settings and the wider society, an "engaged pedagogy" is necessary. This perspective incorporates "anti-colonial, critical and feminist pedagogies for interrogating biases in curricula that re-inscribe systems of domination while simultaneously providing new ways to teach diverse groups of students" (Hooks, 1994, p. 10). Her model of engaged pedagogy, while focused on changing the way in which students and professors work, influences curriculum development and has important contributions to make to the way in which systems change is conceptualized. Freire and Faundez (1989) maintain that "the task for transforming education and society belongs not only to designated leaders, but also to every individual because by 'recreating ourselves, individually and socially, we change society'" (p. 82).

What Processes Help Educational Organizations Move toward Digital Equity?

Complexity is "the degree to which an innovation is perceived as relatively difficult to understand and use" (Rogers, 1995, p. 242). The systemic change needed to create digital equity is complex. It carries significant implications for the teaching and learning culture, the decision-making processes, infrastructure development, and resource allocation, to mention a few. One of the first steps in understanding how to change is to look at the change in relation to the constraints that may be standing in the way. This section of the chapter identifies some constraints currently felt by systems working to become digitally equitable. It then provides a theoretical framework for looking at change and identifies some change model resources for further study.

High on school systems' lists of demands is to be accountable to the learning of their students. The accountability movement's operational model strives to capture the learners' basic knowledge and skills. This is most often accomplished by assessing those skills with multiple-choice testing. Another item on their list is the integration of technology into teaching and learning which often incorporates a nonlinear and problem-based approach to teaching and learning. Students, with technology's assistance, are encouraged to be self-motivated explorers and creators in uncharted territories in partnership with their teacher. The final student product is often a digital creation, demonstrating mastery of content via technology tools.

The intersection of the accountability movement and the integration of technology into teaching and learning in school systems leads to compounding tensions in educational organizations. Teachers and professors are being forced to choose between teaching basic skills for accountability testing and using technology in innovative and beneficial ways. Further, many public school districts have limited and shrinking fiscal and time resources to support their basic programs, yet to maintain computer equipment and provide necessary support requires significant investments (Fishman, Pinkard, & Bruce, 2001). Other factors that may contribute to the perplexing dynamics of today's learning environments include the benefits of class size, higher entry-level teacher salaries, renovation of decayed buildings, responsive school communities, full-day preschool and kindergarten, cross-disciplinary programs in the high schools, innovative arts programs in the elementary schools, and foreign language for middle school students (Cuban, 2001). Senge et al. (2000) describes the increasing stress students and parents feel about schooling. In some communities where parents have the means for private or home schooling, the divisions among the "haves" and the "have-nots" are expanding. Fewer resources are being provided for students with the greatest needs. Nowhere are these changes more necessary and dramatic in scope than in the nation's schools serving low-income and traditionally underrepresented student populations (Becker, 2000c).

The complexities felt by education organizations due to accountability movements, scarce resources, inequality, and technology's potential, among other things, create significant tensions. Resourceful organizations recognize the fact that tension can energize change. The formula that follows reflects one way to tap the energy generated by tension in order to effect change: Shared Dissatisfaction × Shared Vision × Knowledge of Practical Tools and Strategies > the Cost of the Change = CHANGE (Beckhard & Harris, 1977; Garmston & Wellman, 1999; Jacobs, 1994). According to this formula, resistance to change (the cost of change) is overcome if the product of shared dissatisfaction with the present environment meets a common vision of a possible future and doable steps so that people can move toward creating their desired future. When all three of these elements are in place, resistance is overcome and change occurs. For example, the state-based accountability movement arose from the society's tensions associated with poor student achievement and the perception of poor teaching in public schools. When the public combined the vision of standardization and articulated action steps, state after state adopted this accountability strategy. This movement attempts to order and assess the ever-expanding pool of present knowledge students should know and be able to apply. While many resisted this change, it is now standard operating procedure in districts and universities across the nation.

Let's apply the change formula to working toward digital equity. Imagine school systems gathering information about what is and isn't working in their district with regard to technology integration. They seek input from diverse internal populations: students, parents, teachers, administrators, staff and technology professionals. Additionally, they gather information from external professionals such as higher education faculty who place preservice teachers in the their system. Perhaps they solicit information from public institutions that provide Internet and/or computer access to their student population (libraries, community technology centers, etc.). Once this information is gathered, the school system analyzes it to determine current needs. But this isn't enough. What kind of future do they desire? The next step is to work collaboratively with the stakeholders previously mentioned to envision the digitally equitable future they want for each of their students. With this future vision in mind, they then identify the action steps needed to realize their vision. For digitally inequitable schools the first step will be to gain technology access. This means the development of proposals for application to state and federally grant resources, such as the U.S. Government E-rate program. To others, such as Superintendent Riverson's system, it means developing structures, policies, and processes that support teachers to become technology proficient teachers. One step at a time change is made real.

In order to apply these principles, it is important to understand school districts as living systems. Margaret Wheatley (1999) defines a system as "a set of processes that are made visible in temporary structures. These living structures are in no way similar to the solid structures we build. The system continues to develop, to release itself from the old and find new structures as they are required" (p. 23). This adaptation comes through systems change, supported by an organization's ability to continually build capacities for ongoing change. Adaptability in the organization comes from each individual's capacity to learn. Therefore, to foster successful change, school administrators, teachers, and parents, both individually and collectively, find the following skills to be helpful collaborative practices (Senge et al., 2000). These include:

- Personal mastery: a thorough understanding of the current state of the organization and the changes envisioned by the individual.
- Mental models: reflection and inquiry skills focused around developing awareness of the attitudes and perceptions that can influence change.
- Shared vision: a focus on the mutually understood image of the desired future state.
- Team learning: skills of group interaction. "Through techniques like dialogue and skillful discussion, teams transform their collective thinking, learning to mobilize their energies and actions to achieve common goals, and drawing forth an intelligence and ability greater than the sum of the individual members' talents" (p. 32).
- Systems thinking: where people actively think about the way in which the changes proposed apply to the system rather than to a smaller subsection of it.

We believe schools systems that apply systemic change tools can bring about meaningful reform. What are these tools? In addition to the Senge practices and the change formula previously described, the collaborative change tools listed below come from the organization development profession. They help organizations in private and public sectors change. School systems that deploy these tools through consultant assistance, educator/administrator expertise, or organized internal development will be able to move toward the desired state of digital equity.

The Institute for Cultural Affairs (ICA).   ICA is an approximately 25-year-old, worldwide private, non-profit organization. Its aim is to develop and implement methods of individual, community, and organizational development. It offers training programs in group facilitation methods around the world. ICA methods, including discussion, action planning, workshop, and strategic planning, are highly participatory in nature.

Future Search.   This site provides information about Future Search Conferences, an organizational tool for finding common ground, and then building upon that ground to plan for change. Originally developed by Marvin R. Weisbord and Sandra

Janoff, this change tool requires representative participation from diverse groups within an organization and from those whom the organization affects. This type of tool is called a large-scale change model.

The Society for Organizational Learning (SoL).   SoL originated, with Peter Senge's guidance, in 1991 at the Massachusetts Institute of Technology with a mission to "foster collaboration among a group of corporations committed to fundamental organizational change and advancing the state of the art in building learning organizations." SoL's purpose is to "help build organizations worthy of people's fullest commitment, and [we] are committed to any institution and individual that is committed to SoL's purpose and principles. To meet this goal, we discover, integrate, and implement theories and practices for the interdependent development of people and their institutions." SoL's web site is a good resource for systemic change information. It includes a dictionary and frequently asked questions about building collaborative learning communities to affect change.

Twelve Roles of Facilitators for School Change by R. Bruce Williams (1997).   In his book, Mr. Williams, an educational organization developer with 30 years of experience, describes many useful tools that help those working on educational change to help their organization change. He helps educators build the skills needed for group facilitation. These include building trust in three areas: relationships, the change process, and the environment of change.

What Technology Integration Practices Can Organizations Easily Adopt?

Trial-ability is "the degree to which an innovation may be experimented with on a limited basis" (Rogers, 1995, p. 243). The preceding sections of this chapter outline the complexity of school and university systems' change to create digitally equitable environments. Yet even with the complex nature of school change, there are many school districts and universities that successfully integrate technology into their programs and see growth in their students as a result. One of the ways they resolve tensions is through reallocation of resources. This section depicts technology integration practices adopted by successful school and universities in terms of how they use their financial, personnel, and temporal resources.

Financial Resources Allocation

Schools and universities invest increasingly greater amounts of money in technology. Estimates of the money spent on technology for schools in 1998 is over seven billion dollars per year—about 2.7 percent of total expenditures (Anderson & Becker, 2001). But how are those dollars spent? Who makes these decisions? Hardware purchases, estimated at 74 percent in 1998, make up the greatest proportion of expenditures. School administrators in central offices make the majority of decisions about hardware purchases. On average, technology coordinators prefer only 40 percent be spent on hardware with the balance reserved for software and technical support. According to Anderson & Becker (2001), technology coordinators responses are consistent with the conclusions of two national studies: the Presidents

Committee of Advisors on Science and Technology (1997) and the U.S. Congress's OTA report of 1995. Schools using technology advocate for more decision-making control of monetary decisions at the school or teacher level (Anderson & Ronnqvist, 1999).

In low-income school districts where there is less access to family or corporate special funding, successful districts use state and federal grants to build the technology infrastructure and support, tapping into funds for E-rate and state technology challenge grants. In low-income districts where the costs for technology are often high due to older facilities and increased need for security, successful technology innovators use wireless solutions and less costly hardware such as thin clients (limited-function computers) linked to central servers (About Project LemonLink, Lemon Grove School District, CA, 2001; Newsome Park Elementary, About Our School, 2001). These two districts are part of a series of case studies completed by the University of Minnesota's Exemplary Technology Supported Schooling Case Studies Project. The project describes a number of innovative school districts serving low-income and minority students and their implementation of technology (Anderson & Dexter, 2001). These cases portray the use of successful technology in the full context of the culture of the school and the community resources available.

Human Resource Involvement

A number of key individuals are affected by technology innovation in educational organizations. Students, chief school administrators, teachers, management, and information systems (MIS) staff and technology coordinators all have roles to play.

Students. Students have many new roles both within and out of the classroom. Generation Y, for example, trains and then enlists middle and high school students to assist classroom teachers integrate technology into their teaching (Generationwww.Y, 2001). At the University of Minnesota Duluth, undergraduate students are team members with classroom teachers and university faculty, where they contribute equally to the discussion of how technology can help students learn and create technology-infused units of instruction for classroom implementation (APT3 Arrowhead Preparing Tomorrow's Teachers to Use Technology, 2001). In elementary through high school, students are taking on roles of "knowledge manager" and team member in project-based learning activities. Wireless laptops and intranet software such as Lotus Notes or Blackboard support students working on projects in small teams (McGhee & Kozma, 2001).

Administrators. Technology changes chief school administrators' roles in many ways. Rather than planning with a twelve-month budget cycle, timelines for planning technology are better set at a three- to five-year cycle (Levinson & Surrat, 1999). The paradox is that the technology is often outdated in three years, so even with the long view, the planning must be reviewed annually with flexibility and forethought (Levinson & Surrat, 1999). Delegating authority for technology decisions may be difficult for chief school officers because the seemingly most competent staff available such as MIS directors may have limited knowledge of effective technology integration for teaching and learning.

Successful school administrators create teams of professionals from a variety of levels in the organization to develop technology plans (Levinson & Surrat, 1999). These teams include at a minimum MIS staff, technology coordinators, school principals, and teachers.

Innovative programs include university faculty, community leaders, and parents on the teams as well. Chief school officers with well-functioning technology integration programs emphasize time for teacher development and provide reliable technology systems as well as excellent technical support (Dexter & Seashore, 2001). They often apply data mining and data-driven decision making as key strategies.

Teachers.   Teachers in technology-rich environments, in addition to their usual instructional roles, take on the roles of "instructional designer, trainer, collaborator, team coordinator, advisor, and assessment specialist" (McGhee & Kozma, 2001, p. 23). Often working in constructivist or project-based classes, teachers consult and advise students working on projects. They work on advisory teams in the school system to assist with decisions about hardware, software, and networking. Teachers in schools where technology is working well have support systems through which teachers help other teachers and students help teachers to learn the new skills inherent in technology's use (Dexter & Seashore, 2001).

Technology Coordinator and MIS Staff.   The role of the technology coordinator and MIS staff are different in the new configurations of schools integrating technology. They are part of teams working on the long-term tasks of supporting teachers and students, planning training, and purchasing hardware and software, but more importantly are available for the immediate assistance teachers need (Fishman et. al, 2001).

Other Stakeholders.   Parents, legislators, businesspeople, and taxpayers support digital equity by becoming engaged in the change process. One of the first steps is to recognize that society has changed. Another is to accept and support twenty-first-century student needs. These are more complex and require significant expenditures for infrastructure, training, and technical maintenance. As school systems realize that change takes time and human resources, they are creating new positions such as Director of Professional & Organization Development created by the Eden Prairie School District in Minnesota. The responsibilities and qualifications for this job include:

- **Responsibilities:**   Manage, supervise, and coordinate staff development and organizational development in alignment with the district strategic plan.
- **Qualifications:**   Demonstrated ability in the development, delivery, and evaluation of professional development for all staff; excellent organization and management skills; effective written and verbal communication skills; and excellent team, consensus-building, and collaboration skills.
- **Education:**   Masters Degree and background in organizational development, the change process, and group facilitation; research related to teaching and learning theory and practice preferred.

Time Allocation

Schools with strong technology programs allocate considerable amounts of time to instructing teachers at the beginning of the program. Maintenance and enhancement of teacher skills continues throughout the program (Dexter & Seashore, 2001). Teachers receive a variety of different incentives such as laptops or extra pay for using their time to learn the new skills needed to integrate technology (Dexter & Seashore, 2001). They are given time throughout the school year to meet with other teachers to support each other and form professional communities of learners.

Which Models Provide Direction for Successful Systems Change?

Observe-ability is "the degree to which the results of an innovation are visible to others" (Rogers, 1995, p. 244). There are hundreds of school systems and universities engaged in systemic change designed to successfully integrate technology into teaching and learning. This section will highlight three examples that support digital equity, one national program and two system models.

PT3—A National Program to Stimulate Change

The United States Department of Education's Preparing Tomorrow's Teachers to Use Technology (PT3) Program, begun in 1999, is a large-scale change effort. It originated with the observations that while the nation's public school educators have access to technology, few actually use it for teaching and learning in the classroom. Additionally, our nation's public school districts currently do not equitably provide the necessary staff development, technology support, and maintenance structures to realize the potential of technology-integrated educational opportunities. Consequently, the PT3 Program created a mission: to facilitate systemic change at the nation's universities and colleges by supporting cross-institutional networked partnerships among schools, universities, and businesses whose focus is to integrate technology into P–12 and higher education institutions. This mission, if realized, will develop a large cadre of preservice teachers who, upon graduation, will know how to meaningfully apply digital technologies in P–12 school settings across the nation. Steps toward this mission include, but are not limited to: acquiring legislative support for the program, calling for proposals from institutions, awarding grants, holding projects accountable, and developing face-to-face and digital opportunities for dissemination of learning. Over four hundred campuses across the United States are now working with low-income rural and urban schools with traditionally underrepresented students to meaningfully integrate technology into learning environments. Faculty, in-service, and preservice teachers are becoming proficient users of technology in the classroom.

The PT3 vision is dynamic. Representatives of the program's project recently created a new vision: "We envision dynamic e-learning cultures that embrace the inherent contributions of all people as life-long learners to meet the needs of both the individual and the society" (McNabb et al., 2001). With this vision, new steps will be taken along the path toward digital equity. More information about this program is available at http://pt3.org.

Middle School Science Partnership of Universities and Urban Schools (Letus)

Educational researchers and teachers have created five middle school science project-based learning curriculum units with specialized software; but can these be implemented on a large scale in urban school environments? Do students in large urban school environments have the basic skills necessary to learn effectively in a project-based technology-rich curriculum? What changes need to take place within school systems to create effective and sustainable curricula reform on such a large scale? These are the questions faced by researchers from Northwestern University and University of Michigan working in partnership with the Detroit and Chicago Public Schools on the LeTUS project (Krajcik, Marx, Blumenfeld, Soloway, & Fishman, 2000).

> Our approach to reform is one of collaboration, not technology transfer. . . . Rather than change from the outside, we emphasize process, collaborating with teachers and administrators to adapt the innovation so that it is achievable given the constraints of the context, but also true to the underlying premises of the instructional approach (p. 5).

The partnership began with a vision and commitment of the communities to the goals of reform and the challenge of schools systems working collaboratively with universities. Recognizing the mutually beneficial outcomes when students become a force for change, these partners work together to articulate the changes needed in the systems (Letus, 2000). The pragmatic findings based on students' learning and teachers' discovery propel the research conducted by the universities, which in turn, informs the practice in these two school systems. The changing practices pave the way for other large urban districts to move in these new technology-enhanced directions. The partnership has created a web space for school administrators across the country to share the information they have learned about what it takes to integrate technology into school systems. What are the lessons for systemic change that have been learned from this partnership?

The three dimensions of change that the project takes into account as it implements new technology-enhanced teaching and learning involves district policy and management, culture, and capability. The researchers believe that the further away from an innovation on any of the three dimensions, the more challenging it is for the district to implement and sustain change.

The first lesson learned is that teachers need specific curriculum that integrates technology and addresses standards. The technology tools most prevalent in classrooms today are word-processing and presentation software tools. These were developed by businesses, specific to *their* needs, and although these tools can have many appropriate educational applications, teachers and students need more specific tools. While tools have been developed in science, mathematics, and reading, the interface for each is different, creating the need for student and teacher to learn new interfaces each time a new application is used (Fishman et al., 2001). LeTUS and its related projects from the Center for Highly Interactive Computing in Education (Krajcik et al., 2000) have developed a number of software tools that incorporate problem-based inquiry learning into the middle school science curriculum in collaborations between university faculty and teachers.

Often new curriculum also requires teachers to change their teaching approaches. The LeTUS curriculum requires teachers to use constructivist approaches that many teachers are not accustomed to using (Jackson, Stratford, Krajcik, & Soloway, 1994). It can take teachers many years to incorporate new ways of teaching into their practice. The project-based and inquiry-driven science curriculum requires teachers to think in new ways, to organize their teaching differently, and to interface with school administrators responsible for technology (e.g., computer lab teachers and MIS administrators). After preparing teachers to implement the new methods by having summer workshops, the university faculty realized that some of the teachers were not able to successfully implement the curriculum, so changes to the preparation methods were made. More support was provided to classroom teachers and subsequent preparation included more opportunities for the teachers to practice using the curriculum and the technology before using it with their students. Follow-up that demonstrated how to use the software with the types of concept development that a teacher would use with students in class was necessary for success (Krajcik et al., 2000).

The Internet creates special challenges for teachers and school systems. It relies on connections to the world outside of the classroom to expand students learning in ways that have never before been possible. In using the Internet with students, teachers must develop appropriate scaffolds so that the connections students make are meaningfully integrated into their learning. The cycles of activity and work are different than when using more traditional methods. Teachers must monitor students' behavior while on the Internet because the "students who act out in face to face situations will also act out on-line" (Fishman et al., 2001), but it may be more difficult for the teacher to see the behaviors and prevent them. Fishman and his colleagues have also observed student disappointment when teachers or mentors do not respond to student queries during a class period or within a short time of the query.

In the urban school systems of the LeTUS project, the Internet is often not working reliably and predictably, so using it is a gamble for the classroom teacher. There are multiple reasons why the Internet may not be working when the classroom teacher plans to use it, most of which are not within the classroom teachers' control. Typically schools have used a help-desk model that is not functional for the classroom teacher who has no phone in the classroom and needs immediate assistance. Most often the class period or school day is over before the teacher receives assistance. Generic policies and system settings established for Internet security to protect students may hinder instruction because appropriate Internet sites may be blocked.

The educational organization is often structured so that what have been formerly business-oriented departments of "management and information services" (MIS) are responsible for the implementation of technology deployment and support in the schools. The individuals running these departments are "not accustomed to supporting classroom learning, and are not good candidates for coordinating or problem-solving with classroom teachers" (Fishman et al., 2001). It is critical that teachers who use technology for teaching and learning collaborate with administrators in the planning, managing, and implementing of new technologies in classrooms.

A planning model has been developed that involves the following four phases of development: (1) establish a vision of teaching and learning, (2) develop staff's technology skills, (3) redesign curriculum so that it is embedded with technology, and (4) benchmark student and teacher performance and progress (Fishman, Pinkard, & Bruce, 1998). To assist teachers establishing their vision, North Central Regional Educational Laboratory's "Plugged In" framework was used for teachers to assess their "engaged learning" and "high performance technology." It asks teachers to think about their current realities with future goals, very much like Senge's personal mastery described earlier.

Research on the success of the LeTUS model indicates that urban middle school students gained in their knowledge and skills on all of the inquiry based science units (Krajcik et al., 2000); however, there was considerable variability by teacher. Krajcik and his colleagues (2000) suggest that the different levels of student achievement shown among classes may be the result of factors such as differences among the schools and communities in economic security or levels of resources available to teachers.

K–12 Partnership of University, Indian Reservation, and Medium Size Urban School District

The University of Minnesota Duluth (UMD), supported by US Department of Education's PT3 grant, is working in collaboration with the Duluth Public Schools and Fond du Lac Indian Reservation's Ojibwe Schools to create systemic change through technology integration in each institution. Their project focuses on preschool through grade-twelve Ojibwe students, and low-income students in rural and urban settings. The social support structures to facilitate change are small, self-managed educator teams who integrate technology into teaching and learning environments. These teams are called collaboratories. Each collaboratory is composed of a teacher, two university professors—one from education and one from arts and sciences—and three university students. The classroom teacher in each collaboratory brings a unit of instruction to the group and indicates what the students need to learn. The collaboratory determines how technology can assist students' learning the material. It also determines how to use technology for real-time staff development (with support from a technology coordinator) and assists the classroom teacher implementing the plans. In this manner each collaboratory member expands technology proficiency.

During the first year of implementation six collaboratories were formed; at Fond du Lac Indian Reservation Ojibwe Schools: first-grade literacy and middle school science; in Duluth Public Schools: fourth-grade science, elementary school visual arts, high school English, and high school social studies. Systems change issues created tensions at each site. In the subsequent paragraphs we will provide you with two such examples.

All three public schools involved in the implementation had issues related to use of the Internet, responsive support for teachers implementing technology in their classrooms, and MIS administrators being responsible for technology deployment and support but having limited previous knowledge of using technology for teaching and learning by teachers. The issues were very similar to those issues expressed in the urban cities of the LeTUS projects. Some of the solutions were different however.

The high school collaboratory members envisioned a problem-solving structure that would enlighten both the computer technicians and themselves. Therefore, they formed a team composed of their administrators, technology support people, a MIS staff person, and a university researcher, which met regularly to jointly resolve issues the teachers were facing as they tried to implement technology more thoroughly into their curriculum. One of the principle issues across each system was the use of shared folders on a central school or district-based server. The school computers frequently were configured without disk drives, so rather than e-mail work between student and teachers, the teachers found using shared folders easier—when they worked properly. At several critical junctures student work in shared folders inexplicably disappeared. The diverse problem-solving team worked through the seriousness of the issue and designed strategies to minimize this disruption in the future. The team was also instrumental in assisting the MIS staff in configuring computers and acquiring software that was more supportive of classroom-based learning.

At Fond du Lac, the first-grade collaboratory members asked whether the young students would be able to share their knowledge via technology at home with their parents. This question was brought to the Tribe. Consequently, the Tribe decided to support the purchase of computers for the families of the first graders. They would continue this support each year, creating the opportunity for students to share their work and for families to digitally learn at home. The university faculty and technology coordinator assisted the reservation staff in preparing the parents to set up and use the home computers.

Summary

"Bridging [the] gaps and creating a more cohesive sense of community between those living in regions largely outside the digital economy and those within could well represent the greatest challenge of the new millennium" (Kotkin & Moyers, 2000, p. 23).

How do educational organizations systemically change to provide digitally equitable learning environments for their students, teachers, and communities? And as a correlate, how does a nation support the challenge to create digital equity among its citizens? As illustrated in this chapter and throughout this book, our public school organizations are key constructors of the bridge between those who are able to function and contribute in the digital age and those who are not. But, significant fundamental systems change needs to occur. Each organization willing to fully prepare their students for living, working, and civically participating in the twenty-first century, needs to see their organization with a new perspective. We know what the problems are. We know what questions to ask. Given this knowledge, the models for systems change, examples from the field, and a renewed zest for democratic, inter-institutional, and inter-community participation in planning, implementation, development, technical support and maintenance, and dynamic adjustment, we believe the change will be widespread and successful.

Therefore, change initiatives that promote the partnership of teachers, administrators, parents, businesspersons, community members, and university faculty, such as PT3 projects and the LeTUS Program, are essential building blocks for digital equity. Entire communities need to engage in productive conversations to create shared visions of twenty-first-century education organizations with actionable steps to facilitate digitally equitable, sustainable public school change. This type of grassroots effort requires support from traditionally "top down" policymakers. Teachers, parents, administrators, community members, and university professionals, on the other hand, must be willing to engage in what is often time consuming and challenging work to build from the "bottom up." Respectful democratic processes in concert with all partner voices, build ownership for new visions, blue prints for meaningful change, and collective willingness to work toward innovative and digitally equitable structures, processes, and roles.

14 Assessing Equity in Educational Technology

J. DAVID RAMIREZ

FOCUS QUESTIONS

1. What are the critical factors in assessing digital equity?
2. What is the relationship between assessment and educational use of information and communication technologies?
3. What methods are most effective for assessing digital equity?
4. What pitfalls related to equity issues need to be considered in assessments?

Will current and emerging information and communication technologies (ICT) improve learning for all students, especially for diverse and traditionally underserved populations by providing them all with rigorous content and demanding learning opportunities (Means, 1995; Schacter, 1999)? Or will ICT be yet another obstacle to widen the achievement gap between different groups of students (Becker & Ravitz, 1997; Fabos & Young, 1999; Hedges, Konstantopoulos, & Thoreson, 2000)? Systematic group differences in student achievement reflect systemic inequitable learning opportunities. Earlier chapters in this volume describe how ICT might be used to address the specific learning needs of diverse and traditionally underserved populations to eliminate these inequities. This chapter provides a framework for assessing ICT's contribution toward creating equitable learning opportunities for all students.

ICT can help bridge the digital divide to the extent that the teaching and learning context into which ICT is integrated bridges the educational divide. In turn, the effectiveness of the teaching and learning context in bridging the educational divide depends upon the quality, relevance, and appropriateness of the underlying educational research, practice, and policy that define the instructional context. Educational practice, research, and policy are, however, themselves mediated by complex social, economic, and political forces that often go unexamined or unquestioned (Beyer & Apple, 1998; Pea, 1996).

Assessment and accountability need to make explicit how these underlying forces shape what students learn, how they learn, and the criteria and processes used to document what they have learned (Dimitriadis & Kamberelis, 1997). We need a broad theoretical perspective to help us understand how these underlying forces, in isolation and when combined, not only influence the teaching and learning context, educational research agendas, and policies, but how they also determine how ICT is used and its role in promoting or impeding digital equity.

The Importance of Assessing Equity

We live in a world of difference. How each of us responds, personally and professionally, to diversity remains one of our most formidable challenges. Rapid demographic changes in our local communities and the growing interdependence of communities across the globe increasingly present us with opportunities to interact with those who differ from us in such ways as income, race/ethnicity, language, language proficiency, religion, culture, gender, sexual orientation, and special needs. Schools have a central role in helping students develop the skills to successfully respond to these differences. These coping skills include multilingualism, multiculturalism, information literacy, technological fluency, and of course, high levels of knowledge and skills proficiency. Equally important, students need to fully develop democratic citizenship skills that will allow them to negotiate, cooperate, and collaborate for the mutual good in a world of difference. It is within this context that digital equity is assessed.

An assessment of equity considers who is being served and how they are served. Educational equity is concerned with both student access to resources (who has it and who doesn't) as well as the meaningfulness of those resources to students as compared within and between classrooms, schools, and districts. It means affirming that groups of students, regardless of their differences, are provided with appropriate learning opportunities to help them participate in and contribute to a democratic and just society.

Important Factors

Social Context.   Schools are one of the most important institutions, outside of the home, responsible for preparing twenty-first-century citizens. Some view public education as the great equalizer, a tangible effort to provide opportunities to those willing to work hard to realize their aspirations regardless of background, to become full participants in a democratic society. In contrast, others believe that schools function as a mechanism of control, socializing students, according to their differences, to take their rightful places in the existing inequitable social, economic, and political structures (Dimitriades & Kamberelis, 1997; Sleeter & McLaren, 1995). Knowing and understanding how a community defines the purpose of schooling and how schooling is implemented guides us in determining what information to collect and in interpreting results.

Economic Context.   The growing disparity in income by race/ethnicity and gender parallels the differences in the type and quality of educational services and ICT that schools provide to students in these groups. It also, not unexpectedly, parallels the observed differences in student achievement by social class, race/ethnicity, gender, and language (Becker, 2000a; DeVillar & Faltis, 1991); that is, inequities in schools mirror inequities in the larger society. Why is it, then, that despite efforts by states to equalize funding across schools, that some schools are consistently underresourced and others fully resourced? This relationship, between school funding and student achievement, therefore becomes an important factor to assess in evaluating programs, projects, and research.

Political Context.   Many of the issues related to digital equity are political in nature. Why is it that certain differences between people result in inequitable educational treatment and achievement? Who determines how differences in class, race, gender, language, etc., come to be attributes that create opportunity for some and barriers to others? What mechanisms are used to create and sustain inequities? What is the relationship between these areas of difference and the social, economic, and political forces in schools and community?

Lipman (1998) found that the social, economic, and political inequities between groups in a community and the forces that created them are duplicated in schools, creating inequities between corresponding groups of students in learning opportunities and achievement. A serious analysis of digital equity needs to examine more deeply how the social, economic, and political forces outside of schools impact teaching and learning within schools, and in turn determine which and how ICT will be used to either create or impede equitable learning opportunities for all students and the development of democratic citizens. Such systemic analyses are central to the assessment of digital equity and are needed to identify systematic student differences as to who is learning and who is not and to recognize how and why these differences occur.

Educational Reform Context.   The educational reform effort of the past twenty years focused on identifying and strengthening key systemic processes in education that directly impact the quality of teaching and learning with a concern for all students. An assessment of digital equity must necessarily document the educational reform context and identify how ICT is integrated into instruction to understand how these reform efforts are shaping the teaching and learning opportunities provided to all students. Research has taught us a great deal about how ICT can support the elements of educational reform. It supports (a) what is taught, (b) how it is taught, (c) how people in schools work together, (d) how the school/district is organized and managed, (e) how the home, school, and community collaborate to support student learning, and, (f) how to assure systemic accountability (Means & Olson, 1995). We also now understand that effective integration of ICT into teaching and learning, as with systemic educational reform, requires intervention and changes at several levels: national, state, local, community, district, and classroom. A proper assessment of digital equity also requires that we determine how ICT is integrated into each of the elements of reform and within and across each change level.

Most educational reform efforts like the CEO Forum (1997) are fairly generic in approach, providing few, if any, specific recommendations as to how these efforts directly address the unique learning needs of diverse student populations. For example, the Reading First program is a federal initiative to reform literacy instruction by funding specific research-based literacy activities and guiding the development of state reading standards. Yet, these required literacy activities are based on reading research on only monolingual English speakers (Snow, Burns, & Griffin, 1999). Reading First resources assume that the literacy learning needs of English language learners and speakers of non-traditional English are the same as those of middle class native English speakers. (Ramirez, 2001) The result is that both English language learners and speakers of non-traditional English are provided with inappropriate literacy instruction.

If we fail to fully explore the evidence and rationale of the research, policies, and practices underlying a particular instructional program from a diversity perspective, we may provide inappropriate teaching and learning for some students, inaccurately conclude that students and their parents are solely responsible for poor achievement, and never question our teaching and learning practices. Only when we implement diversity-responsive assessments can we monitor and evaluate the progress made toward digital equity. Diversity-responsive assessments make visible the invisible. They identify and reveal why certain processes support or impede access and meaningfulness of learning opportunities for different groups of students. They answer, for example, such questions as how specific attributes of people such as skin color, gender, homelessness, or immigrant status come to be regarded as "markers" around which groups are defined and treated differently and what the processes are that sustain these differences. When we clearly understand what is meant by "difference" and how and why this concept is created and maintained, we can begin to move towards digital equity.

Origin of a Concept of Difference

Social Construction of Identity

The challenge of learning about diversity and equity begins within ourselves as we confront our individual experiences related to difference and privilege within the dominant culture (Van Soest, Canon, & Grant, 2000). This understanding can guide us in identifying constructs and processes directly related to digital equity. A basic premise in multicultural education is that the construction of meaning and identity is a social and cultural act. Identity and meaning develop as each of us interact with others in our community who are different from us. This is a lifelong never-ending process.

Social Construction of Privilege and Oppression

Inherent in our identity is a sense of our status in a given social context, e.g., at home— husband, wife, child, sibling, or parent; at work—employer or employee; at school— principal, teacher, student, or parent; at a child custody hearing—economically stable or economically at risk; at a high school dance—straight or gay; or at a hospital emergency room—rich or poor. Our status in a given social context also defines for us the type and amount of social, economic, and/or political power, that entitles us to certain benefits (privileges) or creates barriers for us to resources and opportunities. However, much as a winner requires that there be a loser, to privilege some necessitates that others be denied comparable access (i.e., subordinated) in a given social context. It is important to note that such privilege comes about not on the basis of personal merit, but because of demographics. Those who knowingly or unknowingly use such unmerited privilege may be considered oppressors or dominant and those that are unfairly denied access as a result of this privilege may be considered the oppressed or subordinated. One outcome of having multiple identities is that as each of us move from one social context to another we may find ourselves in the role of either an oppressor or oppressed. An awareness of these shifting roles and their implications to us provides a shared experience with others on which to begin dialogue and investigate privilege and oppression. Recognizing these dynamics provides an avenue for systematically examining how teaching and learning activities and ICT may enfranchise or disenfranchise different groups of students. The research and principals of multicultural education can inform efforts to identify these dynamics. They can provide a framework for recognizing the processes by which we become oppressed or oppressors in different social contexts (Bell, 1997; Tatum, 1992; Van Soest, Canon, & Grant, 2000). Such a framework can help us focus on key issues, such as institutional racism and social justice.

Origin of Privilege and Oppression

Multicultural education focuses on making explicit the impact of institutional racism. This is done by identifying unnamed assumptions underlying traditional and new pedagogies and questioning their appropriateness for different types of students, e.g., providing only direct instruction and a phonics-based reading program to all students (Kohn, 1999) or assigning all English language learners to an English-only instructional program (Delpit, 1995). By asking who was or was not present and in charge when decisions were made and how these decisions were made and to identify who was privileged or disenfranchised as a result of the decisions and actions taken, begins to reveal the underlying rationale and dynamics of the dominance of one group over another and the mechanisms by which difference is socially constructed and maintained. Assessment should try to answer the questions: who benefits, who loses, and, why?

Critical multiculturalists insist that students deconstruct their educational experiences and work continuously toward equalizing the distribution of privilege and power (McLaren, 1995). Critical multiculturalists are concerned with moving students beyond superficial learning opportunities (such as celebrating holidays of different ethnic groups) into those which help students understand their role in the social change process leading to a just society by (a) relating what they are learning to their lived experiences, (b) clarifying the role of difference in their own lives, (c) understanding the socially constructed origins of difference, (d) recognizing how privileges and barriers flow from the inequities created as a result of these differences, and (e) learning what action they can take individually and collectively to rectify these injustices by creating "opportunities for resistance" (Fabos & Young, 1999). Each of these concepts and approaches helps define important factors in a process or outcome evaluation of an ICT-enriched teaching and learning context.

Impact of Personal Attitudes, Beliefs, and Behaviors

Personal attitudes, beliefs, and behaviors define the learning context and ICT use in schools. As the chapter on access clearly documents, students must have adequate and meaningful access to technology for it to make a difference. Someone, or some group of individuals, makes the decision of how resources will be distributed within districts, states, and across the nation. What social, economic, and political processes affect the distribution of resources to schools? Why is it that these processes and the resultant distribution of resources do not seem to equalize resources to schools? Who decides how resources are distributed? Who benefits and who loses in this process? To what extent does this process advance the cause of justice for all? These questions need answers.

The effectiveness of ICT to support student achievement begins with the quality of the underlying teaching and learning context (Interactive, Inc., 2000). Ultimately, the teacher is the primary determiner of digital equity within culturally diverse classrooms (Brown, Higgins, & Hartley, 2001; Sianjina, 2000). There appears to be a strong relationship between the type of student and the type of instruction they receive based upon teacher beliefs and attitudes about the capabilities of different students (Brown, Higgins, & Hartley, 2001) and the teacher's personal philosophical beliefs about how students learn and the type of instructional strategies that reflect that style of learning (Becker, 2000b). An assessment of digital equity should surface and examine the relationship between observed differences in content and learning activities and any differences in teacher expectations by type of student (i.e., data disaggregated by race, income, language status, gender, special needs, etc.). This is accomplished by documenting how the teacher differentiates instruction while maintaining the same breadth and depth of content standards and holds all students accountable for the same performance standards. Documenting differentiated instruction means more than simply determining whether the teacher is using passive or active learning pedagogy or whether students participate in project-based learning tasks or cooperative learning groups. It means assessing how teaching and learning draw from a student's background knowledge, how assigned learning tasks consider the extent to which a student must speak, read, write, and comprehend English to do a given task, and how teaching and learning consider the distribution and availability of ICT resources to assure equal opportunities to learn for all students.

Assessment and Educational Use of ICT

Banks (1994, p. 5) presents a framework that could be used by schools as a basis for assessing digital equity. He clearly goes beyond the simple notion of integrating cultural information as a means to teach the academic content, instead emphasizing opportunities to develop the skills needed by democratic citizens. He identifies five dimensions of multicultural education: (1) content integration, (2) knowledge construction, (3) prejudice reduction, (4) achievement of an equity pedagogy, and (5) empowerment of school culture and social structure. I use these dimensions as a basis for developing content as well as teacher and student performance standards that explicitly focus on democratic citizenship thereby allowing one approach for the assessment of digital equity (see Table 14.1 at the end of this chapter).

Is ICT used in culturally relevant ways? Pea (1996) notes that computers are not culture free. Rather, their value and use is determined by teacher and student background knowledge and experience. Teachers need to consider cultural differences in how students work, learn, and see the world in selecting ICT tools and determining how they are to be used. Sianjina (2000) asserts that culturally responsive ICT use in a multicultural classroom requires at least six factors: cultural relevance, equitable access, instructional flexibility, cultural awareness, supportive multicultural environment, and ICT integration. Au and Kawakami (1991) state that culturally relevant instruction occurs when teaching and learning activities support differences in learning preferences, language of instruction, and language proficiency. This is demonstrated through the integration of the learner's lived experiences into what is taught, how it is taught, and instructional materials and learning activities. We know that when students are provided with educational ICT learning opportunities that relate to students' experiences (e.g., topics, activities, programs, and resources), their motivation to learn increases (Sianjina, 2000; Wlodkowski & Ginsberg, 1995). These opportunities should be assessed.

What process do teachers use to plan ICT use? The steps taken by a teacher to create a student-centered learning venue are important indicators of the type and quality of the teaching and learning context. Ideally, the teacher is guided by the content and by student and teacher performance standards and follows the process of:

1. Specifying the instructional academic and democratic citizenship objectives
2. Identifying the optimal teaching and learning context
3. Reviewing the composition of the class in terms of diversity
4. Assessing what each student or group knows or does not know
5. Organizing the class into appropriate learning groups
6. Selecting the appropriate instructional ICT and non-ICT materials and strategies to assure full participation and access to the content standards by each student group and by each student within a group
7. Regularly monitoring the progress of each group and individual student with both ICT and non-ICT tools
8. Completing a culminating assessment to determine the achievement of each student and working group
9. Reflecting on how well the unit of practice succeeded in realizing the instructional goals for the unit

Is physical access to ICT a sufficient indicator of digital equity? In a lawsuit brought against the San Francisco Unified School District in 1966, *Lau v. Nichols,* the United States Supreme Court made it very clear that equal learning opportunities does not necessarily indicate the same instructional treatment (1974). What is more important is that the instruction be meaningful to each student. Thus, equitable ICT access is defined in terms of instructional flexibility provided by the teacher and its appropriateness and meaningfulness to the student's current learning needs in terms of developing higher-order thinking, academic language, content knowledge, and social and democratic citizenship skills. Assessment must determine, therefore, not only whether students have physical access to ICT, but also the quality of that physical access.

Is ICT used to support the necessary conditions for learning? Integrating ICT into teaching and learning can benefit high- and low-performing students, improve specific content area skills and knowledge, and foster positive attitudes toward ICT and academic learning and self (Sianjina, 2000). Many necessary conditions for successful learning environments for diverse students can be provided through ICT, such as providing opportunities for cooperative learning, addressing varied learning styles, allowing students to be knowledge producers rather than consumers, and providing activities that develop critical multicultural awareness, improve communication skills, and make learning interesting, fun, and relevant (Soska, 1994). An assessment of digital equity documents how ICT tools are used to create and support these necessary conditions.

Is ICT being used in meaningful ways? Equity in ICT refers to both the physical access to hardware and software and the meaningfulness of this access. One important aspect of meaningfulness is the amount, frequency, and type of student autonomy afforded in the learning process given its contribution to task engagement and learning. From the students' perspective, it means having options as to what they will learn, how they will learn, and how they will be assessed (Wlodkowski & Ginsberg, 1995). It also means "deciding who uses the computer, with whom, at what time, for how long, and for what purpose" (Mislevy, Steinberg, Almond, Haertel, & Penuel, 2000, p. 26). Such instructional flexibility by the teacher demonstrates to students a respect for who they are and what they can do and must be a part of assessment.

Example of a Digital Equity Assessment of ICT-Enhanced Teaching and Learning

Fabos and Young's critical review of research on telecommunication exchange projects (1999) illustrates how integrating diversity issues into an assessment of student learning tasks and activities can make visible inherent inequities in learning opportunities for students and provide a clearer understanding of different patterns of achievement between different groups of students. Telecommunication exchange projects are promoted as providing students with an authentic purpose for communicating. Such projects purportedly help students to develop three important skills: writing, multicultural awareness, and work preparedness. Riel (1992), for example, extols the virtues of AT&T's Learning Circles: (a) students are free to work together productively online without the social encumbrances and challenges one usually finds in face-to-face interactions; and (b) online interactions minimize, if not obviate, any differences that might exist between groups such as skin color, income, special needs, or accent.

However, there is no research evidence to support the underlying assumption of telecommunication projects (Fabos & Young, 1999). Researchers have found that simply providing students with opportunities for socially constructed exchanges will not by themselves lead to improved writing as most students need a modicum of guidance and structure if they are to improve their writing (Walkerdine, 1998), nor to the development of deep multicultural awareness (Dimitriades & Kamberelis, 1997). In fact, providing students with only an opportunity to engage in virtual interactions with peers who differ from them might actually reinforce the male eurocentric bias inherent in much of ICT (Berland, 1998; Damarin, 1998; Fabos & Young, 1999).

What is interesting is that none of the researchers cited, nor Fabos and Young themselves, seem to have sufficiently probed or considered other critical factors that affect the development of student writing skills, e.g., students' language proficiency or teachers' understanding of language development. As presented, all of the researchers assumed that all of the students in the process of developing their writing skills were English proficient. Moreover, none of the researchers questioned whether teachers were sufficiently knowledgeable about language development to provide the necessary feedback to students. With very few exceptions, the majority of teachers in classrooms have little or no understanding of English language development for native English-speaking students, let alone of the specific academic language skills needed for content learning, especially for those that are traditionally underserved. The digital equity assessment process needs to probe for such factors.

Fabos and Young (1999) assert that to develop multicultural awareness, teachers must move students from simply recognizing differences to an understanding of how difference is socially constructed, its implications for advantaging some and disadvantaging others, and the action needed to create and support a more democratic community and society (McCarthy, 1998; Willinsky, 1998). Currently assessments of telecommunication projects fail to address these deeper multicultural issues.

Methodological Considerations

Changing Evaluation Goals

ICT assessment goals evolved over time from simply gathering information to help policy-makers decide whether ICT should be incorporated into the educational system to the current focus on trying to understand exactly how the teaching and learning process can be transformed through ICT. Much of the early evaluation efforts focused on comparing the achievement of students who used ICT to those who did not. Most of these results were inconclusive because of serious methodological problems, e.g., failure to document comparability of instructional strategies between the ICT and non-ICT learning situations being studied or generalizing across different types of technologies (Baker & Herman, 2000).

Current assessment efforts focus on the relationship between ICT and the teaching and learning process. Such efforts tend to focus on studying ICT support of project-based learning. Project-based learning is student-centered, creating opportunities for students to develop the critical thinking and problem-solving skills they will need as adults. Ideally, the teacher as facilitator provides students with activities to help them to "problem-pose" (i.e., to identify a question or issue that they would like to investigate), to develop an action plan to address their question or issue (i.e., establish project goals, objectives, activities, assign responsibilities, timelines, and specify outcomes), to apply what they have learned to their problem and evaluate the results, and to revise their thinking and solution based on what they learned. This approach is generally thematic and interdisciplinary, integrating information and skills across content areas (e.g., language arts, math, science, and social science). The teacher monitors student work and as a critical friend may pose questions for students to consider to further and refine their thinking and to assure that the process addresses grade-level content.

These research efforts focus on both content and process. Key questions include:

- How does ICT transform our notion of what content to access, how to organize it, and how students interact with it?
- How can ICT tools help teachers create, manage, and monitor what is taught and is being learned, such as the integration and acquisition of content standards in student-centered and student-directed project-based learning?
- How can teachers' use of different ICT strategies such as the Internet and multimedia be used to organize and present information to support reflective teaching and collaborative inquiry for the teacher and for the students?

Current research notwithstanding, Haertel and Means (2000) note that we are still only at the frontiers of understanding how ICT can transform teaching and learning.

Increased Focus on Assessing Impact upon Different Types of Students

The majority of federal funding for ICT use in schools is provided to support improvement of services to traditionally underserved populations, e.g., Technology Innovation Challenge Grants, Technology Literacy Challenge Fund, and STAR Schools. It was not surprising then to find that a review of a sample of Challenge Grant and STAR Schools program evaluations revealed that serving traditionally underserved populations was a key reason for seeking funding (Ramirez, 1999). Yet besides noting that students were poor, of color, or English language learners, there was scant identification in any of the proposals of the specific learning issues or interventions that would explicitly address the needs of these students. Each proposal assumed that the instructional goals and objectives would be appropriate for these students. This omission was exacerbated in the evaluations, where all but one of the evaluation reports presented student achievement data for all students taken together. In general, project evaluations did not disaggregate student achievement data by type of student group to identify who was or was not learning. Only by engaging in a more detailed analysis of student achievement data by key diversity factors (e.g., Chinese-speaking female born in Taiwan) is it possible to begin to identify the relative effectiveness of ICT upon student achievement. Moreover, such assessment of ICT must necessarily include for each student group: (1) a clear statement of their specific teaching and learning needs beyond that they are poor, of color, English language learner, migrant, or immigrant; (2) a rationale for the specific teaching and learning activities to be provided; (3) documentation of the amount, frequency, and quality of the teaching and learning activities to be provided; (4) documentation of which ICT were used (amount and frequency of access); (5) documentation of how ICT implementation reflected the desired teaching and learning activities (i.e., amount, frequency, and fidelity of treatment); and, (6) analyses that examine the effect of these activities upon student achievement. The one evaluation that did disaggregate student data did not provide any evidence of a critical inquiry into the appropriateness of the intervention to the needs of their students.

Many current evaluation efforts also suffer the same limitations. Honey, McMillan-Culp, and Carrigg (1999) researched how ICT can be used to improve student learning and teachers' perceptions of student ability. Their study design was guided by two key assumptions. First, systemic change comes about more from the educational reform context into which ICT are integrated than from the technologies themselves, and second, it is important to examine how different ICT can be used to support different school processes as well as the different elements of school change. They wanted to understand how and why ICT could facilitate school change. Through their work they identified eight key reform strategies that were critical to the successful integration of ICT into teaching and learning:

- Instructional leadership at the building level
- Effective school improvement teams
- Extensive professional development in whole-language teaching approaches and cooperative learning
- A strong emphasis on student creativity and the expression of ideas in multiple formats
- An emphasis on providing different points of entry into a task for children working at different ability levels
- A de-emphasis on remediation and an emphasis on learning for all

- Establishment of classroom libraries and media-rich classroom environments
- A multi-text approach to learning that includes the integration of ICT into instruction

While these findings are very helpful in describing contextual factors critical to successful ICT integration, they do not help us understand how the technologies used addressed the specific learning needs of the students involved in their study. A large proportion of the students in Union City are Hispanic, language minority, English language learners, and poor, yet the researchers did not report disaggregated student achievement data. Honey, McMillan Culp, and Carrigg (1999) failed to provide an analysis of the impact these student characteristics had on student learning needs (e.g., by English language development level), or a description of how the specific project activities addressed these needs. While the report does state the importance of allowing students to use multiple formats for presenting what they are learning and of differentiating instruction for students at various skill levels, it does not give sufficient detail or show how these strategies are central to the project. The findings as presented are sufficiently generic that they could apply to any student group in any school context. As Baker and Herman said, "Traditional designs are not doing the job, nor are they really providing the control expected of them, can't capture the outcomes we want to achieve with new technology interventions, and these tend to be variable across and even within specific initiatives as well as over time" (2000, p. 11). Researchers and evaluators need to exert greater effort to improve the quality of ICT evaluations in reference to equity issues.

Assessment Design Issues to Consider

What Is the Social, Economic, and Political Context within Which ICT-Supported Teaching and Learning Occur Both Outside and within the School?

"Unless researchers and educators address the historical and cultural context of dominance within many of these [telecommunications] projects, real pluralism can easily be overlooked as one political and economic system and communication culture is unilaterally favored over another" (Fabos & Young, 1999, p. 237). Table 14.1, at the end of this chapter, draws constructs from the prior discussion of multicultural education and lists key teacher and student performance standards that would be key indicators of digital equity.

What Is the Teaching and Learning Context of the ICT Project?

It is critical that evaluations of digital equity carefully delineate and document the educational equity of the teaching and learning context, as this context shapes both how ICT is used as well as its impact upon the teaching and learning process. Only by fully understanding how ICT can be effective in different teaching and learning contexts for different groups of students can we begin to understand how ICT can be used to guide public policy in the use of ICT to support the unique instructional and learning goals of diverse students in a given classroom, school, and community.

Assessment of digital equity also needs to closely examine the information teachers provide to students, what teachers ask students to do with this information, who created the information provided (i.e., who's voice is reflected in the information), and who designed the teaching and learning context. In addition, it is important to assess how the specific types and uses of ICT help transform the student into a participating member in their local, national, and international community and an advocate for justice.

Haertel and Means (2000) identified information that they felt was important in the teaching and learning context: (a) how the ICT innovation is conceptualized and introduced; (b) the ICT infrastructure within the classroom, school, and district; (c) the type and availability of resources to support the integration of ICT; (d) the prevailing attitudes towards ICT, teaching and learning, and educational reform at the classroom, school, and district levels; (e) the amount and type of support for ICT integration from administrators and school board; and (f) the demographic characteristics of the classroom, school, district, community, and student's home. While this list is helpful in identifying "generic" data that should be collected, Haertel and Means did not address diversity, failed to provide a conceptual framework for describing the role or relative contribution of the teaching and learning data elements to student achievement.

In contrast, Lesgold's (2000) conceptual model describes the educational context. He developed a set of rubrics to assess the degree and quality of implementation of four dimensions that he identified as critical to determining how ICT are used and their impact upon student learning: instructional, ICT infrastructure, educational software, and people maturity. His work more clearly illustrates the type of approach that needs to be taken by evaluators. His conceptual model not only delineates what should be examined and a systematic way of how it should be examined, but facilitates quantitative analyses of the data through use of rubrics as well as guiding the examination of the relationships among and between the constructs within and between each of the four dimensions. Such a quantitative and conceptual approach allows for examination of data across educational contexts and the development of a theoretical model explaining the role of ICT in supporting teaching and learning across educational contexts.

Schum (1994) provides a framework for examining the learning process. He describes three steps for assessing how students learn and how they use what they have learned: (1) define the underlying constructs to be examined; (2) specify the type and forms of evidence (i.e., process and outcome variables); and, (3) delineate the unique characteristics of the teaching and learning context that is considered necessary by theory to most yield the desired outcomes. The strength of Schum's approach is that it forces the evaluation to examine and understand the unique features of a given context and their interaction with and impact upon student learning, as well as the patterns and processes students use to develop and apply what they have learned. Both understandings are needed when assessing ICT-based instruction and learning.

Building upon Schum's work, Mislevy, Steinberg, Almond, Haertel, and Penuel (2000) describe observable student behaviors that can be used to monitor changes in student learning, particularly learning outcomes typically identified in ICT-enhanced project-based learning. They note that it is important for evaluators to carefully identify which unique features of a given learning activity lead students to use different thinking processes or prior knowledge. They also describe how a Web-based environment can be used to monitor and record student work as students search for information, analyze it, and problem-solve. Moreover, such an environment can be easily controlled to modify the type of information and the type of task to be performed, thereby facilitating assessment of specific changes to the learning context and their impact upon how students access, process, and apply information. Thus, a Web-based environment provides a platform for designing research and evaluations that allows for the collection "of data that is keenly contextualized, taking into account the characteristics of students, teachers, classroom, school, district, and community all related to the key program goals and objectives" (Mislevy et al., 2000, p. 23).

Most of the recommendations listed by these researchers only address physical access issues and fail to discuss the equally critical equity issue of meaningfulness. As presented, by failing to mention the unique learning needs of traditionally underserved students and providing a framework for their consideration in the assessment process, the evaluator simply documents who is and who is not learning in a given instructional context without questioning the appropriateness of the instruction, with results possibly reinforcing stereotypes, and failing to consider the larger social, economic, and political systems that contribute to these differences. The exception is Kenway (1998) who does raise the issue of representation of voice and of message to students.

What Research Methodology Is Most Effective?

There are two methodological approaches to examine ICT's impact upon the teaching and learning process, qualitative and quantitative. Qualitative research is a more intensive examination of a particular context. It relies on a number of different types of in-depth and intensive data collection procedures, such as direct open-ended observations, interviews, focus groups, and reviews of documents and artifacts. Qualitative research is most helpful in theory building through synthesis of and reflection on the information collected and in positing critical constructs about their interrelationships. The work by Haertel and Means (2000) discussed above tends to reflect such a qualitative exploratory approach. Because of the intensity of data collection procedures and the resources required, qualitative research is very labor intensive and most suitable for studying a small number of sites at one time. It is particularly suited for evaluation efforts seeking to assess the impact of ICT in a specific teaching and learning context. This strength, however, is also a limitation. Qualitative results cannot be generalized across settings.

In contrast, quantitative research is characterized as a more structured approach to data collection. The evaluator develops a conceptual model delineating his/her assumptions of what data are important and should be collected, how they should be collected (e.g., frequencies and fixed responses) through observations and interviews, and how they should be analyzed (e.g., specification of independent and dependent measures and their interrelationships). Quantitative data collection procedures are designed to gather a fixed amount of data across a large number of sites. The focus of a quantitative approach is upon generalizability, that is, upon describing basic underlying principles across contexts. The work by Lesgold (2000), Schum (1994), and Mislevy, Steinberg, Almond, Haertel and Penuel (2000) are examples of a more quantitative approach. Quantitative methods are limited in that by gathering pre-identified information across a number of sites, there is the risk of ignoring other potentially valuable factors. This is particularly problematic if the goal of the assessment to clearly understand a specific teaching and learning context.

While a qualitative approach provides depth, it lacks breadth. A quantitative approach provides breadth, but lacks depth. Consequently, an assessment design ideally incorporates both qualitative and quantitative methodologies to take advantage of the strengths of each approach and to minimize the limitations of each. This is true of assessments of digital equity issues as well as other research agendas.

What about Comparison Groups?

The major consideration is to assure that the groups to be used for comparison (control and treatment) are in fact initially comparable with respect to all of the major independent and dependent variables. When comparing the achievement of students in an ICT-supported learning environment to that of their peers in a non-ICT learning context, it is essential that the learning tasks and activities in both settings directly reflect the same program goals and objectives, philosophies, and instructional approaches (e.g., project-based learning), and that student characteristics be the same. The two contexts should only differ with regards to the integration of ICT into the teaching and learning context: one group integrates ICT; the other does not.

What Special Considerations Are There for Instrument Development?

Standardized measures assess a limited level and range of student skills, yet ICT projects require broad, deep, and complex student performance and use of higher-order thinking skills. To adequately assess an ICT project, evaluators need instruments that will capture the outcomes of constructivist interventions of extended performance tasks—instruments that will measure the student's ability to learn, to problem-solve, explain, interpret, and apply knowledge in different contexts (Haertel & Means, 2000), as well as how well he/she collaborates, plans, and leads.

Haertel and Means (2000) reviewed educational ICT evaluations and found that few if any specifically targeted and examined the effects of ICT-enabled innovations on student learning. They identified two critical areas for improving ICT evaluations: (a) the development of new assessment approaches to measure student outcomes to include constructivist theories of learning that reflect extended performance tasks (e.g., capacity to problem-solve, explain, interpret, and apply knowledge in diverse contexts), social competencies, and collaboration; and (b) the development of valid and reliable ways to document the teaching and learning context (e.g., constructivist-centered approach; linkages to content, teacher, and student performance standards; and, teacher negotiation of content). It is critical that evaluations not only document that educational ICT worked, but also the factors contributing to this success, i.e., why did it work? To these might be added a third factor, degree of equity.

Evaluators need to develop assessment approaches that reflect an understanding of diversity responsive multicultural and multilingual theories and practices. Currently, evaluation efforts should document the quality and effects of specific ICT implementations: that is, specific ICT tools (software and/or hardware), the teaching and learning context (goals, objectives, type and nature of activities, materials, specified outcomes, and enabling conditions), the characteristics of those participating in this context (teachers and students), and the differential access of each group and subgroup. The focus of such digital-equity-responsive assessment is to make explicit the relationship between the instructional processes implemented, ICT use, unique contextual characteristics, specific student learning needs, and student outcomes.

How Might Data Collection Be Improved?

Finally, given the multiple factors that contribute to improving teaching and learning, evaluators need multiple data collection procedures and instruments: surveys, observations, interviews, focus groups, teacher logs, records of online activity, and reviews of documents. New technologies provide us with a range of options for assessment, for creating new kinds of tasks, for infusing life into assessment, and for interacting with those being tested (Bennett, 1999; Quellmalz & Haertel, 1999). ICT tools are available that allow us to measure students' higher-level inquiry processes, such as how they generate questions and what type of research questions they generate, their project planning processes, their project implementation strategies, the type of data they collect, how they collect, analyze, and interpret data, and how they present findings (Mislevy et al., 2000). Once again, it is as important to understand why an innovation worked as it is to document that it did work.

Cognitive and educational psychology have helped to capture the processes by which people organize data, make inferences, and generalize (Mislevy et al., 2000; Schum, 1994). Theory and research in situative psychology and cognitive psychology serve to highlight the multiplicity and complexity of factors affecting learning, from the characteristics of those in the learning context and the learning context itself, and the myriad interactions of all of these variables leading to a specific outcome. This approach emphasizes understanding the different ways people interact with one another in different social and technological systems and understanding how these different ICT-learning contexts support or impede learning. From an equity perspective, we would integrate into this assessment process what we know about language, race, class, special needs, or any other important area of difference to not only interpret student performance, but also to understand how these areas of difference impact the process of knowing and doing.

To design an assessment instrument, we first need to identify the specific information needed to support the inferences we wish to make. For example, drawing from the preceding paragraph, we would like to make inferences about the "patterns, skills, and knowledge structures that characterize developing expertise" (Mislevy et al., 2000, p. 8). From this perspective, we would determine student achievement by documenting the student's developing knowledge structures, the cognitive processes used, and the procedures used in learning and applying this new knowledge in new contexts.

Contemporary views of how we learn and think reflect notions of situative psychology and constructivist approaches to information processing. Mislevy et al. (2000) proposed two approaches for educational assessment. The first attempts to understand how students learn a given area of knowledge and the second seeks to understand how they use this knowledge by examining what they say and do. They identify three models for educational assessment. In the Student Model, the researcher begins by hypothesizing the expected impact, by defining what should be assessed, and by specifying criteria for determining competence. The theoretical rationale the researcher provides as well as the data that the researcher will collect must explain how the impact of using ICT varies from one ICT environment to another by identifying specific skills and the ways these skills are used in different ICT environments. In the Evidence Model, researchers postulate and articulate how and why certain types of student behaviors in a given task situation are indicators of student competence. In the Task Model, researchers provide a detailed description of (1) the tasks and/or necessary conditions that will produce the desired student behaviors (e.g., type and nature of learning materials, directions, support, and tools), (2) of the student performance/product, and (3) how this performance will be recorded.

Expand and Raise the Quality of Student Assessment through ICT

ICT can be used to measure higher-level inquiry processes (Haertel & Means, 2000). Students can use authoring tools to generate research questions and other tools to plan an experiment, conduct the experiment, collect and organize data, analyze and interpret data, draw conclusions, and disseminate results. ICT can also provide a means for improving how data are managed (e.g., collected, scored, analyzed, displayed, and disseminated).

A Web-based environment provides a very flexible assessment venue. It can host assessment tasks for students, which the teacher can easily modified as needed without changing the format or constructs she is assessing. The Web environment can also allow the researcher to monitor and interact with students, as well as provide rich documentation of the students' reasoning processes.

In sum, the strength of the Mislevy et al. (2000) approach is that it provides a framework for a multilevel research design. With this approach, the researcher gathers data that is contextualized, taking into consideration the characteristics of students, teachers, classroom, school, district, and community and relates these to the key program goals, objectives, activities, and outcomes.

What Should Researchers Consider in Data Analyses?

As the assessment goal in quantitative studies is to measure change over time, it is critical that both program implementation and outcome data are collected and organized to allow for the use of statistical tools that are designed for longitudinal analyses (e.g., hierarchical linear modeling), and have the ability to consider variables from a number of different levels. The statistical methods selected should be sufficiently robust to accommodate missing data and permit estimation of effects at different levels (e.g., at classroom, school, district, home, and community levels).

What Are Potential Sources of Error?

The quality of data is compromised by several factors: (1) limited measures; (2) nonalignment of achievement tests with content standards; (3) reliance on soft self-report data; (4) lack of reliability or validity information; (5) timing (test data arrive too late to be included in analysis); (6) inflexibility of data systems to make changes over time; (7) lack of quality control; and (8) lack of resources to make needed changes to the data system. The overall evaluation effort itself is often challenged by: (1) lack of and maintenance of equipment; (2) inadequate management support; (3) limited teacher skills; (4) limited student knowledge and skills; and (5) failure to document the teaching and learning context and how the project integrated ICT into the context. Any of these problems, especially the last point, will compromise the validity of the evaluation.

A lack of a clear and sustained focus throughout all phases of the assessment process increases the probability of error in the interpretation of results. Bruce and Hogan argued that computer ICT "are actors in social systems" that function within a larger social context (cited in Ba, McMillan Culp, Green, Henriquez, & Honey, 2001, p. 7). Notwithstanding this broad perspective, these researchers narrowly defined digital inequity in terms of the lack of physical access to hardware and software as well as how such resources are used. Their presentation of the research documenting the consistent underachievement of diverse student populations by race/ethnicity, education, geography, income, age, and disability, does not delve into the underlying reasons and mechanisms leading to this systematic underachievement other than to blame the lack of ICT and its use. When they asserted that the level of access to information depends upon the user's assets (education, family, socialization patterns, social networks, peers, and occupational experiences) one is left with the sense that these diverse student groups are somehow at fault for their underachievement. The authors failed to probe into and make visible the underlying forces that have resulted in these specific groups not having the necessary assets or life experiences to be successful (e.g., resources and dynamics within the family, school, and community such as socialization patterns, social networks, peers, and occupational experiences). They failed to inquire about the underlying issues of social, economic, and political power in the United States that determine availability of resources, how they are distributed, to whom, how they will be used, how they will be evaluated, and who will be informed. In short, they, as other researchers (Becker, 2000a; Haertel & Means, 2000; Interactive, Inc., 2000), failed to critically examine the roots for this disparity, thereby indirectly continuing to blame the victim.

In summary, the intent of this paper was to provide some guidance in the assessment of digital equity. Equity was defined as not simply as a requirement to help underperforming students, but as an educational goal central to the development and maintenance of a democratic society. Historical patterns of social, economic, and political forces have functioned to work against a democratic society by advantaging some students and disadvantaging others. Only by systematically questioning the status quo and by identifying inequities can we begin to move towards dismantling injustice and create a more inclusive and equitable teaching and learning context for all students. The goal of an assessment of digital equity is to make explicit the role of underlying forces in shaping teaching and learning and how ICT can and is used to advantage some and disadvantage others. This information is needed to help initiate action towards assuring equal opportunities to learn for all students. While much work has and is being devoted to delineate the optimum teaching and learning contexts for students and for understanding how ICT can be used to support and transform these contexts for maximal benefit to students, unfortunately much of this work appears to assume that all students, regardless of background, will learn in the same way. Greater attention has to be given towards assessing and understanding how these generic innovative educational efforts interact with the specific learning needs of traditionally underserved populations.

Given the range and complexity of issues influencing the teaching and learning processes, I strongly recommend that any assessment of digital equity include an interdisciplinary team using multiple strategies. While evaluators and other educators have identified and continue to identify many of the important traditional methodological pitfalls and to generate solutions, they have given scant attention to developing a deeper understanding of diversity in the teaching and learning process. The assessment process should clearly have diversity as its central focus through careful detailing of the life experiences of the learners and examining the interactions within and between the students' experiences with the teaching and learning context and the role of ICT. The work of researchers and theorists in multicultural education, antiracist education, and critical pedagogy can expand current research efforts to provide a richer and more comprehensive assessment of the teaching and learning context and of the impact of ICT. The assessment task ultimately remains to make the invisible visible, so that we can move toward assuring digital equity for all students.

Questions to Ponder

Knowing Your Students

- How diverse are the students in your classroom? Consider background characteristics such as race/ethnicity, income, parent education, immigrant status, home language, and academic English language proficiency?
- How does this diversity impact the range of access to learning resources in their community, e.g., access to books and technology in the home, in their neighborhood, and community? Are there groups of students that consistently are among the highest achievers? Lowest achievers? Who are they?
- How do these patterns of achievement relate to student characteristics?

Knowing Yourself

- Think of two instances in which you recently felt competent and in control. What factors helped make you feel this way?
- Identify two settings in which you feel incompetent and powerless. What about these settings make you feel this way?
- As a teacher, with which groups of students do you feel most successful? Unsuccessful? Why? Do these feelings reflect different learning expectations between these two student groups? How does this map to the achievement patterns of the different groups of students?
- How do differences in student achievement relate to the factors that make you feel competent or helpless?

Knowing Your School

- What are the background characteristics of the instructional, administrative, and support staff? Are they representative of the students in your school?
- Are all students required to meet the same content performance standards?
- Are all students provided with the same level of educational resources, e.g., fully trained teachers, instructional materials, and enrichment learning opportunities?
- To what extent is instruction differentiated for different groups of students as a function of language proficiency and background knowledge?
- To what extent do instructional materials and instructional strategies build upon a student's prior knowledge and relate content to a student's lived experiences?
- As currently designed and implemented, which groups of students are enfranchised by the teaching and learning in your classroom and school, and which students are disenfranchised?

- Who makes the decisions in your school regarding teaching and learning? Who benefits from these decisions and who loses? What sector of the community is not involved in the decision-making?

Knowing Your Community

- How diverse is your school community?
- Where do the different groups in your community live?
- Where are basic services located in your community, e.g., grocery stores, health and social services, recreation, police, libraries, museums, etc.? Whose neighborhoods have the most access to these services?
- Where are factories and/or industrial buildings located? Whose neighborhoods border these facilities?
- Who makes the decisions in the community? Which sectors of the community have the most social, economic, and political power? Who benefits from these decisions and who loses? How does this pattern match the location of basic services and the location of factories? How do these patterns of power compare to how decisions are made in your district, school, and classroom? Who decides and who benefits? Who is left out and who loses?

TABLE 14.1   **Proposed Standards for Democratic Citizenship**

Dimensions of Multicultural Education	Augmented Content Standards	Indicators of Multicultural Classroom	
		Proposed Teacher Democratic Citizenship Performance Standards	*Proposed Student Democratic Citizenship Performance Standards*
Content Integration	The content in each subject area and discipline draws from different cultures to illustrate key concepts, principles, generalizations, and theories.	Teacher has the cross-cultural knowledge and pedagogic skills to draw from the experiences of different cultures to illustrate key concepts, principles, generalizations, and theories in the subject area or discipline.	Student is able to demonstrate understanding of key concepts, principles, generalizations, and theories in each subject area or discipline drawing examples from a variety of cultures and communities.
Knowledge Construction Process	The content in each subject area and discipline explicitly articulates its underlying assumptions, frames of references, perspectives, and biases as to how knowledge is constructed within it as well as alternative conceptualizations.	Teacher has the knowledge and skills to help students to understand, investigate, and determine how the implicit cultural assumptions, frames of references, perspectives, and biases within a discipline influence the ways in which knowledge is constructed within it.	Student is able to demonstrate understanding, investigate, and explain how underlying cultural assumptions, frames of references, perspectives, and biases within a discipline influence the ways in which knowledge is within it.

(continued)

TABLE 14.1 *(Continued)*

Dimensions of Multicultural Education	Augmented Content Standards	Indicators of Multicultural Classroom	
		Proposed Teacher Democratic Citizenship Performance Standards	*Proposed Student Democratic Citizenship Performance Standards*
Equity Pedagogy	The content in each subject area and discipline supports a range of instructional approaches and strategies that are responsive to the varied academic learning needs of linguistically, culturally, racially/ ethnically, or economically diverse student populations.	Teacher has the knowledge and skills to provide varied modes of presentation, delivery, practice, and applications to accommodate the range of learning needs of linguistically, culturally, racially, and/or economically diverse students.	Student is able to meet grade level content and equity standards regardless of gender, race/ethnicity, culture, language, language proficiency, income level, immigrant or migrant status.
Prejudice Reduction	The content in each subject area and discipline provides a basis for helping students understand difference in our lives and an appreciation and respect for differences.	Teacher has the knowledge and skills to provide learning materials and activities that will help students develop an understanding of difference in our lives (how it develops, why it develops, how it is maintained, and how to change it) as well as an appreciation and respect for differences.	Student demonstrates appreciation and respect in work and play for others who differ in gender, race/ethnicity, language, language proficiency, special needs, income level, immigrant or migrant status. Student understands how difference is socially constructed, why it is constructed, how it is maintained, how it can be changed, and his or her responsibility for helping with this change process.
Empowering School Culture and Social Structure	The content in each subject area and discipline explicitly provides a range of learning opportunities that validate and empower students' perceptions of themselves as learners and producers of knowledge, sufficiently flexible to accommodate a range of learning needs and styles, and that facilitate positive collaboration across different groups.	The teacher has the knowledge and skills to create and sustain a validating and empowering learning and school environment for students as evidenced in grouping and labeling practices, participation rates in all classroom and school activities, comparability of academic achievement across all student groups, as well as how students and faculty interact across different groups.	Student is able to work and play with diverse students.

15 Policy Implications of Moving toward Digital Equity

PAUL RESTA

ROBERT McLAUGHLIN

FOCUS QUESTIONS

1. What policies in the past have been effective in increasing digital equity?
2. What are key digital equity issues and challenges confronting policymakers?
3. What kinds of institutions make the policies that establish the direction and rate of progress of digital equality? What recommendations are those institutions currently supporting?
4. What data is most central in determining progress toward digital equity?
5. What could be accomplished if policymakers at all levels improved their collaboration?

We have witnessed the power of information and communication technologies (ICT) to generate great wealth and prosperity but have also seen that it can "exacerbate economic disparity and magnify existing inequities" in society (Kirschenbaum & Kunamneni, 2001). Inequity of access to technology in schools and communities has been a focus of concern to policymakers, resulting in a number of initiatives by state and federal agencies, industry, and philanthropic organizations to bridge the divide. National reports provide a complex picture for policymakers. On the one hand, the reports note that remarkable progress has been made in increasing the number of classrooms with computers and connections to the Internet. The reports also show, however, that despite these gains, significant differences in access and use of technology continue to exist according to racial and socioeconomic status. The glass may appear to the policymaker as either half empty or half full depending on his or her interpretation of the trends. One view is that the digital divide has largely been addressed and that normal market forces rather than policy initiatives will eliminate the remaining gap (Murdock, 2000). Others point out the continuing patterns of digital inequity and assert that these can only be addressed through effective policy actions at the national, state, and local level. This chapter briefly describes past efforts to achieve digital equity and the current context and challenges confronting policy decisions related to digital equity. Lastly, it provides a number of recommendations to be considered by policymakers related to the roles and responsibilities of national and state government, local educational agencies, and the private and philanthropic sectors in moving toward digital equity.

Past Efforts to Address Digital Equity

The initiatives to address the digital divide represent only the latest in a long history of policy efforts to help address inequities in our nation's schools. One of the first efforts to recognize and correct inequities in schools was initiated by Horace Mann in the early 1800s. He surveyed public schools and found serious inequities in physical facilities, qualifications of teachers, and availability of books, chalk, and writing instruments. Through his leadership, training institutes for teachers were established, new curricula designed, new teaching methods employed, professional standards established, and more funding was made available for teacher salaries, books, and school construction (McCluskey, 1958).

In the past 35 years, there have been a number of policy initiatives at the federal, state, and local levels that have helped to provide access to technology resources for low-income students, students with disabilities, and students in rural isolated areas. At the federal level, the Elementary and Secondary Education Act (ESEA) has represented the U.S. government's single largest investment in elementary and secondary education. It provides targeted resources to help ensure that disadvantaged students have access to quality public education. Originally authorized in 1965 for five years, it has continued to be reauthorized by Congress every five years since. One section of the act, Chapter 1 (later renamed Title I), specifically focuses on improving educational opportunities for disadvantaged students.

A significant portion of the Title I funding was used by schools to acquire technology. In the 1980s, schools frequently used Title I funds to purchase integrated learning systems that provided regimented drill and practice to students in priority areas such as reading and mathematics. Often these systems were sold with the promise of significant gains in students test scores. Many of these systems continue to be used today despite limited evidence of the effectiveness of drill and practice to enhance learning for disadvantaged students (Wenglinksy, 1998). The widespread use of these systems in Title I programs underscores the fallacy that the digital divide can be bridged solely by providing access to technology. As noted in earlier chapters, although gaps in technology access between rich and poor schools have been greatly reduced, significant differences in use of technology remain. In many instances, low-income students continue to use computers for drill and practice while higher income students use computers for higher-order cognitive skills (Wenglinsky, 1998).

Another provision of ESEA, Title III, provided funding for programs such as the Technology Innovation Challenge Grants and Technology Literacy Challenge Grants, many of which focused on addressing underserved populations. Another major federal policy initiative, the E-rate program, has provided connectivity to the Internet for many schools across the country serving low-income students. The Department of Commerce Technology Opportunities Program (TOP) has also provided funding for demonstrations of how digital network technologies can be used to extend and improve the delivery of valuable services and opportunities to underserved communities and schools. Specifically, TOP has provided resources to assist many schools and communities in isolated rural areas to derive the benefits of technology access.

The U.S. Department of Education's Preparing Tomorrow's Teachers to Use Technology (PT3) program, has helped colleges of education address the need for teachers who are able to effectively use the new tools for learning. Federal funding has also been provided to support the development of technology-rich community centers in low-income communities. The Department of Education's 21st Century Community Learning Centers program, for example, has enabled schools to stay open longer, providing a safe place for homework centers, academic enrichment, and technology education programs. The government has also encouraged the federally funded educational research centers and laboratories to provide resources that will help address the digital divide. The regional laboratories and regional technology in education consortia continue to provide extensive professional development resources to help educators make more effective use of technology for all students.

The private and philanthropic sectors have also played a major role in addressing the digital divide. Intel's Teach to the Future program has as its goal to train 100,000 teachers to effectively integrate technology into instruction. The Gates Foundation has funded statewide professional development programs for superintendents and principals designed to enhance their technology leadership skills. PowerUP, an initiative comprised of dozens of non-profit organizations, major corporations, and state and federal government agencies, has installed computer labs in schools, public housing complexes, youth-serving facilities, and community centers throughout the United States and Puerto Rico. Other non-profit organizations, such as the New American Schools Development Corporation, although focused on improving America's schools, have also provided support for effective use of technology to address the needs of underserved students. The cumulative effect of these manifold policy initiatives and efforts has helped to reduce the digital divide significantly (Rowand, 2000).

Although much progress has been made since the 1800s to improve our nation's schools, inequities remain between rich and poor schools in quality of facilities, teaching, and learning resources. Many policymakers recognize that the digital divide represents only one aspect of the larger social divide that includes serious disparities in economic opportunity, education, health, safety, housing, employment, and transportation that is also of concern to policymakers (Morino Institute, 2001). The question confronting policymakers today is, in a context of limited resources, should digital equity be assigned a higher priority than other aspects of the larger social divide? For example, does it warrant a higher priority than renovating deteriorating school buildings, providing health care for all children, or improving housing conditions for the poor? Does the lack of digital equity have unique and profound implications for our society that warrant its receiving higher priority? The major rationale for past national efforts to bridge the digital divide was to prevent the establishment of a permanent underclass of the information poor within our nation. In many ways, this is an extension of what Tapscott (2000) describes as the impact of the digital divide in "splintering society into a race of information haves and have nots, knowers and know-nots, doers and do-nots." The following vision of life in the year 2300 by Jaques Barzun (2000) reflects possible consequences.

> The population was divided into two groups: they did not like the word classes. The first, less numerous, was made up of men and women who possessed the virtually inborn ability to handle the products of techne and master the methods of physical science, especially mathematics—it was to them what Latin had been to medieval clergy. This modern elite had the geometric mind that singled them out for the life of research and engineering. . . . Dials, toggles, buzzers, gauges, icons on screens, light-emitting diodes, symbols and formulas to save time and thought—these were for this group of people the source of emotional satisfaction, the means to rule over others, the substance of shoptalk, the very joy and justification of life. . . . It is from this class—no, group—that the governors and heads of institutions are recruited. The parallel with the Middle Ages is plain—clerics in one case, cybernists in the other. The latter took pride in the fact that in ancient Greek cybernetes means helmsman, governor. It validated their position as rulers over the masses, which by then could neither read nor count (pp. 779–780).

Barzun's vision of a small elite and large underclass, however, is contradictory to the vision of a democratic society where power and participation is distributed among all citizens. Long ago Horace Mann recognized educational inequity as a serious and pernicious threat to democracy and took action to move toward equity in the schools of his day. His innovative efforts have helped shape our entire educational system and continue to serve as a model and inspiration for today's policymakers. The challenge for today's policymaker is to understand the important ways in which the digital divide still exists, and to understand the nature, context and status of the digital divide in order to decide upon the best course of policy action.

Does the Digital Divide Exist?

As is evident from the detailed analysis of the digital divide in previous chapters, policymakers struggling to understand the nature and extent of the digital divide are not only confronted with complex data but with divergent perspectives on how best to define the divide (bridges.org, 2001). In the first surveys by the National Telecommunications and Information Agency (NTIA), the digital divide referred to personal ownership of a computer. Later this definition evolved into access to the Internet and, currently, refers to whether homes/schools have high-speed access to the Internet or slow conventional phone line access to the Internet. The definition of the divide has also been expanded to include other important factors such as the type of use, availability of appropriate content, and quality of teaching. The evolving notion of what constitutes the divide makes it difficult for policymakers to determine what are the key elements of digital equity to be addressed.

Another challenge for policymakers is the differing interpretations of the findings from the national reports addressing technology access in schools and homes. Policymakers read national reports from the National Center for Educational Statistics (Rowand, 2000) indicating that the numbers of computers and access to the Internet in schools serving low-income students has increased rapidly during the past decade. These positive trends, a result of policy initiatives at the national, state, and local level and efforts by corporations and philanthropic organizations, raise questions in their mind about the seriousness of the present divide. Michael Powell, for example, the chairman of the Federal Communications Commission suggested that the digital divide is more of a "Mercedes divide." In other words, everyone would like to have one but you can get where you are going with a less expensive vehicle (Education Week, 2001b) and public funding should not be provided to address this divide. In the same article, similarly, others assert that with the rapid growth of computers and Internet access in schools, the digital divide is now largely closed or will disappear soon through normal market forces without the need of any further special government intervention or initiatives—that it is time to declare victory and move on.

Others, looking at the data in the same reports note that, despite rapid growth in the infusion of technology in schools and homes, serious inequities in access continue to exist. Confronted with these divergent views, it is important for policymakers to understand the present status of the digital divide

Status of the Digital Divide

To illustrate the "good news–bad news" dilemma confronting decision makers, one may analyze the findings of the NCES report *Internet Access in U.S. Public Schools and Classrooms: 1994–2000* (2001). Among the findings is that the ratio of students per instructional computer has improved to a national average of 5 to 1. Consistent with this trend, the nation's poorest schools have made remarkable gains in computer access, improving from a ratio of 17 to 1 in 1994 to 9 to 1 in 2000. The study also found remarkable gains in connecting classrooms to the Internet. From 1994 to 2000 the percent of instructional rooms with Internet access increased from 3 to 77 percent. Although these are promising statistics, the report also notes that significant differences in computer and Internet access remain based on school characteristics. In schools with low concentrations of poor students, 82 percent of instructional rooms had computers with Internet access. This compares to 60 percent of instructional rooms having Internet access in schools with high concentrations of students in poverty (National Education Goals, 2001). A similar pattern occurs between schools with low and high concentrations of minority students. Schools with low concentrations of minority students provide Internet access in 85 percent of the rooms compared to Internet access in 64 percent in schools with high concentrations of minority students. In brief, the report shows that access to computers in poor schools has improved greatly during the past six years, bringing even poor schools closer to the national average (Rowand, 2000). The good news is that great gains have been made in digital equity. The bad news is that substantial differences in technology access continue to exist between schools, based on socioeconomic and racial/ethnicity characteristics.

A similar pattern may be seen in the report *Falling Through the Net: Toward Digital Inclusion*, published by the Department of Commerce in October 2000. The report notes that half of all Americans have computers and project that more than half will be using the Internet by the middle of 2001. Nevertheless, the report indicates that a digital divide remains or has expanded slightly in some cases, despite the rapid growth in Internet access and computer ownership for almost all groups. For example, the report shows that large gaps remain for Blacks and Hispanics when measured against the national average Internet penetration rate. Blacks have a 23.5 percent penetration rate and Hispanics a 23.6 percent penetration rate, compared to 41.5 percent nationally.

The low penetration of computers in low-income homes continues to be a concern to policymakers. Access to computers and the Internet in the home represents a clear advantage for students, enabling them to access vast information resources in completing class learning projects, using word processors to complete papers, and to integrate media resources into their classroom presentations. As noted by the U.S. Department of Commerce, "We are approaching the point where not having access to these tools is likely to put an individual at a competitive disadvantage and in a position of being a less-than-full participant in the digital economy (U.S. Department of Commerce, 2000).

This view is not universally shared and critics of policy initiatives to provide Internet access in the home point out that simply placing a computer in the home does not necessarily ensure that it will be effectively used for educational purposes. Parallels are drawn with television, which also offers rich learning resources that are often little used in the home. Compaine (2001) notes that surveys of Internet use in the home have found that services such as chat rooms, sports, and games top the list of activities for home computers, while news and public affairs information resources are way down on the list of uses.

Critics also point out that defining the digital divide simply in terms of access in the home or at school ignores the fact of access to computers at work. They note that 62 percent of employed Americans go online through their jobs (Pew Research Center, 2000). Thus, those without computers at home or school may have substantial access to technology in work settings. This view is countered, however, by the observation that those with access to the Internet at work are more likely to be more highly educated and in better paying jobs than those who do not have such access.

Tapscott (2000) indicates that there are two extreme perspectives related to issues of access to technology resources. At one extreme are the statists, who argue that the access to the Internet is an essential service and a key infrastructure for any economy and therefore should be planned and controlled by the government. The other point of view is that of the market determinists, who argue that market forces will eliminate the digital divide. They contend that market forces have enabled television, today's primary source of information, to penetrate over 99 percent of American homes. The determinist view is that the present digital divide is analogous to the 1950s when only the wealthier homes were able to purchase televisions. At that time they were rare and expensive devices but are now relatively inexpensive and ubiquitous in all households. They point out that today there is no debate over the television rich and television poor in America. In their view, computer access in low-income homes will continue to increase as the price of computers and Internet access continues to fall. Tapscott notes, however, that the present digital divide has been created, in part, by the market in which the wealthy continue to have better access to information resources and more sophisticated technologies while the poor continue to remain information poor. As new and more powerful technologies emerge, the gap will continue but mutate into new forms of information rich and information poor.

One compelling example of technology continuing to provide wealthier persons with access to far more quality information than lower-income persons is the emergence in recent years of digital libraries of fee-based full-text content. Through such proprietary fee-based online library database services as Ebsco, Wilson Select, Gayle, NetLibrary.com, and Big Chalk's Electric Library, schools, families and individuals in wealthier communities are financing access to high-quality, librarian-catalogued and -indexed information not available via the open Web. Through the non-profit, fee-based databases offered by OCLC, an international association of academic and national libraries spanning 78 nations, schools and universities finance access for their subscribers not only to the higher-quality content of librarian-approved and -catalogued information, but to more than 10,000 times greater quantity of content than is available via the free Web. These for-profit and non-profit full-text instructional, professional development, and research content database providers offer vastly more content at a consistently far higher quality than the open Web, but their services are available only to those who can pay their fees. As important as it is to recognize and celebrate the digital equity achievements that have been realized in recent years in dramatically improving equitable access to hardware and the Web for educators and learners in lower-income schools and communities, policymakers need to remain vigilant regarding the tendency of emerging technologies to continually reinvent the digital divide along new lines.

Digital Divide Is More Than Access to Computers and the Internet

While many policy efforts have focused on providing access to technology, it is increasingly recognized that such access represents a necessary but not sufficient condition for children to derive the benefits of technology-supported learning. As noted in Chapter 1, Creating Educational Access, to achieve digital equity requires that the following conditions be met:

Students and teachers must have access to up-to-date hardware, software, and connectivity. Although the national surveys show that poor schools have made significant gains in the access to technology, in many cases the technology is obsolete. The 2000 report of the National Center for Education Statistics found that more than three-quarters of teachers cited a lack of computers at school as a concern. Nearly two-thirds cited, "outdated, incompatible, or unreliable" computers; and nearly six in ten indicated that "Internet access is not easily accessible (Rowand, 2000).

Students and teachers must have access to meaningful, high-quality, and culturally responsive content along with the opportunity to contribute to the knowledge base represented in online content. There remains a lack of high-quality content and tools to assist and facilitate the learning of students with special needs such as language minority students, children with reading difficulties, and students with disabilities. Underserved students need opportunities to be able to use technology for higher-order thinking skills and creative work rather than being limited to softway and practices that have a focus primarily on drill and practice.

Educators must know how to use digital tools and resources effectively. NASBE (2001) points out that the divide has been reduced in physical access to computers and the Internet, but goes on to say that "the disturbing reality is that the digital divide remains wide in a more pernicious form: inequities in instructional practice" (p. 27). The greater the concentration of students in poverty in schools, the more likely that the computers will be used for drill and practice and the less likely they will be used for higher-order cognitive skills and creative applications.

Access to systems must be sustained by leaders with vision and support for change through technology. A critical variable in creating change within schools is the quality of the leadership. Colleges of education need to assure that future school administrators are able to use technology to enhance their own productivity and, more importantly, understand the ways that technology can be used to enhance learning for all students. Efforts are needed to reach out to the current generation of school leaders to help them better understand the potential of technology to improve learning for all students, including those with special needs.

In brief, the present context for policy reveals, on the one hand, substantial gains in providing physical access to computers and the Internet in schools serving low-income students. On the other hand, as noted in the previous sections of this book, serious inequities continue to exist in access to the Internet and more sophisticated technologies—particularly for poor children, minority youngsters, girls, low-achieving students, rural students, students with disabilities, and children with limited English proficiency (Johnston et. al., 2001). In considering whether a digital divide continues to exist and, if so, what policy actions should be taken, it is important for policymakers to ask the following questions:

■ **How often are students using the Internet and other computer resources to learn?** A growing body of research shows that teachers tend to infuse technology into lessons much less with low-achieving students than with high achievers (Johnston, et. al., 2001). Other studies have indicated that students with higher grades are allowed more in-school computer time than their underperforming peers in spite of a substantial body of evidence suggesting that technology may be of greater benefit to low-achieving than to high-achieving students (President's Committee of Advisors on Science and Technology, 1997). Also, while one school whose computers are located primarily or entirely in computer labs may claim the same student-to-computer ratio as another school that places its computers in classrooms, the opportunities for students to actually use these resources is dramatically greater in the latter school.

■ **What applications are students using?** Previous research has shown that low-achieving and minority students tend to use computers for drill and practice while other students use more programs focused on higher-order cognitive skills (Johnston, et. al., 2001). The lack of fluency in the use of technology-supported cognitive tools can handicap low-income students when they enter higher education (Resta, 1994). Lower expectations by teachers of the technology skills low-income students need can greatly diminish the potential value of providing students with access to learning technology resources.

- **Are the computers able to support sophisticated interactive multimedia programs and communication tools?** A critical factor in the significantly lower rate of computers with Internet access in schools serving low-income students is that in many of these schools, students are working with obsolete machines that belong in a junkyard rather than a twenty-first-century classroom. Many older computers cannot access the Web and multimedia content.
- **Are teachers well prepared to use sophisticated pedagogies and technologies?** Teachers with high levels of knowledge and skill in the use of technology are a critical factor in the power of technology to enhance learning. Unfortunately, children in the highest-minority and lowest-achieving schools are roughly five times more likely to be taught by teachers who failed at least one teacher certification test than children in the lowest-poverty, lowest-minority schools (Grossman, Bempre, & Rossi, 2001). Wealthy school districts are able to recruit teachers with greater qualifications, including technology expertise. In addition, they provide more professional development opportunities than school districts serving high concentrations of low-income students (President's Committee of Advisors on Science and Technology, 1997). Based on these factors, children in poverty are more likely to have teachers less skilled in using technology in their instruction.
- **Is high-quality and relevant content available to meet the needs of the diverse learners?** There remains a lack of high-quality, culturally responsive digital content to address the needs of ethnic minority students and students with limited proficiency in English.
- **Is technical support provided to keep the machines running?** The presence of a technology coordinator or technology support person is less likely to be found in schools serving low-income students compared to those in rich districts (President's Committee of Advisors on Science and Technology, 1997).

Do educators know about digital equity resources and how to tap them? While philanthropists and public and private sector initiatives offer hundreds of millions of dollars in funding and material resources to foster digital equity in education, few educators are aware of them and know how to tap them. As we will discuss later in this chapter, there is evidence that educators, especially in lower-income communities, lack awareness of even the most basic digital equity resources such as how to provide low-income students and their families with free e-mail accounts using any of several hundred free e-mail account providers.

Policymakers must consider the factors described in greater detail in the earlier chapters in determining what, if any, policy actions need to be taken to prevent or reduce the possibility of digital exclusion of individuals. As noted by McNair (2000, p. 11), "Exclusion reduces the capacity of individuals to contribute to—and benefit from—society and the economy. It increases the costs which the unwilling majority have to bear, while sowing the seeds of civil and political instability." The issue for policymakers is to understand that we are at a critical point in the trajectory in moving toward digital equity. Careful consideration of the complex factors comprising the digital divide discussed in the preceding chapters provides the basis for more informed policy decisions that will move the nation toward digital equity.

Policy Implications of the Digital Divide

Based on the current context of the digital divide, what policy issues or actions should be considered at the national, state, and local levels to move toward digital equity during the present decade? What needs to be done to derive maximum benefit from initiatives and expenditures at the national, state, and local educational agencies, industry, and philanthropic organizations? Perhaps the greatest need is for collaborative effort between all sectors to develop a clear and coherent plan that will guide and focus the efforts and commitment of resources to target the most critical factors of the digital divide strategically.

Policy Recommendations at the National Level

As noted at the beginning of this chapter, the federal government and national philanthropic leaders have initiated a number of policies and programs focused on addressing the digital divide. The following are recommendations for the continued leadership of the federal government and national philanthropies in moving toward digital equity.

1. Access to digital equipment and programs. Federal policy initiatives have provided support for technology access and connectivity in schools through various programs such as Title I. We recommend that the federal government continue to provide leadership to assist disadvantaged schools with access to learning technology resources. We also recommend that the federal government continue to gather data and monitor the digital equity situation in schools, homes, and the workplace. National studies of access to computers and the Internet should include information on the capabilities of hardware and bandwidth access to the Internet. Surveys should take into account the extent to which students are using computers that support current educational software programs and provide reasonable bandwidth access to Internet resources. Greater coordination among federal departments may yield more useful surveys of school, home, and work use of digital technologies and provide a more comprehensive picture of progress toward digital equity. The need to generate such information is likely to continue for the foreseeable future.

2. Access to educators who know how to use digital tools and resources. The most critical variable in the potential of the digital technologies to enhance learning is the quality of the teaching. Policies are needed to help assure that teachers are well prepared to use the new tools for learning through encouragement of standards development, teacher certification requirements, teacher education graduation requirements, and both professional development and preservice programs to raise the level of educator abilities. Federal and national philanthropic direction should encourage schools to acquire technology through Title I funding and, in particular, to allocate sufficient funds for professional development. A suggestion by Morino (2000) is the creation of a Digital Peace Corps, consisting of people with technology skills and other disciplines who could work with schools in mentoring teachers in the use of the new tools for learning. However, it is not enough that educators have the skills to use learning technologies effectively; preservice and in-service teacher and administrator development is needed to ensure that they also adhere to high expectations regarding the technology skills that low-income as well as wealthier students can and should develop. Federal and philanthropic initiatives in educator preparation and professional development in technology should promote these crucial goals. Because of the magnitude of the problem of educators' expectations of the technology abilities of lower-income students, it is likely to take many years to make substantial progress in improving these expectations. Because of the dynamically evolving nature of learning technologies, national policymakers will need to continue for years, perhaps permanently, to create and revise policies to ensure that educators become and remain skilled in using learning technologies effectively.

3. Access to meaningful, high-quality and culturally responsive content. In the past, the federal government has helped support the research and development of high-quality digital content through grants from the National Science Foundation and U.S. Department of Education. The federal government may explore new partnerships with philanthropists and the private sector in development of culturally responsive curriculum. Since educational publishers often consider such content as "thin market" materials, such a partnership may provide sufficient incentive to the private sector to develop culturally appropriate content. Similar to investments in Sesame Street that have helped countless disadvantaged children—as well as all children—to learn, public–private partnerships might be formed to develop high-quality culturally responsive learning resources for children both in school and at home. As with the concern regarding lower educator expectations of the technology capabilities of lower-income students, the magnitude of the challenge of providing America's increasingly diverse student population with culturally relevant content will require a sustained effort over the coming decade, if not longer.

4. Access to creating, sharing, and exchanging digital content. An important part of the mission of the federally supported educational research laboratories and centers is to help school systems and educators understand the extensive body of research in human learning and the implications for the use of technology to enhance learning of all children. As noted earlier, disadvantaged students often only use technology for tutorial and drill-and-practice programs, whereas other students use the technology as a cognition and communication tool. It is important that the labs and centers, as well as federal and philanthropic programs, focus on disadvantaged students and help educators understand the importance of providing digitally excluded children with opportunities to create and share knowledge and to exchange digital content with others. ThinkQuest is one example of a philanthropic initiative that assists such children to develop Web publishing opportunities and skills.

5. Access to high-quality research on the application of digital technologies to enhance learning. A long-standing role of the federal government is that of supporting systematic research and development on the ways information and communication technologies may be used to enhance learning. This role should continue in areas such as:

- Basic research in learning sciences
- Research and development of new technology tools, content, and sophisticated technology-supported applications of pedagogy and assessment
- Empirical studies of technology applications in schools to determine the most effective ways of using technology to enhance learning
- Identifying and disseminating information on exemplary models and best practices of use of technology to enhance learning for disadvantaged students.

6. **Access to national leadership in digital equity.** Perhaps the most important role of the federal government is that of providing leadership in moving toward digital equity. This role includes:

- Disseminating information from national surveys about progress toward digital equity
- Facilitating new partnerships between the government and private and philanthropic organizations to assure more effective focusing of resources to achieve the greatest gains toward digital equity
- Collaborating with state educational agencies and national professional associations to develop and promulgate standards for student technology fluency and fluency of teachers in the use of sophisticated technologies and pedagogies for learning
- Supporting states in their efforts to transform state tests to reflect the higher-order knowledge and skills and authentic assessments of learning that are enabled through technology.

7. **Leveraging student testing results to assess impacts of technology investments.** In recent years, state and federal policies have been developed to mandate intensified student testing efforts. It is possible that these results will show uneven impacts of local learning technology investments on student learning results. Policymakers should be cautious about concluding, based on these results, that technology investments should be decreased because, in far too many schools, the failure of technology investments to contribute more substantially to student learning outcomes is a direct result of how local technology plans are developed. In the great majority of school districts, technology specialists and a small group of technology-savvy educators develop local technology plans. While the goal of the plans is to support identification, adoption, and instructional use of powerful learning technologies, it is rare that the planners take explicitly into account building-level and districtwide priorities for improving targeted student learning results of greatest local concern. As a result, many educators regard technology resources and professional development as a distraction from and not a direct contribution to their efforts to improve their students' most problematic learning results. Federal, philanthropic, state, and local policies are needed to more authentically ground local technology planning and professional development in local consensus-driven efforts to improve student results of greatest shared concern at the building and district levels. Only then can the contributions of technology investments to student testing results be fairly assessed.

Policy Recommendations at the State Level

A comparable effort needs to be made at the state level to better coordinate efforts among state educational agencies and the private and philanthropic centers in moving toward digital equity. Since states have the responsibility for teacher certification standards and preservice program approval, efforts are also needed to assure that all schools meet the basic standards for access and effective use of technology to improve learning for all students. Recommendations include:

1. **Developing standards for teacher fluency in use of the new tools for learning.** A number of states have developed state standards for both student and teacher technology

fluency based on the national educational technology standards developed by the International Society for Technology in Education. States will need to review and update their standards on a regular basis to incorporate new technologies and pedagogies such as project-based and collaborative learning, guided inquiry, and telementoring. States will also need to consider the standards to be used for certification of teacher preparation programs including evidence that future teachers are well prepared to use the new tools for learning.

2. Developing standards for technology access in schools. Although state funding formulas for schools vary considerably, it is helpful for states to develop minimum standards for physical access to technology. The standards should be used in assessing schools, and should include measures such as student-computer ratios, connectivity in classrooms, bandwidth, and frequency and type of use of technology in instruction. Disadvantaged schools with limited technology resources and funding resources might then be assigned a higher priority for funding in future state technology initiatives. While development of such standards has been and can quickly be accomplished in many states, the need to monitor compliance with such standards will remain a long-term state responsibility.

3. Providing access to digital equipment and high-quality content. States can use the power of state purchasing contracts and agreements and use their leveraging power to negotiate discounted rates from vendors of hardware and high quality digital content. Many of the long-standing textbook review policies and procedures may need to be updated based on the increased use of digital content in the schools. States also should work to remove barriers for schools to the acquisition of needed technology resources and digital instructional and professional development content by themselves negotiating or helping LEAs to negotiate discounted rates with vendors for needed learning technology resources.

4. Gathering data and monitoring digital equity in schools across the state. The state should play a leadership role in monitoring and publicizing the progress of schools toward digital equity. Specific information on level of technology access could be included as part of the information reporting requirements of schools. Information such as number and type of computer, numbers of classrooms with Internet access, bandwidth of connections, etc., could be incorporated into state-mandated reports. The information provided by such reports would help the state identify schools requiring additional assistance or resources to meet state standards. The Technology Inventory used by the State of Maryland provides one example of an instrument used by a state to assess the status of technology in schools (Johnson, et. al., 2001). States especially should require that local technology plans identify what specific student learning result indicators they most want to improve through their technology investments and efforts. All such data should be made public.

Policy Recommendations for the
Business–Industry/Philanthropic Sector

Corporations, local businesses, and philanthropic organizations have made significant investments to address the digital divide and have been key players in national, state, and local efforts to address it. The nation's corporations, through coalitions such as PowerUp and the CEO Forum, have helped focus national attention on the importance of technology access in schools and homes. Business and industry have also provided computer access to schools and community-based organizations, and local businesses have adopted low-income schools and made equipment, wiring, professional development, and technical support resources available to schools. The National Cable Television Association's members have pledged, for example, to provide a free cable modem for every school in the nation. Philanthropic organizations have also made significant investments in technology resources for low-income schools and communities. The following recommendations are offered to assure that the investments will have the greatest impact in moving toward digital equity.

1. **Developing strategic investment models to achieve high-impact change.** As noted by Morino (2000), greater use of strategic investment models is required to achieve the maximum impact of investments made by the corporate and philanthropic sectors in addressing the digital divide. Corporations and foundations must work closely with government agencies to target resources for maximum benefit to low-income schools and communities and move beyond funding through grant applications to more strategic investment models. The investments should be long-term, going beyond the typical 2–3-year patterns of support to provide funding for a 4–6-year period tied to performance criteria. A major criterion for funding should be the extent to which schools and community organizations have proven leadership and strong track records in addressing the needs of the students and community, and how effective technology investments are in improving locally problematic student learning results. Investments in schools or community organizations without strong leadership and commitment will yield few benefits.

2. **Creating and maintaining national, state, and local coalitions of business leaders and foundation executives to address the digital divide.** Chief executive officers of corporations and foundations have significant influence on national, state, and local policy initiatives. Their leadership is critically needed in addressing the digital divide and helping to assure that policies and programs to bridge the digital divide are linked to broader strategies for social change. The leadership may be provided either through existing or new coalitions of leaders that will help focus national, state, and local attention on the ongoing need to move toward digital equity.

3. **Provide leadership in focusing investments in schools and communities.** Leaders of business and philanthropic organizations should play a key role in reviewing current funding resources addressing the divide and exploring ways to better orchestrate investments to have the highest impact. A common situation confronting schools is the ability of parent organizations in higher-income schools to generate more funding for additional technology resources to enrich learning opportunities than those in low-income schools. This creates a dilemma for school district policymakers who are concerned about inequities between schools in technology resources. Business leaders can help ameliorate this ongoing problem by focusing their investments on the schools or communities with greatest needs.

The Need for "Policy Alignment"

As noted above, policymakers in different societal sectors (e.g., foundations, government, and business) can mobilize different kinds of resources to foster digital equity in schools and communities. Working at different levels, local, state, and national policymakers in these sectors have varying degrees of access to resources to affect digital divide concerns. To an impressive extent, policymakers at these levels and across these sectors have invested a tremendous amount of the financial, material, and human resources available to them to address the digital divide. As a result, much progress has been made, yet considerable waste and inefficiency persist, because policymakers do not inform one another about their policy efforts, let alone fashion their own policies in a conscious attempt to complement other policy initiatives. What has not yet occurred with regard to the digital divide is a true *alignment* of policy efforts that spans local, state, and national levels and cuts across public, philanthropic, and business sectors.

For example, many of the nation's largest corporations (AOL Time Warner, Microsoft, Cisco, etc.) and corporate philanthropies annually invest hundreds of millions of dollars to provide individuals and families in low-income communities with hands-on access to hardware, software, connectivity, and training and support to use them. Meanwhile, the federally funded community technology centers program has spurred the creation of hundreds of technology centers in housing projects, shopping centers, and other public locations in economically distressed neighborhoods, enabling low-income youths and adults to access learning technology resources and training. Through the U.S. Department of Education's Technology Literacy Challenge Fund alone, the federal government provided nearly a half billion dollars in FY 2001 to assist schools to purchase hardware, software, and connectivity. Through state and local technology initiatives, further funding, training, and material resources are provided to educators and learners in lower, moderate, and wealthier communities. Yet, few educators know about resources available to lower-income students and their families to give them hands-on access to learning technologies outside the school. While corporate, philanthropic, and government policymakers invest billions of dollars to provide digital equity resources for lower-income communities, many educators and policymakers are unaware of these resources, and opportunities to more effectively use these resources to provide the maximum benefits to schools and communities are often lost.

Research has consistently shown that when learners and educators have regular access to learning technologies at home as well as at school, their basic literacy and technology skills are greatly improved (Salpeter, 2000). Without asking corporate and philanthropic donors to increase their digital equity investments, great gains could be achieved in student learning by ensuring that educators are informed when students and their families can use community-based learning technology resources to support their school-based learning. For instance, through a nationwide Boys and Girls Clubs initiative, lower-income youths can get substantial free training in learning technologies and free access to computers and Microsoft Office suite applications. Through Community Technology Centers, students in many urban low-income housing projects can access computers and software, establish e-mail accounts, and learn how to use these resources. Through hundreds of for-profit and non-profit initiatives, anyone can easily create an e-mail account. Through a national initiative of the American Libraries Association, anyone can go into a public library and gain free access to the Internet for Web browsing and e-mail. Educators armed with this knowledge are much better able to assist lower-income students and their families to obtain and learn how to use such important learning technologies to augment and support their school-based technology skill development. By working together more effectively, educational policymakers and philanthropists can thus better enable educators to point low-income students and their families to valuable learning technology resources.

Here is another example of one way in which better policy alignment, easily achieved, can yield great returns. In 2001, the Council for Opportunity in Education, a non-profit national organization that provides information, professional development, and other supports for educators working in such federally funded TRIO Programs as Upward Bound and Talent Search, conducted a national survey of the leaders and staff in these programs to assess their access to learning technology resources. TRIO programs annually serve 700,000 low-income youths and young adults, helping them to enter and successfully complete college. Students with comparable demographic characteristics not in TRIO programs are more likely to go to prison than to college. Fortunately, these programs are highly effective and more than 80 percent of their clients do remain engaged and successful in education. However, in 2001, only 70 percent of Upward Bound and Talent Search personnel had Internet connectivity—and only 50 percent had an e-mail account.

It is unacceptable that our digital equity policies remain so woefully unaligned that tens of thousands of dedicated, skilled TRIO educators making profound differences in the quality of life for hundreds of thousands of low-income students should remain uninformed about their capacity to access resources like free e-mail accounts. Far too many TRIO program educators remain uninformed by corporate, philanthropic, and public sector policymakers about the resources that policymakers and businesses have invested to provide free e-mail accounts to anyone with connectivity, free access to high-quality instructional content (e.g., the Worldcom Foundation's Marco Polo initiative), access to tools to create free classroom and school Web sites (e.g., the AOL@School program), and many other kinds of free, high-quality learning resources. Two factors appear to contribute to the generally low awareness among TRIO educators about these resources and how to access and use them. First, few TRIO educators possess high levels of technology skill while those who are publicly and philanthropically funded to provide professional development and technical assistance (e.g., regional technology in education consortia) have not made any systematic effort to provide outreach and support. Second and more vexing, it appears that many TRIO educators—and perhaps many K–12 educators in general who serve predominantly low-income communities—have become so discouraged by the effects of their students' persistent poverty that it is difficult for them to remain hopeful that valuable learning resources are truly available for the asking. Thus, those who do possess considerable technology literacy and knowledge of digital equity resources and who are funded to provide them should be required by policymakers to make more proactive efforts to outreach to educators serving low-income learners, encouraging them to take full advantage of such resources.

This is what we mean by improved "policy alignment"—making sure that those who most need awareness and support are targeted to receive it. The fragmentation that characterizes otherwise highly encouraging policy initiatives should be addressed in an explicit, sustained manner.

Savvy educators know the wisdom of admonishing their students to "work smarter, not harder." While hard work is essential for real progress in addressing the digital divide, policymakers need to undertake a concerted effort to work smarter. Basic elements of an aligned policy system, using existing resource investment levels more effectively, include such steps as:

- Developing a shared map at the local, state, and national levels of the kinds of digital equity investments being made across the public, business, and philanthropic sectors, so that policymakers in each sector know who is investing what resources for whom and toward what ends.

- Compiling this information on a regular basis and providing it to educational policy leaders at the local, state, and national levels, with the understanding that educational leaders (e.g., state departments of education, the National Science Foundation and U.S. Department of Education, and national education organizations such as the National Education Association) will in turn undertake a periodic rigorous effort to inform educators within their jurisdictions and memberships.

- Bringing educational policy leaders together on a periodic basis at the local level, at the state level, and at the national level, to explore how they will ensure that through their respective dissemination vehicles (newsletters, Web sites, listserves, professional development conferences, training of trainer programs, etc.) all current K–12 educators will know how and why to tap digital equity resources.

- Making sure that educators working at the classroom, building, and district level receive this information in a very succinct, highly readable, and actionable form so that they can quickly tell what resources they can tap, what benefits they and their students would likely reap, and how to access those resources.

- Working with policymakers in educator preparation to ensure that preparation program faculty include information about digital equity resources in their curriculum, clinical placement, supervision and assessment of preservice teachers, counselors, and administrators. Policies regarding state teacher certification and preservice program approval should require that preparation programs prepare future educators and administrators to tap digital equity resources effectively.

- Working with local, state, and national in-service providers to ensure that they too integrate awareness of digital equity issues, strategies, and resources into their professional development services and content.

- Framing federal educational research policy to provide a steady stream of research funding to monitor progress achieved in addressing current digital divide challenges and to provide early warning about emerging technologies that might generate substantial new digital divide inequities.

Each of the policy alignment strategies above requires few resources other than the time and expense to convene policymakers in person and electronically on a periodic basis. The primary barrier to meaningful policy alignment is not one of cost, but of reluctance to give up territoriality, share credit, and work together for a shared goal. The digital divide is likely to persist in constantly mutating forms, given the rapidly evolving nature of technology. Through improved policy alignment, we will be much more likely to respond meaningfully and quickly to digital divide inequities and, perhaps, even to anticipate them and prevent the often terrible human toll which they can exact.

Summary

We have seen how technology has transformed all aspects of society including science, business, engineering, and the arts. Just as medical practice has been transformed as a result of new medical diagnostic and treatment technologies, so are new information and communication technologies and learning pedagogies beginning to transform the teaching–learning process. It is critical that specific groups within our society not be excluded from the benefits of these new developments. As noted in the report *From Access to Outcomes* (Morino Institute, 2001):

> The window of opportunity is small, and the price of inaction would almost certainly be far steeper than the cost of action. The consequences of inaction would take two forms. First, enormous opportunities would be missed, through the loss of financial and social contributions that people in low-income communities could be empowered to make. Second, tens of billions of dollars would be added to entitlement payments and other social payments. It is no exaggeration to conclude that if we do not dramatically increase the size and effectiveness of our efforts, we could cement a permanent underclass in our society.

Not only must digital equity, therefore, continue as a priority goal of policymakers, but efforts to move toward digital equity also must be mobilized, focused, and coordinated to prevent the development of a permanent underclass in our society.

CONCLUSION

Technology's Promise

GWEN SOLOMON

From the earliest computer tutorial programs to the powerful, interactive, multimedia software and websites of today, content providers and developers have recognized that there is something about this new technology that could enhance what students learn and the ways in which they learn it. We also know that as new technology tools evolve, students will have more options for learning opportunities. Yet they will need to know more to compete successfully in society. The process of creating new tools for learning is evolutionary—and we don't yet know what the newest, most powerful technologies will provide in terms of educational tools in the future—but we're clear that technology holds a significant promise for learning as well as a challenge for those who are teaching.

We can look at some of the practical ways in which technology already enriches learning: word processing for the writing process, spreadsheets for mathematical manipulation and graphing, presentation programs for displaying ideas and reports, access to vast libraries and experts for research, and more. While not all learners are yet using these applications to best advantage, there is significant progress.

Concurrently, the potential for technology-enhanced learning increases with interactive simulations and modeling tools, virtual field trips, software for publishing and website development, and other technologies that enable students to create and control their learning. With the expansion of resources enabled by broadband technologies and the World Wide Web, a rich assortment of tools is available for creating and sharing knowledge. A premise of this book is that education will build significantly on these successes.

In regard to access to computers and connectivity, data show that the digital divide still exists. The 2000 U.S. Census tells us that while "more than half of today's schoolchildren have access to the Internet at home, and schools are leveling the playing field by providing access to children who do not have computers at home," we are at a critical stage (Newburger, 2000, p. 5). This makes our current challenge even greater, especially since, as the authors clearly indicated, we must reframe the conversation.

The digital divide is no longer just about hardware and connections; instead it is about what students are able and encouraged to do with them. In much of this book we have focused on what we have learned about diverse learners, content, educators, and educational leadership. Since the role of schooling in this country has always been to create an educated citizenry who can become contributing members of our democratic society and to prepare young people for the workplace, today's technology tools can make an enormous difference in our ability to reach these goals. Those who have access to technology and to its best uses can scale intellectual heights, become self-actualized individuals, and improve their economic status. For these reasons the insights in these chapters are significant.

Before turning to a summary of the key points from each chapter and their implications, we must acknowledge that technology is able to provide, promote, and enhance learning as no other tool that has come before. In fact, research shows that students who use technology for higher-order thinking skills improve their scores on standardized tests (Wenglinsky, 1998). In addition to easily measured quantitative impacts, there are qualitative results that may turn out to be even more important—that students are revising written work more . . . and meeting their research needs online.

However optimistic we are and however much progress we have made in using technology in education and in achieving digital equity, we know that there are certain areas that continue to need improvement. The chapters in this book addressed both areas of concern and potential solutions as they focused on the issues we face in the twenty-first century. The book is divided into sections that help us to understand past and current progress, examples of success, and future needs.

Section One: Setting the Stage

The "digital divide" is often confused with the notion of access to hardware. While many people have yet to gain equitable access to equipment and to the world's telecommunications infrastructure, there is much more to consider. Even when access is available, what does this mean? This section presented the perspective that while historically this country developed policies and laws to provide access to whatever infrastructure was considered essential, many real barriers to effective use were overlooked. In these chapters, discussed briefly below, we learned about the forms of access and the barriers to achieving the best uses of technology for learning, and we heard from those on the edge of the digital divide, who must deal daily with critical human and educational issues and find solutions.

Creating Educational Access

Summary

Chapter 1, Creating Educational Access, presented a historical framework from which to understand current efforts to achieve digital equity. It began by connecting the current digital divide to divides in education in general and to access to electronic information. It continued with examples of how the leadership in this country has committed to providing access to public education, electricity, telephony, and now to information. Authors Wiburg and Butler concluded with four components of access that define our goals: access to equipment, access to meaningful and high-quality content, access to knowledgeable educators, and access to leadership that supports systems of digital equity. These issues frame much of the discussion in chapters that follow.

Implications

The conversation has changed. While there have been evolutionary gains in providing access to equipment through programs such as the federal E-rate, access to hardware and connectivity are not sufficient for optimal use of technology for student learning. In this chapter, we learned what the other key components of access are. Thus the major implication is that school systems must look at funding priorities differently to make sure that their investment is put to best use.

Barriers to Equity

Summary

School systems, perhaps even more than any other part of society, are slow to change. Systems protect the status quo until there is evidence of a better way. Within education, entrenched bureaucracy and political and public resistance make change difficult, but authors Fulton and Sibley pointed out in Chapter 2, Barriers to Equity, that today's schooling "must change to meet the educational demands of a changing society. . . . In the U.S., the question is no longer one of access; it is what kind of access, for whom, when, and for what purposes." This chapter elaborates on the critical components needed for digital participation that were introduced in Chapter 1 and expands on the importance of leadership that has clear goals, visions, and understandings of how technology can support learning. To overcome the barriers and achieve equity, the authors believe, "the engine for pursuing this vision is leadership, and the fuel is funding." Without this vision, they maintained, the digital divide will lead to an even more troubling "didactic divide."

Implications

The goal for the future is full educational opportunity in our digital age. Beyond access to equipment, to achieve this goal, students need access to meaningful, high-quality, and culturally responsive content, and an opportunity to contribute their knowledge. Their teachers must be helped to use digital tools and resources effectively and school systems must have leaders who have vision and will support positive change through technology.

Factors of the Divide

Summary

Those on the front lines, the educators and those who work with them, are responsible—and held accountable—for integrating technology into curriculum so that students learn more, better, faster, differently, and equitably. The vast majority of educators are dedicated, sincere individuals, who often are not prepared well enough to help students use technology in the most powerful ways. Yet they are deeply concerned about the issues that cause inequity in general and digital inequity in particular. In this chapter, Factors of the Divide, author Wiburg presented the voices of K–12 teachers and of teacher educators at the college level who face the digital divide every day and who identify the issues with which we must deal for digital equity to become a reality.

Implications

Understanding the factors that cause inequity is only the first step. Once empowered by knowledge, people must confront the economic, political, cultural, and pedagogical factors that affect society and schooling in an electronic age. The next step for a just and thoughtful society is to address inequitable factors for economically and geographically isolated students and those with special needs, language and cultural diversity, and other factors that lead to their being disenfranchised. What each of the factors discussed in this chapter has in common is the need to empower individuals within diverse communities to use technology to better meet their own needs.

Section Two: Power and Literacy

This section was about power and how the people who make decisions have power—over their own lives and the lives of others. These chapters explored the meaning of power and looked at a prerequisite for gaining it—literacy. While the world understands literacy to be the ability to understand and communicate, there are new literacies that govern in the twenty-first century, including those that resulted from new technologies. There is also a desire to expand literacy to include culturally diverse ways of knowing and communicating. In order to gain and wield power, learners and those who work with them must understand the new world and how to be literate in new ways.

Empowering Individuals, Schools, and Communities

Summary

Power is not elusive. It is always clear who has it and who does not. Chapter author Pittman defined empowerment as "the ability to make something happen, to effect change that can make a difference in people's lives, schools, communities, and the continuous creation of capacity." The question is who has this ability. People are empowered when they have access to the technology, expertise, and capital they need to build a better tomorrow. Pittman pointed out, "In a digital age, individuals, schools, and communities are empowered when training and computers provide opportunities to help them access information for decision making that fundamentally transforms their lives by expanding their capacity to achieve greater levels of human performance and citizenship through high-quality education."

Implications

We know that technology can make a difference in people's lives, and that people have a greater impact when they feel empowered to use it. For education, students must have access to computers and to the Internet when and where they need them. They must be empowered to learn by researching, creating, designing, and by being in charge of their own learning. Learning is powerful when it is self-directed and culturally responsive to today's multicultural and multilingual society. Thus, teachers must get the training and support to understand for themselves how new ways of teaching provide more opportunities for them and for their students to grow. When teachers learn how to offer twenty-first century learning opportunities, it will empower them to empower their students. To revolutionize learning and teaching, we must find ways to revolutionize society by using technology to create and support communities of learners and develop new models and resources for making our world a better place.

Defining and Designing Literacy for the 21st Century

Summary

Traditionally, we are literate when we can negotiate the written word and communicate with others. In this era of computers and telecommunications, there are new literacies as well. Traditional literacy means being able to read and write. Specifically, we expect adults to be able to read a book, perhaps in a language other than English, and to write. Yet any definition of literacy must include a functional component. People must be able to fill out a job application or apartment rental agreement. Being literate in the 21st century also means having technological literacy skills, negotiating information and communications technologies. To be successful in high-end work environments, people will need to navigate and understand the Internet effectively, use applications software, and more. Individuals without these literacies will not succeed.

Implications

If students are to acquire all these literacies, education must value student cultures. In schools, we should find ways to help learners become "technology literate" in a way that is different from the conventional approach to literacy. Yet author Rocap pointed out that it is necessary to help teachers to understand how technologies can mitigate an inequitable status quo. Methodologies too often ignore multicultural learning, multiple intelligences, and other approaches to intellectual development that honor diversity. They fail to eliminate cultural biases that interfere with comprehension and interpretation. Digital equity is broader than disseminating current technologies and their uses. It is about putting technology in the service of poor and underserved communities to help solve persistent problems and improve life chances and outcomes.

Section Three: Learners and Technology

Digital equity has not yet reached many students who are not empowered and who lack the literacies needed to negotiate our digital society. Among these students are physically challenged and learning disabled students, English language learners, those in other than mainstream cultures, and females. Once aware of the diverse needs of diverse learners, educators can create solutions, and we can achieve digital equity for all learners.

As authors Schrum and Bracey pointed out in Chapter 10, Refocusing Curricula, the curriculum in our schools is really a multilayered configuration. The curriculum includes an officially stated curriculum, an operational curriculum (educators' day-to-day activities and materials), and an additional "hidden" curriculum. The hidden curriculum includes all the institutionalized perspectives on gender, class, race, and authority even though these perspectives are not always made explicit. This hidden curriculum is woven throughout the activities that occur in schools and is typically so subtle that even those involved in perpetuating it are unaware of its existence.

Connections across Culture, Demography, and New Technologies

Summary

Technology can be a tool for cultural preservation, cultural homogenization, or to support multiple cultural perspectives. Chapter author Ingle approached the issue from the perspective that media, methods, and materials are out of sync with the cultural antecedents of those students who need excellent schooling most. His focus was on who is or is not learning, what is being taught, where the learning is taking place, why learning does or does not take hold, and how students acquire learning—all within a broader context of understanding the impact of technology on culture and culture on technology. These twin concerns of technology and cultural diversity have become more prevalent given the fact that the United States is experiencing a radical population demographic shift, which is changing the color and the cultures of its citizenry, and in particular, the student demography in our classrooms.

Implications

Technology must be used as a tool for developing culturally responsive information and enhancing learning by promoting culturally responsive curriculum. The focus must be on interrelated human and cultural behaviors, attitudes, social and cultural actions and thoughts, as well as economic, political, technological, and demographic trends in society. Where our knowledge and understanding of the characteristics and attributes of a particular technology are synchronized with the characteristics and behaviors of the users, the messages or content being delivered over the medium, and the operating conditions or environment for use, we tend to get the best and most widespread use of the technology. Orchestrating interconnections provides new opportunities for using technology in culturally responsive ways.

Technology and Native America: A Double-Edged Sword

Summary

Many cultures and perspectives exist within our society, and some have beliefs that currently conflict with the use of technology. Instead of automatic acceptance of technology, in some cases there is questioning about philosophical and even spiritual and ethical issues. As one case in point, author Delgado explained that the Native American worldview identifies balance and harmony with the environment and includes a reverence for nature and the natural world. Digital knowledge has a place in this integrated and harmonious world, but the long-term effects are not yet understood. It may be that technology can help to reverse the academic underachievement of Native students.

Implications

Few comprehensive attempts have been made to create a body of content and teaching models that are founded on American Indian educational philosophy. Along with this development must come the principles for using technology. The direction of digital media needs broader attention and research, and offers educators the opportunity to promote creative innovation that will attract, retain, and challenge Native students. It is the author's belief that a multidisciplinary approach that addresses the Native cultures in the framework of the curriculum will open the doors to technology in a way that is appropriate and progressive to Native peoples without disrespecting the inherited way of knowing.

Building Learning Communities

Summary

While technology can transform education for all learners, for a large number of students with disabilities, technology may serve as the lifeline to learning. Students with disabilities use special technology called assistive technology to communicate, participate in lessons, complete schoolwork, learn, and move about their school. Beyond having access to assistive technologies, when students with special education needs have access to instructional technologies in the same ways as their mainstream peers, they can participate in a more equitable learning experience. Technology has the power to narrow the equity gap in education for children with disabilities.

Implications

Employing technologies equitably for students with disabilities remains a challenge. There is no single, simple solution. The needs of students with cognitive impairments differ from those with emotional disorders, from those with physical challenges, and from those with sensory impairments. Even within these groups, there is no single solution, since even students identified with the same label demonstrate a broad range of needs with regard to education and/or technology. Thus the biggest challenge, according to authors Staples and Pittman, is individualizing education well and matching individuals to the technology that will help them. More research into what works, where it works, how it works, and why it works will make a difference. Creating accessible websites will make a difference. Preparing educational leaders, educators, and future educators to understand the issues and to implement technology effectively is essential to success for the most vulnerable and misunderstood of our student populations.

Gender Issues and Considerations

Summary

Electronic and visual media play a large role in shaping our identities, and part of this process is differentiated depending on whether we are female or male. Messages carried in much of current media promote common gender stereotypes, which can have negative effects on learning. If we look at digital content, a male perspective often dominates. Typically, boys are more interested in technology for technology's sake while girls appreciate technology for its use in solving social and everyday problems. Boys are more likely to play games and run educational software while girls are more likely to use word processing and creativity software.

Implications

Approaches to technology use in schools should reflect gender preferences and should include software that meets the needs of both genders as well. If technology is introduced as a means to an end, as a tool for in-depth research or for making a multimedia presentation, in the arts and humanities as well as in the sciences, young women are as likely to use it with an enthusiasm comparable to young men. When this happens, stated authors Schrum and Geisler, it may result in more female students having an interest in careers in technology and engineering as well as increasing their interest in using technology as a learning tool. Everyone should pay close attention to the subtle messages in media and educational materials and should encourage software companies to invest in programs that appeal to both genders.

Refocusing Curricula

Summary

Building meaning and understanding happens when learning is encompassing rather than restrictive. When students are fully engaged, taking charge of their own learning, and performing higher-order skills, for example, their learning is permanent. When students are required to do such tasks as rote memorization for standardized testing, learning is often transitory. Since we first saw computers in classrooms in the early 1980s, educators have understood that if they could harness the power of this new technology and find the best applications, it could change teaching and learning. The road has been paved with underpowered computers, lack of vision and understanding, and inappropriate use of technology—but the future is promising. Current understanding of how technology enhances learning leads us to view interactive, collaborative, project-based activities as the way to both engage learners and empower students to drive their own intellectual development.

"In such a classroom," Schrum and Bracey pointed out, "students don't 'learn' technology; technology provides the tools for authentic learning; students are active, rather than passive; educators encourage a diversity of outcomes; educators evaluate learning in multiple ways, beyond traditional paper-and-pencil tests, and educators and students move from individual efforts to being part of learning teams, which may include students from all over the world."

Implications

Integrating technology is complex, and using software or websites requires close review for instances of bias or hidden agendas. Schrum and Bracey presented questions for product review: "What assumptions are embedded in the program's goals? Whose perspectives dominate the program? Whose voices are included and whose are left out of the dialogue and program? What messages are promoted?" After considering educational materials for classroom use, it is worthwhile to look carefully at the types of activities that are designed to support equity for all students. We must encourage the creation of content that is interactive, collaborative, project-based, intellectually stimulating, and culturally responsive.

Section Four: Road Map to the Future

In Section Three, we learned about considering the needs of learners when planning for technology use. In addition, it is necessary to devise methods of enabling all learners to use technology for self-enhancement and learning. Thus, in the final set of chapters, the authors discussed how to enable people to harness technology for their own purposes, how to help educators and educational leaders prepare for teaching, and how to assist schools as they undergo organizational change in the 21st century. Several authors discussed the seriousness of assessing technology's impact on student learning. Ultimately, the authors focused on how we must look toward our national and local leaders to create policies that will indeed create digital equity and a more perfect society.

Professional Development for Change

Summary

A substantial number of teachers report that they do not use computers and other technologies regularly for instruction, especially teachers in districts with minority enrollments.

Using classroom technology effectively requires time for learning and developing good applications, but districts have often resorted to quick fixes and simple solutions that have led to disappointing results in how technology is integrated into schools. The K–12 education community is beginning to recognize the limitations inherent in accepted practice—both in student and teacher learning. By providing teachers with effective methods for technology integration, and by giving them time to learn and adapt those models and strategies, professional development experiences can have significant impact on classroom practice. There must be a substantial connection between technology and the professional preparation and continued development of teachers and educational leaders.

Implications

Model programs can serve as a basis for those who are seeking to implement similar initiatives. Some of the strategies in creating professional development programs include having key parties working together, respecting teachers as professionals, responding to feedback, tailoring instruction and adapting content to meet the needs of diverse groups, and having (or establishing) a close connection between curriculum and technology. Authors Gonzales and Sanchez pointed out that what is needed are professional development models that can help educators most effectively bridge the technology divide. The challenge will be for reformers to create programs that are equitable, affordable, sustainable, and scalable, and that capture the opportunities offered by emerging technologies.

Leadership for a Changing World

Summary

Leadership is possibly the single most important element in creating the systemic, sustained transformation of learning communities required to meet the challenges that face education today. Effective leaders not only understand that new strategies and technologies can transform teaching and learning, but they also facilitate the planning, communicating, resource acquisition, and staff development necessary to make that transformation happen. The key characteristics of effective leadership are vision, collaboration, informed reflection, creative resource management, and perseverance.

Implications

Competent guidance of current leaders and creative preparation of the next generation of leaders are key elements of educational reform. To respond to the challenges of a rapidly changing world, authors Allen and Wing explained, leaders of tomorrow must be change agents who are willing to take risks and create new rules, roles, and responsibilities in response to emerging issues and trends. They must have expert knowledge of research and best practices in order to improve teaching and learning continuously to the benefit of every child using advanced technologies. They must be skillful in creating and sustaining true collaborations within the educational community so that all members, especially teachers, understand and act upon the most effective strategies—including digital solutions—to reduce inequity and further the academic achievement all children.

Building Meaningful Organizational Change

Summary

Systems change is difficult because it requires the approval of most members of the community. In school systems, things have been done the same way for decades. What makes any particular new action likely to take hold? Factors that support change include relative advantage, cultural compatibility, complexity, trial-ability, and observe-ability. The discrepancy between our present school culture and our ever-increasingly digitally savvy and reliant society is the paramount digital divide.

Implications

When new factors create a disturbance of the status quo, according to authors Keenan and Karp, the resulting tension can energize change. If the product of shared dissatisfaction with the present environment finds a common vision of the future and doable steps so that people can move toward creating their desired future, they can overcome resistance to change. A participative approach leads to sustained organization development and cultural transformation because people develop a commitment to the change and a willingness to work toward it. Working collaboratively promotes understanding of the current state of the organization, awareness of attitudes that can influence change, shared vision, group process, and systems thinking. Above all, people must understand and accept the goal of change—in this case, to provide an equitable society that underlies creating tension around technology use.

Assessing Equity in Educational Technology

Summary

The effectiveness of information and communication technologies in improving teaching and learning depends upon the context in which they are used. Defining these contexts is crucial for identifying and interpreting student outcomes, and as such, is a critical and necessary step in any assessment and accountability process. For example, we must consider how the quality, relevance, and appropriateness of the teaching and learning contexts are shaped by underlying factors, i.e., the specific educational research, practices, and policies used to define these contexts. Yet none of these factors occur in isolation; complex social, economic, and political forces influence each. Assessment and accountability should appraise the role of diversity as well as these forces in defining and shaping what students are learning, how they are learning, and how their learning is measured. Making diversity issues central to assessment and accountability of teaching and learning contexts can help identify inherent inequities in learning opportunities for students, provide a better understanding of different patterns of achievement between different groups of students, and identify strategies for maximizing digital equity.

Implications

Given the range and complexity of issues influencing the teaching and learning processes, assessment of digital equity requires multiple strategies. Author Ramirez stated that diversity should be central to an evaluative process in order to examine interactions between student experiences with teaching and learning in general and the role of instructional technology specifically. The work of researchers in multicultural education, antiracist education, and critical pedagogy provide rich and comprehensive perspectives to help guide efforts to examine the teaching and learning contexts to assure digital equity.

Policy Implications of Moving toward Digital Equity

Summary

Based on the success of past efforts of the federal and state governments, local education agencies and communities, and private and philanthropic sectors, substantial progress has been made in moving schools and students toward digital equity. Based on these positive trends there are those who indicate that it is time to claim victory over the digital divide and to move on to other policy priorities. However, despite enormous gains, significant differences in access and use of technology continue to exist by racial and socioeconomic status. The question confronting policy-makers today is—in a context of limited resources, should digital equity have a higher priority than other aspects of the larger social divide, or will efforts to overcome other inequities ultimately have a positive effect in promoting digital equity?

Implications

Digital equity must continue as a priority goal of policy-makers, and efforts to move toward digital equity must be mobilized, focused, and coordinated to prevent the development of a permanent underclass in our society. Policy decisions can promote the goal of educational digital equity. Authors Resta and McLaughlin established that leadership is needed at all levels, including federal, state and district education agencies, corporations and foundations, to create new, collaborative, and innovative policy initiatives to help this nation move toward digital equity. Partnership forged among national, state, and local agencies and between the public and private sectors can optimize limited resources and align policies and initiatives to derive the maximum benefit from the multiple efforts over time.

REFERENCES

Abbott v. Burke, 153 N.J. 480, 710. 2d 450 (1998). Retrieved July 10, 2001, from http://nces.ed.gov/edfin/litigation/Citation.asp

Abbott v. N. J, 710 A.2d 450, 153 N.J. 480, 126 Ed. Law Rep. 258 (1998). Retrieved December 28, 2001, http://www.faculty.piercelaw.edu/redfield/library/case-abbott1.nj.html

Abdal-Haqq, I. (1996). *Making time for teacher professional development.* Washington, DC: ERIC Clearing House on Teaching and Teacher Education. ERIC Identifier: ED400259.

About Project LemonLink, Lemon Grove School District, CA. (2001). Retrieved November 1, 2001, from http://www.lgsd.k12.ca.us/lemonlink

Adams, D. W. (1995). *Education for extinction: American Indians and the boarding school experience, 1875–1928.* Lawrence, KS: University Press of Kansas.

Adams, S., & Burns, M. (1999). *Connecting student learning and technology.* Austin, TX: Southwest Educational Development Laboratory.

Alaimo, K., Olson, C. M., Frongillo, E. A., Jr., & Briefel, R. R. (2001). Food insufficiency, family income, and health in US preschool and school-aged children, *American Journal of Public Health, 91*(5), 781–786.

Alaska Native Knowledge Network. (2001). *Alaska Native Knowledge Network.* Author unknown. Retrieved July 17, 2001 http://www.ankn.uaf.edu/

Allen, N. J., & Crawley, F. C. (1998). Voices from the bridge: Worldview conflicts of Kickapoo students of science, *Journal of Research in Science Teaching, 35*(2), 111–132.

Allen, N. J., Christal, M., Perrot, D, Wilson, B., Grote, B., & Earley, M. A. (1999). Native American schools move into the new millennium, *Educational Leadership, 56*(7), 71–74.

Allen, N. J., Christal, M., & Resta, P. (2002). Technology and tradition: The role of technology in American Indian schools. *TechTrends, 46*(2), 50–55.

Alonso, A. A. (2001). *Leadership in the superintendency: Effectiveness in an age of standards-based reform.* Qualifying Paper. Graduate School of Education, Cambridge, MA: Harvard University.

Altwerger, B., & Saevedra, E. (1999). Forward. In C. Edelsky (Ed.). *Making justice our project: Teachers working toward critical whole language practice.* (pp. vii–xii). Urbana: National Council of Teachers of English.

American Association of School Librarians & Association for Educational Communications and Technology (1988). *Information power: Guidelines for school library media programs.* Chicago, IL: American Library Association or Washington, DC: Association for Education Communications and Technology.

American Association of University Women (AAUW). (1998). *Separated by sex: A critical look at single-sex education for girls.* Washington, DC: AAUW Educational Foundation.

American Association of University Women (AAUW). (2000). *Tech savvy: Educating girls in the new computer age.* Washington, DC: AAUW Educational Foundation.

Americans with Disabilities Act of 1990, Pub. L. No. 101-336.

Anderson, K., & Evans, C., (1996). The development of the canonical story grammar model and its use in the analysis of beginning reading computer stories. *Reading Improvement, 33*(1), 2–15.

Anderson, R. E., & Becker, H. J. (2001, July). *School investments in instructional technology,* Retrieved August 31, 2001, from http://www.crito.uci.edu/tlc/findings/report_8/

Anderson, R. E., & Dexter, S. L. (2000, December). *School technology leadership: Incidence and impact.* Retrieved January 10, 2001, from http://www.crito.uci.edu/tlc/findings/report_6

Anderson, R. E., & Dexter, S. L. (2001). *University of Minnesota's exemplary technology supported schooling case studies project.* Retrieved November 1, 2001, from http://education.umn.edu/edutech/etips/supports/Research.html

Apple Computer, Inc. (1998). *Achieving equity and excellence in the classroom.* Cupertino, CA: Educational Affairs Division, Apple Computer Company.

APT3 Arrowhead Preparing Tomorrow's Teachers to Use Technology (2001). Retrieved August 15, 2001, from http://www.d.umn.edu/~apt3www

Archer, J. (2000). The link to higher scores. In R. D. Pea (Ed.), *The Jossey-Bass reader on technology and learning* (pp. 112–127). San Francisco, CA: Jossey-Bass.

Armitage, D. (1993). Where are the girls? Increasing female participation in computer, math, and science education. In D. Carey, R. Carey, D. A. Willis, & J. Willis (Eds.), *Technology and teacher education* annual—1993 (pp. 19–24). Charlottesville, VA: Association for the Advancement of Computing in Education.

Au, K. H., & Jordan, C. (1981). Teaching reading to Hawaiian children: Finding a culturally appropriate solution. In H. T. Trueba, G. P. Guthrie, & K. H. Au (Eds.), Culture and the bilingual classroom: Studies in classroom ethnography (pp. 139–152). New York: Newbury House.

Au, K. H., & Kawakami, A. J. (1991). Culture and ownership: Schooling of minority students. Childhood Education, 67(5), 280–84.

Autor, D. H., Levy, F. & Murnane, R. J. (2001, June). The skill content of recent technological change: An empirical exploration. Social Science Research Network Paper Collection. Retrieved November 13, 2001, from: http://papers.ssrn.com/paper.taf?abstract_id=272691

Ba, H., McMillan Culp, K., Green, L., Henriquez, A., & Honey, M. (2001). Effective technology use in low-income communities: Research review for the America Connects Consortium. New York: Center for Children and Technology.

Baker, E. L., & Herman, J. L. (2000, September 27). Draft SRI 9 29:Technology and evaluation. Educational Ressearch and Development Centers Program, PR/Award Numb er R305B60002, Office of Educational Research and Improvement, U.S. Department of Education. Retrieved June 10, 2002, from http://www.sri.com/policy/designkt/baker1.pdf

Baldwin, G. (1995). Public access to the Internet: American Indian and Alaskan Native Issues. In B. Kahin & J. Keller (Eds.), Public access to the Internet (pp. 137–153). Cambridge, MA: MIT Press.

Bandura, A. (1986). Social foundations of thought and action: A social cognitive theory. Upper Saddle River, NJ: Prentice Hall.

Banks, J. (1994). Multiethnic education: Theory and practice (3rd edition). Boston, MA: Allyn and Bacon.

Banks, J., & Banks, C. (1997). Multicultural education: Issues and perspectives. Boston, MA: Allyn and Bacon.

Barrera, R. L. & Jiménez, R. T. (2000). Literacy practices for Latino students. National Clearinghouse for Bilingual Education (Contract No. T295005001).

Bartolomé, L. I. (1998). The misteaching of academic discourse: The politics of language in the classroom. Boulder, CO: Westview.

Barzun, J. (2000). From dawn to decadence: 500 years of Western cultural life. New York: HarperCollins.

Beck, J., & Wynn, H. (1998). Technology in teacher education: Progress along the continuum. ERIC Digest.

Washington DC: ERIC Clearinghouse on Teaching and Teacher Education. ERIC Identifier: ED424212.

Beck, L. (1994). Reclaiming educational administration as a caring profession. New York: Teachers College Press.

Becker, H. J. (1985). National survey of instructional uses of school computers. Center for the Social Organization of Schools. Baltimore, MD: Johns Hopkins University.

Becker, H. J. (2000a). Findings from the Teaching, Learning, and Computing Survey: Is Larry Cuban right? Education Policy Analysis Archives, 8(51). Retrieved November 15, 2000, from http://epaa.asu.edu/epaa/v8n51/

Becker, H.J. (2000b). SNAPSHOT #7 Subject and teacher objectives for computer-using classes by school socio-economic status. Center For Research On Information Technology And Organizations. Retrieved November 11, 2001, from http://www.crito.uci.edu/tlc/findings/snapshot7/

Becker, H. J. (2000c). Who's wired and who's not: Children's access to and use of computer technology. In M. Shields, (Vol. Ed.), The future of children: Children and computer technology, 10(2) 44–75. David and Lucile Packard Foundation.

Becker, H. J. (2001, April). How are teachers using computers in instruction? Paper presented at the meeting of the American Educational Research Association, Seattle, WA.

Becker, H. J., & Ravitz, J. L. (1997). The equity threat of promising innovations: The Internet in schools. Paper presented at the annual meeting of the Society for the Psychological Study of Issues, Chicago, IL.

Becker, H. J., & Riel, M. M. (2000). Teacher professional engagement and constructivist- compatible computer use. Irvine, CA: Center for Research on Information Technology and Organization. University of California, Irvine, and University of Minnesota.

Becker, H. J., & Sterling, C. (1987). Equity in school computer use: National data and neglected considerations. Journal of Educational Computing Research, 3(3), 289–311.

Beckhard, R., & Harris, R. (1987). Organizational transitions. Reading, MA: Addison-Wesley.

Bell, E. (2001, December 25). State being pressured on teacher credentials: New bill requires qualification in 4 years. San Francisco Chronicle. Retrieved January 14, 2002, from http://www.sfgate.com/cgi-bin/article.cgi?file=/chronicle/archive/2001/12/25/MN65715.DTL&type=printable/

Bell, L. A. (1997). Theoretical foundations for social justice education. In M. Adams, L. A. Bell, & P. Griffin (Eds.), Teaching for diversity and social justice: A sourcebook. New York: Routledge.

BellSouth. (2001). *Bellsouth grant guidelines: Gaining ground.* Retrieved July 2001, from: http://www. bellsouthfoundation.org/grants/guidelines/v-core.html

Benne, K. D., & Tozer, S. (Eds.). (1987). *Eighty-sixth yearbook.* Chicago, IL: The National Society for the Study of Education.

Bennett, D. (2000). The role of gender in the design of electronic learning environments for children. *Tech Learning's Well-connected Educator Journal,* Retrieved August 1, 2001, from http://www.techlearning. com/db_area/archives/WCE/archives/ennett.htm/

Bennett, D., & Brunner, C. (in press). *Gender and technological imagination: Using multimedia to support alternative visions for girls and technology.* Proceedings for the 108th Convention of the American Psychological Association.

Bennett, R. E. (1999). Using new technology to improve assessment. *Educational Measurement: Issues and Practice, 18,* 5–12.

Benton Foundation (2001). *Digital divide network.* Retrieved July, 2001, from http://www.digitaldivide network.org/content/sections/index.cfm

Benton, L. (1997, August/September). Connection for success: Young children, computers and software. *Closing the gap: Computer technology in special education and rehabilitation.* Retrieved October 30, 2001, from http://www.closingthegap.com/cgi-bin/ lib/libDsply.pl?a=1108&b=5&c=1

Berber, B. (1984). New technology and women's education in Sweden. In S. Acker (Ed.), *World yearbook of education 1984: Women and education.* New York: Kogan Page.

Bereiter, C. (1994). Implications of postmodernism for science, or science as progressive discourse. *Educational Technology, 29,* 3–12.

Bereiter, C., & Scardamalia, M. (1993). *Surpassing ourselves: An inquiry into the nature and implications of expertise.* Chicago, IL: Open Court.

Berland, J. (1998). *Cultural technologies and the evolution of technological cultures.* Paper presented at the WWW and Contemporary Cultural Theory Magic, Metaphor, and Power Conference. Drake University, Des Moines, IA.

Berliner, D. C., & Biddle, B. J. (1995). *The manufactured crisis: Myths, fraud, and the attack on America's public schools.* New York: Addison-Wesley.

Bernstein, J. (2000). *IT and the new economy: Macro, jobs, and gender.* Washington, DC: Economic Policy Institute.

Beyer, L. E. & Apple, M. W. (Eds.) (1998). *The curriculum: Problems, politics, and possibilities.* Albany, NY: SUNY Press.

Bialo, E., & Sivin, J. (1990). *Report on the effectiveness of microcomputers in school.* Washington, DC: Software Publishers Association.

Bigelow, B. (1995). On the road to cultural bias: A critique of "The Oregon Trail" CD-ROM. *Rethinking Schools,* (Fall), 14–18.

Bill & Melinda Gates Foundation. (2001). *Native American access to technology program.* Retrieved July 17, 2001, from http://www.gatesfoundation.org/ learning/publicinfoaccess/nativeamerican.htm

Binns, J. C., & Branch, R. C. (1995). Gender stereotyped computer clip-art images as an implicit influence in instructional message design. In D. G. Beauchamp, R. A. Braden, & R. E. Griffin (Eds.), *Imagery and visual literacy* (pp. 315–324). Rochester, NY: International Visual Literacy Association.

Blumberg, A. (1985). *The school superintendent: Living with conflict.* New York and London: Teachers College Press.

Bobiwash, R., & Afele, J. (2001). Summary issue of culture and technology. *The Earth Watch Institute Journal, 20*(2), 5–6.

Boe, G., & Gilford, D. (1992). Summary of conference proceedings. In G. Boe & D. Gilford (Eds.), *Teacher supply, demand, and quality: Policy issues, models, and data bases* (pp. 21–62). Washington, DC: National Academy Press.

Boethel, M., & Dimock, V. (1999). *Constructing with technology: A review of the literature.* Austin, TX: Southwest Educational Development Laboratory.

Bohren, J. (1999). *Coordination and restructuring the instructional technology for preservice and graduate teacher education.* Interview at University of Cincinnati, Teachers' College.

Bottge, B. A., & Hasselbring, T. S. (1999). Teaching mathematics to adolescents with disabilities in a multimedia environment. *Intervention in School & Clinic, 35*(2), 113–117.

Bowers, C. A. (1988). *The cultural dimensions of educational computing: Understanding the non-neutrality of technology.* New York: Teachers College Press.

Bowers, C. A. (2000). *Let them eat data: How computers affect education, cultural diversity, and the prospects of ecological sustainability.* Athens, GA: University of Georgia Press.

Bransford, J., Brown, A. L., & Cocking, R. R. (Eds.). (1999). *How people learn: Brain, mind, experience, and school.* Washington DC: National Academy Press.

Braun, L. (1993). Help for all the students. *Communication of the ACM, 36*(5), 66–69.

Brewer, J. (2000, February 9). Statement of Judy Brewer, U.S. House Subcommittee. Retrieved on June 22,

2002, from http://www.w3.org/WAI/References/200002-Statement.html

bridges.org (2001) *Spanning the digital divide: understanding and tackling the issues.* Retrieved December 2001, from http://www.bridges.org/spanning/index.html

Brinkley, E. H. (1999). *Caught off guard: Teachers rethinking censorship and controversy.* Boston, MA: Allyn and Bacon.

Brown, M. R., Higgins, K., & Hartley, K. (2001). Teachers and technology equity. *Teaching Exceptional Children, 33*(4), 32–39.

Brownell, G. (1993). Macintosh clip art: Are females and minorities represented? *Journal of Research on Computing in Education, 26*(1), 116–129.

Brunner, C. (1991). Gender and distance learning. In L. Roberts & V. Horner (Eds.), *The annals of political and social science* (pp. 133–145). Beverly Hills, CA: Sage Publishers.

Bryant, D. P., & Bryant, B. (1998). Using assistive technology adaptations to include students with learning disabilities in cooperative learning activities. *Journal of Learning Disabilities, 31*(1), 41–45.

Bryant, D. P., Bryant, B. R., & Raskind, M. H. (1998, September). Using assistive technology to enhance the skills of students with learning disabilities. *Intervention in School & Clinic, 43*(1), 53–59.

Buller, K. (1999). *Who heads the National Indian Telecommunications Institute NITI,* Retrieved Jan. 29, 2001, from www.niti.org/fcc199.htm

Bullough, R. V., & Baughman, K. (1997). *"First year teacher" eight years later: An inquiry into teacher development.* New York: Teachers College Press.

Bureau of Labor Statistics. (2000). *Women's earnings in 2000.* Washington, DC: U.S. Department of Labor, Bureau of Labor Statistics. Retrieved November 20, 2001, from http://www.bls.gov/pdf/cpswom2000.pdf

Burnett, G. (1994). *Technology as a tool for urban classrooms* (Digest Number 95). Washington, DC: ERIC Clearinghouse on Urban Education, Office of Educational Research and Improvement.

Bush, G. (2000). Transforming the federal role in education so that no child is left behind. *West Wing Connections (Education).* Retrieved October 5, 2001, from http://www.whitehouse.gov/infocus/education/

Business-Higher Education Forum. (2002). *Investing in people: Developing all of America's talent on campus and in the workplace.* Retrieved January 10, 2002, from http://www.acenet.edu/bookstore/pdf/investing_in_people.pdf

Butler, D. (2000). Gender, girls, and computer technology: What's the status now? *Clearing House, 73*(4), 225–230.

Butler-Pascoe, M. E., & Wiburg, K. (2002). *Technology and teaching English language learners.* Boston, MA: Allyn and Bacon.

Byrne, E. (1993). *The shark syndrome.* London: The Falmer Press.

Cajete, G. (1994). *Look to the mountain.* Asheville, NC: Kivaki Press.

Caleb, L. (2000). Design technology: Learning how girls learn best. *Equity & Excellence in Education, 33*(1), 22–25.

Callister, T. A., Jr., & Dunne, F. (1992). The computer as doorstop: Technology as disempowerment. *Phi Delta Kappan, 74*(4), 324–326.

Carroll, T. (2001). *Leaders as change agents.* Presentation for the Fall Institute of the Technology Leadership Academy, September 14–16, 2001, Austin, TX.

Carter, B. (1996). Hold the applause! Do accelerated reader ™ and electronic bookshelf ™ send the right message? *School Library Journal. 42*(10), 22–25.

Carter, R., & Kirkup, G. (1990). *Women in engineering.* London: Macmillan Education.

Carvin, A. (2000a, May). *Beyond access: Understanding the digital divide.* Keynote address at the NYU Third Conference, New York. Retrieved December 3, 2001, from http://www.benton.org/Divide/thirdact/speech.html

Carvin, A. (2000b, November, December). More than just access: Fitting literacy and content into the digital divide equation. *Educause Review,* 38–47.

Cassell, J. (1998). Storytelling as a nexus for change in the relationship between gender and technology: A feminist approach to software design. In J. Cassell & H. Jenkins (Eds.), *From Barbie to Mortal Kombat: Gender and computer games* (pp. 298–322). Cambridge, MA: MIT Press.

Castellani, J. D. (2000). Strategies for integrating the Internet into classrooms for high school students with emotional and learning disabilities. *Intervention in school & clinic, 35*(5), 297–308.

Castells, M. (2000). *The rise of the network society* (Vol. 1). UK: Blackwell Publishers.

Cattagni, A., & Farris-Westat, E. (2000). *Teacher use of computers and the Internet in public schools.* National Center for Education Statistics (NCES). Stats in Brief. Washington, DC: U.S. Department of Education, Office of Educational Research and Improvement. NCES 2000-090.

Cattagni, A., & Farris-Westat, E. (2001). *Internet access in public schools and classrooms: 1994–1999.* Stats In Brief. National Center for Education Statistics (NCES). Retrieved August 31, 2001, from http://www.edu/gov/NCES/pubs

Center for Language Minority Education & Research (CLMER). (2001). Speaking of technology: Raising voices, linking wisdom. In G. D. Klerd, (Ed.), *Virtual p: Technology education and community*. David Ramirez Interview. Pacific Southwest Regional Technology in Education Consortium. Retrieved July 5, 2001, from http://psrtec.clmer.csulb.edu/virtualp/21stcen.htm

Center for Public Policy Priorities (1998). *History of school finances in Texas: Measuring up*. Retrieved December 28, 2001, from http://www.cppp.org/kidscount/education/finance2.html

Center for Research on Information Technology and Organizations. (1998). *Teaching, learning, computing: A national survey of schools and technology*. Retrieved November 30, 2001, from www.crito.uci.edu/tlc/html/methodology.html

Century Foundation. (2001). *Digital promise*. Liberty Concepts. Retrieved on November 30, 2001, from http://www.digitalpromise.org/

Century Foundation. (2002). Digital Promise. Status Report: Very Good News. (April, 2002) Retrieved May 17, 2002, from http://www.digitalpromise.org/status_report.asp#april2002

CEO Forum on Education and Technology. (1997, October). *Year 1 report: From pillars to progress: Integrating education and technology*. Retrieved on November 30, 2001, from http://www.ceoforum.org/reports.cfm

CEO Forum on Education and Technology (1999, February). *Year 2 report: Professional development: A link to better learning*. Retrieved December 6, 2001, from http://www.ceoforum.org/reports.cfm?RID=2

CEO Forum on Education and Technology. (2000). *Year 3 report: School technology and readiness report*. Retrieved October 5, 2000, from http://www.ceoforum.org/downloads/report3.pdf

CEO Forum on Education and Technology. (2001). *Year 4 report: Key building blocks for student achievement in the 21st century: Assessment, alignment, accountability, access and analysis*. Retrieved December 12, 2001, from http://www.ceoforum.org

Chang, H., Honey, M., Light, M., Light, D., Moeller, B., & Ross, N. (1998, April). *The Union City story: Education reform and technology, students' performance on standardized tests, CTC Reports*. New York: Center for Children & Technology, Education Development Center.

Chapman, G. (2001). Paying for net foils 'public space' idea. *Los Angeles Time*. Retrieved on November 17, 2001 from http://www.digitalpromise.org/latimes_5_6.asp

Childers, T., & Post, J. (1975). *The information poor in America*. Metuchen, NJ: Scarecrow Press.

Children's Partnership. (2001, April). *Young Americans and the digital future campaign: National fact sheet*. Washington, DC: Author. Retrieved December 3, 2001, from http://www.childrenspartnership.org/youngamericans/factsheet.html

Choy, S. P., & Chen, X. (1998). Toward better teaching: Professional development in 1993–94. National Center for Education Statistics (NCES). NCES 98–230. *Toward better teaching: Professional development in 1993–94*. Retrieved July 2001, from http://nces.ed.gov/pubs98/teaching9394/chapter1.html

Cifuentes, L., & Murphy, K. L. (2000). Promoting multicultural understanding and positive self-concept through a distance learning community: Cultural connections. *Educational Technology Research and Development, 48*(1), 69–83.

Clinchy, E. (2001). Needed: A new educational civil rights movement, *Phi Delta Kappan 82*(7), 498–498.

Clyde, A. (2001). Bobby approves: Web accessibility for the print disabled. *Teacher Librarian, 28*(4), 52–54.

Coalition to Diversify Computing (2000). Retrieved on July 15, 2001 from www.npaci.edu/Outreach/CDC/news/antonia_stone.htm

Cobern, W. W. (1990). *World view theory and science education research: Fundamental epistemological structure as a critical factor in science learning and attitude development*. Cincinnati, OH: National Association for Research in Science Teaching.

Cockburn, C. (1988). *Machinery of dominance: Women, men, and technological know-how*. Boston, MA: Northeastern Press.

Cognition and Technology Group at Vanderbilt. (1997). *The Jasper project: Lessons in curriculum, instruction, assessment, and professional development*. Mahwah, NJ: Lawrence Erlbaum.

Coleman, J. G. (1993). *The early intervention dictionary: A multidisciplinary guide to terminology*. Bethesda, MD: Woodbine House.

Coley, R. J., Cradler, J., & Engel, P. K. (1997). *Computers and classrooms: The status of technology in U.S. schools*. Princeton, NJ: Educational Testing Service.

Colonia, S. (2001). From *The forgotten Americans, PBS online*. Retrieved on July 10, 2002, from http://www.pbs.org/klru/forgottenamericans/press/facts.htm

Comer, J. P. (1988). Educating poor minority children. *Scientific American, 259*(5), 42–48.

Compaine, B. (2001). Re-Examining the digital divide. In B. Compaine, (Ed.). *The digital divide: Facing a crisis or creating a myth*. Boston, MA: MIT Press.

Computer Refurbishing Program Monograph. Cincinnati, OH: The University of Cincinnati.

Conger, J. (1989). *The charismatic leader*. San Francisco, CA: Jossey-Bass.

Conte, C. (1997, July 21). *The learning connection: Schools in the information age*. Benton Foundation.

Retrieved August 31, 2001 from http://www.benton. org/Library/Schools/two.html

Cooper, M. (2000). *Disconnected, disadvantaged, and disenfranchised: Explorations in the digital divide.* Retrieved May 16, 2001, from http://www.consumers union.org/pdf/disconnect.pdf

Cope, B., & Kalantzis, M. (Eds.). (2000). *Multiliteracies: Literacy learning and the design of social futures.* London and New York: Routledge.

Cormier, C., Folland-Tillinghast, A., & Skau, L. (1998, February/March). *Closing the gap: Computer technology in special education and rehabilitation.* Retrieved October 30, 2001, from http://www.closingthe gap.com/cgi-bin/lib/libDsply.pl?a=1006&b=1&c=1

Cradleboard Teaching Project. (1999). *Cradleboard curriculum.* Nihewan Foundation: Retrieved July 24, 2001, from http://www.cradleboard.org/curriculum/ curricul.html

Crombie, G., & Armstrong, P. I. (1999). Effects of classroom gender composition on adolescents' computer-related attitudes and future intentions. *Journal of Educational Computing Research, 20*(4), 317–327.

CTCNet. (2001). *Community technology centers.* Retrieved on December 14, 2001 from http://www.ctcnet.org/

Cuban, L. (1976). *The urban superintendent: A century and a half of change.* Bloomington, IN: Phi Delta Kappan Educational Foundation.

Cuban, L. (1986). *Teachers and machines: The classroom use of technology since 1920.* New York: Teachers College Press.

Cuban, L. (1988). *The managerial imperative and the practice of leadership in schools.* Albany, NY: SUNY Press.

Cuban, L. (1998, October 14). The superintendent contradiction. *Education Week,* Retrieved August 15, 2001, from http://www.edweek.org

Cuban L. (2000). Paper presented at the January, 2000, School Technology Leadership Conference of the Council of Chief State School Officers, Washington, DC.

Cuban, L. (2001). *Oversold and underused: Reforming schools through technology 1980–2000.* Cambridge, MA: Harvard University Press.

Cummings, J., & Sayers, D. (1995). *Brave new schools: Challenging cultural illiteracy through global learning networks.* New York: St. Martin's Press.

Cummins, J. (1986, March). Cultures in context: Using classroom computers for cultural interchange and reinforcement. *TESL Canada Journal/Revue TESL Du Canada, 3*(2), 13–14.

Damarin, S. K. (1998) Technology and multicultural education: The question of convergence. *Theory Into Practice, 37*(1), 11–19.

Darling-Hammond, L. (1997). *The Right to learn: A blueprint for creating schools that work.* San Francisco, CA: Jossey-Bass.

Darling-Hammond, L. (1998). Teacher learning that supports student learning. *Educational Leadership, 55*(32), 6–11.

Darling-Hammond, L. (1999a). *Teacher quality and student achievement: A review of state policy evidence.* Seattle: Center for the Study of Teaching and Policy, a National Research Consortium, University of Washington (lead institution). Retrieved January 14, 2002, from http://depts.Washington.edu/ctpmail/ PDFs/LDH_1999.pdf

Darling-Hammond, L. (1999b). Unequal opportunity. *Brookings Review, 16*(2), 28–32.

Darling-Hammond, L. (2000). Teacher quality and student achievement: A review of state policy evidence. *Education Policy Analysis Archives 8*(1). Retrieved November 7, 2001, from http://epaa.asu.edu/epaa/ v8n1

Darling-Hammond, L., & Ball, D. (1997). *Teaching for high standards: What policymakers need to do.* A report prepared for the National Education Goals Panel. 1–39.

Davidman, L., & Davidman, P. T. (1994). *Teaching with a multicultural perspective: A practical guide.* New York: Longman.

Dede, C. (1985). New information technologies, the knowledge-based economy and education. *Educational Media International 2*(2), 2–8.

Dede, C. (1998). The scaling-up process for technology-based educational innovations. In C. Dede (Ed.). *Learning with technology* [ASCD yearbook 1998] (pp. 199–215). Alexandria, VA: Association for Supervision of Curriculum Development.

Dede, C. (2000a). Emerging influences of information technology on school curriculum. *Journal of Curriculum Studies. 32,* 281–303.

Dede. C. (2000b, May) Implications of emerging technologies for states' educational policies, in *2000 State Educational Technology Conference Papers.* State Leadership Center, Council of Chief State School Officers.

De Jean, J., Upitis, R., Koch, C., & Young, J. (1999). The story of "Phoenix Quest": How girls respond to a prototype language and mathematics computer game. *Gender and Education, 11*(2), 207–223.

Delgado, R., & Stefancic, J. (Eds.). (2001). *Critical race theory: An introduction.* Albany, NY: SUNY Press.

Deloria, V. Jr. (1971). *Of utmost good faith.* San Francisco, CA: Straight Arrow Books.

Delpit, L. D. (1986). Skills and other dilemmas of a progressive Black educator. *Harvard Educational Review, 56*(4), 379–385.

Delpit, L. D. (1988). The silenced dialogue: Power and pedagogy in educating other people's children. *Harvard Educational Review, 58*(3), 280–298.

Delpit, L. D. (1995) *Other people's children: Cultural conflict in the classroom.* New York: New Press.

Depree, M. (1989). *Leadership is an art.* New York: Dell.

De Vaney, A. (1998). Can and need educational technology become a postmodern enterprise? *Theory into Practice, 37*(1), 72–80.

DeVillar, R. A., & Faltis, C. J. (1991) *Computers and cultural diversity: Restructuring for school success.* Albany, NY: SUNY Press.

DeVillar, R. A., Faltis, C. J., & Cummins, J. P, (Eds.) (1994). *Cultural diversity in schools: From rhetoric to practice.* Albany, NY: SUNY Press.

Dexter, S., & Seashore, K. (2001, April). *It's OK to be stupid: Contributions to professional community makes to exemplary technology use.* A symposium paper presented at American Educational Research Association, Seattle, WA.

Dimitriadis, G. and Kamberelis, G. (1997). Shifting terrains: Mapping education within a global landscape. *The Annals of the American Academy of Political and Social Science, 551,* 137–150.

Doherty, K. M., & Orlofsky, G. F. (2001). Technology Counts 2001: Student survey says: Schools are probably not using educational technology as wisely or effectively as they could. *Education Week, 20*(35), 54–48. Retrieved on June 22, 2002, from http://www.edweek.org/sreports/tc01/tc01article.cfm?slug=35student_survey.h20

Donahue, P. L., Finnegan, P. L., Lutkus, A. D., Allen, N. L., & Campbell, J. R. (2001). National Center for Education Statistics Office of Educational Research and Improvement (2000). *The nation's report card: Fourth-grade reading 2000,* NCES 2001-499.

Donahue, S. (2001). Immigrant students: Overlooked and underserved. *American Language Review.* Los Angeles, CA: The Journal of Communication & Education.

Donaldson, G., & Sanderson, D. (1996). *Working together in schools.* Thousand Oaks, CA: Corwin Press.

Donlevy, J. (2000). Closing the digital divide: Elite schools—transforming special education in public and private settings. *International Journal of Instructional Media, 27*(1), 1–21.

Drucker, P. (1998). From capitalism to knowledge society. In D. Neef (Ed.), *The knowledge economy* (pp. 15–34). Boston, MA: Butterworth-Heinemann.

Dyer, C., & Choksi, A. (2001). Literacy, schooling and development: Views of Rabari nomads, India. In B. V. Street (Ed.), *Literacy and development: Ethnographic perspectives* (pp. 27–39). New York: Routledge.

Ebert, T. (1991). Writing in the political: Resistance (post)modernism. *Legal Studies Forum 15*(4), 291–303.

Edelsky, C. (1996). *With literacy and justice for all* (2nd edition). London: Taylor and Francis.

Education Development Center, Center for Children & Technology with the Union City, New Jersey, Board of Education. (2000, August 15). *The transformation of Union City: 1989 to Present.* Retrieved on November 20, 2001, from http://www2.edc.org/cct/cctweb

Education Week. (1998). *Technology counts, 1998.* Washington, DC: Education Week.

Education Week (2001a). Dividing lines. In Technology counts 2001: The new divides: Looking beneath the numbers to reveal digital inequities, *Education Week 20*(35).

Education Week (2001b). Technology counts 2001: The new divides: Looking beneath the numbers to reveal digital inequities, *Education Week 20*(35).

Edyburn, D. L. (2000). Assistive technology and students with mild disabilities. *Focus on exceptional children, 32*(9), 1–24.

Elmore, R. F. (2000, Winter). Building a new structure for school leadership. *American Educator,* 6–44.

Engestrom, Y., Miettinen, R., & Punamaki, R. L. (Eds.). (1999). *Perspectives on activity theory.* Cambridge, UK: Cambridge University Press.

Evans, C. (1995). *Prejudice, educational policy, and the transmission of Spanish as a family language.* Unpublished manuscript, University of Arizona.

Fabos, B., & Young, M. (1999). Telecommunication in the classroom: Rhetoric versus reality. *Review of Educational Research; 69*(3), 21–59.

Fessler, R., & Ungaretti, A. (1994). Expanding opportunities for teacher leadership. In D. Walling (Ed.), *Teachers as leaders: Perspectives on the professional development of teachers* (pp. 211–222). Bloomington, IN: Phi Delta Kappa Educational Foundation.

Fink, E., & Resnick, L B. (2001). Developing principals as instructional leaders. *Phi Delta Kappan, 82*(2), 598–606.

Fishman, B., Pinkard, N., & Bruce, C. (1998). Preparing schools for curricular reform: Planning for technology vs. technology planning. In A. Bruckman, M. Guzdial, J. Kolodner, & A. Ram (Eds.), *International conference on the learning sciences* (pp. 98–104). Atlanta, GA: AACE.

Fishman, B., Soloway, E., Krajcik, J., Marx, R., Blumenfeld, P. (2001, April). *Creating scalable and systemic technology innovations for urban education.* Paper presented at American Education Research Association, Seattle, WA.

Fort Peck Increasing Native Teachers. (1999, Winter). *Tribal College Journal of American Indian Higher Education, 11*(2), 30–31. Mancos, CO: American Indian Higher Education Consortium.

Franklin, J. (2001). The diverse challenges of multiculturalism. *Education Update, 43*(2), 1, 3, 8. Alexandria, VA: American Association for Curriculum Development.

Freire, P. (1972/1994). *Pedagogy of the oppressed.* New York: Continuum.

Freire, P. (1982). *Education for critical consciousness.* New York: Continuum.

Freire, P. (1992/1998). *Teachers as cultural workers: Letters to those who dare teach.* (D. Macedo, D. Koike, and A. Oliveira, Trans.). Boulder, CO: Westview Press.

Freire, P., & Faundez, A. (1989). *Learning to question: A pedagogy of liberation.* New York: Continuum.

Friedman, T. L. (2000). *The lexus and the olive tree.* New York: Anchor Books.

Fullan, M. (1993). *Change forces: Probing the depths of educational reform.* London: The Falmer Press.

Fullan, M. (1999). *Change forces: The sequel.* London: The Falmer Press.

Fullan, M., & Stieglbauer, S. (1991). *The new meaning of educational change* (2nd edition). New York: Teachers College Press.

Fulton, K. & Sibley, R. (2001, June). Survey of Educators at North Central Regional Lab Leadership Summit, Napierville, Il. Unpublished data.

Furger, R. (1998). *Does Jane compute? Preserving our daughters' place in the cyber revolution.* New York: Warner Books.

Futrell, M. (1994). Empowering teachers as learners and leaders. In D. Walling (Ed.), *Teachers as leaders: Perspectives on the professional development of teachers* (pp. 119–135). Bloomington, IN: Phi Delta Kappa Educational Foundation.

Gale, X. L., & Gale, F. G. (1999). Introduction. In X. L. Gale & F. G. Gale (Eds.), *(Re)visioning composition textbooks: Conflicts of culture, ideology, and pedagogy* (pp. 3–13). Albany, NY: SUNY Press.

Gardner, H. (1993). *Multiple intelligences: The theory in practice.* New York: Basic Books.

Garmston, R., & Wellman, B. (1999). *The adaptive school: A sourcebook for developing collaborative groups.* Norwood, MA: Christopher-Gordon.

Garrison, J., & Yi, D. (2001, August 23). School wants laptop on every desk, *LA Times.* Retrieved September 15, 2001. http://www.latimes.com/editions/orange/la-000068309aug23.story

Gee, J. P. (2000). New people in new worlds: Networks, the new capitalism and schools. In B. Cope & M. Kalantzis (Eds.), *Multiliteracies* (pp. 43–68). London: Routledge.

Gehring, J. (2001). Technology Counts 2001: Not enough girls. *Education Week, 20*(35), 18–19.

Generationwww.Y. (2001). *Teaching with technology.* Retrieved November 1, 2001 from http://genwhy.wednet.edu

Gersten, R., & Woodward, J. (1994). A longitudinal study of transitional and immersion bilingual educational programs in one district. *The Elementary School Journal. 95*(3), 223–239.

Gibbs, N. (2001). *Amexica.* TIME magazine, June 11, 2001.

Ginsberg, R., & Berry, B. (1997). The capability for enhancing accountability. In R. Macpherson (Ed.), *The politics of accountability: Educative and international perspectives* (pp. 43–61). Thousand Oaks, CA: Corwin Press.

Gipson, J. (1997). Girls and computer technology: Barrier or key? *Educational Technology, 37*(2), 41–43.

Glass, T. E., Bjork, L., & Brunner, C. C. (2000). *The study of the American school superintendency 2000: A look at the superintendent of education in the new millennium.* Arlington, VA: American Association of School Administrators.

Gmelch, S. B., Daniels, R., Ramira, R., Arkie, J., & Bobiwash, R. (2001). Indigenous Internet. *Earth Watch Institute Journal, 20*(2), 6.

Goals 2000: Educate America Act. (1994, March 31). Pub. Law 103–227 (108 Stat. 125).

Golding, P., & Murdock, G. (1986). Unequal information: Access and exclusion in the new communication market place. In M. Ferguson, (Ed.). *New communication technologies and the public interest: Comparative perspectives on policy and research* (pp. 71–83). London: Sage Communications in Society Series.

Gollnick, D. M., & Chinn, P. C. (1986). *Multicultural education in a pluralistic society* (2nd edition). Columbus, OH: Merrill.

Gonzales, C., Pickett, L., Hupert, N., & Martin, W. (2001, April). *Regional educational technology assistance (RETA) program: Impact on teaching practice.* Paper presented at American Educational Research Association, Seattle, WA.

Gonzalez-Bueno, M. (1998). The effects of electronic mail on Spanish L2 discourse. *Language Learning and Technology, 1*(2), 55–70.

Gooden, A. R. (1996). *Computers in the classrooms: How teachers and students are using technology to transform learning.* San Francisco, CA: Jossey-Bass and Apple Press Publication.

Graham, S., Berninger, V. W., Abbott, R. D., Abbott, S. P., & Whitaker, D. (1997). Role of mechanics in composing in elementary school students: A new methodological approach. *Journal of Educational Psychology, 89,* 170–182.

Graham, S., Harris, K., MacArthur, C. A., & Schwartz, S. S. (1991). Writing and writing instruction with students with learning disabilities: A review of a program of research. *Learning Disabilities Quarterly, 14,* 89–114.

Greene, J. P. (2001). *Graduation rates in the United States.* In a presentation to the Black Alliance for Educational Option and The Manhattan Institute.

Greenlee-Moore, M., & Smith, L. (1996). Interactive computer software: The effects on young children's reading achievement. *Reading Psychology, 17*(1), 43–64.

Greeno, J. G., Colins, A. M., and Resnick, L. B. (1997). Cognition and learning. In D. Berliner and R. Calfee (Eds.), *Handbook of educational psychology* (pp. 15–47). New York: Simon & Schuster Macmillan.

Grossman, K., Beaupre, B., & Rossi, R. (2001, September 7). *Poorest kids often wind up with the weakest teachers.* Chicago Sun Times. Retrieved November 11, 2001, from http://www.suntimes.com/special_sections/failing_teacher/part2/cst-nws-main07.html

Grover, K. (2001). *American Indian schools connect for the 21st century.* Access America. Retrieved on July 10, 2002, from http://www.accessamerica.gov/docs/indian.html

Gutiérrez, F. (1988, March 15). Poor may be left out at high-tech fee libraries. *The Los Angeles Times:* Calendar Section.

Gutierrez, K., Rymes, B., & Larson, J. (1995). Script, counterscript, and underlife in the classroom: James Brown v. Board of Education. *Harvard Educational Review, 65*(3), 445–471.

Haag, P. (2000). K–12 single-sex education: What does the research say? *ERIC Digest* Champaign, IL: ERIC Clearinghouse on Elementary and Early Childhood Education. ERIC Identifier: ED444758.

Haberman, M. (1991). The pedagogy of poverty versus good teaching. *Phi Delta Kappan, 73*(4): 290–295.

Habermas, J. (1971). *Knowledge and human interests.* Boston, MA: Beacon Press.

Haertel, G., and Means, B. (2000). *Stronger designs for research on educational uses of technology: Conclusion and implications.* Center for Innovative Learning Technologies, SRI International. Retrieved on June 20, 2002, from http://www.sri.com/policy/designkt/synthe1b.pdf

Haigler, K. O., Harlow, C., O'Connor, P., & Campbell, A. (1994). *Literacy behind prison walls: Profiles of the prison population from the national adult literacy survey.* Washington, DC: National Center for Education Statistics.

Halcón, J. J. (2001). Mainstream ideology and literacy instruction for Spanish-speaking children. In M. L. Reyes & J. J. Halcon (Eds.), *The best for our children, critical perspectives on literacy for Latino students* (pp 65–77). New York: Teachers College Press.

Halley, W. D., & Valli, L. (1999). The essentials of effective professional development. In L. Darling-Hammond & G. Sykes (Eds.), *Teaching as a learning profession: Handbook of policy and practice* (pp. 127–150). San Francisco, CA: Jossey-Bass.

Hamilton, K. (2001). Historically Black colleges strive to bring campus communities up to technological speed. *Black Issues in Higher Education, 18*(2), 30.

Hanor, J. H. (1998). Concepts and strategies learned from girls' interactions with computers. *Theory into Practice, 37*(1), 64–71.

Harper, D., & GenerationYes (2000). Generation Yes News. Revolutionary Curriculum to Help Schools national study, with six pupils for each terminal. Technology and equity issues. *Technology & Learning:* 38–47.

Harris Corporation. (2001). Communication Equipment: Annual report. Retrieved from on June 24, 2002, from http://www.harris.com/harris/ar/01/

Harris, J. B. (1998). Activity structures for curriculum-based telecollaboration. *Learning and Leading with technology, 26*(1), 6–15.

Hascall, R. (1996, June 9). S. D. leads in student-computer ratio: State's schools rank first in a national study, with six pupils for each terminal. *Argus Leader,* 1D.

Hativa, N. (1988). Computer-based drill and practice in arithmetic. Widening the gap between high-achieving and low-achieving students. *American Educational Research Journal, 25*(3), 366–397.

Hawley, S, & Brasey, H. (2001). Partnering to make a difference. *Community Access to Technology Computer Refurbishing Program Monograph.* Cincinnati, OH: The University of Cincinnati.

H.R. 1804. Goals 2000: Educate America Act. One Hundred Third Congress of the United States of America At the Second Session. Retrieved on June 20, 2002, from http://www.ed.gov/legislation/GOALS2000/TheAct/

Heath, S. B. (1983). *Ways with words: Language, life and work in communities and classrooms.* New York: Cambridge University Press.

Hedges, L. V., Konstantopoulos, S., & Thoreson, A. (2000, February) *Technology: Research designs for the next decade.* Menlo Park, CA. SRI International.

Heidegger, M. (1962). *Being and time.* New York: Harper and Row.

Henwood, F. (1998). Engineering difference: discourses on gender, sexuality and work in a college of technology. *Gender and Education, 10*(1), 35–49.

Hess, F. M., & Leal, D. L. (1999). Computer-assisted learning in urban classrooms: The impact of politics, race, and class. *Urban Education, 34*(3), 370–388.

Hickenbotham, M., & Schamber, S. (2001). Linking to life beyond the reservation: The Takini story. *Learning and Leading with Technology, 28*(8), 22–27.

Higgins, E. L., & Raskind, M. (2000). Speaking to read: The effects of continuous vs. discrete speech recognition systems on the reading and spelling of children with learning disabilities. *Journal of Special Education Technology, 15*(1). Retrieved October 30, 2001, from http://jset.unlv.edu/15.1T/higgins/first.html

Hirsch, E. D. (1987). *Cultural literacy: What every American needs to know.* Boston, MA: Houghton Mifflin.

Honey, M. (2002). New approaches to assessing students' technology-based work. In N. Dickard, (Ed.), *Great expectations, leveraging America's investment in educational technology.* Washington, DC: Benton Foundation, Communications Policy Program, Educational Development Center, Inc. Center for Children and Technology. Retrieved January 4, 2002, from http://www.benton.org/e-rate/greatexpectations.pdf

Honey, M., Brunner, C., Bennett, D., Meade, T., & Tsen, V. (1994). *Designing for equity: A new approach for girls and engineering. Final report to the National Science Foundation.* New York: Center for Children and Technology.

Honey, M., Carrigg, F., & Hawkins, J. (1998). Union City online: An architecture for networking and reform. In C. Dede (Ed.), *Learning with technology* [1998 ASCD yearbook] (pp. 121–140). Alexandria, VA: Association for Supervision and Curriculum Development.

Honey, M., McMillan Culp, K., and Carrigg, F. (1999). Perspectives on technology and education research: Lessons from the past and present. *The Secretary's Conference on Educational Technology,* 1999. Washington, DC. Retrieved from http://www.ed.gov/Technology/TechConf/Tech/1999/whitepapers/paper1.html

Honey, M. & Moeller, B. (1990). Teacher's beliefs and technology integration: Different values, different understandings. *CTE Technical Report,* Issue No. 6. Retrieved November 11,2001 from http://www.edc.org/CCT/ccthome/reports/tr6.html

Hooks, B. (1984). *Feminist theory from margin to center.* Boston, MA: South End Press.

Hooks, B. (1990). *Yearning: Race, gender, and cultural politics.* Boston, MA: South End Press.

Hooks, B. (1994). *Teaching to transgress: Education as the practice of freedom.* New York: Routledge.

Horn, L. J., & Chen, X. (1998). *Toward resiliency: At risk students who make it to college.* Washington, DC: U.S. Department of Education Office of Educational Research and Improvement.

Howard, E. R. & Sugarman, J. (2001). Two-Way immersion programs: Features and Statistics. *ERIC Digest [On-line],* Retrieved on June 17, 2002, from http://www.cal.org/ericcll/digest/intheirownwords.html

Howe, H. II., & Edelman, M. W. (1985). *Barriers to excellence: Our children at risk.* Boston, MA: National Coalition of Advocates for Students.

Howell, R. D., Erickson, K., Stanger, C., & Wheaton, J. E. (2000). Evaluation of a computer-based program on the reading performance of first grade students with potential for reading failure. *Journal of Special Education Technology, 15*(4). Retrieved October 30, 2001 from http://jset.unlv.edu/15.4T/tHowell/first.html

Hoy, W. K., & Tarter, C. J. (1995). *Road to open and healthy schools.* Thousand Oaks, CA: Corwin Press.

Hoyle, J. F. (1972). *The learning climate inventory.* Oxford, OH: Miami University School Climate Research Project.

Hoyle, J. F. (1995). *Leadership and futuring: Making vision happen.* Thousand Oaks, CA: Sage.

Hoyle, J. F., English, F., & Steffy, B. (1994). *Skills for successful school leaders* (2nd edition). Arlington, VA: American Association of School Administrators.

Hurley, K., & Shumway, P. (1997, October/November). Features of award winning software for special need students. *Closing the gap: Computer technology in special education and rehabilitation.* Retrieved October 30,2001, from http://www.closingthegap.com/cgi-bin/lib/libDsply.pl?a=1022&b=5&c=1

Huston-Tillotson College (1999). *Huston-Tillotson Catalog.* Austin, TX: Huston-Tillitson.

Huston-Tillotson College (2001). *Texas technology funds awarded.* Retrieved on December 10, 2002, from http://www.htc.edu/abouthtc/whatsnew.asp

Ideadata.org (2001). *Childcount 1999–2000.* Washington, DC: Author. http://www.ideadata.org/

Indian Country Today. (2000, December 6). Smoke signals now travel the Web. *Indian country today.* Retrieved July 12, 2001 from http://www.indiancountry.com/articles/lifeways-2000-12-06-02.html

Individuals with Disabilities Education Act Amendments of 1997, Pub. L. No. 105-17, § 602, U.S.C. 1401 [On-line]. Retrieved on January 14, 2002 from http://www.ed.gov/offices/OSERS/IDEA/the_law.html

Individuals with Disabilities Education Act of 1990, Pub. L. No. 101-476.

Ingersoll, R. (2001) Teacher turnover and teacher shortages. *American Educational Research Journal, 38*(4), 499–534.

Ingle, H. T. (1987). *The role of the new information media and technology within the Hispanic community: A policy research inquiry.* Claremont, CA: The Tomás Rivera Center for Policy Studies.

Ingle, H. T. (1992). A nation of learners: The demographics of access to video and telecommunications. In *New visions for video: Use of cable satellite broadcast, and interactive systems for literacy and learning* (pp. 1–53). Washington, DC: Office of Technology Assessment and The Annnenberg Washington Program for Communication Policy Studies.

Ingle, H. T. (1998). *Sharpening the Issues and Shaping the Policies: The Role of the New Information Media and Technology Within the U.S. Hispanic Community.* Claremont, California: The Tomás Rivera Center, A National Institute for Policy Studies.

Ingle, Y. R. (1987). *A descriptive study of the preferred learning styles of Mexican-American and Chicano university students.* Unpublished Master's Thesis Presented to the Faculty of California State University, Chico.

Inness, S. A. (1998). Introduction. In S. A. Inness (Ed.), *Delinquents & debutantes: Twentieth-century American girls' cultures* (pp. 1–15). New York: New York University Press.

Innis, H. A. (1951). *The bias of communication.* Toronto, Canada: University of Toronto Press.

Intel® (2001). *Intel® corporation: Teach to the future.* Retrieved December 28, 2001, from http://www.intel.com/education/teach/

Interactive, Inc. (2000). *Creating practical evaluation templates for measuring the impact of instructional technology.* Retrieved July 2, 2001, from http://www.ed.gov/Technology/techconf/2000/interactive.pdf

International Society for Technology Education (2001). *Technology standards for school administrators: Profile of a technology-leading superintendent,* Draft v3.0.

Irving, L. (1998, July 10). In Benton Foundation, *Losing ground bit by bit: Low-income communities in the digital age,* p. 4. Retrieved September 3, 2001, from http://www.benton.org/Library/Low-Income/home.html

Irving, L. (1999, January 27) Assistant Secretary of Commerce for Communications and Information, Remarks, *The Ed Tech Challenge: Training Our Youth for the 21st Century,* at the Mississippi Educational Technology Luncheon, Jackson, Mississippi, [as prepared]. Retrieved August 31, 2001, from http://www.ntia.doc.gov/ntiahome/speeches/edtech12799.htm

Jackson, S. L., Stratford, S. J., Krajcik, J., & Soloway, E. (1994). Making dynamic modeling accessible to precollege science students. *Interactive Learning Environments, 4*(3), 233–257.

Jacobs, R. (1994). *Real time strategic change.* San Francisco, CA: Berrett-Koehler.

Johnson, D. (2001). Next frontiers: Classrooms of the future. *Newsweek.* Retrieved December 28, 2001, from http://www.msnbc.com/news/645535.asp?cp1=1

Johnson, S. (1997). *Interface culture: How new technology transforms the way we create and communicate* (1st edition). San Francisco, CA: HarperCollins.

Johnson, S. M. (1996). *Leading to change: The challenge of the new superintendency.* San Francisco, CA: Jossey Bass.

Johnston, R. C. (2001). "Money matters." In technology counts 2001—The new divides. *Education Week, 20*(35), 14–15.

Johnston, R. C., Reid, K. S., Gehring, J., Manzo, K. K., Zehr, M. A., Fine, L., Bushweller, K., & Trotter, A. (2001, May 10). Technology counts 2001. *Education Week.* Retrieved on June 20, 2002, from http://www.edweek.org/sreports/tc01/tc2001_default.html

Joo, Jae-Eun. (1999). Cultural issues of the Internet in classrooms. *British Journal of Educational Technology, 30*(3), 245.

Ka'awa, M., & Hawkins, E. (1997). Incorporating technology into a Hawaiian language curriculum. In J. Reyhner (Ed.), *Teaching Indigenous languages* (pp. 151–157). Flagstaff, AZ: Northern Arizona University.

Kafai, Y. B., & Sutton, S. (1999). Elementary school students' computer and Internet use at home: Current trends and issues. *Journal of Educational Computing Research, 21*(3), 345–362.

Kahin, B., & Keller, J. (Eds.). (1995). *Public access to the Internet.* Cambridge, MA: MIT Press.

Kamil, M. L., Mosenthal, P. B., Pearson, P. D., & Barr, R. (Eds.). (2000). *Handbook of Reading Research, Volume III.* Mahwah, NJ: Lawrence Erlbaum Associates.

Kaplan, L. S., & Owings, W. A. (2001). Teacher quality and student achievement: Recommendations for principals. *NASSP Bulletin, 85*(628). Retrieved January 10, 2002, from http://www.nassp.org/news/bltn_tch_qul_stdnt_ach1101.html

Katz, C., & Serventi, J. (2001). Schools for a new millennium. *Learning and Leading with Technology, 28*(8), 36–41, 62.

Kaye, H. S. (2000). *Computer and Internet use among people with disabilities* (Disability Statistics Center, San Francisco, Report No. 13). Abstract retrieved October 30, 2001, from http://dsc.ucsf.edu/UCSF/spl.taf?_from=default

Kaye, J. (1999). *Online news hour: Digital divide.* Retrieved September 17, 1999, from www.pbs.org/newshour/

Kennedy, M. (1992). The problem of improving teacher quality while balancing supply and demand. In G. Boe & D. Gilford (Eds.), *Teacher supply, demand, and quality: Policy issues, models, and data* (pp. 65–108). Washington, DC: National Academy Press.

Kenway, J. (1998) Pulp fictions? Education, markets and the information super-highway. In D. Carlson and M. W. Apple (Eds.), *Power/knowledge/pedagogy: The meaning of democratic education in unsettling times* (pp. 61–91). Boulder, CO: Westview Press.

Kinnaman, D. (1970). Technology and equity. *Technology & Learning 14*(7), 70.

Kinser, J., Pessin, B., & Meyertholen, P. (2001). From the fields to the laptop. *Learning and Leading with Technology, 28*(5), 14–17, 48.

Kirschenbaum, J., & Kunamneni R. (2001). *Bridging the organizational divide: Toward a comprehensive approach to the digital divide.* Retrieved September 14, 2001, from http://www.policylink.org/pdfs/Bridging_the_Org_Divide.pdf

Kleiman, G. M. (2000). Myths and realities about technology in K–12 schools. In D. T. Gordon (Ed.), *The digital classroom: How technology is changing the way we teach and learn* (pp. 7–18). Boston, MA: Harvard Education Letter.

Kleinfeld, J. (1998). *The myth that schools shortchange girls: Social science in the service of deception,* Washington, DC: The Women's Freedom Network. Retrieved November 20, 2001, from http://www.uaf.edu/northern/schools/myth.html

Knapp, L., & Glenn, A. (1996). *Restructuring schools with technology.* Boston, MA: Allyn & Bacon.

Knox, C., & Anderson-Inman, L. (2001). Migrant ESL high school students succeed using networked laptops. *Learning and Leading with Technology, 28*(5), 18–21, 52–53.

Knupfer, N. N. (1997). Gendered by design. *Educational Technology, 37*(2), 31–37.

Knupfer, N. N. (1999). Gender, technology and instructional design. In R. Branch & M. A. Fitzgerald (Eds.), *Educational media and technology yearbook* (pp. 22–29). Englewood, CO: Libraries Unlimited.

Koch, M. (1994). No girls allowed! *Technos, 3*(3), 14–19.

Koedinger, K. R., Anderson, J. R., Hadley, W. H., & Mark, M. A. (1995). Intelligent tutoring goes to school in the big city. In *Proceedings of the 7th World Conference on Artificial Intelligence in Education,* Charlottesville, VA: Association for the Advancement of Computing in Education.

Kohl, H. (1995). *'I won't learn from you': And other thoughts on creative maladjustment.* New York: New Press.

Kohn, A. (1999). *The schools our children deserve: Moving beyond traditional classrooms and "tougher standards".* Boston, MA: Houghton Mifflin Company.

Koppenhaver, D. A., & Yoder, D. E. (1992). Literacy learning of children with severe speech and physical impairments in school settings. *Seminars in Speech and Language, 13*(2), 143–153.

Koschmann, T. (Ed.). (1996). *CSCL: Theory and practice.* Mahwah, NJ: Lawrence Earlbaum.

Kotkin, J., & Moyers, S. (2000). *The new geography: How the digital revolution is reshaping the American landscape.* New York: Random House.

Kozol, J. (1991). *Savage inequalities:* Crown Publishers.

Krajcik, J., Marx, R., Blumenfeld, P., Soloway, E., & Fishman, B., (2000, April). *Inquiry based science supported by technology: Achievement and motivation among urban middle school students.* A paper presented at American Educational Research Association, New Orleans, LA.

Kramarae, C. (Ed.). (1988). *Technology and women's voices.* New York: Routledge & Kegan Paul.

Kraus, L. E. (1998, March). *Teaching mathematics to students with physical disabilities using the World Wide Web: ThePlaneMath Program.* Paper presented at the California State University Northridge Conference, Los Angeles, CA.

Kumer, D., & Wilson, C. (2000). Computer technology, science education, and students with learning disabilities. In *The Jossey-Bass reader on technology and learning* (pp. 197–208). San Francisco, CA: Jossey-Bass.

Lachman, L., & Taylor, L. (1995). *The leadership challenge.* San Francisco, CA: Jossey-Bass.

Lambert, L. (1998). *Building leadership capacity in schools.* Alexandria, VA: Association for Supervision and Curriculum Development.

Lankshear, C., with Gee, J. P., Knobel, M., & Searle, C. (1997). *Changing literacies.* Buckingham. UK: Open University Press.

Lau v. Nichols (1974). 414 US 563. Retrieved on June 25, 2002, from http://caselaw.lp.findlaw.com/scripts/getcase.

Lave, J., & Wenger, E. (1991). *Situated learning: Legitimate peripheral participation.* Cambridge, UK: Cambridge University Press.

Lavoie, R. (1996). *How difficult can this be?* [Video]. Washington, DC: Public Broadcasting Service.

Lazarus, W., & Lipper, L. (2000). *Online content for low-income and underserved Americans: The digital divide's new frontier.* Santa Monica, CA: The Children's Partnership. Retrieved November 30, 2001 from http://www.childrenspartnership.org/pub/low_income/index.html

Lazarus, W., & Mora, F. (2000, March). *Online content for low-income and underserved Americans: The digital divide's new frontier.* Retrieved August 15, 2001, from The Children's Partnership. http://www.childrenspartnership.org/pub/low_income/executive summary.html

Lazzaro, J. (2000, March). Talking windows apps and websites. *Byte,* 1–6.

Lemke, C., & Coughlin, L. (1998, July 10). *Technology in American schools: Seven dimensions for gauging progress.* Milken Exchange. RetrievedSeptember 21, 2001, from http://www.mff.org/publications/publications.taf?page-158

Lemke, J. L. (1997). Metamedia literacy: Transforming meanings and media. In D. Reinking, M. McKenna, M. Labbo, L. & R. D. Kieffer (Eds.), *Literacy for the 21st century: Technological transformations in a post-typographic world.* Hillsdale, NJ: Lawrence Erlbaum.

Lenhart, A., Rainie, L., & Lewis, O. (2001). *Teenage life online: The rise of the instant-message generation and the Internet's impact on friendships and family relationships.* Pew Internet & American Life Project. Retrieved on June 22, 2002, from http://www.pewinternet.org/reports/pdfs/PIP_Teens_Report.pdf

Lenhart, A, Simaon, M, Graziano, M. The Internet and Education: Findings of the Pew Internet & American Life Project (Sept.2001) Retrieved May 17, 2002 http://www.pewinternet.org/reports/pdfs/PIP_Schools_Report.pdf

Lesgold, A. (2000) *Determining the effects of technology in complex school environments.* U.S. Department of Education. Center for Innovative Learning Technologies, SRI International. Retrieved on June 20, 2002, from http://www.sri.com/policy/designkt/lesgold2.pdf

Letus, The Center for Learning Technologies in Urban Schools. (2000). Retrieved August 15, 2001, from http://www.letus.org/aboutus.htm

Leu, D. J. (2000). Literacy and technology: Deictic consequences for literacy education in an Information age. In M. L. Kamil, P. B. Mosenthal, P. D. Pearson, & R. Barr (Eds.), *Handbook of Reading Research* (Vol. III, pp. 743–770). Mahwah, NJ: Earlbaum.

Levin, D., Stephens, M., Kirshstein, R., & Birman, B. (1998). *Toward assessing the effectiveness of using technology in K–12 education.* Washington, DC: U.S. Department of Education, National Center for Educational Statistics.

Levin, H., Glass, G., & Meister, G. (1984). *Cost effectiveness of four educational interventions,* Project Report No 84-A11 Stanford, CA: Institute for Research on Educational Finance and Governance.

Levinson, E. & Surrat, J. (1999, January). What should superintendents know and do with technology? *Converge Magazine.* Retrieved on June 10, 2002, from http://www.convergemag.com/Publications/CNVG Jan99/techfromtop/techfromtop.html

Levy, F., Meltsner, A., & Wildavsky, A. (1974). *Urban outcomes: Schools, streets and libraries.* Berkeley, CA: University of California Press.

Lewis, L, Parsad, B., Carey, N., Bartfai, N., Farris, E. (1999, January). *Teacher quality: A report on the preparation and qualifications of public school teachers.* National Center for Education Statistics (NCES). Retrieved August, 2001, from http://nces.ed.gov/pubs99/1999080/index.htm

Lewis, R. B. (1997). Changes in technology use in California's special education programs. *Remedial and Special Education, 18*(4), 233–242.

Lewis, R. B. (1998). Assistive technology and learning disabilities: Today's realities and tomorrow's promises. *Journal of Learning Disabilities, 31*(1), 16–27.

Lindsey, R. B., Robbins, K. N., & Terrell, R. D. (1999). *Cultural proficiency: A manual for school leaders.* Thousand Oaks, CA: Corwin Press.

Lipman, P. (1998). *Race, class, and power in school restructuring.* Albany, NY: SUNY Press.

Little, W. (1993). Teachers' professional development in a climate of education reform. *Education and Policy Analysis, 15*(1), 129–151.

MacArthur, C. A. (2000). New tools for writing: Assistive technology for students with writing difficulties. *Topics in Language Disorders, 20*(4), 85–100.

Macedo, D. (2000). The colonialism of the English only movement. *Educational Researcher, 20*(3) 15–24.

MacMillan, D., & Reschly, D. (1998). Overrepresentation of minority students: The case for greater specificity or reconsideration of the variables examined. *The Journal of Special Education, 32*(1), 15–24.

Madigan, D. (1993). The politics of multicultural literature for children and adolescents: Combining perspectives and conversations. *Language Arts, 70,* 168–176.

Mander, J. (1991). *In the absence of the sacred: The failure of technology & the survival of the Indian nations.* Sierra Club Books.

Manzo, K. K. (2001). Academic record. *Education Week, 20,* 22–23.

Maryland State Department of Education. (2001). *Technology Inventory Summary. Where Do We Stand in 2001.* Retrieved on November 13, 2001 from: http://msde.aws.com/digitaldivide.asp.

Maslow, A. H. (1943). A theory of human motivation. *Psychological Review, 50,* 370–396.

Matthews, C. E., & Smith, W. S. (1994). Native American related materials in elementary science instruction. *Journal of Research in Science Teaching 31*(4), 363–380.

Matthews, J. (2001). Nontraditional thinking in the central office. *The School Administrator, 6*(58), 6–11.

McAdoo, M. (2000). The real digital divide: Quality not quantity. In D. T. Gordon (Ed.), *The digital classroom: How technology is changing the way we teach and learn* (pp. 143–150). Boston, MA: Harvard Education Letter.

McCarthy, C. (1998) *The uses of culture.* New York: Routledge.

McCluskey, N. G. (1958). *Public schools and moral education: The influence of Horace Mann, William Torrey Harris, and John Dewey.* New York: Columbia University Press.

McGhee, R., & Kozma, R. (2001, April). *New teacher and student roles in the technology-supported classroom.* A symposium paper presented at American Educational Research Association, Seattle, WA.

McGowan, E. (2001). *Five models of mentoring relationships.* Qualifying Paper, Graduate School of Education. Cambridge, MA: Harvard University.

Mcilwee, J. S., & Robinson, J. G. (1992). *Women in engineering: Gender, power and workplace culture.* Albany, NY: SUNY Press.

McKenzie, J. (1999). *How teachers learn technology best.* Bellingham, WA: FNO Press.

McLaren, P. (1995) White terror and oppositional agency: Towards a critical multiculturalism. In C. Sleeter and P. McLaren (Eds.), *Multicural education, critical pedagogy, and the politics of difference,* (pp. 33–70). Albany, NY: SUNY Press.

McLuhan, M. (1960). Classrooms without walls. In E. Carpenter & M. McLuhan (Eds.), *Exploration in communication.* Toronto, Canada: Beacon Press.

McLuhan, M. (1964). *Understanding media: The extension of man.* New York: McGraw-Hill.

McNabb, M., McCombs, B., Riel, M., Rose, R., Nelson, D., Braun, H., Barrett, H., & Bransford, J. (2001, August). *PT3 Vision.* Paper presented at PT3 Grantees Meeting, Washington, DC.

McNair, S. (2000) *The emerging policy agenda in learning to bridge the digital divide.* Center for Educational Research and Innovation. Paris: Organization for Economic Co-Operation and Development.

Mead, M. (1994/1995, December/January). Enriching the reading process with software. *Closing the gap: Computer technology in special education and rehabilitation.* Retrieved October 30, 2001 from http://www.closingthegap.com/cgi-bin/lib/libDsply.pl?a=1031&b=14&c=1

Means, B. (Ed.). (1995). *Technology and education reform.* San Francisco, CA: Jossey-Bass.

Means, B., & Olson, K. (1995). *Technology's role in education reform.* Menlo Park, CA: SRI, International.

Menkart, D., Lee, E., & Okazawa-Rey, M. (Eds.). (1998). *Beyond heroes and holidays.* Washington DC: Network of Educators on the Americas.

Merriam-Webster's New World Dictionary (2000). (10th edition). New York: Simon & Schuster Macmillan Company.Metheny, R. (1997, October/November). Curriculum adaptations: Improving student success. *Closing the gap: Computer technology in special ed-*

ucation and rehabilitation. Retrieved October 30, 2001, from http:///www.closingthegap.com/cgi-bin/lib/libDsply.pl?a=1020&b=3&c=1

Metheny, R. (1997, October/November). Curriculum adaptations: Improving student success. *Closing the gap: Computer technology in special education and rehabilitation.* Retrieved October 30, 2001, from http://www.closingthegap.com/cgi-bin/lib/libDsply.pl?a=1020&b=3&c=1

Meyrowitz, J. (1986). *No sense of place: The impact of electronic media on social behavior.* New York: Oxford University Press.

Milken Exchange on Educational Technology. (1998, July 10). *Technology in American schools: Seven dimensions for gauging progress.* Retrieved June 20, 2002, from http://www.milkenexchange.org/policy/Discrepancy_full.pdf

Milken Exchange on Educational Technology. (1999). *Transforming learning through technology: Policy roadmaps for the nation's governors.* Santa Monica, CA: Milken Family Foundation. Retrieved November 30, 2001, from http://www.ericsp.org/pages/digests/roberts.htm

Milone, M. N., & Salpeter, J. (1996). Technology and equity issues. *Technology & Learning, 16*(4) 38–41, 44–47.

Mineta, N. Y. (2000) *Falling through the net: Toward digital inclusion.* Economics and Statistics Administration, National Telecommunications and Information Administration. U.S. Department of Commerce. Retrieved on May 18, 2002 from http://www.ntia.doc.gov/ntiahome/fttn00/Falling.htm#36

Mirenda, P., Wilk, D., & Carson, P. (2000). A retrospective analysis of technology use patterns of students with autism over a five-year period. *Journal of Special Education Technology, 15*(3), 5–16.

Mislevy, R. J., Steinberg, L. S., Almond, R. G., Haertel, G., & Penuel, W. (2000) *Leverage points for improving educational assessment.* Princeton, NJ: Educational Testing Service and SRI International.

Moll, L. C. (1992). Bilingual classroom studies and community analysis: Some recent trends. *Educational Researcher, 21*(2), 20–24.

Moll, L. C., Amanti, C., Neff, D., & González, N. (1992). Funds of knowledge for teaching: Using a qualitative approach to connect homes and classrooms. *Theory into Practice, 31*(2), 132–141.

Moore Lappe, F. & Du Bois, P. M. (1994). *The quickening of America: Rebuilding our nation, remaking our lives.* San Francisco, CA: Jossey-Bass.

Morales-Gómez, D. & Melesse, M. (1998). Utilizing information and communication technologies for development: The social dimensions. *Journal of Information Technology for Development, 8*(1), 11.

Morino Institute. (2001). *From access to outcomes: Raising the aspirations for technology initiatives in low-income communities.* Retrieved December 3, 2001, from http://www.morino.org

Morino, M. (2000). Policy & philanthropy: Keys to closing the digital divide. *Address at Networks for People 2000 Conference.* Technology Opportunities Program, National Telecommunications and Information Administration. U.S. Department of Commerce, October 30, 2000.

Morritt, H. (1997). *Women and computer based technologies: A feminist perspective.* Lanham, MD: University Press of America.

Moses, R. P., & Cobb, C. E. Jr. (2001). *Radical equations: Math literacy and civil rights.* Boston: Beacon Press.

Moursund, D. (1999). *Will new teachers be prepared to teach in a digital age: A national survey on information technology in teacher education.* Santa Monica, CA: Milken Exchange on Education Technology (with the International Society for Technology in Education).

Moursund, D. (2001). The learner and teacher sides of the digital divide. *Learning & Leading with Technology, 28*(5), 4–5, 48.

Muir, M. (1994). Putting computer projects at the heart of the curriculum. *Educational Leadership, 51*(7), 30–32.

Mumtaz, S. (2001). Children's enjoyment and perception of computer use in the home and the school. *Computers & Education, 36,* 347–362.

Murdock, D. (2000) *Digital divide? What digital divide?* The CATO Institute. Retrieved September 10, 2001, http://www.cato.org/daily/06-16-00.html

Murnane, R., Levy, F., & Autor, D. (2001). The skill content of recent technological change: An empirical exploration. *Social Science Research Network Paper Collection.* Retrieved on November 13, 2001, from: http://papers.ssrn.com/paper.taf?abstract_id=272691

Murphy, J. T. (1991). Superintendents as saviors: From the Terminator to Pogo. *Phi Delta Kappan, 72*(7), 507–515.

Murray, T. (1995). Gender equity in the mathematics classroom: Separate and equal. *The Nueva Journal, 35*(3), 1–4.

Murtha, J. P. & Larson, J. B. (2000). *Technological call to arms.* Retrieved May 1, 2000, from http://www.ndol.org/ndol_ci.cfm?kaid=124&subid=159&contentid=817

Musgrove, M. (2001, September 16). The search for intelligent life online. *Washington Post Magazine.*

Nachmias, R., Mioduser, D., & Shemla, A. (2001). Information and communication technologies usage by students in an Israeli high school: Equity, gender, and inside/outside school learning issues. *Education and Information Technologies, 6*(1), 43–53.

National Association of State Boards of Education (NASBE). (2001). Any time, any place, any path, any pace: Taking the lead on e-learning policy. In *NASBE's report.* Retrieved October, 2001, from http://www.nasbe.org/e_Learning.html

National Congress of American Indians (date unknown). *American Indians and the digital divide: Education.* National Congress of American Indians: Retrieved July 12, 2001 from http://www.ncai.org/indianissues/DigitalDivide/ddeducationl.htm

National Commission on Excellence in Education (1983, April). *A nation at risk.* Retrieved June 6, 2001, from http://www.ed.gov/pubs/NatAtRisk/risk.html

National Council on Disability. (2001). *Investing in independence: Transition recommendations for President George W. Bush.* Washington DC: Author.

National Education Goals Panel. (1995). Building a nation of learners. *The national education goals report 1*(1), 39–41. U.S. Department of Education Government Printing Office. Washington, DC: Author.

National Education Goals Panel Report (2001). More high school graduates enrolling in college; 39 states increase college enrollments; Racial gap in matriculation goes from 14 to 9 percent. *National education goals panel report.* U.S. Government Printing Office. Washington, DC. Author. Retrieved July 5, 2001, from http://www.negp.gov. and http://nces.ed.gov/pubs98/teaching9394/chapter1.html

National Education Technology Standards for Students and Teachers (NETS). (2000). *Connecting curriculum and technology.* The International Society for Technology in Education. Printed by ISTE in cooperation with the U.S. Department of Education, *1*(1) 4–6.

National Office for the Information Economy. (2000). Digital divide. Retrieved July 25, 2001, from http://www.noie.gov.au/projects/access/accessibility/index.htm

National Telecommunications and Information Administration (NTIA). (1998). *Falling through the net II: New data on the digital divide.* Retrieved on July 15, 2001, from http://www.ntia.doc.gov/itiahome/net2/

National Telecommunications and Information Administration (NTIA). (1999). *Falling through the net: Defining the digital divide.* Retrieved on November 30, 2001, from http://www.ntia.doc.gov/ntiahome/fttn99/contents.html

National Telecommunications and Information Administration (NTIA). (2000). *Advanced telecommunications in rural America: The challenge of bringing broadband services to all Americans.* Boulder, CO: Author.

Negroni, P. J. (2000, September). A radical role for super-intendents. *The school administrator web edition,* Retrieved on August 10, 2001, from http://www.aasa.org/publications/sa/2000-09/negroni.htm

Net day (2001). *A model for empowering schools and community's online portal.* Retrieved July 13, 2001, from http://www.netday.org/about.htm_

Neuman, D. (1990). Beyond the chip: A model for fostering equity. *School Library Quarterly, 18,* 158–164.

Neuman, M. & Simmons, W. (2000). Leadership for student learning. *Phi Delta Kappan, 82*(1), 9–12.

Newburger, E. (2000). *Poverty: 1999 highlights. Washington, DC: U.S. Census Bureau.* Retrieved on July 10, 2002, from http://www.census.gov/hhes/poverty/poverty/99hi.html

Newmann, F. M., King, M. B., & Rigdon, M. (1996, September 15). *Accountability and school performance: Implications from restructuring schools.* ERIC Identifier: ED412631.

New Mexico Department of Education. (1999). *New Mexico's educational technology plan: A road map to student success.* Santa Fe, NM: Author.

Newsome Park Elementary (2001). *All about us.* Retrieved November 1, 2001 from http://npes.nn.k12.va.us/mission.html

Newsweek (2000, September, 18), *The New American,* p. 48.

Nieto, S. (1996) *Affirming diversity: The sociopolitical context of multicultural education.* New York: Longman.

Norman, D. (1993). *Things that make us smart: Defending human attributes in the age of the machine.* Reading, MA: Addison-Wesley.

North Central Regional Educational Lab (NCREL) (n. d.). Retrieved on July 15, 2001, from http://www.ncrel.org/sdrs/lwteach1/tsld008.htms

Norton, P. & Wiburg, K. (1998). *Teaching with technology.* Fort Worth, TX: Harcourt-Brace.

Office of Technology Assessment, U.S. Congress (OTA). (1983). *Information technology and its impact on American education.* Washington, DC: Superintendent of Documents, U.S. Government Printing Office.

Office of Technology Assessment, U.S. Congress (OTA). (1987). *Trends and status of computers in schools: Use in Chapter I programs and use with limited English proficient students.* Washington, DC: OTA, Science, Education, and Transportation Program.

Office of Technology Assessment. U.S. Congress (OTA). (1989) *Power on: New tools for teaching and learning.* Washington, DC: U.S. Government Printing Office. Retrieved November 30, 2001, from http://www.wws.princeton.edu/~ota/ns20/year_f.html/index.html

Office of Technology Assessment. U.S. Congress (OTA). (1995). *Teachers & technology: Making the connection.* Washington, DC: U.S. Government Printing Office. Retrieved on November 30, 2001, from http://www.wws.princeton.edu/~ota/ns20/year_f.html/index.html

Ohlemacher, S. (2001, November 4). Test scores reveal width of racial gap. *Plain Dealer Reporter.* Retrieved November 11, 2001,http://www.cleveland.com/news/plaindealer/index.ssf?/xml/story.ssf/html_standard.xsl?/base/news/10048698192732956.hml

Ojito, M. (2001). Better housing is the big issue in a poor district, *NY Times, 90*(51), 840.

O'Meara, S., & West, D. (1996). *From our eyes.* Aurora, ONT: Garamond Press.

Ortmeir, C. (2000). Project Homeland: Crossing cultural boundaries in the ESL classroom.

Osher, D., Woodruff, D., & Sims, A. (2000, November). *Exploring relationships between inappropriate and ineffective special education services for African American children and youth and their overrepresentation in the juvenile justice system.* Paper presented at the Minority Issues in Special Education Conference, Harvard University, Cambridge, MA.

Oswald, D., Coutinho, M., & Best, A. M. (2000, November). *Community and school predictors of over representation of minority children in special education.* Paper presented at the Minority Issues in Special Education Conference, Harvard University, Cambridge, MA.

Paisley, W. J. (1984). *Rhythms of the future: Learning and working in the age of algorithms.* Stanford, CA: Stanford University, Institute for Communication Research.

Papert, S. (1987). Computer criticism and technocentric thinking. *Educational Researcher, 16*(1), 22–30.

Parks, D. R., Kusher, J., Hooper, W., Flavin, F., Yellow Bird, D., & Ditmar, S. (1999). Documenting and maintaining Native American languages for the 21st century: The Indiana University model. In J. Reyhner, G. Cantoni, R. St. Clair, and E. Parsons Yazzie (Eds.), *Revitalizing Indigenous languages.* Flagstaff, AZ: Northern Arizona University.

Parks, S. (1999). Reducing the effects of racism in schools, *Educational Leadership 56*(7) 14–18.

Paul, D. G. (2000). Rap and orality: Critical media literacy, pedagogy, and cultural synchronization. *Journal of Adolescent and Adult Literacy, 44*(3), 246–252.

Payne, R. K., (1998). *A framework for understanding poverty* (revised edition). Baytown, TX: RFT Publishing.

Payzant, T. (1995). Public interview on August 20, 1995, conducted by the Boston School Committee in the

Boston Public Library's Rabb Lecture Hall, Boston, MA.

Pea, R. D. (1996). Learning and teaching with educational technologies. In H. J. Walberg, and G. D. Haertel *Educational psychology: Effective practices and policies.* Berkeley, CA: McCutchan Publishers.

Pemberton, G. (1993). *On teaching America's new majority students: Problems and strategies.* Stanford, CA: Center for Educational Research and Effective Teaching.

Peters, M., & Lankshear, C. (1996). Critical literacy and digital texts. *Educational Theory, 46,* 51–70.

Pew Research Center's Internet & American Life Project. (2001). *Who's not online.* Retrieved September 21, 2001, from http://www.pewinternet.org/reports/toc.asp?Report=21

Phillips, S. U. (1983). *The invisible culture, communication in classroom and community on the Warm Springs Indian Reservation.* Prospect Heights, IL: Waveland Press.

Pittman, J. (1999). *A study of professional development, research, practices, and policies to prepare inservice teachers in new technologies: Implications for training standards in new technologies.* A published dissertation. Ames, IA: Iowa State University.

Pittman, J. (2000). *Community access to technology study.* Cincinnati, OH: University of Cincinnati Press.

Porter, A. C., Garet, M. S., Desimone, L., Yoon, K. S., & Birman, B. F. (2000). *Does professional development change teaching practice? Results from a three-year study.* Washington, DC: U.S. Department of Education.

Posner, G. J. (1992). *Analyzing the curriculum.* New York: McGraw-Hill.

Postman, N. M. (1992). *The surrender of culture to technology.* New York: Knopf Publishers.

Postman, N. M. (1995). *The end of education: Redefining the value of schools.* New York: Knopf Publishers.

Power UP: Helping youth succeed in the digital age. (2001). *What is Power Up?* Retrieved July 5, 2001, from http://www.powerup.org

Preparing Tomorrow's Teachers to Use Technology, PT3 (2000). Retrieved August 15, 2001, from http://pt3.org

President's Committee of Advisors on Science and Technology: Panel on Educational Technology (1997). *Report to the President on the use of technology to strengthen K–12 education in the United States.* Retrieved September, 2001, from http://www.ostp.gov/PCASTA/k-12ed.html#exec

Provenzo, Jr., E. F., Brett, A., & McCloskey, G. N. (1999). *Computers, curriculum, and cultural change: An introduction for teachers.* Mahwah, NJ: Lawrence Erlbaum.

Prucha, F. P. (Ed.) (1990). *Documents of United States Indian Policy* (2nd edition). Lincoln, NE: University of Nebraska Press.

Puma, M. J., Chaplin, D. D., & Pape, A. D. (2000). *E-rate and the digital divide: A preliminary analysis from the integrated studies of educational technology.* Washington, DC: The Urban Institute.

Quellmalz, E., & Haertel, G. D. (1999). *Breaking the mold: Technology-based science assessment in the 21st century.* Menlo Park, CA: SRI International.

Raine, L. (2001). *Education and the Internet: Internet tracking report.* Pew Internet Project. Retrieved on November 13, 2001, from: http://www.pewinternet.org/reports/toc.asp?Report=30

Ramirez, J. D. (1992) Executive summary: Longitudinal study of structured English immersion strategy, early-exit and late-exit bilingual education programs for language minority children. *Bilingual Research Journal 62*(4), 427–446.

Ramirez, J. D. (1999). *Diversity responsive evaluations.* Presentation at the Education Evaluation Summit, Office of Educational Research and Improvement, U.S. Department of Education. Ann Arbor, MI.

Ramirez, J. D. (2001) Bilingualism and literacy: Problem or opportunity? A synthesis of reading research on bilingual students. *Reading Research Symposium.* In Office of Bilingual Education and Minority Language Affairs, Washington, DC: U.S. Department of Education. U.S. Government Printing Office.

Real Bird, L. (2001, July 12). *Preserving Native American culture and language.* Presentation for the New Mexico State University American Indian Bridges Program of the Social Sciences and Humanities and the American Indian Bridges Program of Bio-Medical Science, Las Cruces, NM.

Reid, K. S. (2001). Technology counts 2001: Racial disparities. *Education Week, 20*(35), 16–17.

Reinking, D., McKenna, M. C., Labbo, L. D., & Kieffer, R. D. (Eds.). (1998). *Handbook of literacy and technology.* Mahwah, NJ: Lawrence Erlbaum.

Renchler, R. (1993, May). Poverty and learning. *ERIC Digest 83.* Eugene, OR: ERIC Clearinghouse on Educational Management.

Resnick, M., & Fink, E. (2001). Developing principals as instructional leaders. *Phi Delta Kappan, 82*(8), 598–610.

Resnick, M., Rusk, N., & Cooke, S. (1999). The computer clubhouse: Technological fluency in the inner city. In D. A. Schon, B. Sanyal, & W. J. Mitchell (Eds.), *High technology and low-income communities* (pp. 263–285). Cambridge, MA: MIT Press.

Resta, P. (1994). Minorities and the new information technologies in higher education: Barriers and Opportunities. In M. J. Justiz, (Ed.), *Minorities in higher education.* American Council of Education Book Series. Phoenix, AZ: Oryx Press.

Reyes, M. L. (2001). Unleashing possibilities: Biliteracy in the primary grades. In M. L. Reyes & J. J. Halcon (Eds.), *The best for our children: Critical perspectives on literacy for Latino students* (pp. 65–77). New York: Teachers College Press.

Rice, M. L., & Wilson, E. K. (1999). How technology aids constructivism in the social studies classroom. *Social Studies, 90*(1), 28–34.

Riddle, W., & White, L. (1994). Variations in expenditures per Pupil within the states: Evidence from census data for 1989–90. *Journal of Education Finance, 19*(13), 358–362.

Riel, M. (1992). Making connections from urban schools. *Education and Urban Society, 24*(4).

Rifkin, J. (2000). *The age of access: The new culture of hypercapitalism, where all of life is a paid-for experience.* New York: Random House.

Riley, L. A., Nassersharif, B., & Mullen, J. (1999, July). *Assessment of technology infrastructure in Native communities* (Economic Development Administration Rep. No. 99-07-13799). Washington, DC: U. S. Department of Commerce.

Riley, R. (1998). *The challenge for America: A high quality teacher in every classroom* (National Press Club annual address). Retrieved September 15, 1998, from http://www.ed.gov//Speeches/980915.html

Ritzer, G. (1993/1996). *The McDonaldization of society.* Thousand Oaks, CA: Pine Forge Press.

Rivera, J., and Poplin, M. (1995). Multicultural, critical, feminine, and constructive pedagogies seen through the lives of youth: A call for the revisioning of these and beyond: Toward a pedagogy for the next century. In. C. Sleeter & P. McClaren (Eds.), *Multicultural education, critical pedagogy, and the politics of difference* (pp. 222–244). Albany, NY: SUNY Press.

Roach, R. (2001). Building African American e-culture. *Black Issues in Higher Education 17*(25), 42.

Rocap, K. (1999). *Diversity and technology integration.* Presentation to regional participants, Pacific Southwest Regional Technology in Education Consortium, San Diego, CA.

Rogers, E. M. (1986). *Communications technology: The new media in society.* New York: The Free Press.

Rogers, E. M. (1995). *Diffusion of innovations.* New York: The Free Press.

Roschelle, J. M, Rob, D. P., Hoadley, C. M., Gordin, D. N. & Means, B. M. (2000). Changing how and what children learn in school with computer-based technologies. In M. Shields, (Vol. Ed.), *The future of children: Children and computer technology:* Vol. 10, No. 2 (pp. 76–101). Menlo Park, CA: David and Lucile Packard Foundation with SRI International.

Rose, M. (2001). Bridging the digital divide, *American Teacher, 85*(5), 10, 11, 16.

Rosser, S. V. (1990). *Female-friendly science: Applying women's studies methods and theories to attract students.* New York: Pergamon Press.

Rowand, C. (2000). *Public school teachers' use of computers and the Internet.* National Center for Education Statistics (NCES). NECS 2000-090. Washington, DC: Author.

Rozack, T. (1994). *The cult of information: A neo-Luddite treatise on high tech, artificial intelligence, and the true art of thinking.* Berkeley, CA: University of California Press.

Sadker, M., & Sadker, D. (1986). Sexism in the classroom: From grade school to graduate school. *Phi Delta Kappan, 67*(7), 512–515.

Sadker, M., & Sadker, D. (1994). *Failing at fairness: How America's schools cheat girls.* New York: Macmillan International.

Sadker, M., & Sadker, D. (1997). *Teachers, schools, and society.* New York: McGraw-Hill.

Sadker, M., Sadker, D., & Klein, S. (1991). The issue of gender in elementary and secondary education. In G. Grant (Ed.), *Review of research in education* (pp. 269–334. Washington, DC: American Educational Research Association.

Salpeter, J. (2000). Taking stock: What does the research say about technology's impact on education? An interview with David Dwyer. *Technology and Learning Magazine. 20*(11). Retrieved on June 20, 2002, from http://www.techlearning.com/db_area/archives/ TL/062000/archives/interv.html

Sánchez, G. I. (1940/1996). *Forgotten people: A study of New Mexicans.* Albuquerque, NM: University of New Mexico in cooperation with University of New Mexico Center for the American West.

Sandholtz, J. H., Ringstaff, C., & Dwyer, D. C. (1997). *Teaching with technology: Creating student-centered classrooms.* New York: Teachers College Press.

San Miguel, G., Jr., & Valencia, R. R. (1998). From the Treaty of Guadalupe Hidalgo to Hopwood: The educational plight and struggle of Mexican Americans in the southwest. *Harvard Educational Review, 68*(3), 353–412.

Sayers, D. (1995). Language choice and global learning networks: The pitfall of Lingua Franca approaches to classroom telecomputing. *Education Policy Analysis Archives, 3*(10).

SCANS (1991). *What work requires of schools: A SCANS report for America 2000* (Secretary's Commission Report). Washington DC: U.S. Department of Labor.

Scardamalia, M., & Bereiter, C. (1999). Schools as knowledge-building organizations. In D. Keating & C. Hertzman (Eds.), *Today's children, tomorrow's soci-*

ety: The developmental health and wealth of nations (pp. 274–289). New York: Guilford.

Schacter, J. (1999). *The impact of educational technology on students' achievement: What the most current research has to say.* Milken Exchange on Educational Technology.

Schall, P. L., & Skeele, R. W. (1995). Creating a home-school partnership for learning: Exploiting the home computer. *The Educational Forum, 59*(Spring), 244–249.

Shashaani, L. (1994). Gender differences in computer experience and its influence on computer attitudes. *Journal of Educational Computing Research, 11*(4), 347–367.

Schnaiberg, L. (2001). Technology counts 2001. In state of the states. *Education Week Report 20*(35), 10–11, 97.

Schofield, J. (1995). *Computers and classroom culture.* New York: Cambridge University Press.

Schön, D. A., Sanyal, B., & Mitchell, W. J. (Eds.). (1999). *High Technology and Low-Income Communities: Prospects for the Use of Advanced Information Technology.* Cambridge, MA: MIT Press.

Schon, D. A. (1987) *Educating the reflective practitioner.* San Francisco, CA: Jossey-Bass.

Schrum, L., Geisler, S., & Wise, C. (2000). *Tech 4 Success: Evaluation of an after-school computer program.* Athens, GA: University of Georgia.

Schum, D. A. (1994). *The evidential foundations of probabilistic reasoning.* New York: Wiley.

Scott, H. J. (1980). *The Black school superintendent: Messiah or scapegoat?*

Senge, P. (1990). *The fifth discipline: The art and practice of the learning organization.* New York: Doubleday Currency.

Senge, P. (1999). *The dance of change: The challenges of sustaining momentum in learning organizations.* New York: Currency-Doubleday.

Senge, P., Cambron-McCabe, N., Lucas, T., Smith, B., Dutton, J,. & Kleiner, A. (Eds.). (2000). *Schools that learn: A fifth discipline fieldbook for educators, parents, and everyone who cares about education.* New York: Doubleday.

Shannon, P. (1990). *The struggle to continue: Progressive reading practice in the United States.* Portsmouth, NH: Heinemann.

Shashaani, L. (1994). Gender differences in computer experience and its influence on computer attitudes. *Journal of Educational Computing Research, 11*(4), 347–367.

Shashaani, L. (1997). Gender differences in computer attitude and use along college students. Journal of Educational Computing Research *16*(1) pp. 27–51.

Sharp, S. (2001). Bridging the digital divide. *THE Journal, 28*(10), 10–12.

Short, P., & Greer, J. (1997). *Leadership in empowered schools.* Columbus, OH: Merrill, Prentice Hall.

Sianjina, R. R. (2000). Educational technology in the diverse classroom. *Kappa Delta Pi, 37*(1), 26–29.

Skeele, R. W. (1993). Technology and diversity: Resolving computer equity issues through multicultural education. In D. Carey, R. Carey, D. A. Willis, & J. Willis (Eds.), *Technology and teacher education annual—1993* (pp. 550–553). Charlottesville, VA: Association for the Advancement of Computing in Education.

Skerry, P. (2002). Beyond sushiology: Does diversity work? *Brookings Review, 20*(1), 20–23. Retrieved on June 22, 20, from http://www.brook.edu/dybdocroot/press/review/winter2002/skerry.htm

Sleeter, C. & McLaren, P. (1995) Introduction: Exploring connections to build a critical multiculturalism. In C. Sleeter and P. Mclaren (Eds.), *Multicultural education, critical pedagogy, and the politics of difference* (pp. 5–32).

Sleeter, C. E. (1996). *Multicultural education as social activism.* Albany, NY: SUNY Press.

Smerdon, B., Cronen, S., Lanahan, L., Anderson, J., Iannotti, N., & Angeles, J. (2000). *Teachers' tools for the 21st century: A report on teachers' use of technology.* Retrieved December 6, 2001, from http://nces.ed.gov/pubs2000/2000102C.pdf

Smith, L. B. (1999). *The socialization of excelling women with regard to a technology career: Guides and pathtakers.* Unpublished Dissertation. Athens, GA: The University of Georgia.

Smith, R. A. (1997). Remarks made at the October 1997 Advisory Panel Meeting of the Urban Superintendents Program, Harvard Graduate School of Education, Cambridge, MA.

Smith, R. C. (1996). *They closed their schools: Prince Edward County, Virginia, 1951–1964.* Farmville, Virginia: Martha E Forrester Council of Women.

Smylie, M., & Conyers, J. (1991). Changing conceptions of teaching influence the future of staff development. *Journal of Staff Development, 12*(1), 12–16.

Snow, C. E., Burns, M. S., & Griffin, P. (Eds.) (1998). *Preventing reading difficulties in young children.* Washington, DC: National Academy Press.

Solomon, G. (1992). The computer as electronic doorway: Technology and the promise of empowerment. *Phi Delta Kappan, 47*(4), 327–329.

Soska, M. (1994) An introduction to educational technology. *Directions in Language and Education, 1*(1), 1–7.

South Dakota Department of Education (2001). *South Dakota repeats as national leader in school technology.* Retrieved on December 28, 2001, from http://www.state.sd.us/deca/

Sparks, D. (2000). It all comes down to the teacher. *Journal of Staff Development, 21*(4). Retrieved December

6, 2001, from http://www.nsdc.org/educatorindex. htm

Sparks, D., & Hirsch, S. (1997). *A new vision for staff development.* Oxford, OH: Association for Supervision and Curriculum Development and National Staff Development Council.

Spillane, J. P., Halverson, R. & Diamond, J. B., School of Education and Social Policy, Northwestern University. (1999, April). *Distributed leadership: Toward a theory of school leadership practice.* Paper prepared for presentation at the Annual Meeting of the American Educational Research Association, Montreal, Canada.

Spring, J. (1996). *The cultural transformation of a Native American family and its tribe 1763–1995.* Mahwah, NJ: Lawrence Erlbaum.

Stage, E. K., Kreinberg, N., & Eccles-Parson, J. (1987). Increasing the participation and achievement of girls in math, science, and engineering. In A. Kelly (Ed.), *Science for girls?* (pp. 100–133). Philadelphia, PA: Open University Press.

Staples. A. H., & Pugach, M. C. (2000). *Year 1 progress report of the Technology and Urban Teaching Project.* Milwaukee, WI: University of Wisconsin-Milwaukee.

State of the Internet: USIC report on use and threats (2000). Retrieved January 14, 2002 from http://www.usic.org

Stedman, J., & Riddle, W. (1998). *Goals 2000: Educate America Act implementation status and issues.* Congressional Research Report prepared for Members of Congress. 95–502 EPW. November, P.L. 106-25.

Stellin, S. (2001, April 11). Bandwidth constraints begin to worry schools. *New York Times,* p. A19.

Stern, G. M. (1999, October). Changing our view of the border: High hopes for UTEP Borderlands Project. *The Hispanic Outlook in Higher Education,* p. 24–26.

Stigler, J. W., & Hiebert, J. (1999). *The teaching gap: Best ideas from the world's teachers for improving education in the classroom.* New York: Free Press.

Stout, C. (1995, March). Education, access to telecommunications technology, and equity. *The Computing Teacher* 22(6), 37–39.

Street, B. V. (Ed.). (2001). *Literacy and development: Ethnographic perspectives.* New York: Routledge.

Sullivan, B. (1999). Professional development: The linchpin of teacher quality. *Professional Development, 18,* 1–10. Retrieved December 6, 2001, from http://www.ascd.org/readingroom/infobrief/9908.html

Sunstein, C. (2001). *Republic.com.* Princeton, NJ: Princeton University Press.

Swain, C., & Pearson, T. (2001). Bridging the digital divide: A building block for teachers, *Learning and Leading with Technology, 28*(8) 10.

Swisher, K., & Hoisch, M. (1992, January). Dropping out among American Indians and Alaska Natives: A review of studies. *Journal of American Indian Education, 31*(2), 3–23.

Swisher, K. & Tippeconnic III, J. (1999). *Next steps.* Charleston, NC: Clearinghouse on Rural Education and Small Schools.

Tanchak, T. L., & Sawyer, C. (1995). Augmentative communication. In K. F. Flippo, K. J. Inge, & J. M. Barcus (Eds.), *Assistive technology: A resource for school, work, and community* (pp. 57–85). Baltimore, MD: Paul H. Brookes Publishing Co.

Tapscott, D. (1999). *Growing up digital.* New York: McGraw-Hill Professional Publishing

Tapscott, D. (2000) The digital divide. In *The Jossey-Bass Reader on Technology and Learning,* p. 127–154. San Francisco, CA: Jossey-Bass.

Tatum, B. D. (1992) Talking about race, learning about racism: The application of racial identity development theory in the classroom. *Harvard Educational Review, 62*(1), 1–24.

Technology Counts 2001. The new divides. *Education Week Report 20*(35), 10–11, 97. Retrieved on June 22, 2002, from http://www.edweek.org/sreports/tc01/tc01article.cfm?slug=35execsum.h20

Technology Leadership Academy (October 23, 2000). *Online assessment tools.* Retrieved September 25, 2001, from http://www.edb.utexas.edu/academy/planning.html

TERC. (2000). *Eyes to the future: Middle school girls envisioning science and technology in high school and beyond.* Cambridge, MA: Terc, Inc. Retrieved November 14, 2001, from http://www.terc.edu/etf/about. html

Texas Center for Educational Computing (1998). Images of technology in Texas schools: Report number twenty-four. Retrieved on December 14, 2001, from http://www.tcet.unt.edu/images/i24.pdf

Thackara, J. (2001). *The design challenge of pervasive computing: Interactions, 8*(3), 47–51.

Tharp, R. G., & Yamauchi, L. A. (1994). *Effective instructional conversation in Native American classrooms.* Santa Cruz, CA: The National Center for Research on Cultural Diversity and Second Language Learning.

Thinkquest, Inc. (2001). *Thinkquest.* Retrieved on November 30, 2001, from http://www.thinkquest.org

Thom, M. (2001). *Balancing the equation: Where are women and girls in science, engineering, & technology?* Washington, DC: National Council for Research on Women.

Thompson, B. (2001, September 16). Learning to be wired. *The Washington Post Magazine,* p. 18.

Thompson, E., Bull, G. & Willis, J. (1998). *Society for Information Technology in Education mission state-*

ment. Retrieved July 1999, from http://www.aacte. org/site/default.htm

Thorkildsden, R. (2001). Executive summary of research synthesis on quality and availability of assistive technology devices. Retrieved July 27, 2001, from http:// atadvocacy.phillynews.com/docs/atedresearch.html

Todman, J. (2000). Gender differences in computer anxiety among university entrants since 1992. *Computers and Education, 34*(1), 27–35.

Tomlinson, C. A. (1999). *The differentiated classroom: Responding to the needs of all learners.* Alexandria, VA: Association for Supervision and Curriculum Development.

Tomlinson, C. A. (2001). *How to differentiate instruction in mixed-ability classrooms.* (2nd edition). Alexandria, VA: Association for Supervision and Curriculum Development.

TOP (2002). *Technology Opportunity Program.* Retrieved on June 22, 2002, from http://www.ntia.doc.gov/ otiahome/top/

Torrez, N. (2000). *Developing culturally consonant curriculum using the technology of the new millennium.* Paper presented at the American Association of Colleges of Teacher Education, Chicago, IL. Eric Identifier: ED 440 058.

Tuijnman, A. (2000). Benchmarking adult literacy in America: An international comparative study. *International adult literacy survey monograph series.* Washington DC: U.S. Department of Education.

Turkle, S. (1984). *The second self: Computers and the human spirit.* New York: Simon and Schuster.

Turkle, S. ([1995] 1997). *Life on the screen: Identity in the age of the Internet* (Reprint edition). New York: Simon and Schuster

Turkle, S., & Papert, S. (1990). Epistemological pluralism: Styles and voices within the computer culture. *Signs: Journal of Women and Culture in Society, 16*(1), 128–154.

Uchitelle, L. (1997). Making sense of a stubborn educational gap. *Week in Review Section,* The New York Times (August 15, 1997), pp. 1 & 5.

Unicode Consortium (1991). *Unicode Home Page.* Retrieved on June 22, 2002, from http://www.unicode. org/

University of Nebraska–Lincoln. (n.d.). Traumatic brain injury and assistive technology: Case studies. Retrieved on June 17, 2002 from http://ricketts.unl.edu/ tbi/AT/case.html

Upitis, R. (1998). From hackers to Luddites, game players to game creators: Profiles of adolescent students using technology. *Journal of Curriculum Studies, 30*(3), 293–318.

Urban League of Cincinnati (2001). Retrieved, November, 2001, from http://www.gcul.org/programs.htm

U.S. Census Bureau. (2000, September 26). *Poverty: 1999 highlights.* Washington, DC: Author. Retrieved July 15, 2001, from http://www.census.gov/hhes/ poverty/poverty99/pov99hi.html

U.S. Department of Agriculture (2001). News release (May 21, 1999) Retrieved on July 15, 2001 from http://www.usda.gov/rus/electric

U.S. Department of Commerce. (1993, September). *"We the . . . first Americans"* [Economics and Statistics Administration, Bureau of the Census, WE-5.] U.S. Government Printing Office, 350–631.

U.S. Department of Commerce. (1994). *National Information Infrastructure: Progress report.* Washington, DC: U.S. Department of Commerce.

U.S. Department of Education (1995). *Seventeenth annual report to Congress on the implementation of the Disabilities Education Act.* Retrieved March 22, 1998, from http://www.ed.gov/pubs/OSEP95AnlRpt

U.S. Department of Education. (2000a). *E-learning: Putting a world-class education at the fingertips of all children.* The National Educational Technology Plan. Retrieved on May 23, 2002, from http://www. ed.gov/Technology/elearning/e-learning.pdf

U.S. Department of Education (2000b). *Learning without limits: An agenda for postsecondary education— Theme 4.* Retrieved on June 5, 2002, from http://www. ed.gov/offices/OPE/AgenProj/report/theme4.html

U.S. Department of Education Web-based Education Commission. (2000). *The power of the Internet for learning: Moving from promise to practice.* Retrieved on November 30, 2001 from http://www.webcommission.org

U.S. Department of Labor, The Secretary's Commission on Achieving Necessary Skills (SCANS) (2000). *Learning a living: A blueprint for high performance, a SCANS report for America, 2000.* Retrieved on June 5, 2002, from http://www.scans.jhu.edu/NS/HTML/ Index.htm

U.S. Internet Council and International Technology and Trade Associates (2000). *State of the Internet 2000.* Washington, DC.

Vaill, P. (1996). *Learning as a way of being.* San Francisco, CA: Jossey-Bass.

Valencia, R. (Ed.). (1999). *The evolution of deficit thinking.* Bristol, PA: Falmer Press.

Valenzuela, A. (1999). Subtractive schooling. *U.S.-Mexican youth and the politics of caring.* Albany: SUNY Press.

Van Soest, D. Canon, R., and Grant, D. (2000). Using an interactive website to educate about cultural diversity and societal oppression. *Journal of Social Work Education, 36*(3), 463–479.

Vásquez, O. (1994). A look at language as resource: Lessons from La Clase Mágica. In M. B. Arias & U.

Casanova (Eds.), *Bilingual education: Politics, practice, and research* (pp. 199–224). Ninety-second Yearbook of the National Society for the Study of Education, Part 2. Chicago, IL: University of Chicago Press.

Vygotsky, L. S. (1962). *Thought and language.* Cambridge, MA: MIT. Press.

Vygotsky, L. S. (1978). *Mind in society: The development of higher psychological processes.* Cambridge, MA and London, UK: Harvard University Press

Waddell, C. (1999). Understanding the digital economy: Data, tools, and research. Retrieved May 10, 2001, from http://www.icdri.org/the_digital_divide.htm

Waddock, S. A. (1995). *Not by schools alone: Sharing responsibility for America's education reform.* Westport, CT: Praeger.

Waks, L. & Roy, R. (1987). Learning from technology. In K. D. Benne & S. Tozer (Eds.), *Society as educator in an age of transition* (pp. 24–53). Chicago, IL: The National Society for the Study of Education.

Walkerdine, V. (1998). *Counting girls out: Girls and mathematics.* London: Bristol, PA: Falmer Press.

Wallace, J. (2001). *Digital equity toolkit.* Montpelier, VT: National Institute for Community Innovations. Retrieved on January 14, 2002, from www.digital-equity.org

Wallace, R. (1995). *From vision to practice.* Thousand Oaks, CA: Corwin Press.

Warschauer, M. (2000). The changing global economy and the future of English teaching. *TESOL Quarterly, 34*(3), 511–535. Washington, DC: Howard University Press.

Weinberg, M. (1977). *A chance to learn.* Cambridge, MA: Cambridge University Press.

Weissglass, J. (2001). Racism and the achievement gap, *Education Week, 20*(43). Retrieved on June 22, 2002, from http://www.edweek.org/ew/ewstory.cfm?slug=43weissglass.h20

Wenger, B. L., Kaye, H. S., & LaPlante, M. P. (1996). *Disabilities among children* (Disability Statistics Center, San Francisco, Report No. 15). Abstract retrieved from http://dsc.ucsf.edu/UCSF/spl.taf?_from=default

Wenglinsky, H. (1998). *Does it compute? The relationship between educational technology and student achievement in mathematics.* Published by ETS Policy Information Center. Retrieved August 31, 2001 from http://www.ets.org/research/textonly/pic/dic/preack.html

West Wing Connections. (2001). *Fulfilling America's promise to Americans with disabilities.* Retrieved July 27, 2001, from http://www.whitehouse.gov/news/freedominitiative/freedominitiative.html

Wetzel, K., & Chisholm, I. (1998). An evaluation of technology integration in teacher education for bilingual and English as a second language education majors, *Journal of Research on Computing in Education, 30*(4), 379–397.

Wheatley, M. J. (1999). *Leadership and the new science: Discovering order in a chaotic world.* San Francisco, CA: Berett-Koehler.

White House, 2001, Fulfilling America's promise to Americans with disabilities. Retrieved July 27, 2001, from the World Wide Web: http://www.whitehouse.gov/news/freedominitiative/freedominitiative.html

Whiting, B., & Edwards, C. P. (1988). *Children of different worlds.* Cambridge, MA: Harvard University Press.

WICHE. (1987). *From minority to majority: Education and the future of the southwest.* Boulder, CO: WICHE Regional Policy Committee on Minorities in Higher Education.

Wilder, G. Z. (1996). *Correlates of gender differences in cognitive functioning.* New York: College Entrance Examination Board.

Williams, R. B. (1997). *Twelve roles of facilitators for school change.* Arlington Heights, IL: IRI/Skylight Training and Publishing.

Willinsky, J. (1998) *Learning to divide the world: Education at empire's end.* Minneapolis, MN: University of Minnesota Press.

Wilson, C. A. & Martin, B. (2000). Race, poverty, and test scores: A model of the determinants of test scores in Toledo. *The Negro Educational Review. 51*(1/2), 23–36.

Wlodkowski, R. J. & Ginsberg, M. B. (1995). A framework for culturally responsive teaching. *Educational Leadership, 53*(1), 17–21.

Yau, R. (1999, Fall/Winter). Technology in K-12 public schools: What are the equity issues? *Equity Review.* Retrieved July 2001, from http://www.maec.org/techrev.html

Young, Jeffry, R. (2001, November 9). Does "digital divide" rhetoric do more harm than good? *The Chronicle of Higher Education* (pgs. A52–A53).

Zehr, M. A. (2001). Technology counts 2001: Language barriers. *Education Week, 20*(35), 28–29. Retrieved on June 22, 2002, from http://www.edweek.org/sreports/tc01/tc01article.cfm?slug=35lep.h20

Zhang, Y. (2000). Technology and the writing skills of students with learning disabilities. *Journal of Research on Computing in Education, 32*(4), 467–478.

Zorkocy, Peter. (1982). *Information technology: An introduction.* White Plains, NY: Knowledge Industries Publications.

R E S O U R C E   L I S T

with Information on the Digital Equity Portal

PAT LASTER

CHERYL GRABLE

The resource section begins with an explanation of the Digital Equity Portal and continues with annotated sites collected from the different chapters. The sites were used as resources by the authors or specified as sites to be referenced for additional information on a subject. All sites are functional at the date of printing, but may change. The "portal" is continually updated and offers the reader access to a variety of sites.

Digital Equity Portal

Sponsored by National Institute for Community Innovations
Developed with funds from a PT3 grant from U.S. Department of Education

PURPOSE:
The purpose of an Internet "portal" is to collect information about a specific topic. The purpose of the Digital Equity Portal is to assist educators in increasing the use of technology in classrooms, thereby providing digital equity for more students.

CONTENTS:
The Digital Equity Portal is a virtual library of educational resources designed to help educators expand their use of technology and the Internet in their teaching and learning. The Digital Equity Portal points users to information on the Web about strategies and resources educators can use to address each of the five dimensions of digital equity:

- Access to tangible learning technology resources: hardware, software, wiring, and connectivity
- Access to educators skilled in using these resources for teaching and learning
- Access to high-quality digital content
- Access to digital content relevant to one's culture
- Opportunities to create one's own digital content

The resources included in the Digital Equity Portal are catalogued using metatags, and each one includes a description linked to the purpose of the portal.

A new user of the Digital Equity Portal is asked to register by identifying topics that the user wishes to explore. The Portal is "customized" for the new user from registration information, and resources about the selected topics are highlighted for the user in future visits to the site. Furthermore, the user will be notified via e-mail of new resources related to the favorite topics.

New resources are frequently added to the Digital Equity Portal, and users are invited to recommend Internet-based resources that will be helpful to others.

The Digital Equity Portal also features resources such as the Digital Equity Tool Kit, designed to help educators and non-profit organizations to increase connectivity and use Internet resources.

www.digital-equity.org/portal.cgi

Joy Wallace [joywallace@attbi.com]

Digital Equity Resources

4-H Virtual Farm   The bird egg is an excellent educational subject for the study of embryology. This section is designed to help you obtain a better understanding of incubation and embryonic development.

www.ext.vt.edu/resources/4h/virtualfarm/poultry/poultry_incubation.html

ABC News: Studies in Bilingual Education   Bilingual education is an instructional program for limited English speaking students that teaches academic subjects in their native languages so that students will be able to join English-only classes.

www.abcnews.go.com/sections/us/DailyNews/bilingualed_research.html

Able Net, Inc.   *AbleNet* offers practical products and creative solutions for teaching children with disabilities. Its tools are specially designed to fuel the imagination—whether you're new to simple assistive technology, are already a technology expert, or are a classroom teacher or teacher trainer.

www.ablenetinc.com

Asian Studies WWW Virtual Library   The Asian Studies WWW VL is one of the key sections of the prestigious WWW Virtual Library Project initiated in 1992 by the CERN's WWW development team.

http://coombs.anu.edu.au/WWWVL-AsianStudies.html

AskERIC   *AskERIC* is a personalized Internet-based service providing education information to teachers, librarians, counselors, administrators, parents, and anyone throughout the United States and the world interested in education.

http://ericir.syr.edu

BellSouth Foundation   BellSouth Corporation established the BellSouth Foundation in 1986. The new foundation was created with one purpose: improving the quality of education in the Southeast. The company, itself new, realized that strengthening the South's economy and improving life chances for all Southerners depended upon a highly skilled work force and an informed and active citizenry, and that education was the cornerstone to building this future.

   www.bellsouthfoundation.org

Benton Foundation   The Benton Foundation seeks to articulate a public interest vision for the digital age and to demonstrate the value of communications for solving social problems.

   www.benton.org

Beyond the Individual—Social Antimony in Discussions of Piaget and Vygotsky   A paper by Michael Cole, University of California, San Diego and James V. Wertsch, Washington University, St. Louis, centering on the primacy of cultural mediation on education, and using the discussions of various commentators on the ideas of Piaget and Vygotsky.

   www.massey.ac.nz/~ALock/virtual/colevyg.htm

Cadamujer   A Latino/Spanish language online magazine for women.

   www.cadamujer.com

Center for Research on Information Technology and Organizations   (Becker's Teaching, Learning and Computing survey)—Teaching, Learning, and Computing: 1998, a National Survey of Teachers and Schools. This is a report on research begun in 1997 with surveys on teacher beliefs and practices, measures of changes in teaching practices, and technology use and school-level investments in technology hardware, software, and training and teacher support.

   www.crito.uci.edu/tlc/html/tlc_home.html

Center for the Study of White American Culture   The Center for the Study of White American Culture (the Center) supports cultural exploration and self-discovery among white Americans. It encourages a dialogue among all racial and cultural groups concerning the role of white American culture in the larger American society.

   www.euroamerican.org

The Center for World Indigenous Studies' Fourth World Documentation Project   The Center for World Indigenous Studies (CWIS) is an independent, non-profit [U.S. 501(c)(3)] research and education organization dedicated to wider understanding and appreciation of the ideas and knowledge of indigenous peoples and the social, economic, and political realities of indigenous nations.

   www.cwis.org

Chicano/Latino Net   "Building Chicana/o Latina/o Communities Through Networking"— A website designed to provide Chicanos/Latinos with a comprehensive, searchable directory of links to sites and information on the World Wide Web.

   http://latino.sscnet.ucla.edu

Community Technology Centers Networks (CTCNet)   A national, non-profit membership organization of more than 600 independent community technology centers where people get free or low-cost access to computers and computer-related technology, such as the Internet, together with learning opportunities that encourage exploration and discovery.

   www.ctcnet.org

Currents in Electronic Literacy: Constructivism Online—A Survey of Freshman Writing Distance Learning Courses   A report by Dan Melzer about his survey of twenty online freshman writing courses "to find out if these cybercomp classes have the kind of discussion and collaboration most writing teachers value in their conventional classrooms."

   www.cwrl.utexas.edu/currents/archives/fall99/melzer/Introduction.html

Digital Promise   Digital Promise seeks to develop public policies that will focus on the nation's essential public interest needs in the new media environment. Its goal is to galvanize local public interest resources that are essential to the strength and quality of our society, to halt the encroachment of purely marketplace values upon the missions of our public service institutions, and to use the powerful new digital tools to enable those not-for-profit institutions to move outside their walls to widen their audiences and bring their educational and informational resources, essential services, and cultural programs to all citizens.

   www.digitalpromise.org

Encyclopedia Britannica   For-fee online access to Encyclopedia Britannica.

   www.britannica.com/premium

Ethnic Grocer   A site for thousands of the world's most sought-after cooking ingredients, recipes, and ideas.

   www.ethnicgrocer.com

European Crosspoint Anti-Racism Webpage   The Crosspoint is the Net's biggest collection of links in the fields of human rights, antiracism, refugees, women's rights, antifascism, Shoah, etc. This site also links to Jewish organizations, migrant organizations, and others.

   www.magenta.nl/crosspoint

Facing History and Ourselves National Foundation, Inc.   For more than 25 years, Facing History has engaged teachers and students of diverse backgrounds in an examination of racism, prejudice, and antisemitism in order to promote the development of a more humane and informed citizenry.

   www.facing.org

Falling Through the Net   This site provides information about efforts to provide all Americans with access to the Internet and other information technologies as well as reports and information about the digital divide.

   www.digitaldivide.gov

Femina Femina was created in September of 1995 and debuted online to provide women with a comprehensive, searchable directory of links to female-friendly sites and information on the World Wide Web.

www.femina.com

Future Search A worldwide service network providing public/non-profit sector future searches in all cultures for whatever people can afford.

www.futuresearch.net

Gender-Related Electronic Forums Gender-Related Electronic Forums is an annotated, frequently updated, award-winning listing of publicly-accessible e-mail discussion forums (also known as "lists" or "listservs") related to women or to women-focused gender issues.

www-unix.umbc.edu/~korenman/wmst/forums.html

Generation Yes Generation Yes develops revolutionary curricula that help schools effectively use technology.

http://genyes.org/news.php

Global Learning and Observations to Benefit the Environment (GLOBE) GLOBE is a worldwide hands-on, primary and secondary school-based science and education program.

http://globe.fsl.noaa.gov

Hmong Homepage The WWW Hmong Homepage, first made available on the Internet in March, 1994, is a volunteer effort bringing together a collection the Internet-based resources related to Hmong news and current events, issues, history, publications, and culture. This site is an official Asian Studies WWW Virtual Library Associate site.

www.stolaf.edu/people/cdr/hmong

Indian Country Today The nation's leading American Indian News Source.

www.indiancountry.com

Informal Education Encyclopedia: Paolo Freire—Humanism and Learner-Centered Empowerment "Perhaps the most influential thinker about education in the late twentieth century, Paulo Freire has been particularly popular with informal educators with his emphasis on dialogue and his concern for the oppressed."

www.infed.org/thinkers/et-freir.htm

The Institute for Cultural Affairs (ICA) The Institute of Cultural Affairs is a worldwide private, non-profit organization. Its aim is to develop and implement methods of individual, community, and organizational development.

www.icaworld.org

Internet Public Library The Internet Public Library (IPL), is a public service organization and learning/teaching environment at the University of Michigan School of Information.

www.ipl.org

Latina Style "We are the premier site for the Contemporary Hispanic Woman, providing real tools and tips for your busy lifestyle."

www.latinastyle.com

Latinos and the InfoHighway This policy brief is designed to address the issues affecting the Latino community as existing telecommunications policy is overhauled.

www.cgs.edu/inst/trc_super1.html

LatinoWeb A website designed to provide Latinos with a comprehensive, searchable directory of links to Latino-friendly sites and information on the World Wide Web.

www.latinoweb.com

The Louvre The official website of the museum.

www.louvre.fr

Maryland State Department of Education (Technology Inventory) "The . . . graphs [at this site] provide quantitative summaries that document the digital divide that exists in Maryland Schools. The data has [sic] been compiled using the most up-to-date information currently available on technology resources in Maryland Schools as of December 2000 and data from the State's 'Free and Reduced Meals Program' database (FARMS)."

http://msde.aws.com/digitaldivide.asp

Mujer Futura An online Spanish-language magazine.

www.mujerfutura.com

Multicultural Pavilion of the University of Virginia The Multicultural Pavilion provides resources for educators, students, and activists to explore and discuss multicultural education; facilitates opportunities for educators to work toward self-awareness and development; and provides forums for educators to interact and collaborate toward a critical, transformative approach to multicultural education.

http://curry.edschool.virginia.edu/curry/centers/multicultural

Mundo Latino A Spanish-language website with a comprehensive directory of links to Latino-friendly and Spanish-language sites on the World Wide Web.

www.mundolatino.org

National Association for Ethnic Studies A web page providing links to ethnic studies programs at various universities, ethnic websites, and other ethnic resources.

www.ksu.edu/ameth/naes/ethnic.htm

National Center for Education Statistics NCES is the primary federal entity for collecting and analyzing data that are related to education in the United States and other nations.

http://nces.ed.gov

Native American Resources for Teachers and Students   A website providing links to Native American resources on the Internet.

>   http://indy4.fdl.cc.mn.us/~isk/mainmenu.html

Nativeweb   Resources for indigenous cultures around the world.

>   www.nativeweb.org

Nizcor   A website containing links related to the Holocaust.

>   www2.ca.nizkor.org/index.html

NPR Online: National Survey of American Adults on Technology, National Survey of American Kids on Technology   An NPR report on a poll by National Public Radio, the Kaiser Family Foundation, and Harvard's Kennedy School of Government concerning people's attitudes toward computers and the Internet, and a separate survey of children age 10–17 showing their attitudes and access to modern technology at school.

>   www.npr.org/programs/specials/poll/technology

Online Content for Low Income and Underserved Americans: The Digital Divide's New Frontier   A strategic audit of activities and opportunities.

>   www.childrenspartnership.org/pub/low_income

PBS   The official website of the Public Broadcasting System.

>   www.pbs.org

PBS Digital Divide Series   Digital Divide shines a light on the role computers play in widening social gaps throughout our society, particularly among young people. By providing equitable and meaningful access to technology, we can ensure that all children step into the 21st century together.

>   www.pbs.org/digitaldivide

PBS: A Science Odyssey   A biography of Jean Piaget on the Science Odyssey People and Discoveries website.

>   www.pbs.org/wgbh/aso/databank/entries/dh23pi.html

Power Up—Bridging the Digital Divide   Launched in November, 1999, PowerUP is composed of dozens of non-profit organizations, major corporations, and state and federal government agencies that have joined together to ensure that America's underserved youth acquire the skills, experiences, and resources they need to succeed in the digital age.

>   www.powerup.org/what_is.shtml

RETAnet   The Latin America Data Base (LADB) is an online publisher and information resource. LADB produces three weekly electronic publications (*Sourcemex, NotiCen,* and

NotiSur) and maintains an online searchable database of over 24,000 articles (from back issues of LADB publications as well as Latin American journals).

> http://ladb.unm.edu/retanet

Society for Organizational Learning (SoL)   A global learning community dedicated to building knowledge about fundamental institutional change. Their aim is to help build organizations worthy of people's fullest commitment, and they are committed to any institution or individual that is committed to SoL's purpose and principles.

> www.solonline.org

Stagecast Creator™   A program that allows adults and children as young as 8 to build their own simulations and games and to publish them on the World Wide Web. Authors create characters and show them how to change and move. The characters can be made to do different things depending on what other objects are around them.

> www.acypher.com/creator

ThinkQuest   A global network of students, teachers, parents, and technologists dedicated to exploring youth-centered learning on the Net. ThinkQuest is an online community where young people learn, teach, mentor, discover, research, and grow through ThinkQuest programs.

> www.thinkquest.org

Traces   A website of links related to Mexico, including tourism, shopping online, investments, and entertainment.

> www.trace-sc.com/index1.htm

TumbleBooks   TumbleBooks Inc. is a new media company based in Toronto, Canada. They have created an innovative e-book format for children's books called TumbleBooks™. These animated picture books, complete with sound, music, and narration, are experienced off-line in a free, proprietary software application called the TumbleReader™. TumbleBooks Inc. produces original content or converts existing books into the TumbleBook™ format.

> www.tumblebooks.com

Urban League of Cincinnati Programs and Services   A local group providing a wide range of services designed to strengthen the African American community at all levels.

> www.gcul.org/programs.htm

USAC Schools and Libraries Division   The Universal Service Administrative Company (USAC) is a private, not-for-profit corporation that is responsible for providing every state and territory in the United States with access to affordable telecommunications services through the Universal Service Fund. All of the country's communities—including remote communities—such as rural areas, low-income neighborhoods, rural health care providers, public and private schools, and public libraries—are eligible to seek support from the Universal Service Fund.

> www.sl.universalservice.org

The U.S. Holocaust Memorial Museum   National museum for the documentation, study, and interpretation of Holocaust history.

   www.ushmm.org

U.S. Race and Ethnicity Resources—Action without Borders   This is a global network of individuals and organizations working to build a world where all people can live free and dignified lives. Action without Borders is independent of any government, political ideology, or religious creed. Its work is guided by the common desire of its members and supporters to find practical solutions to social and environmental problems, in a spirit of generosity and mutual respect.

   www.idealist.org

Vandergrift's Feminist Websites   The sites provided here are very useful to those who are interested in knowing more about feminists, feminism, women's studies, and women's issues.

   http://scils.rutgers.edu/~kvander/Feminist/femsites.html

Virtual Whale Watching   Online virtual whale watching expedition in Victoria, British Columbia.

   www.whalewatch.ca

Worldcom Foundation's Marco Polo   The Marco Polo program provides no-cost, standards-based Internet content for the K–12 teacher and classroom, developed by the nation's content experts. Online resources include panel-reviewed links to top sites in many disciplines, professionally developed lesson plans, classroom activities, materials to help with daily classroom planning, and powerful search engines.

   www.wcom.com/marcopolo

GLOSSARY

ADHD Attention Deficit Hyperactivity Disorder is "a group of symptoms believed to be caused by slight abnormalities in the brain. Symptoms include lack of ability to attend, impulsivity, distractibility, clumsiness, and hyperactivity." (Coleman, 1993, p. 25)

assistive technology Refers to any item, piece of equipment, or product system, whether acquired commercially modified, or customized, that is used to increase, maintain, or improve functional capabilities of individuals with disabilities. Examples of assistive technology (AT) include calculators, wheelchairs, augmentative communication devices, computers, specialized software, and picture communication symbols.

cerebral palsy A nonprogressive neuromuscular condition resulting from injury to the brain before, during, or after birth.

developmental disability A severe, chronic disability of an individual five years of age or older that: (a) is attributable to a mental or physical impairment or combination of mental and physical impairments; (b) is manifested before the person attains age 22; (c) is likely to continue indefinitely; (d) results in substantial functional limitation in three or more of the following areas of major life activity: (i) self care; (ii) language; (iii) learning; (iv) mobility; (v) self-direction; (vi) capacity for independent living; (vii) economic sufficiency; and (e) reflects individual's need for lifelong services."

digitized speech Human voice recordings.

FAPE Free Appropriate Public Education. " . . . *special education* and *related services* that: (a) are provided at *public* expense, under public supervision and direction, and without charge; (b) meet the standards of the *SEA,* including the requirements of this part; (c) include preschool, elementary school, or secondary school education in the State; and (d) are provided in conformity with an *individualized education program (IEP)* that meets the requirements under §§300.340–300.350."

high incidence disabilities Those disabilities which comprise the majority of individuals with disabilities (i.e., learning disabilities, language disabilities, attention deficit hyperactivity disorder).

IDEA Individuals with Disabilities Education Act. Signed into law in 1990 and reauthorized in 1997, it provides legal mandates relative to the free appropriate public education of children and youth with disabilities, aged birth through twenty-one.

learning disabilities IDEA regulations define a learning disability as "a disorder in one or more of the basic psychological processes involved in understanding or in using spoken or written language, which manifest itself in an imperfect ability to listen, think, speak, read, write, spell or do mathematical calculations" 34 Code of Federal Regulations §300.7(c)(10).

self-efficacy "[T]he belief in one's abilities to organize and execute the series of action necessary to manage prospective situations" (Bandura, 1986, p. 391).

synthesized speech Computer generated speech. Typically sounds rather robotic.

word prediction Software program which suggests word choices as the user types individual letters. Suggestions are typically made based on frequency, grammar, and recency.

INDEX